KING, COURT AND CAPITAL

AN ANTHOLOGY OF KANNADA LITERARY SOURCES FROM THE VIJAYANAGARA PERIOD

VIJAYANAGARA RESEARCH PROJECT MONOGRAPH SERIES

General Editors
JOHN M. FRITZ, University of Pennsylvania
GEORGE MICHELL, London
K.R. RAMAKRISHNA, KAS, Karnataka Department of Archaeology and Museums

Vol. 1. *Pots and Palaces* by Carla M. Sinopoli

Vol. 2. *The Ramachandra Temple at Vijayanagara* by Anna L. Dallapiccola, John M. Fritz, George Michell and S. Rajasekhara

Vol. 3. *The Vijayanagara Courtly Style* by George Michell

Vol. 4. *Religious Traditions at Vijayanagara as Revealed through its Monuments* by Anila Verghese

Vol. 5. *The Irrigation and Water Supply Systems of Vijayanagara* by Dominic J. Davison-Jenkins

Vol. 6. *Sculpture at Vijayanagara: Iconography and Style* by Anna L. Dallapiccola and Anila Verghese

Vol. 7. *Anegondi: Architectural Ethnography of a Royal Village* by Natalie Tobert

Vol. 8. *Vijayanagara: Architectural Inventory of the Sacred Centre* (in 3 volumes) by George Michell and Phillip B. Wagoner

Vol. 9. *King, Court and Capital: An Anthology of Kannada Literary Sources from the Vijayanagara Period* translated by C.T.M. Kotraiah and edited by Anna L. Dallapiccola

Jacket Illustration by Graham Reed:
Royal hunter; sculptural relief from the Mahanavami platform at Hampi

KING, COURT AND CAPITAL

AN ANTHOLOGY OF KANNADA LITERARY SOURCES FROM THE VIJAYANAGARA PERIOD

Translated by C.T.M. Kotraiah

Edited by Anna L. Dallapiccola

with a Foreword by John M. Fritz

MANOHAR
AMERICAN INSTITUTE OF INDIAN STUDIES
NEW DELHI
2003

First published 2003

ISBN 81-7304-532-1

Published by
Ajay Kumar Jain for
Manohar Publishers & Distributors
4753/23 Ansari Road, Daryaganj
New Delhi 110002

Typeset by
A J Software Publishing Co. Pvt. Ltd.
New Delhi 110005

Printed at
Lordson Publishers Pvt. Ltd.
Delhi 110007

CONTENTS

FOREWORD

AN ARCHAEOLOGICAL PERSPECTIVE

From the beginning, this Anthology has concentrated on "non-religious" texts that have as their chief subject the king and court, as well as the people, artefacts and habitats that surrounded them. Though many of these works recount stories about the great people of the realm to convey the religious doctrines propounded by the authors, vivid accounts do emerge of courtly life, such as intrigue, romance, marriage, council and war. In this way, we can fashion a surprisingly complete picture of the lives of kings, queens, attendant women, princes, commanders, guards, gatekeepers, messengers and foreign visitors. That we are less informed about the points of view of servants, agriculturalists, merchants, soldiers and even priests is hardly surprising given the bias of the authors and the social environment in which they wrote.

It would be naïve for us to expect any precise correspondence between the locations and events described in these texts and the actual places and events of the Vijayanagara period. Some of the authors lived in the capital and others may have visited it. Very few of the works that C.T.M. Kotraiah has consulted purport to describe the Vijayanagara capital, an exception being the *Pampasthana Varnanam*; most deal with mythical courts and cities that already had been described by countless storytellers in earlier times.

Created in a cultural tradition that extended back many centuries, these Kannada texts should be understood first and foremost as literary artefacts. It is probable that the roles of conventional forms and representation, versification and audience were as significant in determining the organization and content of texts as the personal observations of the poets or the events to which they refer. No doubt, courtly gossip and witty remarks in Devaraya's Pansupari bazaar at Vijayanagara, for example, were expressed according to quite different literary conventions that had a closer relationship to the daily life of the capital. On the other hand, it seems reasonable to assume that the content of these texts had some relationship to the life experience of the Vijayanagara poets and their courtly patrons. We believe that these texts convey a good deal about the idiom according to which members of the Vijayanagara literati understood their world. This language included elaborate and lengthy enumerations of the objects with which patrons embellished their lives; items of food and drink, jewellery and costumes, weapons and military equipment, plants and animals.

There is also some discussion of the structures and locales in which the authors and their patrons conducted their lives, and which may perhaps be related to the archaeological record of the Vijayanagara site. The texts also indicate the relationships between people and things. For example, they specify the kinds of objects that could be used appropriately by a particular person in a particular venue. Furthermore, they testify to the preferred relationships between the different members of the court, especially between kings and their family members, spiritual advisors, ministers and attendant women. At another level, these texts convey a sense of the ideal world to which members of the court aspired. If they do not detail a particular hunt, courtly reception or marriage feast, they at least inform on the essential qualities of such events, "as they were wished to be." Such works are embedded in "historical reality," even if they convey this reality in a quite different manner from historiographic traditions from other parts of the world. (There is even one source, the *Shri Krishnadevarayana Dinachari*, which purports to narrate events that are known from other historical sources, including Krishnadevaraya's war against the Gajapatis.)

How then are we who are concerned with the material form of the Vijayanagara capital to understand these literary sources? If they do not describe "historical things", can they still help us to shed light on the documented remains of the Vijayanagara capital? Some passages refer to things that already have been observed archaeologically. For example, the *Jivandhra Charite* mentions the presence of boulders outside a fortification wall that would impede access by attacking forces (see Section 2.4). Such boulder fields were noted by Portuguese visitors to Vijayanagara (Sewell 1980) and have been observed at the pre-Vijayanagara site of Kummata (Patil 1991), as well as at Vijayanagara itself (Sinopoli and Morrison at press). Other passages suggest features that might be observed through scientific excavation of ruined buildings; thus, for instance, the *Ramanatha Charite* states that the walls of houses within a fort were painted with pictures and decorated with mirrors (Section 2.7). While painted bands and some small figures have been observed on the surviving basements of Vijayanagara palace structures, no figurative painting on the walls has been recorded. If such paintings existed, they were either so damaged by the destruction of these buildings as to leave almost no record, and/or recovery techniques were inadequate to observe them. Traces of small mirrors have been found during excavation of one palace in the so-called Noblemen's Quarter (Balasubrahmanya, personal communication), and cautious uncovery of other such structures might indicate further instances. Other equally ephemeral features are also not likely to be preserved, and we must exercise caution in postulating the presence of hanging textiles, jewelled inlays and metallic pinnacles, even though such elements are common enough in the literature.

At an architectural scale, the texts also suggest different types of structures and rooms to be found in a palace complex: according to one text, a gymnasium, stables, a garden, pleasure tank, pavilion with painted murals, court hall, store house, treasury and queens' apartments (Section 3.2). Another source describes the constituent elements of a king's palace: the stables, an armory, theater, painting gallery, council chamber, study and pleasure pavilion, as well as a front hall, audience hall and outer court (Section 3.3). It would surely be a mistake for us to assume that a particular palace complex at Vijayanagara would have contained any of these elements, let alone the elements mentioned in other texts. But we can propose the use of different spaces and structures and scientifically test these propositions based on the form and associated artefacts of each functional type (Fritz 1972).

The same investigative method can be followed at an urban scale. Some specific elements referred to in the literary sources are easily identified at the Vijayanagara site: gateways, fort walls, roads, temples and elite residences. However, their disposition may not be according to a particular text (Section 4.1). Other urban elements might yet be identified through careful documentation of surface remains and future excavation: shops, bazaars and non-elite houses. The city as described in the texts consists of many different neighbourhoods, each defined by the kinds of people who live there. The *Ramanatha Charite* lists more than three dozen occupational groups that may have been spatially segregated (Section 4.5). The *Shivatattva Chintamani* suggests the spatial relation of some groups when it refers to a street in which wealthy people lived in mansions and jewellers worked in nearby shops, while a street of concubines was not far away (Section 4.3). Scientific archaeology carried out on a large scale might one day discover neighbourhoods and identify the groups who lived there. At Vijayanagara, one such neighbourhood has already been excavated—the Noblemen's Quarter (Devaraj and Patil 1996)—but the artefacts that might contribute to the identification of the people who lived in these different areas have yet to be consistently collected and analysed.

Looking beyond the instrumental use of these texts to name, identify and explain the material record of the Vijayanagara site, we can appreciate the richly expressive view of the Vijayanagara world as the poets and their patrons might have understood it. In the ideal world a king was learned in the arts and devout, respectful of the advice of learned and holy men, expert in strategy and astute—even wily—in his dealings with his advisors, family, friends and adversaries. He exercised self-control in all things, was generous to his kin, servants, and supplicants and upheld traditional law. He was ready to act heroically and to go to war. But he was not taken over by the pursuit of sensual pleasures, intolerance or unwarranted anger. At the same time he was expected to be wealthy and display his riches and power through his largesse to charity and religion, the strength of his army and fortresses and the splendour of his household. The scale and opulence of his palace, the beauty of his jewels and clothing, his rare perfumes, and the magnificence of his state rituals all contributed to the king's glory. His household included his family members, numerous beautiful and sensuous women and even his state elephants and horses. This magnificence he supported through taxes that were not burdensome to his subjects. He also encouraged agriculture and commerce. In contrast, Shulman (1985) has suggested that such a prescriptive model can be burdensome even to the point of tragedy.

In conclusion, we may read these Kannada texts of the Vijayanagara period on several levels: as literary formulas, as indications of components of the material world of the elite, as evocations of an ideal world in which the elite wished to see themselves or as elements of cultural patterns through which elites coped with the tensions between an ideal, poetical world and the untidy and threatening world of the everyday (Shulman 1985). Those readers who are not concerned with the ambiguities of the material record of Vijayanagara, however, are invited to share the enjoyable experience of entering into this richly poetical world; part reality, part convention, part creative exposition.

References

Devaraj, D.V. and C.S. Patil, eds., 1996, *Vijayanagara: Progress of Research, 1988-1991*, Mysore, Directorate of Archaeology and Museums, Government of Karnataka.

Fritz, J.M., 1972, "Archaeological Systems for Indirect Observations of the Past", in M.P. Leone, ed., *Contemporary Archaeology: A Guide to Theory and Contributions*, Carbondale, pp. 135-87.

Patil, C.S., 1991, "Mummadi Singa, Kampila and Kumara Rama" and "Kummata", in D.V. Devaraj and C.S. Patil, eds., *Vijayanagara: Progress of Research, 1987-88*, Mysore, Directorate of Archaeology and Museums, Government of Karnataka, pp. 179-216.

Sewell, R., 1980 (reprint), *A Forgotten Empire* (*Vijayanagar*), New Delhi.

Shulman, D.D., 1985, *The King and the Clown: In South Indian Myth and Poetry*, Princeton.

Sinopoli, C.M. and K.D. Morrison, at press, "The Regional Landscapes of the Imperial City of Vijayanagara: Report on the Vijayanagara Metropolitan Survey Project", in K.R. van Kooij and E. Raven, eds., *South Asian Archaeology 1999*, Groningen.

JOHN M. FRITZ

PREFACE AND ACKNOWLEDGEMENTS

As an archaeologist and architectural historian involved for many years in documenting and interpreting the material record of Vijayanagara, we have felt keenly our lack of capability with respect to south Indian languages. This shortcoming is not unique; indeed it is shared with several other foreign scholars and even with some of our colleagues from north India. As our research at Vijayanagara progressed over the years, we became increasingly aware of a rich body of contemporary prose and poetical sources in Kannada and Telugu that lay beyond our reach, in the absence of English translations. It was with this desire to understand the relevant indigenous literary background to Vijayanagara that we approached Sri C.T.M. Kotraiah, a highly respected Kannadiga archaeologist with a long-standing interest in the Vijayanagara site and the Vijayanagara period in general. This scholar confirmed that a host of Kannada literary sources did indeed exist, but none of these were available in English. Fortunately for us, we were able to persuade Kotraiah to trawl through the various published Kannada language texts of the Vijayanagara period and advise us about their contents. When he revealed that these prose and poetic works contained a wealth of detail on topics such as royal architecture and town planning, courtly life and ceremonies, entertainments and festivals, the practice of war and hunting and even the costumes and eating habits of the period, we immediately recognized the relevance of these subjects to our attempts to interpret the material evidence of the Vijayanagara site and the activities of its elite population.

Thus it came about that we commissioned Kotraiah to translate into English a set of passages covering these and other related subjects to be found in the various literary works of the period that might be pertinent to our archaeological and art historical investigations. While Kotraiah makes no claim at being a scholar of Kannada literature, his experience as an archaeologist has made him particularly sensitive to the types of data that would help us understand the material dimensions of the Vijayanagara site. To this end, we devised a numerical outline listing an elaborate set of categories on king, court and capital that might potentially be found in the selected texts. Kotraiah carefully excerpted data for each of our categories, arranging the materials according to our numerical outline. These excerpts varied from complete translations to summaries or simple abstracts of the information that was to be found in these sources.

Over the next three years, Kotraiah presented us with an impressive and ever growing stack of materials. As we went through this rapidly increasing mass of typescript, it soon became apparent that we would require the services of an expert editor and compiler. Again, fortunately for us, Prof. Anna L. Dallapiccola, with whom we have collaborated over many years, was prepared to take on this arduous task. As a scholar specializing in the visual expressions of Vijayanagara culture, she was fascinated to read through the translations, which presented a literary portrait of the period as imagined by contemporary authors and poets. It is thanks to Dallapiccola that Kotraiah's texts came to be organized in the perceptive and instructive manner that we have in this volume, thereby greatly aiding the general reader. In her overall role as compiler and editor, Dallapiccola was expertly helped by Janet McAlpin, who acted as a consultant editor, giving an inspired final polish to the format and language of the various chapters. Without the fruitful interaction of these three experts, this publication would have never reached this final form.

Of course, no academic publication such as this is possible without financial support. Funds to sustain Kotraiah derived from grants to the Vijayanagara Research Project given by the Special Currency Programme of the Smithsonian Institution in Washington, as administered through the American Institute of Indian Studies in New Delhi. In this regard, we are once more indebted to Ms. Francine C. Berkowitz, Director, Office of International Relations of the Smithsonian, and Dr. Pradeep R. Mehendiratta, Director General, American Institute.

Other funds covering production and publication expenses of the volume have been raised by generous contributions from a number of personal friends, most of whom have visited the site and witnessed our team in action. They include Alain Adam, E. Alkazi, Norman Braden and George Copland, George and Louise Browning, Cathy Curran, Elizabeth Chatwin, John Eskenazi, Phillip and Helen Jessup, Peter and Elbrun Kimmelman, Sue Kirby and John Goldring, Tony Korner, Dino and Edmee Leventis, David and Janet Harper, Julia Hodgkin, Eleanor Schwartz, Peter and Margaret Stern, Alex and Jo Wodak, and a donor who wishes to remain anonymous.

As with previous volumes in the Vijayanagara Research Project Monograph Series, Ramesh Jain has acted as a highly responsible publisher, with B.N. Varma as an ever-vigilant production manager. We are grateful to both for maintaining high standards while seeing our ninth monograph through the press.

To all of these individuals and institutions, we tend our grateful thanks.

JOHN M. FRITZ and GEORGE MICHELL
Co-Directors of the Vijayanagara Research Project
Editors of the Vijayanagara Monograph Series

INTRODUCTION

LITERARY AND CULTURAL CONTEXT

Kannada, along with Telugu and Tamil, was one of the most important languages spoken in the Vijayanagara empire. Its literature is among the most varied and prolific of southern India.

Literary developments

Apart from numerous inscriptions dating from the sixth and seventh centuries AD, the earliest surviving work in Kannada is the *Kavirajamarga* by Shrivijaya dating from the mid-ninth century. Early Kannada literature from then until the twelfth century shows a marked Jaina influence. Most of the authors were Jainas and their works were either translations from the Sanskrit, or imitations of the format set by Sanskrit and Prakrit Jaina literature.

The situation changes dramatically in the twelfth century with the emergence of Virashaivism. Under the influence of its founder, Basava, a new linguistic style was created. The old ornate language of the *champu kavyas* (a mixture of verse and prose) became obsolete. Basava adopted the terse and direct language of the common people. His doctrine inspired a vast literary output, mainly consisting of religious topics, couched in a poetic prose, the *vachana*, a literary form typical of Virashaiva devotional literature. In its wake, new poetic metres, some deriving from folk ballads and popular songs, came into usage. Literary production focused on the importance of *bhakti*, rather than on typically Jaina themes, such as the transience of human life and the present world, and on renunciation.

The death of the charismatic figure of Basava dealt a severe blow to the Virashaiva community, which subsequently split into various groups. This, compounded with the Muslim invasion of southern India at the close of the thirteenth century and the subsequent political instability, marked the end of the primacy of Virashaivism in Karnataka.

Apart from Jaina and Virashaiva influence, there was a third important element that played a determinant role in Kannada literary history. This was the Shaiva and Vaishnava inspired *bhakti* movement, which was very strong in the neighbouring Tamil country. The devotion to a personal god found a fertile ground among the Kannada-speaking masses. Rama and Krishna, from being mere *avataras*, became supreme gods in their own right. Preachers vied with each other to propagate the new cults: devotional hymns were composed and disseminated throughout Karnataka by wandering bards.

During the fourteenth century, at the beginning of the Vijayanagara period, a new kind of popular literature emerged in southern India as the by-product of numerous devotional movements. Its language was straightforward, immediate, and the verses could be recited or sung. The appeal of this new type of poetry spread rapidly and by the mid-fourteenth century it was employed by poets of different backgrounds. Jaina authors discarded their old mannerisms and used simple metres. Shaiva and Vaishnava authors chose to write in Kannada instead of Sanskrit, thereby initiating a substantial production of devotional works.

There was also a revival of Virashaivism after a period of stagnation of over a hundred years. Virashaiva activity was concentrated mainly in southern Karnataka. From here, its influence spread again throughout the region, recovering the losses it had sustained and attracting the masses anew. An impressive body of this type of literature was produced between 1336 and 1565.

The authors and their backgrounds

From the vast literary output of the Vijayanagara era it has been necessary to limit the choice of topics presented in this Anthology. These have been selected to complement the data obtained from epigraphic, archaeological and art historical research, attempting, as far as possible, to recreate the atmosphere of the Vijayanagara period, allowing for the poetical flights of fantasy of the authors. The excerpts are drawn from 27 of the most relevant Kannada works written between *ca.* 1345 to 1585. The majority of the consulted texts is written in verse, especially in *shatpadi* (and its six varieties), *sangatya* and *champu* (mixture of rhyme and prose), and only very rarely in prose.

The authors come from different religious and cultural backgrounds: Jaina, Virashaiva, Vaishnava or Shaiva. Except for some technical or secular works, most of them composed poetry inspired by their own creed, refusing in no uncertain terms to tackle other subjects. As far as it is possible to ascertain given the paucity of information, their social background was very diverse. Some, such as Deparaja are reputed to be courtly figures. It has even been suggested that Deparaja, the author of the *Sobagine Sone*, was the psuedonym of the emperor Devaraya II. Other authors, such as Mangarasa III and Kanakadasa, were *dandanayakas* (local chieftains); Srutakirti was a Jaina ascetic and Bhattaleshvara a Sanskrit scholar and priest, while Chandrashekhara and Kalyana-Kirti were court poets.

Jaina literature

Eleven works in this Anthology represent Jaina literature. These concentrate on two main themes: the lives of the *tirthankaras* and the edifying stories illustrating the main tenets of Jainism.

A number of Jaina authors chose to compose poems on the life of a *tirthankara* whom they particularly revered. Three such works are represented here. Soon after the establishment of the Vijayanagara dynasty, Bahubali Pandita composed the *Dharmanatha Purana* (*ca.* 1352), which is the last example of the almost obsolete literary form of *champu.* Around 1457, Ratnakaravarni wrote the *Bharatesha Vaibhava Sangraha,* perhaps one of the most important works of Kannada literature. The versatile Mangarasa III was the author of the *Nemijinesha Sangati* (*ca.* 1508).

The genre of edifying stories was popular from the early period of Kannada Jaina literature. These had an educational aim in that they illustrated the Jaina doctrine and its fundamental principles. An example of this type of literature in its refined form is Bhaskara's *Jivandhra Charite* of 1424. The story, which is known from Sanskrit and Tamil literature, had a particular appeal; thus Terakanambi Bommarasa took up the same theme (*ca.* 1485). Among the other well known works in this kind are the *Nagakumara Charite* (*ca.* 1425) and *Jnanachandrabhyudhaya* (1439) by Kalyana-Kirti, the *Sanatkumara Charite* by Terakanambi Bommarasa (*ca.* 1485) and the *Samyukta Kaumudi* by Mangarasa III (*ca.* 1508). This type of literature ends with the *Vijayakumari Charite* by Srutakirti (*ca.* 1567). Although most, if not all these narratives, are drawn from classic Sanskrit, Prakrit or Tamil, the authors felt free to alter their subject according to their inspiration, thereby incorporating some valuable observations on contemporary social and religious life.

Virashaiva literature

Excerpts from twelve Virashaiva works have been included in this Anthology.

Among the diverse kinds of Virashaiva literature, the most important are narratives focusing on the life of Basava and other prominent Virashaivas. One of the most famous is the *Padmaraja Purana* by Padmanaka (*ca.* 1385). The poem deals with the career of Kereya-Padmarasa, a minister at the court of Narasimha Ballala.

Three other significant works in this category are the *Prabhulinga Lile* by Chamarasa (*ca.* 1430), an account of the life of the mystic, Allama, also known as Allama Prabhu, the ideologist of the Virashaiva movement; the *Proudharayana Kavya* by Adrishya-Kavi (*ca.* 1430), a poem narrating the life of the Virashaiva saints and Shaiva devotees; and the *Amalabasava Charite*, the life of Basava, by Singiraja (*ca.* 1500). Finally, one of the most significant authors of the period under review, Virupaksha Pandita, composed the *Channabasava Purana* (*ca.* 1585), a biography of the nephew of Basava.

The compilations of Virashaiva mythology constitute another related literary genre. The most important of these is the *Shivatattva Chintamani* (*ca.* 1450) composed by Lakkannadandesha. Two slightly earlier works, the anonymous *Virupaksha Shataka* (*ca.* 1410) and the *Pampasthana Varnanam* by Chandrashekhara (*ca.* 1430), focus on Hampe and its environs, celebrating its mythical background and sanctity.

Shaiva and Vaishnava literature

Under the patronage of the Vijayanagara rulers, both Shaiva and Vaishnava faiths flourished. Brahmin writers, who until this period continued to cultivate Sanskrit, now started to produce works in Kannada to spread their creed among the masses. Some of them rendered the great Sanskrit epics into Kannada, while others became wandering bards (*dasas*), preaching in simple language the philosophy of the Upanishads. These changes appealed to the people and increased religious fervour. Four works by Vaishnava authors are included here; three are inspired by the great epics and one by the *Bhagavata Purana*.

Based on a Sanskrit work with the same title, the Kannada *Jaimini Ashvamedha* by Lakshmisha (1345-47) focuses not so much on Yudhisthira's *ashvamedha-yajna*, as on the figure of Krishna, portrayed here as the supreme god. The next work is Kumara Vyasa's *Airavata* (*ca.* 1430), which is an elaboration of an episode of the *Mahabharata*. Here, too, Krishna plays a pivotal role in the unfolding of events. Kumara Vyasa was also responsible for a very successful Kannada version of the epic, the *Bharata*, where he omitted the last eight books of the original *Mahabharata*. The sequel to Kumara Vyasa's work, the *Karnataka Krishnaraya Bharata*, was composed by Timmanna (*ca.* 1510), one of the court poets of Krishnadevaraya, by order of the king. The *Ramayana* was recast into Kannada by various authors. In the present selection are some excerpts from the Virashaiva version of the poem *Kaushika Ramayana* by Battaleshvara (*ca.* 1500).

In this period two Kannada versions of the *Bhagavata Purana* were composed. Among the works inspired by the events narrated in this Purana, one of the most important is Kanakadasa's *Mohana Tarangini* (*ca.* 1550), a work rich in descriptions of contemporary life.

Semi-historical literature

In this Anthology are two works belonging to this category: Nanjunda Kavi's *Ramanatha Charite* (*ca.* 1525) is a romantic narrative interspersed with some historical facts, while the *Shri Krishnadevarayana Dinachari*, the so-called diary of Krishnadevaraya by Timmaya and Mallaya, is one of the very few prose works in Kannada literature. The *Shri Krishnadevarayana Dinachari* presents something of a problem since recent scholarship suggests the possibility that it may be a translation into Kannada of the Telugu *Rayavachakamu* composed either in the late sixteenth or the early seventeenth century at the Nayaka court of Madurai. In spite of these doubts, the *Krishnadevarayana Dinachari* is included here as it is an important testimony to the pivotal role played by Krishnadevaraya in southern Indian history.

In addition to the literary genres that have already been mentioned, there are also numerous collections of verses of religious inspiration (*shatakas*), as well as treatises on poetics, lexicography, medicine, astrology and erotics. An exceptional work of fundamental importance for the study of food is the *Supa-Shastra* by Mangarasa III (*ca.* 1508). It is the only surviving cookery book of the Vijayanagara period.

Cultural context

The internal evidence gleaned from the works in this Anthology suggests that poems were composed and recited in a courtly milieu. The fact that a number of the authors of this group of texts were court poets demonstrates that recitation or public reading of literary composition was part of the cultured life in the palace, as indeed was the reading of and commenting on sacred texts, which still plays an important role in religious institutions and meetings in southern India.

Some works, such as the Jaina *Bharatesha Vaibhava Sangraha* or the Virashaiva *Shivatattva Chintamani,* were intended to strengthen the faith in the moral principles in one or the other of the faiths obtaining in the Vijayanagara period. The same applies to those works eulogizing the life of some prominent religious figure, such as the *Padmaraja Purana* or the *Channabasava Purana.* Some of the authors were very keen to parade their knowledge of various disciplines, as demonstrated by the lengthy passages on moral conduct, cult and ritual, as well as statecraft. Other texts, such as the *Sobagina Sone, Ramanatha Charite* and *Mohana Tarangini,* which were filled with romantic episodes and adventures, catered to a wider audience. It must be noted, however, that even the works with an ideological agenda had plenty of entertaining passages, no doubt intended to retain the attention of their audience.

The majority of the texts seems to express the points of view of either the Vijayanagara ruler and his courtly advisors or of the religious establishment. Criticism was probably not openly expressed. No doubt, conflicts and differences of opinion existed, but these were voiced through veiled allusions and subtle tongue-in-cheek hints that would only have been picked up by those involved in the scheming and politics at court or in religious institutions.

The question arises here of how can we know that the observations contained in the texts actually refer to Vijayanagara. Poets such as Lakkannadandesha, Adrishya-kavi and Ratnakaravarni lived or visited Hampe and were familiar with the courtly life at the capital. It is most probable that they incorporated their observations into their works. As far as the other authors are concerned, especially those who lived at a great distance from the capital, such as Kalyana-kirti of Karkala, it is conceivable that they described their own local environment, adding some details that they may have heard from passing dignitaries and travellers who had actually visited the capital. It is clear, however, that beneath all the poetical exaggerations and flights of imagination, all these works reflect various facets of life in the Vijayanagara period as seen from different vantage points.

An ideal world

The texts in this Anthology give a picture, albeit idealized, of the life of king, court and capital in the Vijayanagara period. This vision is due, at least partly, to the rules of Kannada poetics, according to which there are eighteen topics which should be treated in a poetic work, ranging from landscape, such as the sea or mountains, to battles, and from politics to love (see Appendix III).

The poets conjure up an ideal world filled with magnificent visions of verdant, well-watered, fertile lands, yielding rich crops, surrounded by mountain ranges rich in metals and precious stones. The capital, built according to the traditional rules of Hindu architecture, is inhabited by contented citizens of all castes, mindful of their place in society, and pursuing their own activities. The king himself, surrounded by able ministers, lives and acts in accordance with the rules established by the *dharmashastras* (law-treatises), while his policies follow those of the *nitishastras* (treatises on politics). Needless to say, religious practices are scrupulously followed; religious personalities, regardless of their creed, are duly revered; and temples and religious establishments are richly endowed. The court fosters the development of literary pursuits and the arts, as well as encouraging civic works such as the building of channels, reservoirs and tanks. The return of a victorious army, a royal visit to a pleasure garden, a royal wedding and the birth of a prince, are all occasions for public rejoicing and lavish bestowing of gifts and donations to religious mendicants and needy citizens.

Despite the overall urge to portray a pristine society, there are the occasional tales of violence, adultery, jealousy, lust and hatred. These basic instincts are generally used as a pretext to turn the unsavoury aspects of life into a topic for edification and meditation. Accounts of battles, sieges of fortresses and other war operations have at times a remarkable spontaneity, demonstrating that the authors were familiar with the current tactics of warfare and methods of defence. This, of course, did not prevent them taking off into a world of fantasy, enumerating magical weapons allegedly also used in warfare.

The same freshness of approach is found in the passages describing markets and bazaars teeming with busy vendors and buyers. The wares on offer in the shops and the bustle of the streets, the various betting shops and taverns, and the quarters of the concubines invite us to participate in the excitement of the scene. Vijayanagara was famous as one of the best-stocked markets of its time; possibly a number of details which percolated into the poetic works are drawn from personal observation. This is especially true of the description of costumes, jewellery, household items, buildings and pavilions, many of which have their visual counterpart in the sculpture and painting of the period.

The Anthology

The present work consists of 25 chapters arranged into six parts.

Part One, The Setting, contains descriptions of landscapes, cities of various types, their amenities, such as palaces, temples, streets, markets, civic works and charitable institutions, and agriculture and forestry. Chapter 5 considers the perception of the Vijayanagara area as the locus of mythological events and hence as a hallowed spot.

Part Two, The King, is concerned with courtly life. The intricate courtly etiquette is explored at length in the section on royal visits and receptions and in the section on the bestowing of honours. Particularly important is Chapter 7, The Ideal Ruler in the Ideal State, in which the authors vie with each other in displaying their knowledge of treatises on statecraft and law.

Part Three, Polity, has vivid accounts of the organization of the army, enrolment tactics, layout of the encampment, types of weapons and strategic formations of the army, as well as breath-taking descriptions of cities and fortresses under siege.

Part Four, Pleasures of the Court, deals with courtly pastimes such as hunting parties, visits to the royal gardens and water-sports; royal banquets with extensive comments on the bill of fare and dining etiquette, and even actual cooking recipes; and royal weddings and royal patronage of the arts. The buoyancy of courtly life, its pomp and pageantry is rendered here in the most glowing terms. Royal weddings, as described in Chapter 19, provided ample scope for the poets to dwell lovingly on the minutest details of dress, makeup and ritual, all of which, no doubt, were highly appreciated by their audience.

Part Five, Religious Life, is devoted to festivals and rituals. Chapter 21 has a brief description of the Mahanavami festival, which in the fourteenth century was still a simple affair in contrast to the grand event described in great detail by sixteenth-century foreign visitors. Private worship and royal visits to temples and monasteries are discussed in Chapter 22. Of special interest is the account of a *sati* ceremony at the end of this chapter.

Part Six, Everyday Life, Beliefs and Pastimes, records daily life. Chapter 23 has various accounts of the dreams of the mothers-to-be, forecasting the birth of religious personalities or princes, and proceeds with several narratives detailing the various ceremonies that celebrate a royal birth. Omens, magic spells and traditional medicine are explored in Chapter 24, and finally Chapter 25 is a brief survey of the various pastimes indulged in by different categories of citizens: betting games, board and other indoor games, martial sports and others.

Three appendices follow the Anthology.

Appendix I gives essential summary information about the 27 texts that have been consulted and their authors. The material is presented in chronological order, according to the dates assigned to the authors by the editors of the various texts.

Appendix II is a glossary of Kannada terms and their English equivalents. Unfortunately, it was not always possible to find English equivalents for all the food preparations mentioned in the excerpts, since many of these are now obsolete. The same applies to a number of plants, flowers and military and other equipment.

Appendix III contains explanations of some of the recurring phrases, such as "the eighteen persons at the service of the king" and "the proverbial 56 countries".

Note to the reader

The excerpts comprising the Anthology have been selected and arranged according to various topics. Their order, of course, does not conform to the sequence in the original sources. At the end of each paragraph a reference is given indicating the source, chapter and verse. The texts have been paraphrased rather than translated literally; occasionally the translator has conflated material from different chapters of the same work into a coherent narrative. This is noted in the appropriate references.

The authors were obsessed with long enumerations and the reader will perhaps be surprised to find long lists, of plants, trees, flowers, jewels and other items, all of which end with the word "etcetera" or the expression "and others". These abrupt endings are not the whim of the translator, but are in the original text, as if the poet would leave it to the imagination of his listeners to muse on the almost indescribable variety and wealth he is trying to convey through his enumeration. The terms of the lists follow the same order as that given in the original texts.

References

Desai, P.B., "Language and Literature (iii) Kannada", in H.K. Sherwani and P.M. Joshi, eds., *History of Medieval Deccan (1295-1724)*, vol. II, Hyderabad, 1974, pp. 35-55.

Mugali, R., *History of Kannada Literature*, New Delhi, 1975.

Narasimha Char, D.L., "Kannada Literature under Vijayanagara (1336-1565 A.D.)", in *Vijayanagara Sexcentenary Commemoration Volume*, Dharwar, 1936, pp. 347-66.

Narasimhacharya, R., *History of Kannada Literature*, reprint, New Delhi, 1988.

Ramanujan, A.K., *Speaking of Shiva*, Harmondsworth, 1973.

Rice, E.P., *A History of Kannada Literature*, reprint, New Delhi, 1982.

Wagoner, P.B., *Tidings of the King. A Translation and Ethnohistorical Analysis of the Rayavacakamu*, Honolulu, 1993.

ABBREVIATIONS OF SOURCE TEXTS

A	*Airavata* (No. 9)
AC	*Amalabasava Charite* (No. 17)
BVS	*Bharatesha Vaibhava Sangraha* (No. 14)
CP	*Channabasava Purana* (No. 27)
DP	*Dharmanatha Purana* (No. 2)
J	*Jnanachandrabhyudaya* (No. 11)
JB	*Jaimini Bharata* (No. 1)
JCB	*Jivandhra Charite* by Bhaskara-Kavi (No. 6)
JCT	*Jivandhra Charite* by Terakanambi Bommarasa (No. 16)
KKB	*Karnataka Krishnaraya Bharata* (No. 22)
MT	*Mohana Tarangini* (No. 25)
NC	*Nagakumara Charite* (No. 12)
NS	*Nemijinesha Sangati* (No. 20)
PK	*Proudharayana Kavya* (No. 10)
PL	*Prabhulinga Lile* (No. 7)
PP	*Padmaraja Purana* (No. 3)
PV	*Pampasthana Varnanam* (No. 8)
R	*Ramayana* by Battaleshvara (No. 18)
RC	*Ramanatha Charite* (No. 24)
S	*Shivatattva Chintamani* (No. 13)
SC	*Sanatkumara Charite* (No. 15)
SK	*Samyutka Kaumudi* (No. 21)
SKD	*Shri Krishnadevarayana Dinachari* (No. 23)
SoS	*Sobagina Sone* (No. 5)
SuS	*Supa Shastra* (No. 19)
VC	*Vijayakumari Charite* (No. 26)
VS	*Virupaksha Shataka* (No. 4)

The numbers after each title refer to the sequence of source texts as they appear chronologically in Appendix I (pp. 137-54). The citations at the end of each extract in the Anthology quote the above abbreviation, together with the chapter(s) and verse(s) of the original manuscript, followed by the page reference(s) in the published work given for each source text in Appendix I.

ANTHOLOGY

PART ONE

THE SETTING

Chapters 1 to 6, which constitute the first part of this work, set the larger scene of the extracts to follow. They describe fortified cities, their palaces and temples, markets, streets, waterworks, charitable institutions, forests, agriculture and floriculture. This information is generalized, conforming, by and large, to the appropriate themes and rules of poetic composition. Thus the poets conjure up an ideal world in which mountains yield plenty of minerals and precious stones, fields are verdant and fertile, rivers have plenty of water, and the capital city is built according to the tenets of architectural treatises and inhabited by citizens who are ruled by a just king, all leading an exemplary life.

In Chapter 2, the town and its fortifications are explored in some detail, together with the marvellous yet improbable description of the layout and fort of Manipuram, the famed capital of Babhruvahana and other similar fortified cities. A number of interesting details about actual fortifications, such as the various elements of a fortress and the typology of fortification systems, emerge from the poetic narrative.

In Chapter 3, the depiction of the palaces with their innumerable halls, among which the audience hall has pride of place, gives the poets ample scope to vie with each other's imagination. Perhaps the most striking is the description of Babhruvahana's audience hall (see Section 3.11), with its 10,000 pillars sheathed in gold and its wealth of marble, mirrorwork, gold-plated statues and dazzling gems, in which, according to the poet Jaimini, it would have been "difficult to decide whether it was day or night". Not only are the public rooms deemed worthy of the poets' attention: private audience halls, secret council chambers, rear courtyards with marvellous gardens, storerooms, bathhouses, gymnasia, terraces, roof pavilions partly open to the sky in order to admire the moon at night, and finally the private apartments of the king, queen and princess, are all painstakingly described. There is information on wall decoration such as textiles and murals; mention is also made of various types of cots, lamps, and other objects such as special containers for water and baskets of betel-nuts and leaves. Special attention is given to the various kinds of incense and other perfumes which were either burnt or sprinkled on the floors of the private apartments.

The city has, of course, a number of temples. Although shrines and religious cults are among the most important topics in these poems, the buildings are only very cursorily mentioned. (For the ritual activities that are the main focus of the authors' attentions see Chapter 22.)

One of the most vivid sections of this part is undoubtedly Chapter 4, which offers a vibrant description of the town, with its streets laid out in a grid, and its various quarters inhabited by the representatives of various professions such as philosophers, scholars, merchants and hunters. Next are its bustling markets where anything under the sun can be purchased: textiles, brassware, precious stones, groceries, cosmetics, flowers and perfumes. These last two items are intimately connected with the "street of the concubines", a theme which fascinated authors, giving them ample scope to dwell on feminine charms and elegance. Of the substantial number of descriptions of "street of the concubines", the four most informative have been reproduced here. Another relevant theme dealt with in this chapter is the provision of water and various types of hydraulic devices. Finally, the section on charitable institutions centres on the free feeding-houses and water-sheds, which were constructed along the main roads of the country to provide travellers and pilgrims with food and refreshments, and a place to rest in the course of their journeys.

Vijayanagara is dealt with exclusively in Chapter 5. This opens with the two most relevant legends related to the town: the marriage of Virupaksha and Pampa, and the founding of the city by the sage Vidyaranya. It then proceeds with a description of Vijaya-nagara, its surroundings, the numerous holy places, the distinguished sages who lived there, and of Hemakuta hill. The chapter concludes with a list of the names of the deities wor-shipped in the city.

Chapter 6, the last of this part, is concerned mainly with forestry, agriculture and agricul-tural products. The poets have here compiled substantial lists of plants, trees, shrubs and flowers. Although it is not always possible to determine the exact identity of all of the plants, these enumerations are particularly valuable as they give an insight into what was grown and consumed in this period.

Chapter 1

TOWN AND COUNTRY

This chapter deals with idealized descriptions of hilly and verdant landscapes, blessed by abundant rains and rivers, in which nestle towns built according to the traditional tenets of architecture and inhabited by law-abiding citizens. One of these is the capital of the kingdom of Vidyanagara (Vijayanagara) ruled by the famous king Devaraya II (1424-46), also known as Proudharaya. The chapter ends with a brief description of training grounds for martial sports outside the city of Hosamaledurga.

1.1 The region of Kousaladesam

The *Dharmanatha Purana* describes the Kousala region as follows.

The country [Bharatakshetra] was situated to the south of the mountain [Meru?]. One of its six parts was known as Kousaladesam. It was rich in forests that yielded many kinds of products, and it had plenty of minerals such as gold and diamonds. There were large fields in which different types of crops were cultivated and a great number of water reservoirs, tanks and ponds, which irrigated the paddy and sugarcane crops.

It was a wealthy country and its inhabitants were prosperous, as could be seen from the piles of grain. A number of streams and rivulets flowed throughout the year. In the gardens on the banks of these water courses there were lush creepers of betel-leaves. [...]

Crabs, fish, alligators and swans teemed in the ponds, rivers, streams. In the fields were sugarcane, paddy and other crops, which attracted parrots and other birds. The deer, lured by the corn, were driven away by girls whose job it was to guard the fields. (*DP*, I, 68-81; pp. 14-16)

That lovely country had main roads that were shaded by trees and creepers. At places there were shady resorts which served as [charity] water-huts where travellers could have cool and fragrant drinking water and various kinds of sweet and ripe fruits. These huts were managed by beautiful young ladies. (*DP*, I, prose & 90; p. 18)

1.2 The capital of the Chadura country

A detailed account of a metropolitan city is given by the *Sobagina Sone* in the following passage on the capital of the Chadura country.

Around the city there were high mountains and rivers. The city was surrounded by a fortification wall. Beyond the wall one could see towering, white storeyed buildings. It was a prosperous place. A wide variety of trees and plants laden with flowers and fruit grew there. There were tanks, lakes, ponds with lotuses in full bloom, and fields with abundant sugarcane crops.

In the gardens of the city there was a large variety of birds, bees and butterflies; there were cuckoos, parrots, peacocks, cranes, swans and other birds. Groups of young girls moved about in the plantain groves and paddy fields, driving away the sparrows and other birds. (*SoS*, XVII, 50-7; pp. 241-3)

[Some] streets were crowded with elephants, horses and princesses sent as tributes by the kings of vanquished kingdoms. (*SoS*, XVII, 59; p. 243)

The streets were skirted on both sides by storeyed buildings. Flags and banners made of coloured silk fluttered above their roofs. [In some houses] were swings with golden peacock motifs. Many entrance gates were decorated with festoons of mirrors.

There were streets with shops for clothes, brass-ware, pearls, diamonds, military equipment such as armour, and perfumery shops from which wafted the fragrance of [different] flowers.

Handsome, elegantly dressed ladies wore tasteful ornaments, which produced harmonious sounds while they gracefully walked through the street. They could be seen in the main street and on the golden swings in the pleasure gardens. (*SoS*, XVIII, 4-7; pp. 247-8)

Some [persons] were engrossed in playing dice, betting, and gambling. They bet conspicuous amounts of money, sometimes even large gems and various kinds of diamonds. These casinos were visited by princes and nobles, too, who occasionally wagered even their elephants and horses. There was also the street of the concubines in which one could see all kinds of people: young lovers, paramours, adulterers, poets and rogues. There were those who sang, gambled, composed poems, painted pictures and played on the *vine*; those who acted and danced; those who listened to [the recitation] of works by Bharata and to the *Kokashastra*; and those who watched the performances of jugglers and magicians. Together they produced a tremendous noise.

Further on there was the palace of the king at whose front was a imposing gateway studded with gems. It was guarded by stout elephants.

In the upper apartments of the beautifully painted guard-houses were soldiers holding shining swords and other weapons including the traditional twelve [types of weapons]. Occasionally from the guard houses came the sound of the *doude* and *dindima.*

There were stables for elephant and horses. In them too, one could hear the sound of instruments such as the *kahale*, *kinnari*, *tappate*, flute and *nissala.* A wind instrument was blown at regular intervals to announce the time. (*SoS*, XVIII, 4-19; pp. 247-50)

1.3 The kingdom of Vidyanagara and its capital

The *Proudharayana Kavya* has the following passage on the kingdom of Vidyanagara and its capital.

Of the 56 kingdoms of Bharatakhanda, the kingdom of Kuntala was one of the important ones, like a jewel [on the forehead of a lady]. It was beautiful and prosperous. It had a number of wealthy cities, towns and villages. All of them, invariably, had temples dedicated to Shiva, as well as tanks, canals filled with water, and gardens and groves with various kinds of trees and plants bearing fruits, nuts, etcetera in plenty, ensuring thus the welfare of the population. In all directions one could see cultivated fields with well-grown paddy, crops of sugarcane, and trees bearing pomegranates, lemons, grapes, jack-fruits and oranges. Plenty of flowers bloomed in the gardens, which were filled with bees, parrots, cuckoos, peacocks, etcetera. At special places on the roadside there were free feeding-houses and charity water-pavilions.

These houses for the use of the travellers were mainly managed by beautiful young ladies, who were a great attraction for the public. They stood in enticing poses at the entrance of the pavilions holding jars of water in their hands, and bantered with the weary travellers. Thus they laughed and enjoyed themselves. (*PK*, I, 32-4; pp. 9-10)

The city known as Vidyanagara stood out in that kingdom like the nose-ornament on the face of a beautiful lady. It was surrounded by a tall fortification wall surmounted by beautiful merlons. Bastions and towers were placed at regular intervals all along it. On top of the bastions were tall staffs with flags and banners fluttering in the air. The gates were embellished with gems. Inside the fort there were two well laid-out main streets, the *chandra-vidhi* and *surya-vidhi*, both lined with shops.

Good and noble-minded citizens inhabited the metropolitan city. They were intelligent, rational, clever, rich and flirtatious; they were conversant with the many languages learned in all the 64 branches of knowledge; they were devotees of the supreme god.

This city, with no equal on earth, was ruled by Proudharaya, who had a minister, Jakkanacharya, an ardent Shaiva devotee. (*PK*, I, 36-9; pp. 10-11)

Similar accounts of other cities are also found in the *Ramanatha Charite*, *Jivandhra Charite* by Bommarasa, and *Vijayakumari Charite.*

1.4 Training grounds for animals and men

In the description of Hosamaledurga in the *Ramanatha Charite* there is an interesting reference to the training grounds on the outskirts of the city.

On the outskirts of the town were grounds for the training of war elephants and horses by their masters. The elephants were classified into four categories: *mriga* (swift like an antelope or ferocious like a wild beast), *manda* (slow moving or dull), *bhadra* (extraordinarily strong) and *sankirna* (of complex or mixed qualities). (*RC*, IV, 69; p. 67)

There were other elephants that were used during functions such as the royal coronation. Similarly, there were the finest breeds of horses, trained by experts in the trade. (*RC*, IV, 71-3; pp. 67-8)

There were also arenas where fights were held between bisons and between rams, and where boxers exercised. (*RC*, IV, 74-9; pp. 68-9)

In other places, brave soldiers and princes practised using various kinds of weapons. (*RC*, IV, 80-2, p. 69)

At the centre of the fort there was a huge building, the arsenal. (*RC*, IV, 85, p. 70)

Chapter 2

FORTIFIED CITIES

In this selection of texts there are a number of descriptions of cities and forts. Generally, all the accounts portray the "ideal city" laid out according to the rules prescribed by the treatises on architecture.

2.1 The city of Manipuram

The earliest and the most detailed description of a fortified city is that of Manipuram, the capital of Arjuna's son Babhruvahana, from the *Jaimini Bharata.*

The city was surrounded by a fortification wall. [Its towers and bastions] were adorned with gold and silver sheaths and studded with precious stones such as diamonds, rubies, lapis-lazuli, red gems and others. Even the rampart walls were similarly decorated. Festoons of rubies and corals and clusters of beautiful pearls hung from the roof-eaves. Painted figures were seen on the towered gateways and filigree work enhanced the doors. The storeyed buildings within that fort were also embellished with golden sheaths. Being whitewashed, they were easily distinguishable above the [rampart] walls. Apart from tall buildings, the fortified city had a main street called *raja-marga.* The main attraction was the palace of the king at the centre. Numerous flags and banners, some decorated with paintings, were hoisted there, together with other embellishments such as garlands, festoons, tassels of precious stones and bunches of beads and pearls. A deep moat surrounded the city. The fort wall had eight bastions upon which were raised flags and banners. Important gateways, efficiently and strictly controlled by guards, were similarly beautified. It was a busy town; thousands of people [of different professions and on different errands], horses, elephants, carts, officers and others passed in and out of the gateways at all times. (*JB*, XVII, 6-10; pp. 186-7)

2.2 The fort at Pampakshetra

The second passage quoted here is an account of the sacred site of Pampakshetra (Hampe) from the *Pampasthana Varnanam.*

The sacred centre [Pampakshetra], with rich woodlands and thick groves situated on the outskirts, looked as if its outermost fortification wall was painted green [on account of the lush vegetation]. The various parts of that fort were richly decorated: the fort wall with gold plate, the doorways with diamonds, the door-lintels with topaz stones, the basements with crystal, the walls with gems of a reddish hue, the platforms [raised seats] with coral, the pavilions with pearls, the steps with moonstones, the upstairs apartments with rubies, the statues with sapphires, the windows with lapis-lazuli, the entrance festoons with emeralds and the pot-shaped finials with gold plate; the banners and flags were of silk. Inside that fort, were cool pleasure gardens, lakes and ponds crowded with people enjoying themselves, main streets such as the *soma-vidhi* and *surya-vidhi,* as well as smaller lanes and sumptuous residential buildings. In short, it was like the city of the gods, but six times better in all respects. Pampakshetra was a famous centre for Shiva's devotees who thronged to the place where Shaiva rituals and festivals were regularly performed throughout the year. Among the most popular [of these] were *Shivaratri, Shani-trayodashi, Somavara, Pashupatavratam* and others. In the centre of this renowned town were the palaces of the nobles and other subordinate rulers, large mansions of rich individuals, various beautiful residences of virtuous gentry, tastefully decorated tall buildings, finely-finished homes, storeyed buildings with open pavilions at the top, houses inhabited by religious persons, towering entrance gateways and many more. They were all arranged in planned rows and tastefully embellished. The presiding deity of that place was the *jyotirlinga,* Virupakshamahadeva. (*PV*, I, 40-53; pp. 12-15)

2.3 The fort at Kalyani

The *Shivatattva Chintamani* describes the fort at Kalyani as follows:

Proceeding further towards the city, one could see its fort with its bastions and ramparts. There were stone slabs projecting from the fort's wall [used to hold stones to be thrown down in the course of a battle]. There were also mechanical contrivances with decorative animal faces [boar, lion, tiger and the like], which were used to forcefully eject stones and other fighting equipment such as balls, shots, spikes, spears, firearms, huge logs of wood, etcetera.

The fort had been provided with bent entryways, on which were [sculpted] tiger faces [to scare away or prevent the entry of enemies, or used as auspicious marks]. The entrances had strong doors and locks. (*S*, XXXI, 6; p. 250)

2.4 The fort of the Bedas

The following account of the fort of the Bedas is drawn from the *Jivandhra Charite* by Terakanambi Bommarasa.

[The Bedas] built a fort at the border of the kingdom to attack the [usurper] king. It had a wide moat filled with water. The fort had been provided with suitable entrance gateways on the four sides. On top of the wall were impressive series of merlons and towering bastions.

There were ramparts, platforms, bastions, towers and tall posts with fluttering flags and banners. Large numbers of war drums and other musical instruments were stored on the ramparts. There were heaps of sand, thick and long ropes, pointed wooden spears, arrows, storehouses filled with gun powder, granaries [and other war requirements]. There were also gymnasia where soldiers practised their fighting skills. Outside the fortification wall, a number of trees had been planted, interspersed with boulders of various sizes, to prevent direct access to the fort wall by troops on horses and elephants. (*JCT*, VIII, 7-14; pp. 56-7)

2.5 The parts of a fort

The *Amalabasava Charite* gives a precise nomenclature for the various parts of a fort:

Giri (peak-like towers), *konte* (fort wall), *agalu* (moat or ditch), *tene* (merlons), *alaveri* (rampart wall), *attale* (bastion), *makara* (device in the form of a crocodile) and *durga* (stronghold or citadel). (*AC*, XXXV, 24; p. 367)

2.6 Typology of fortification systems

The *Shri Krishnadevarayana Dinachari* specifies four kinds of fortified places:

Giri-durga (fort on a peak or mountain), *sthala-durga* (fort in a plain), *vana-durga* (fort in a forest) and *jala-durga* (fort on a river island). (*SKD*, I, prose; p. 10)

The last three excerpts in this section deal with descriptions of forts and give an insight into the layout of the towns within the fort.

2.7 Fortified towns I

The following account is drawn from the *Ramanatha Charite.*

All the streets within the fort had rows of beautiful houses, shining in the lustrous light produced by the precious gems and diamonds set into their walls. On the tops of those buildings were rows of oil lamps. There was no house that had not been decorated with mango leaves, festoons, pinnacles, mirrors, banners and bunches of greenery. Furthermore, the walls were painted with pictures or portraits and the basements were inlaid with stones. Each house had a well that was fitted with a mechanical contrivance for lifting up water, as well as a swing of green creepers. (*RC*, IV, 97-100; p. 72)

2.8 Fortified towns II

The following description is drawn from the *Mohana Tarangini.*

The city had a strong and massive fortification wall. In the construction of that stone fort a binding agent [of mud or lime mortar] had been used. (*MT*, XX, 5; p. 293)

A deep and wide moat encircled the fort. It was full of alligators, crocodiles, hippopotamus, large fish, big tortoises, crabs and other creatures. (*MT*, III, 4; p. 44 & XX, 11; p. 295)

At strategic positions, the fort wall had bulwarks and bastions. The bastions were all strong, sturdy and adequately tall. Canopies, topped with metal pinnacles, embellished them and created a pleasing view from a distance. Soldiers were stationed here, equipped with all kinds of weapons: spears, *marulkai* ("deceptive hand" devices), bows and others. (*MT*, III, 7; p. 45; XX, 5-14; p. 295)

The fort had large gateways at appropriate places. The doors of the main gate were lavishly ornamented. (*MT*, III, 10; p. 46)

The main gate was flanked by two huge sculptures of lions seated on their rumps; their mouths were wide open and their eyes cast ferocious looks. This gate was known as *puli-mukha* (tiger-faced). (*MT*, III, 9; p. 45; XX, 12; p. 295)

The [side] wings of the fort gates were fitted with strong and heavy latches for securing them when closed. They were so heavy that they could only be moved by elephants using their trunks. The fort had sixteen secret openings [posterns] and 32 narrow passageways. (*MT*, XX, 13-14; p. 295)

2.9 Fortified towns III

The last description of a fortified town is drawn from the *Channabasava Purana.*

There was an open area on the outskirts of the fortification where proficient and skilled martial-arts masters trained the young princes. The ground was also used for riding elephants and horses, and for practising the use of various weapons. Beyond that ground were deep moats, which surrounded the fortification wall and spread out for a long distance to the right and left. The fort wall had a number of tall bastions and battlements set at regular intervals. It also had 360 large gateways, appropriately placed. The width of that fortified enclosure was something like 48 *yojana-vistirna.* Within it were 120 *chandra-vidhis* and *surya-vidhis.* (*CP*, XI, 30-4; pp. 124-5)

Chapter 3

PALACES AND TEMPLES

This chapter is divided into four parts: three deal with the palace complex, including the reception and residential zones; the fourth is devoted to excerpts describing temples, both Hindu and Jaina, their halls, tanks and pavilions.

The palace

3.1 The palace complex

This selection starts with the description of Babhruvahana's palace from the *Jaimini Bharata*, which gives an insight into the various parts of the complex.

There was a pavilion for taking showers, a pavilion with a bed of soft tender leaves, a pavilion arranged in such a way to admit cool and fragrant breezes, a pavilion with platforms [or seats] made of marble, a pavilion or bower of creepers, a pond with fresh water skirted by cool sand heaps and shady trees and a roof[top] pavilion open to the sky. (*JB*, XXX, 36; p. 375)

3.2 Parts of the palace

The visit of a Shaiva mendicant gives the author Adrishya-Kavi the opportunity to enumerate various structures in the royal palace in his *Proudharayana Kavya.*

A Shaiva mendicant wished to see the palace of the king. This was promptly arranged by the minister, who gave the necessary instructions to an attendant. The mendicant entered the palace, following the attendant; he saw the gymnasium house, the stables, the garden, the pleasure tank with pure water, the pavilion decorated with murals, the court hall, the upper storeys, the storehouse, the treasure-house and the apartments for the 120 queens. (*PK*, XXI, 8-9; p. 293)

3.3 The palace and its subsidiary structures

This exhaustive account of a palace complex is drawn from the *Ramanatha Charite.*

The king's palace looked like a beautiful well-built ship with fluttering flags anchored in the midst of a vast ocean, the capital. The palace complex included a number of auxiliary structures such as stables for elephants and horses, an armoury with sophisticated weapons, an elegant theatre, a gallery with paintings, a council chamber, a study pavilion, a pleasure pavilion decorated with precious stones and other pavilions embellished with gold and gems. There were lofty storeyed buildings with tall towers whose sloping roofs were covered with a golden sheath. The roofs [of the pavilions were embellished] with corals and the doorways with gems. The front hall and the audience hall were resplendent with golden sheaths with beautifully-worked floral patterns. The outer court of the palace was filled with horses, elephants, soldiers, supplicants, ministers and ambassadors from other courts. (*RC*, V, 1-8; pp. 77-8)

3.4 Auxiliary structures

The *Dharmanatha Purana* has numerous descriptions of audience halls, bathing halls and adjacent dressing rooms, queens' apartments with attached audience and concert hall, marriage pavilion and other structures. Noteworthy is a brief mention of the gold-plated delivery apartment which "had been sterilized by heating", as well as the *chandra-shale* (moon-hall), partly open to the sky.

In the middle of the city were the stables for the [royal] horses and elephants, which were close to the king's palace. They were embellished with precious stones of green and blue. There were also armouries. These [buildings] were disposed in many rows. The king's vast assembly hall was at the centre of the metropolis, similar to a fully-blown lotus in the water of a tank. The king's palace was a majestic structure, seven storeys high and with upper apartments, all embellished with precious stones. It had tall towers with pot-shaped finials on the roofs. All the seven storeys were provided with halls. (*DP*, I, prose, 148-54; pp. 29-31)

Around the king's palace were the mansions of the queens, who often spent their time in the upper apartments. The wells were in the rear courtyards [of these palaces]. (*DP*, I, 158-60; pp. 31-2)

Within the king's palace there was a vast *puja* room built of shining stones. (*DP*, I, 162; p. 32)

There was the king's treasury where gems of different kinds were stored in heaps. (*DP*, I, 164; p. 32)

The whole palace was embellished by fixing, at the appropriate places, numerous flags, banners, tender leaves and sprouts, twigs, tassels of pearls, branches with fruits and other decorations. (*DP*, I, 167; p. 33)

3.5 Halls in the palace

In this passage from the *Ramanatha Charite*, the rendering of the restless lovelorn queen wandering through the palace, trying to find solace, gives the poet an excuse to mention, albeit very briefly, its various halls and pavilions.

One day, after bathing and dressing, the lovelorn queen, accompanied by her attendants, went to a hall on the terrace of a palace [called the] *chandra-shale* and sat on a seat in the shape of a lotus flower. (*RC*, XXIV, 166-8; p. 83, II)

Then, feeling restless, she visited other pavilions, but to no avail. She went to the hall decorated with paintings [or murals], the hall for theatrical performances, the audience hall and the hall for sports and games. (*RC*, XXV, 23; p. 89, II)

3.6 Garden in the palace's rear courtyard

In the same text is a charming description of the rear courtyard of the palace.

The [rear] courtyard of the palace had a beautiful pleasure garden. In the middle of it was a big mango tree. [One day], the queen went there, sat under the tree and looked at the pigeons, deer, peacocks, swans, parrots and other birds and animals, all playfully enjoying themselves. (*RC*, VII, 56-9; pp. 118-19)

3.7 Halls in the queen's palace

After describing the secluded garden in the rear courtyard of the palace, the *Ramanatha Charite* enumerates the halls in the queen's palace. A brief account of her private garden in the courtyard is given in the next excerpt, from the same source.

[In the queen's palace] were other halls such as the *chitra-shale* (hall with paintings or murals), *saitya-shale* (hall of coolness), *chandra-shale* (hall whose wooden roof was partly open to the sky, so as to allow the moonlight to fall inside), *bhadra-mantapa* (auspicious or lovely pavilion), *latavane* (pavilion of creepers and bushes), *mohana-mantapa* (charming pavilion) and *nelevada* (house with upper storeys). (*RC*, XXVI, 67-73; pp. 115-16, II)

3.8 Courtyard of the queen's palace

The courtyard attached to the palace of the queen had a number of bowers, all thickly covered with plants and creepers of different kinds, and pleasure ponds. It was full of tall trees, thick shrubs, dense bushes and verdant creepers. There were different types of plants, both ornamental and fruit-bearing; in short, it was a beautiful pleasure garden. (*RC*, XXXII, 23-9; pp. 228-9, II)

The last two excerpts of this section, drawn from the *Ramanatha Charite* and the *Channabasava Purana*, are both noteworthy for the wealth of detail regarding furniture, including various types of cots and other elements of interior decoration, of two very different palaces. The first is an underground palace in which a prince, unjustly persecuted by his own father, absconds; the second is a magnificent construction built according to the principles of architectural science, sited at the centre of the town. Particularly interesting here is the mention of sculptures, murals, hangings, floor decorations and containers filled with aromatic substances and cosmetics.

3.9 The prince's palace

An underground palace was built for the prince who was hiding from his father. It had the following facilities: sleeping chamber, bathing house, dining hall, main hall, front court hall and study hall. It was lavishly decorated with all kinds of gems. The basement [of the room] was decorated with blue sapphires, while rows of gems of the most exquisite kinds adorned the dressing room. There were different kinds of cots: one made of leaves and twigs, one with a beautiful canopy, one with a very soft mattress and one on a swing. Large containers were filled with perfumes and cosmetics such as camphor, musk, saffron coloured paste, sandal-paste, cool-scented water, *punugu* and civet-musk. There were also a basket of betel-leaves and a large bowl. (*RC*, XXXVI, 44-9; pp. 320-1, II)

3.10 The minister's palace

The palace was located at the centre of the fortified city, at one end of the bazaar. It had auxiliary structures such as elephant-stables, horse-stables, armoury, royal treasury and stores. (*CP*, XI, 47; p. 128)

By order of the minister, another palace was built nearby. It was designed by qualified architects according to the principles of the architectural treatises. It looked as if it had been the work of Vishvakarma because of the precious stones used in the construction and the exquisite attention to the details.

Its basement was [embellished] with sapphires, its walls with crystals or quartz and its pillars with diamonds; green emeralds were embedded in the beams. The capitals were adorned with diverse gems, while corals were fixed on the roof rafters and topazes on the doors; the shutters were covered with glittering gold sheaths.

In this palace were a number of apartments: bathing room, kitchen, dining hall, council hall, hall for dance performances, wardrobe, horse-stable, audience hall, concert hall and sleeping chamber. In addition, there were auxiliary structures for storing treasures and valuables of various kinds. The store-houses were meant for groceries such as oil, *ghee*, vessels containing other liquids, jaggery and food grains. Close by were the residential quarters for the servants entrusted with different services.

The palace had doors and gateways [decorated with] a variety of designs. The walls were embellished with metal sculptures and with murals. There were also painted bands and decorative drawings in fragrant colours on the floors and on the skirtings. Pot-shaped finials were [fixed] at appropriate places; tassels, festoons and tapestries embroidered with pearls and gems were hung tastefully.

The palace [complex] had six entrance gates, which had terraces, storeys and towers [embellished] with various kinds of precious stone, gems and pearls.

There was a pleasure garden with a large variety of trees, plants and creepers. It had a beautiful pond [for water sports], artificial hillocks and tastefully decorated pavilions raised on platforms. (*CP*, V, 47-52; pp. 52-3)

Reception

3.11 Public audience hall

This section opens with the detailed account of the magnificent audience hall in Babhru-vahana's palace in Manipuram, from the *Jaimini Bharata*. As in the previous two excerpts, gold, precious stones, lamps, marble and reflecting surfaces play a major role in the decoration of the hall, along with sculptures and paintings. Particularly intriguing are the references to the statues of young women in poses, and to objects and paintings brought from all over the world.

The audience hall was a square structure with 10,000 pillars. Its basement was of shining marble. The platform was decorated with green emeralds, the walls with sapphires, the pillars with diamonds, the bracket figures with lapis-lazuli, the corbels with shining gems of reddish colour, the beams with topazes and the curved roof-eaves with rubies. There were tassels of pearls and statues set with corals and the roof was covered with a sheath of gold.

In the hall were [metal] statues of attractive maidens shown in different stances: decorating or fixing a flower [in the hair], applying a *tilaka* to the forehead, turning the head to the side out of resentment or bashfulness, applying collyrium to the eyelashes, looking intently into a mirror and singing softly. They were shown in different dance poses and various expressions, playing the *vine* and other musical instruments, showing love marks on their face or body and so on. They were so realistic that one could mistake them for living beings. Their glittering [appearance] added to the illumination of the hall.

There were various images of birds: swans, cranes, partridges, peacocks, peahens, parrots, ducks, ruddy geese, herons and cuckoos. They were so exquisitely rendered as to seem alive.

Figures of lions, tigers, elephants, horses, and carts dragged by horses were also displayed here, along with art objects, mainly paintings, from various places on the earth.

That grand hall was decorated with precious stones, such as bluish sapphires, pure white pearls, lotus-coloured rubies and deep orange-pink corals, all casting different shades depending on their lustre. The light in the hall was such that it was difficult to decide whether it was day or night.

The marble floor was treated with fragrant substances such as musk and civet, while the walls were decorated with designs executed with red saffron. The fragrance of various burning substances such as sandalwood chips permeated the hall. There were metal images of ladies cupping their palms in such a way as to form oil lamps. The oil that fed the lamps was of fragrant camphor. There were many such figures, suitably placed according to the requirements. (*JB*, XVII, 23-7; pp. 190-1)

3.12 Private audience hall

The same text affords us a glimpse of the ruler, seated in state in his private audience hall, surrounded by his entourage. Particularly interesting are details such as the two female fly-whisk-bearers flanking the king, the "background music" playing all the while, the persons attending the meeting, the procedure followed by an arriving prince to gain access to the king and, finally, the actual reception of the prince carrying a confidential message that is opened and read in a secret chamber.

The audience hall was decorated with gems and diamonds. The throne on which the king was seated was at its centre. He was flanked by ladies holding fly-whisks. There were also subordinate kings, learned brahmins, ministers, writers, priests, debators, poets, singers, panegyrists, actors, dancers, experts in religious discourses and many others; music was played.

A prince arrived at the gates of the hall and alighted from his horse. Through the gate-keeper, he sent word to the king that he had arrived and wished to meet him. The message was passed from one entrance to the next until it reached the seventh one, where the most trusted among the gate-keepers, holding a staff in his hand, carried the message to the king, conveying it through the usual heralds. (*JB*, XXX, 44-7; p. 377)

At that, the king stepped down from the throne and went to receive the visiting prince, who was a great devotee of Vishnu. He embraced him and led him by the hand to the audience hall. He then enquired about the welfare of his parents and other matters. (*JB*, XXX, 44-9; pp. 377-8)

The visiting prince delivered a sealed and confidential letter sent by the king, his father. On receiving it the king got up, asked everybody else to remain in the audience hall, and proceeded to the secret council chamber accompanied by his son. There, once the seal was removed, he read the letter and was pleased with its contents. After that he returned to the audience hall. (*JB*, XXX, 44-52; p. 378-9)

3.13 Council chamber

The *Dharmanatha Purana* reveals the architectural features of the secret council chamber.

The princes [from different kingdoms] met in a council chamber for a secret consultation. The structure was circular, without windows and sound-proof. (*DP*, XIII, 8 prose; p. 344)

Residence

Particular care is given to the rendering of the refined ambiance of the sleeping apartments of the royal family. Camphor, musk, *vetiver*-screens, floral wreaths, floors sprinkled with sweet-scented water and a bed made of sandalwood with golden decoration and covered by soft pillows and mattresses provide the backdrop for a visit of the queen to the king's private room.

3.14 The queen visits the king at night

One night the queen, elaborately made up with the help of her assistants and ladies-in-waiting, set out for the decorated bedchamber. She was led there by her ladies, who were carrying hand-lamps. The chamber was provided with screens made of the fragrant root called *vetiver*. Sweet-smelling cool water was sprinkled on the screens, so that when the breeze passed through them small droplets would humidify the air. The whole room had been perfumed by spreading camphor, sandal and musk powder of exquisite quality. The strong fragrance could be smelt outside, wafting from the ventilation holes in the ceiling. (*DP*, VI, prose; p.133)

There was a golden bedstead decorated with sandalwood carvings. Seven mattresses were piled on it, one upon the other. These were made of soft swans' feathers. On them were silk spreads and silk blankets. A pure white curtain was there, too. On the bedstead were a large number of floral garlands. (*DP*, VI, 17, and prose; pp. 133-4)

In this room were silver containers filled with specially treated betel-nuts, tender betel-leaves, camphor powder, mixed lime and other fragrant edible powders, pots filled with sweet-smelling cold water, a number of lights and other necessary items which the king and the queen would require in the course of the night. (*DP*, VI, prose; p. 134)

3.15 The king's sleeping apartments

The following description of the king's sleeping apartments, one of the most elaborate of its kind, is drawn from the *Mohana Tarangini*. This passage is particularly interesting for its precise description of the furniture in the room and the reference to murals depicting love scenes.

The passage leading to the sleeping chamber [of the king] was embellished on both sides by statues holding lit torches in their raised right hands. Some of them were placed in richly framed wall niches. At regular intervals there were pegs supporting decorative arrangements consisting of festoons of various kinds of leaves, flowers, tree branches, coloured tapestries, hangings and bunches of pearls and beads. The flowers used were jasmine, *jaji, sampige, surahonne, nanda, padari* and *parijata.*

Along the walls of the bed chamber, too, there were many statues carrying lit torches. The metal statues were studded with jewels and diamonds. The wall space had been tastefully decorated with murals representing the stories and sports of Rati and Manmatha. In the middle of the chamber there was a richly decorated and canopied cot with a thick and soft mattress covered with numerous flower buds, so as to make it softer and cooler.

As soon as the cot was occupied by the king, the young and beautiful ladies of his entourage stood on either side and started singing his praises. The pleased king presented them with silk clothes, jewellery, perfumes and other fragrant substances. Thereafter, they took leave of him.

Some of the young ladies went to fetch the queen. She entered the chamber and, according to the custom, offered the king betel-nuts with camphor and white tender betel-leaves smeared with lime paste. Then they enjoyed the night pleasantly in many ways. The king was awakened in the morning by the court ladies singing and playing on various instruments. (*MT*, XXII, 7-38; pp. 322-6)

3.16 The queen's sleeping apartments

The *Ramanatha Charite's* description of the queen's apartments follows by and large that given in the previous excerpt. Among the new elements mentioned here are the pet birds typical of the women's quarters.

The bed chamber was glittering with gold decorations; the bedstead was embellished with jewels of nine different kinds and shone like lustrous marble. On it was a mattress of soft feathers. The room was decorated with numerous floral garlands and lit by bright lamps. There were pet birds, such as talking parrots and cooing pigeons, and a large round vessel made of pure white marble containing fragrant thick sandal paste. A perfumed substance, *kunkuma-rasa*, of reddish colour was stored in a golden vessel. A frankincense burner filled the air with redolent smoke, while musk powder was stored in another large round bowl. The queen awaited the imminent arrival of her husband in this beautifully decorated chamber. (*RC*, VIII, 9-13; pp. 129-31)

3.17 A princess's sleeping apartments

The following account of the sleeping chamber where the princess rests with her attendants and musicians, is drawn from the story of prince Vikrama and princess Patrini given in the *Sobagina Sone*. This passage is remarkable for the vivid portrait of the princess and her sleeping attendants, and the attention with which the various toiletry items, musical instruments and other personal belongings are observed.

The sleeping chamber of the princess was in the upper part of the palace. There was a jewelled bedstead with a mattress made of soft swan feathers upon which the princess was resting. [....]

Two trusted ladies-in-waiting were sleeping on either side of the cot. (*SoS*, XXIII, 24, 25 & 50; pp. 326 & 330)

Around the bed were placed fans, containers, fly-whisks, water-jugs, spittoons, caskets for collyrium, mirrors, combs, fresh fragrances to be sprinkled on the fans and ornaments and necklaces used by the princess. The ladies-in-waiting who carried these objects when accompanying her were also sleeping.

Some musicians, having placed the instruments near their heads, slept near the cot of the princess. There were players of stringed instruments, such as *dandige, vine, kinnari* and *saramandala*, as well as of flute, cymbals and the like. Other attendants were sleeping near the pet birds or animals of which they were in charge such as parrots, *koyil*, peacocks, swans, deer and musk deer. (*SoS*, XXIII, 27-9; p. 326)

There were flower baskets, vessels containing perfumed water, caskets with fragrant cream, betel-leaves, lime, incense burners and camphor boxes. (*SoS*, XXIII, 32; p. 327)

Temples

The *Mohana Tarangini* and *Vijayakumari Charite* both describe temples in their urban context.

The excerpts from the first text focus more on auxiliary structures, such as temple tanks, dwellings for the brahmins, temple halls and free feeding-houses, than on the actual temples. The second text, however, has an exhaustive description of a Jaina temple and its surroundings.

3.18 Temples in the city

In the city within the fort was a number of temples, in the proximity of which were tanks. These were mainly for ritual purposes. Around the temples were rows of houses of learned men, from which [the sounds of] instrumental music and the recitation of *mantras* and scriptures incessantly flowed. (*MT*, XX, 15-16; pp. 295-6)

3.19 Temple tanks and pavilions

Numerous pavilions in which the devotees could meditate were on the banks of the tanks within the temple enclosures. The tanks were provided with a series of white marble steps. There were also auxiliary structures where free feeding was provided for scholars, brahmins, students, travellers and others. (*MT*, III, 42-6; pp. 52-3)

The same text goes on to mention another auxiliary building, the *moksha-mantapa* (salvation pavilion). (*MT*, XXIV, 70; p. 357)

3.20 The Vijaya Parshvanatha temple

From all directions, that temple looked imposing because of its towering *gopura,* sanctuary, tall superstructure, numerous fluttering banners and flags and, above all, the golden pinnacle over the sanctuary.

Its pillars were studded with precious stones, such as green emeralds, corals, sapphires, rubies and others, which produced a dazzling light inside the temple. Its main entrance and central hall were beautiful. (*VC*, I, 65-71; pp. 7-8)

On either side of that temple were the dwellings of the devotees and the monasteries of their preceptors. There one could see learned scholars engaged in philosophical discussions, debates and other such activities. The musicians who played and sang in the course of the daily rituals lived there also. There were other devotees engaged in various religious duties, such as observing the prescribed *vratas*, worshipping, listening to discourses and serving the mendicants, preceptors and others. (*VC*, I, 75-7; p. 8)

Chapter 4

MARKETS, STREETS, WATERWORKS AND CHARITABLE INSTITUTIONS

This chapter begins with a fairly detailed account of a town, its layout and its inhabitants, and then goes on to give vivid descriptions of contemporary life, including markets bustling with activity, vendors and merchandise, and finally streets inhabited by special communities such as the hunters or concubines. Although the rendering of the town with its streets laid out in a precise grid and its division into various well-defined quarters may have been inspired by treatises on urban architecture, the lively depictions of the crowds populating the streets and bazaars and of the wares on offer in the shops is based, at least in part, on the authors' observations. The last two sections of this chapter deal with provision of water, and charitable institutions.

Urban layout

4.1 A town and its inhabitants

The most detailed description of a town and its inhabitants is in the following passage drawn from the *Mohana Tarangini.*

Within that walled city were a number of streets laid out in a grid pattern. The city was fairly large and had two main streets, known as *chandra-vidhi* (moon-street) and *surya-vidhi* (sun-street), the former running from south to north, and the latter from east to west. They looked beautiful with rows of storeyed buildings on both sides. In them were some temples whose tall towers and glittering gold pinnacles drew the attention of the onlookers from a distance, shining most attractively in the sunlight. There were also rows of private houses and storeyed houses belonging to rich noblemen. (*MT,* XX, 17-18; p. 296)

There were also other streets with shops and stalls on both sides. The shops [or the warehouses] sold various commodities including essential items such as food, luxury goods and valuable merchandise. There were normally separate streets for different professions such as merchants and their shops, artisans and their workshops, wrestlers, weight-lifters, learned men, teachers, scribes and concubines. (*MT,* III, 18-41; pp. 51-2)

Residential buildings, with upper storeys were fitted with grilled or latticework windows for good ventilation and natural light. (*MT,* XVI, 55; p. 23)

The streets of the city were lit at night. (*MT,* XVIII, 5; p. 253)

4.2 Layout of a town

Another description of the layout of the town and its social structure is found in the *Vijaya-kumari Charite.* It is the only passage in the present selection that pointedly refers to untouchables.

The city had a number of well laid-out streets called *chandra-vidhi* and *surya-vidhi.* In the middle of them was the palace of the king with its towering structures, the tops of which had been adorned with golden pinnacles set with gems.

Close to the king's palace were the homes and the mansions of subordinate kings, princes, ministers, court accountants, court astrologers and a large number of other royal service personnel. (*VC,* I, 78-81; p. 9)

The areas outside the fort walls were inhabited by lower-class people such as washermen, barbers, potters, carpenters, agriculturists and others. At a further distance lived the untouchables such as *holeya, madiga, krura-karmi* and others.

People of all the above-mentioned castes lived in streets reserved for them as established by tradition without violating it. (*VC,* I, 104-6; p. 11)

4.3 The streets and shops of the city of Dwarka

The lively streets of Dwarka are thus described in the *Jaimini Bharata.*

The city was densely populated, crowded with people plying all possible trades and professions. There were large numbers of elephants and horses, as well as people of the servant class such as *chauri*-bearers and umbrella-bearers. There were richly dressed and adorned pleasure-seeking persons, all briskly walking in the streets pursuing their own business. The noise was tremendous.

On either side of the main street there were attractive multi-storeyed mansions, in which one could see beautiful young ladies sitting and enjoying themselves. These houses were glamorously decorated with golden festoons, flagstaffs, pinnacles, mirrors, banners, fly-whisks, umbrellas and other adornments. On their roofs were open pavilions in which sat young ladies, well-dressed, perfumed and beautifully made up.

On the same street were the jewellers' shops. They had on display heaps and piles of all the nine kinds of precious and rare stones and gems, diamonds and gold. The shops of prosperous and wealthy merchants were on the same street.

Lovely young ladies carrying caskets filled with fragrant perfumes were waiting for their clients in the street of the concubines. They had adorned themselves with various kinds of beautiful and fragrant flowers, and were standing or pacing in front of their houses waiting for their lovers. In a street nearby were attractive girls selling flowers and floral garlands.

The houses of the concubines, all with showy and well-decorated front porticoes, occupied both sides of the street. There were young girls of all types, all with their own attendants who assisted them in various ways. Men in amorous mood roamed about, visiting the concubines. Some concubines engaged their clients in all kinds of sweet talk and romantic conversation; others played chess and indulged in pranks and flirtations.

A number of scholars from various countries assembled opposite the palace to meet the king and obtain material support from him.

Very near the palace people were engaged in a variety of games and entertainments: cock-fights, ram-fights and races with pigeons and other birds. There were elephant and horse races, as well as persons engrossed in games such as dice and chess and other kinds of betting. (*JB*, VI, 9-39; pp. 63-70)

4.4 Scholars and philosophers in Kalyani

The following passage from the *Shivatattva Chintamani* describes the city of Kalyani as home to scholars of various faiths.

People of different faiths lived there. All were sincere devotees, well-read in the scriptures, and leading pious and religious lives. There were numerous temples and monasteries where music was played, fragrant incense was burnt and priests uttered their prayers. (*S*, XXXI, 8-11; pp. 250-1)

Learned people spent their time in religious practices, philosophic discussion and debates. Among their other occupations were the stringing of *rudraksha* beads, the preparation of *vibhuti*, the arrangement of flowers and sacred leaves, and the colouring of the cloths required in the course of the rituals. Others prepared the cotton wicks for the oil lamps. Some were engaged in studying different branches of religious literature, interpreting the texts and commenting and debating on them. (*S*, XXXI, 15; p. 252)

4.5 Professions and urban context

The *Ramanatha Charite* has also a substantial section on the streets of the town. This passage focuses on the different professional groups dwelling in them.

There were separate streets inhabited by people of different professions: temple priests, brave warriors, accountants, washermen, garland-makers, army officials, drama actors, comedians, honoured governors (or subordinate rulers), officers, door-keepers, barbers, fort guards, fort watchmen, trainers of war elephants, trainers of war horses, logicians, merchants, gymnastic masters, music masters, learned teachers, dancers, scholars, poets, personnel of the mint, painters, bronze [or brass]-smiths, masons, carpenters, blacksmiths, spies, persons sharpening swords, cobblers, attendants to the royal bath, palace officers, low categories of service personnel, etcetera. (*RC*, IV, 110-15; pp. 74-5)

Markets

4.6 Bazaar streets I

The following passage from the *Mohana Tarangini* has the most comprehensive bazaar description. Especially interesting is the mention of money changers, overseas traders and estate agents.

In the capital were shops dealing in various commodities, including valuable and sometimes unique or rare items of jewellery. (*MT*, XX, 19; p. 296)

These shops were on either side of long streets. Some of them sold only a specific item and these specialized outlets were separated from the other shops. There one could find edible and aromatic items such as camphor, musk of various kinds and others. Some other [shops] were dealing only in medicinal herbs; roots, their essences, mineral mixtures and so on. There were shops selling dry fruits, such as dates, but fresh dates, grapes, jaggery, dry coconut-kernel and others, were also on offer. The next group of shops dealt mainly in grains such as wheat, grams and rice.

Further on were the stalls of the artisans, artists, bronze-smiths, blacksmiths, goldsmiths, those selling sculptures in stone and metal and those selling various types of metal weapons for warfare, hunting, etcetera. Some of the goldsmiths were almost exclusively manufacturing gold cots and sculptures.

Jewellers sold ornaments of gold, precious stones and pearls. Among these were gem-studded bangles, waist girdles, belts, festoons and others. There were also some shops which sold only precious and valuable gems of various sorts and weights and pearls.

The diamond-cutters had their own stalls where they were engaged not only in cutting the diamonds into various shapes and sizes, but also in polishing and fixing them.

There were some others whose main business was to evaluate diamonds and precious jewellery and to negotiate transactions with the customers.

Some merchants were dealing exclusively in gold coins, which they kept in heaps. These coins were from the 56 different countries. Besides gold coins, they also traded in solid gold.

At the same place, but on platforms, were artisans known as *chinnavaradaru*. Their job was to extract gold from wax balls, which had absorbed it from the touchstones used by the merchants when testing the purity of the gold before settling the price of the deal.

In some parts of the market there were overseas traders who in the course of their voyages had amassed large quantities of wealth and foreign objects. They were waiting to dispose at a negotiable price those items that were either unwanted or in excess. The next class of merchants was that in charge of real estate. Their range of business included gardens, cultivated fields, virgin fields and others. There were also those who dealt in horses, elephants, chariots and even mercenaries. (*MT*, III, 18-30; pp. 47-50)

4.7 Bazaar streets II

Merchants and traders are vividly described in the following passage from the *Vijayakumari Charite.*

There were a number of quite prosperous traders and merchants. Some of their shops displayed all the nine kinds of gems, in heaps. The traders were very experienced; they could judge the fineness of gold without using the touchstone and the weight [of the metal] without using the balance. In the course of their transactions they adopted all the tactics to make a profit from the customers while handling touchstones, balances, specimen pieces of gold, wax balls and so on. They also traded (exchanged) in coins of smaller denomination, such as *haga, visa, kasu, arekasu* and *bale.*

There were other shops in which bronze wares such as *harivana, talige, battalu, tatte,* mirrors, pinnacles and others were for sale. Different [shops] traded in woven silks and other cloths, herbal medicines, sandal paste, flowers and lotus wreaths, jasmine and perfumed substances, such as various types of musk, saffron and camphor, as well as fresh betel-leaves and others. There were streets inhabited by the concubines who shrewdly carried on their trade, making money. They were assisted by musicians, dancers and other artists. In a different locality, a number of merchants dealt honestly in food grains. (*VC*, I, 82-103; pp. 9-11)

4.8 A perfume shop

Descriptions of markets and bazaars are very frequent and are always filled with interesting information. The *Padmaraja Purana*, for instance, has a lively rendering of shops selling cloth, jewellery, makeup and perfume.

[In that city] was a market street where one could see all manner of shops. There were those with heaps of cloths of different varieties and hues, golden, blue, red, etcetera, and merchants seated in them attracting prospective buyers. There were also those of the money-lenders(?) with brokers happily engaged in their business. In other [shops], rich merchants were transacting the sale of different kinds of gems and diamonds. (*PP*, VIII, 76-8; p. 154)

Some ladies managed shops specializing in toiletries, make-up and other articles required by women. Among the merchandise on offer were fragrant substances, such as *mriganabhi*, saffron, camphor and *agaru*, and perfumes such as *sadu* and *javadi.* The alluring ladies running the shops looked like the embodiment of different fragrances themselves. There were also those selling different kinds of beautiful and sweet-smelling flowers and garlands. (*PP*, VIII, 77-84; pp. 155-6)

4.9 The flower market

Flower and perfume shops were sited either near or in the quarters inhabited by the concubines. The following is a charming description of the flower market from the *Channabasava Purana.*

In the street of the concubines there was a market in which only flowers and floral wreaths were on sale. These were required by the young prostitutes and the clients calling on them. The flowers in that market were sweet smelling and emitted fragrances which enchanted young lovers. The flowers on offer were *ketaki* (fragrant screwpine), *mallige* (jasmine), *sampige* (a kind of *champaka*), *padiri* (a trumpet-shaped flower of pale red colour), *kumuda* (water-lily), *champaka* (a fragrant yellow flower), *bandhuka* (a red flower), *kamala* (lotus) and *himabhiru* (a white flower). (*CP*, X, 3-4; pp. 95-6)

Streets

4.10 The street of the hunters

The *Sobagina Sone* describes thus the street inhabited by the hunters.

Further ahead there was the street of the hunters, which was recognized by the nests and cages hanging outside the houses. [Here], birds like parrots, peacocks and others were kept in cages. The hunters living in that street were engaged in various activities such as knitting nets and mending bows and arrows. (*SoS*, XVIII, 20-1; p. 251)

They were selling the products of their activity: various kinds of animals, their meat, skins, tusks and heads to decorate the walls, their cubs and precious pearls [supposedly found in the heads of elephants]. Their wives sold deer and fawns with tied legs, as well as birds of various kinds that they captured alive. Among these were birds which could speak, dance, walk with elegant gait, jump or stand still. (*SoS*, XVIII, 24; p. 251)

The ladies, with ivory bangles on their forearms, described the qualities of the birds in various ways in order to entice the buyers. (*SoS*, XVIII, 28-31; pp. 252-3)

Further ahead was the abode of the chief hunter, in front of which were nests, fowl-houses and cages serving as shelters for birds of various kinds. Watch-dogs guarded the house, which was decorated with soft colourful feathers of various birds such as peacocks and swans.

On the side of the main door, there was the wife of the chief hunter; it was as if the goddess of the forest was standing there. In her ears she had peacock's feathers and tender leaves covered her body; she wore ornaments of pearls and on her arms were bangles of ivory. A parrot perched on her wrist. The dark-complexioned huntress had leg ornaments studded with red rubies and sapphires. She wore ornaments made of pearls and an orange-coloured garment covered her body and head. In that attire and with her handsome, well-developed limbs, she looked as beautiful as a statue. (*SoS*, XVIII, 35-43; pp. 254-5)

The street of the concubines is one of the great themes, together with the vibrant descriptions of bazaars and shops. One of the most common excuses for introducing the topic is the account of a nightly stroll of a prince and his followers in convenient disguise. The authors vie with each other to conjure up a vision of luxury, in which exquisitely dressed and bejewelled young ladies entertain visitors in their elegantly furnished houses. Incidental to these poetic descriptions of domestic extravagance is some interesting detail on architecture and interior decoration.

4.11 The street of the concubines I

The first excerpt is drawn from the *Jaimini Bharata.*

In the front verandahs of the concubines' houses were swings decorated with peacock motifs, *makara-toranas,* flags displaying the fish emblem (symbol of love) and calling-bells. On the tops of the buildings, the upper apartments were surmounted by attractive rows of golden pinnacles. Beautiful young ladies, all well trained in the art and secrets of their profession, lived there. Some of them were mature and proficient in classical music and playing the *vine*; some conversed fluently and intelligently; some recited romantic literary works; and some were refined connoisseurs of theatrical performances, poetic compositions and dramas. Some were engrossed in playing indoor games like *nettapagade* or *chaduranga* with their lovers and entertaining them in various ways. Sometimes the ladies had fun in talking coquettishly to their pet birds, such as parrots, peacocks and swans.

In other houses, the concubines were engaging their assistants in the preparation and conditioning of various fragrant substances: camphor, sandal paste or powder, *kumkuma* and musk. Others, while waiting for their lovers, were exchanging pleasantries amongst themselves and taking pride in their profession. In one house a lady was seen intently playing the *vine*; another was enjoying herself on a swing; a third one was playing with a ball. They were all young and beautiful. (*JB*, VIII, 86-99; pp. 156-60)

4.12 The street of the concubines II

This second description is drawn from the *Padmaraja Purana.* Particularly interesting is the mention of the old prostitutes instructing their charges in the subtle arts of seduction.

As the moon was rising, the young concubines appeared and started attracting their lovers. The whole street resounded with music played in the classical 62 modes, while some ladies were practising classical dance. They lived in the houses on both sides of the street, and one could see them singing, dancing, flirting and talking in the manner prescribed in the [treatises] called *Bharata* and *Koka.* (*PP*, VI, 7-8; p. 67)

Aged ladies taught their young daughters the arts of enticing and pleasing their visiting lovers. The ladies were all beautiful, although in different ways. They were masters in the art of seducing their lovers by various means such as gestures, postures, looks, behaviour, etcetera. They were very tactful, yet at the same time shrewd in extracting money from their clients. (*PP*, VI, 10-17; pp. 67-9)

In some places the ladies played chess and other games with their lovers, engaging at the same time in cryptic conversations with amorous double meanings. (*PP*, VI, 20; p. 70)

4.13 The street of the concubines III

This elaborate description of the street of the concubines, culminating in the seduction of a member of the royal family, is drawn from the *Nemijinesha Sangati.*

The prince was persuaded by his friend, who was a womanizer, to pay a visit to the street where the concubines lived and carried on their profession. At first they went into that part [of the town] where flower garlands were on sale. The stalls were managed by young flirtatious ladies who, while engaging in their business, were fully aware of their attractions, enhancing these by their gestures, stances, expressions and manner of talking. Further on were the houses of the concubines. Some were storeyed buildings on the terraces of which the ladies were moving with the grace of *apsaras*, while other [ladies] were walking in the street with their characteristic subtle coquetry.

The halls of these buildings were provided with a large number of eye-catching, trellised gilded screens. The sloping eaves of the roofs at the fronts of the houses were tastefully decorated with gems. On the walls of the buildings were attractive paintings.

The concubines stood at the front of the building, enticing their lovers. They were all beautifully and elegantly dressed. They wore a variety of ornaments made of gold, pearls, large-sized gems and diamonds. They wore the finest silks and perfumed themselves with different varieties of musk. (*NS*, X, 45-58; pp. 196-8)

Some of them were playfully addressing their pet parrots with endearing terms, but those terms were [actually] meant to attract the attention of the passers-by. The prince and his friend listened to those expressions of love and proceeded further, disregarding the amazed gaze of the ladies. (*NS*, X, 59-67; pp. 198-9)

After having walked for a time they saw an elephant coming into the street. In order to make way for it they stood aside and chanced into the main door of a concubine's residence. Immediately, the assistants of the lady of the house approached the prince, inviting him to while away the time inside until the elephant had passed. As soon as he entered, the main door was closed behind him and he was taken to the upper apartment. Soon the lady appeared before him, tastefully dressed, looking like the goddess of love. (*NS*, X, 72-6; pp. 200-1)

She sat by his side, and soon her assistants placed before them a game board called *nettapagade*, which she invited him to play. The board was marked with the diagrams [specific to the game]. (*NS*, X, 77, 78 & 79; p. 201)

They played the game several times until she led him by the hand to the apartment on the terrace. (*NS*, X, 80-3; pp. 201 & 202)

4.14 The street of the concubines IV

The *Mohana Tarangini* describes the street of the concubines as follows:

The houses of the concubines were situated in a separate quarter within the fortified city. That quarter was planned and built by an expert architect according to the prescriptions of the ancient texts, so as to make it suitable for their profession. (*MT*, III, 12, 32; pp. 46 & 50)

The houses skirted both sides of the street. They had spacious halls and upper storeys with projecting balconies that were used by the beautiful young ladies to attract the male customers passing on the road [below]. On the fronts of the houses were also platforms adjoining the main halls. The ladies, tastefully dressed and bejewelled, adorned with flowers and perfumed, stood [on the verandahs] at the entrances in various attractive poses inspired by sculptures. The four traditional kinds of ladies were represented there.

Some of them were proficient singers of different *ragas*; others played on different musical instruments; others, again, danced in the traditional styles. All this was to attract customers and to please them in various ways.

In the centre of those houses were open courtyards where the ladies and their paramours spent some time resting after having enjoyed to the full each other's company. Some of the ladies, attractively dressed and wearing jewellery and perfumed flowers, moved freely in the street. Lewd persons, afraid of being identified, moved about stealthily at night, clad in black woollen blankets. In order to avoid any possible trouble, the city watchmen went round those streets at night, carrying sticks and occasionally beating them on the ground, as a sort of warning to the people. When the ladies and their lovers were disturbed by the movements of the watchmen, they cursed at them. There were bawds plying their trade along with the concubines.

In some parts of the same quarter, there were persons indulging in the nefarious and obscene Shakti worship, in the course of which both men and women consumed intoxicants and ate fried food prepared from eggs, flattened rice, fried rice and fried gram, and took to sensual enjoyment in various ways. (*MT*, XVIII, 22-105; pp. 257-73)

Near the houses, for the convenience of the resident concubines, their patrons and assistants, there were some stalls dealing in betel-nuts and leaves, fragrant sandal paste, varieties of fragrant flowers and floral garlands, and fine foods, sweets and fruits. The vendors were mostly young ladies. (*MT*, III, 13-20; pp. 46-7)

In another part of the same quarter of the city, there were some storeyed buildings with square halls on the side of the road. In those halls one could see foreigners from the 56 countries engaged in betting games. (*MT*, XX, 19-26; pp. 297-8)

Waterworks

Water supply was a crucial factor in Indian town planning: the construction of tanks, digging of wells and building of channels were great projects, sometimes funded by royal families or wealthy individuals. The following extract recounting the building of a tank is drawn from the *Padmaraja Purana*.

4.15 Construction of a water tank

One day the king and his chief minister were seated in audience. An officer of a certain place [Velapura] appeared before them and said that although the kingdom had been blessed with enough irrigation facilities of both kinds [that is, rain-fed and man-made], his town lacked water. A reservoir was therefore needed to irrigate the fields around his town and make it prosper. On hearing that, the king ordered the minister to make the necessary provisions and arrangements for the construction of a tank at Velapura. Then the chief minister, accompanied by other ministers, went to the treasury and gave an order for 12,000 gold coins to be handed over to the officer of Velapura. He also checked that the transaction was entered in the account book of the treasury. Then he ordered the officer to construct a tank at his place, utilizing the money. (*PP*, V, 37-40; pp. 86-7)

[After some time] the king decided to inspect the tank of that place and the minister agreed and their itinerary was made public. They rode on their horses accompanied by a large retinue. (*PP*, VI, 23-5; p. 99)

In the king's party were ministers, commanders, governors, feudal rulers, princes, warriors, generals, officers, poets, musicians, debators, learned scholars, flirtatious persons, philosophers, scholars, artists, service personnel of some 72 departments, elephants, horses, chariots and infantry, besides relatives, servants, citizens, etcetera. The whole party was preceded by musicians playing loud music. (*PP*, VI, 27-30; p. 100)

The tank, together with its [lengthy] *bund*, had strongly-built stone sluices, sluice wells, canals and channels. It was full of water and the irrigated lands below it had well-grown healthy crops, while the gardens were filled with varieties of fruit-bearing trees. (*PP*, VI, 69-76; pp. 110-12)

While describing a superb garden on the outskirts of Kalyani, the *Shivatattva Chintamani* mentions various types of water-lifting devices and other hydraulic works, without, however, going into details. (*S*, XXXI, 5; p. 250)

4.16 Water-providing systems

A list of water-providing systems is given in this excerpt from the *Ramanatha Charite*.

On the outskirts of the fortified town there were a number of waterworks [for the different needs of the people and their domestic animals]: *kola* (ponds in pleasure gardens), *kere* (water reservoir mainly for agricultural purposes), *bavi* (well), *bagarege* (small spring pit on the bank of a dried up river), *doni* (trough for collecting water), *done* (natural pond in rocks), *dirghike* (elongated pond), *orate* (water-spring for subterranean water), *kaluve* (channel), *benche* (small temporary reservoir) and *palla* (stream, rivulet). (*RC*, IV, 67; pp. 66-7)

Charitable institutions

Sheds providing water and food in which travellers could rest are frequently mentioned. These were generally situated along the highways, near some shady grove or in a garden. Descriptions of these charitable institutions are found in the *Prabhulinga Lile* (*PL*, XIV, 4-5; p. 173) and *Proudharayana Kavya* (*PK*, I, 33-4; pp. 9-10), as well as in the *Padmaraja Purana* and *Mohana Tarangini*, extracts from which are reproduced below.

4.17 Charity water-sheds I

Among the most informative passages is the following drawn from the *Padmaraja Purana*.

The walls [of the sheds] were made of roots of fragrant grass; leaves and flowers covered the roof; stems of plantain trees were used as pillars and sugarcanes as rafters. Fragrant roots of *mudivala* were used as ropes to bind the various parts of the hut together. Leaves of the *ashoka* tree, spread on the floor, served as mattresses. [....]

They [the sheds] were managed by attractive young ladies who also did the serving. White marble storage containers were filled with cool and fragrant water. Furthermore, there was curd rice, porridge with buttermilk and *vileya* mixed with edible camphor for the use of the travellers. Trees of various kinds grew near the pavilions; [they were] shade-giving, flowering and fruit-bearing trees. [....] (*PP*, VIII, 8-9; p. 137)

4.18 Charity water-sheds II

The *Mohana Tarangini* has the following account:

Charity water-pavilions for supplying drinking water freely to travellers and citizens were set up by philanthropists. These were established at places where there were no other water sources, such as tanks or wells, for the use of thirsty travellers and others. The pavilions were generally built under or near big mango trees, which offered cool shade for the travellers to rest and relax. In these centres, cool and fragrant water was stored in mud pots. Sometimes the water flowing in nearby streams was collected in bamboo pipes and carried to these pavilions. Moreover, opposite the pavilions there were shady canopies made of green leaves, branches of trees, fragrant *khus*-grass and the like, for the comfort and pleasure of the public. Attractive banners tied to long poles fluttered in the air, indicating the location of these civic amenities. Beautiful young ladies were usually serving in those establishments. They waited on the visitors and supplied them with cold water. The very sight of those attractive ladies was an added delight to the relief of those tired and thirsty travellers and other visitors. (*MT*, II, 26-32; pp. 37-8)

The roads converging on those centres were usually skirted by beautiful, fully grown and shady trees. In addition to the arrangements for the free supply of drinking water to the public, other amenities were provided. Visitors were served curd rice, which had been made more tasty with the addition of a small quantity of raw ginger. Another item, freely supplied there, was cool water mixed with jaggery.

Strictly orthodox Shrivaishnava brahmins were given facilities to cook their own food and dine in privacy. They were freely given betel-nuts, edible camphor and fragrance extracted from flowers. (*MT*, II, 32-4; p. 38)

4.19 Public feeding-houses

Another charitable institution that was established for the convenience of travellers and pilgrims was the free-feeding house. One of these is described in the following passage from the *Channabasava Purana*.

The country's highways were dotted with public feeding-houses for the benefit of travellers and pilgrims who could have free food and drink there. Attractive young ladies supplied water to the thirsty, pouring it from metal vessels. Many persons visited these houses and spent longer there than originally intended, mainly because of the ladies managing them. (*CP*, XI, 14-16; pp. 120-1)

In the charity feeding-houses, the hungry travellers were served a variety of tasty dishes: a fine selection of cooked rice, *ghee*, soup, various vegetable dishes, different kinds of minced raw vegetables, pickles and condiments, sweets, milk sweets, sweet rice, fruit juices of different kinds, curds, buttermilk and others. (*CP*, XI, 13; p. 120)

Chapter 5

GODS, SHRINES AND SACRED PLACES AT VIJAYANAGARA

The three parts of this chapter focus on Vijayanagara and its environs as a sacred area, Pampakshetra. In the first part, the mythological background of the site is explored in two legends which were instrumental in the development of Vijayanagara as a holy place. The first legend, which appears in the *Channabasava Purana,* is the narrative of the various incidents which eventually led to the marriage of Shiva and Parvati, here called Shive or Girije. According to local tradition, these events happened on the banks of the Tungabhadra river and on nearby Hemakuta hill. The second legend, from the *Shri Krishnadevarayana Dinachari,* narrates how the sage Vidyaranya resolved to build a city bearing his name and the miraculous events which determined the selection of the appropriate site. While the first legend is concerned with the Shaiva background of the area, the second establishes a link between Vijayanagara and the *Ramayana,* particularly with the monkey kingdom of Kishkindha.

The second part of this chapter is devoted to sacred landscape. It stresses the notion of Vijayanagara and its environs, Pampakshetra, as the most sacred region in the whole of the subcontinent. Excerpts from the *Pampasthana Varnanam* and *Ramanatha Charite* enumerate its numerous holy lakes and hermitages that were once inhabited by the most renowned among the mythical *rishis.*

The third and last part, Vijayanagara as a sacred city, contains two descriptions of the city: the most informative comes from the *Shivatattva Chintamani,* while the other, which focuses on Hemakuta hill, is drawn from the *Channabasava Purana.* A final extract from the *Pampasthana Varnanam* gives a list of the deities worshipped in the Vijayanagara area.

Myths

5.1 The burning of Kama and the marriage of Shiva and Girije

The following version of this famous myth is drawn from the *Channabasava Purana.*

Giriraja and his wife Mene had no issue for a long time. In order to obtain the blessings of Shive (Parvati), Mena started meditating on the goddess. After a long penance, Shive, pleased with Mena's prayers, condescended to be born as her daughter.

Shive, in her aspect as Dakshayani, had jumped in the fire at her father's place while he was conducting a *yagna.* The prayers of Mena gave her an opportunity to be reborn as her daughter.

Now Shive was born as the child of Giriraja and his wife, and was called Girije. In the course of time she attained a marriageable age.

After Dakshayani's death, her husband, Shiva, retired heartbroken to Hemakuta hill on the banks of the Tungabhadra to perform austerities. The gods were eager that he should end his penance, fall in love with Girije, marry her and beget a son who, as foretold, would free them from the harassment of Tarakasura. So Narada, the divine go-between, approached Giriraja and persuaded him and Mena to send Girije to attend the meditating Shiva-Virupaksha, thereby paving the way for their marriage and the begetting of a son.

In order to succeed, the gods requested Madana, the god of love, to disturb Shiva and attack him with his flowery arrows. Madana, aware of the risk to his own life which this scheme entailed, agreed, although reluctantly, for the sake of the gods. (*CP,* XXXIV, 2-41; pp. 342-52)

Madana attacked Shiva seated in penance at Pampakshetra. The disturbed Shiva opened his third eye, out of which emanated the flame which burnt Madana to ashes. Yet there was no response to Girije's advances. She then commenced severe penance at

Pampakshetra to win the favour and hand of Shiva. (*CP*, XXXV, 3-35; pp. 353-61)

At the end of that penance, Shiva agreed to marry Girije. The wedding took place following the traditional practices. (*CP*, XXXVI & XXXVII; pp. 363-93)

5.2 The founding of Vijayanagara

The *Shri Krishnadevarayana Dinachari* contains the following myth about the sage Vidyaranya and his founding the city of Vidyanagara.

Vidyaranya learned the various branches of philosophy in Kashmir. His *guru*, from whom he received the *chintamani-mantra* was the scholar Misra. With the help of this *mantra*, Vidyaranya acquired supernatural powers: he concentrated his mind on the goddess Lakshmi and told her that he wished to found a city bearing his name, in which she should reside for the prosperity and happiness of its citizens. Because of this city, his name would be forever remembered. The goddess accepted Vidyaranya's invitation and requested him to lead the way, without [once] looking backwards, while she would follow him to the place intended for the new city.

The sage started from Kashmir and passing through Ujjain, Kolhapur and other places he reached Kishkindha. There he bathed in the Tungabhadra river, paid homage to Virupaksha of Hampe and eventually climbed Matanga hill to survey the site and select a suitable place for his city. While he was there, his attention was attracted by an unusual sight: a shepherd's dog was hunted down by a hare, not vice-versa. The surprised sage inquired from the elderly residents the meaning of this episode. He was told that in the past, Matanga hill was the residence of the great sage Matanga. The region around it was the famous Kishkindha, where the two brother monkey kings Vali and Sugriva had lived, quarrelled and eventually fought against each other. In the course of one of those quarrels, Sugriva fled from his stronger brother Vali and sought refuge in Matanga's hermitage. The sage took pity on Sugriva, offering him protection and cursing Vali, thus preventing him from climbing the hill. From that day on, the hill became a sanctuary for all persecuted living beings, whether animal or human.

On hearing this marvellous account, Vidyaranya decided to build his city at this site. He thought of the three rulers, his contemporaries: the Ashvapathi (Lord of cavalry) [probably the sultan of Bijapur, whose main strength was the cavalry], Gajapathi (Lord of elephants) [probably the king of Kalinga, who bore this title,] and Narapathi (Lord of infantry) [probably a reference to the Vijayanagara king whose army consisted mainly of infantry]. He decided that of those three rulers the Narapathi was the best, so he resolved to build the city for him. Vidyaranya proposed that the plan of the city should look like a human body and that its foundations were to be laid at the most auspicious moment in order to ensure that it would forever survive. [Accordingly], the Vastupurusha (tutelary god of the site) was to be established at the appropriate moment with all the necessary pomp and circumstance. Furthermore, he visualized the city [completed] with [all of] its palaces, temples, forts, bastions, nine gateways, streets and markets. He then confided his plan to a trusted disciple and together they fixed the auspicious time for laying the foundation stone of the new city: [this was] the end of the year 1125 of the Shalivahana era, in the year called Prabhava (the first of the cycle of the Shaka era), at midnight on the new moon day of the month of Chaitra (the first month of the Hindu calendar, corresponding to April-May). On that occasion, all the astrologers and ritual specialists assembled to calculate the position of the constellation Trisanku and that of the pole star. They fixed the north-south and the east-west directions, consecrated the images of Brahma, Vishnu and Shiva, and then invoked the god of the site, Vastupurusha. His gold image was installed near the *japa-kamba* (a pillar near which prayers are uttered) which was [set into] a deep pit. This was done to ensure that the city survived for 3,400 years. But at the time of its consecration, the image of the Vastupurusha was inadvertently shaken by the followers of Vidyaranya. When the sage noticed this, he remarked that the city would survive only 360 years. So far 25 monarchs have sat on its throne and 300 years have elapsed. (*SKD*, I, prose, pp. 3-5)

Sacred landscape

5.3 Description of Pampakshetra I

The *Pampasthana Varnanam* gives the following account of Pampakshetra, describing it as the most sacred place of the whole subcontinent, graced by the presence of the most distinguished *rishis*.

The continent was surrounded by oceans and to the north there was a glittering mountain range. To the south lies the famous and prosperous region, Kuntaladesha, where there were numerous Shaiva sacred places such as [the mountains] Meru, Mandara and Kailasa, and [the cities] Kashi, Kedara, Prayaga, Sourashtra, Mahakala (Ujjain), Shrisaila, Kalahasti, Kanchipuram, Arunagiri (Tiruvannamalai), Rameshvara, Gokarna and others. Among these [sacred places], Pampakshetra was the most sacred and everlastingly revered. It was a great religious and spiritual centre. [Pampakshetra] was provided with four entrance gateways sited at the four cardinal points, each under the protection of a deity: Kinnareshvara presided over the eastern [gate], Jambukeshvara over the southern [gate], Someshvara over the western [gate] and Vanibhadreshvara over the northern [gate].

Known as Pampakshetra after its tutelary deity, Pampabhavani, the place was famous on account of numerous *siddha-lingas*, holy tanks, holy hermitages, unparalleled holy lakes with blooming lotuses and forests, in which lived ascetics and hermits. (*PV*, I, 15-17; p. 5)

Such was the sacredness of the place that even wild animals which usually fought against each other lived peacefully together, each in their own way. Among these were the *bherunda* (a mythical, double-headed ferocious and gigantic bird) and *entadi* (a mythical animal with eight legs), lions and elephants, bisons and tigers, deer and others. (*PV*, I, 19; p. 5)

The river Tungabhadra, sacred on account of its origin, added to the sanctity of the place by flowing nearby.

On both banks of the sacred Tungabhadra were numerous hermitages inhabited by revered ascetics, such as Vasishtha, Vamana, Kapila, Gouramukha, Bharadwaja and Sakalya, and holy lakes, such as Tara-tirtha, Koti-tirtha, Naga-tirtha, Mainayaka-tirtha, Kapila-tirtha, Shaiva-tirtha, Yamya-tirtha, Varuna-tirtha, Pitru-tirtha, Brahma-tirtha, Rudra-tirtha and Deva-katha-tirtha.

The river, with its sand-covered banks, lagoons, brooks and rivulets, whose ever-flowing water formed foamy waves, was an amazing sight. Its beauty was enhanced by playful swans floating in rows on the water, lotus flowers, tender shoots of creepers and plants and other flowers. (*PV*, I, 21-24; pp. 6-7)

To the south of that place were three sacred peaks called Rishyamukha, Matanga and Hemakuta. Apart from the Vishnusarovara abutting the river near the Matanga hermitage, there were numerous sacred ponds. The famed Malyavanta hill was to the west. Further to the west was the renowned Hemakuta with the hermitage of Agastya and others, groves inhabited by ascetics, and ponds and lakes overflowing with clear water. Their beauty was enhanced by lotuses and other flowers in full bloom and tender creepers. (*PV*, I, 26-9; pp. 7-8)

Nearby one could see the children of the *rishis* and the cubs of various animals peacefully playing together. Among them were the cubs of lions, tigers, elephants, deer, antelopes and monkeys; there were the chicks of peacocks and the young of snakes. (*PV*, I, 31; p. 9)

The densely forested Hemakuta appeared like a green-emerald pendant attached to the pearl-white necklace formed by the clear water flowing in the nearby canals. The water of those perennial canals nourished the groves and gardens that yielded various kinds of fruit, flowers and other crops. [....]

In addition, there were other varieties of large trees with evergreen sprouts and twigs, ever-blossoming flowers, young fruits that were never astringent and ripe [fruits] that were never bitter to the taste. The entire area was filled the whole year round with the fragrance exuded by all the trees and flowers. It was similar to the garden of the gods. (*PV*, I, 33-4; pp. 9-10)

In short, the rich woodland appeared to be the outermost fortification wall, although of green colour, of that place [Pampakshetra]. (*PV*, I, 37-40; pp. 11-12)

5.4 Description of Pampakshetra II

The following is an account of Pampakshetra from the *Ramanatha Charite.*

In the Kuntala country, among the sacred places, such as Shri-Kailasa (Shrishaila), Ketara, Kanchi-pura, Gokarna, and others, the most renowned is Pampakshetra, which has a number of hermitages and sacred *tirthas.* (*RC*, II, 74,75; p. 31)

The beautiful river Tungabhadra flows near it. Geese and swans play in its clear water among fully-blown lotuses, plants, creepers, a wide variety of flowers and plentiful fish.

Near to the river is a sacred pond known as Manmatha-kunda. Its beauty is enhanced by water lilies and lotuses in full bloom, among which are swans, ducks and other birds. (*RC*, II, 84-6, 92; pp. 33-4)

On its banks the foliage of plants and trees cast a dark shadow over the water. (*RC*, II, 94; p. 34)

At the centre of the sacred Pampapuri is the [temple] enshrining the lord of the universe, the Virupaksha-*linga.* (*RC*, II, 107; p. 36)

Vijayanagara as a sacred city

5.5 Description of Vijayanagara city I

The *Shivatattva Chintamani* has the following description of the city of Vijayanagara during the reign of Devaraya II and his minister Lakkana-dandesha, the author of this work.

It was a place inhabited by citizens whose actions were committed to the welfare of others, who were truthful and compassionate, who achieved what they desired and enjoyed, who followed the right conduct and were devotees of Shiva, and who pursued righteousness and knowledge, [and so on].

Because of this situation, peace, victory, prosperity and welfare reigned supreme in that place. Thus it was known as Devarajendra-pura, the city of the emperor Devaraja. But its proper name was Vijayanagara. Vijayanagara city was the centre of the activities of thousands of Shaiva and other devotees, who pursued their religious, spiritual, literary and other activities. They invariably followed an exemplary conduct and lived simple lives. Their abodes were in caves, rock-shelters and hermitages situated on Matanga hill, Malyavanta hill, Anjenadri hill and other [locations].

One of these pious persons was Gurumurthi Ondettinayya. He lived in a *matha* he had built on the car street opposite the Pampapati temple in Hampe. Besides other activities, he generously fed the needy and supplied them with water and clothes. The Pampavadhuvara (Virupaksha) temple was situated on Hemakuta [hill]. Pampakshetra was a place with many sacred tanks and hermitages teeming with saintly persons, kings and poets, [alive] with various activities.

The temple of Pampapati was a magnificent structure with a number of glittering pinnacles, with walls and pillars covered with gold sheath, doors set with diamonds, platforms studded with topazes, hanging tassels of natural pearls and garlands of rubies and other precious stones.

There were a number of educational institutions, in which could be heard recitations from the ancient scriptures such as the *Vedas* and *Upanishads* and all kinds of *shastras,* discourses and debates on metaphysical matters, *mantras* and compositions in praise of Shiva [and other gods].

The place was provided with four vast gateways. Each had, as a presiding deity, an aspect of Shiva: Kinnareshvara in the east, Jambukeshvara in the south, Someshvara in the west and Vanibhadreshvara in the north. Virupaksha was in the centre.

Numerous devotees worshipped Virupaksha and his consort Pampambike, placed at the centre of innumerable Shiva *lingas (Shivalinga-koti).*

Nearby was the perennially flowing river Tungabhadra, filled with pure and holy water for the use of the inhabitants.

Other deities, which were worshipped from old by mythical ascetics, were near the main one (Virupaksha). These were Rambheshvara, Nateshvara, Shambhu-muktishvara, Mallikarjunalinga, Ramalakshmaneshvara, Mahakaleshvara, Markandeshvara, Indreshvara, Someshvara, Nagneshvara, Shankareshvara, Aghoreshvara, Nageshvara, Chikka-Pampadevi, Ketara-devaru, Chaya-Mallikarjuna, Varuneshvara, Vayuveshvara, Kubereshvara, Jadeya-Shankaradevaru, Patalagangeya Somashekhara, Lokapavana-devaru, Kotishankaradevaru and Ekantarameshvara.

In the proximity of the place there were eleven sacred ponds:

Manmatha-tirtha, Soma-tirtha, Mahakala-tirtha, Tara-tirtha, Surya-tirtha, Vatsa-tirtha, Tapya-tirtha, Markandeya-tirtha, Gajashva-sukhara-tirtha, Kadambari-tirtha and Brahma-tirtha.

There were other *tirthas* attached to the hermitages: Vashishtashrama-papavinasi-tirtha, Badarikashrama-dashashvamedha-tirtha, Malyavanta hill, Runa-vimochana-tirtha, Yaksha-tirtha, Gada-tirtha, Dhanu-tirtha, Shankha-chakra-tirtha and Padmadala-tirtha.

Some other holy lakes were Vatsanabhi-tirtha, Agni-tirtha, Rama-tirtha, Pitru-tirtha, Mangalya-tirtha and Sri-Rudrapada-tirtha. Furthermore, the benevolent Vireshvara could be seen [enshrined in a temple] on the summit of Matanga hill. (*S*, XXXVIII, 206-40; pp. 431-7)

Pampakshetra has been associated with certain mythological incidents such as the burning of the god of love (Smara), the marriage of Girije (Pampa) and the granting of boons to Rati.

Hence it was the seat of great Shaiva teachers like Kriyashaktiraya, Dakshinamurti-yati, Gurumurti-yakashavasi-yati [and many others]. (*S*, XXXVIII, 245-48; pp. 438-39)

There were two chariots, one for Virupaksha and the other for Pampa. (*S*, XXXVIII, 254; p. 440)

5.6 Description of Vijayanagara city II

The description of the city in the *Ramanatha Charite* follows the usual stereotypes. After vividly depicting its verdant surroundings, the poet elaborates on the theme of the ideal town.

The city was provided with a shining fort built of stone and surrounded by a moat filled with water. All this added to the beauty of the place. The fort was provided with towering bastions, battlements and ramparts. Within the fortified city were many tall, multi-storeyed buildings with flags and banners and pinnacles decorating their roofs. There were streets known as *chandra-vidhi* and *surya-vidhi.*

Walls, doors, platforms and corbels, pillars and beams of the storeyed buildings were tastefully embellished with pearls, jewels of various kinds and diamonds.

In the buildings were shops dealing in gems, such as pearls and rubies, in addition to bronze and gold articles. Some others sold camphor and musk; others, again, sold toilet requisites. There were shops for silk cloth and for white betel-leaves. Young ladies were walking in the streets shopping.

On the terrace of those buildings were open pleasure pavilions allowing in sunlight during the day and moonlight during the night. Their roofs were decorated with glistening finials, flags and banners. In these terrace pavilions, beautiful dancing girls could be seen. (*RC*, III, 57-89; pp. 46-51)

The abode of Shiva was a prominent landmark of sacred Pampapura. It was glittering. All its parts were embellished with precious stones such as blue sapphires, crystals, emeralds, lotus coloured rubies, pearls and topazes. The upper storeys too were ornamented with gems, while rubies of different hues decorated the steps and pavilions. Matanga hill and the Tungabhadra (river) near the temple [of Virupaksha] looked like a high fort wall and a deep moat. (*RC*, III, 91-6; pp. 52-3)

The temple precincts had oil lamps fixed on stands. The temple had a towering entrance gateway. The image of Virupaksha could be seen in this temple. (*RC*, III, 104-8; pp. 54-5)

5.7 Description of Hemakuta hill

This description of Hemakuta in the *Channabasava Purana* introduces the passage on the mythical events (see Section 5.1) reputed to have happened there.

Kanakachala (or Hemakuta), the hillock on the bank of the Tungabhadra, looked like a fully-caparisoned elephant sent by Brahma for the use of the supreme god Shri Virupaksha during the ceremony. The rugged huge rocks in the ravines were comparable to the sturdy tusks of that elephant. The other lofty peaks seen around there resembled the abodes of other important gods, such as Rudra, Vishnu, Brahma and others situated around Kailasa, the abode of Shri Virupaksha. Furthermore, Hemakuta hill looked like a throne for Shiva while granting audience. The site had mines which yielded high quality gems and diamonds. The woods around it were full of tall and shady trees, some bearing fruits, and also creepers and large plants. There were wild animals and other fauna and waterfalls of pure water which resembled mercury. (*CP*, II, 8-11; p. 14)

Hemakuta hill consisted of a large expanse of sheet rock and peaks of bluish granite. (*CP*, XXXIV, 15; p. 345)

It was situated on the bank of the Tungabhadra. In its ever-flowing waters, swans and *konche* (heron-like bird) played amid lotus blossoms. The banks of the river were covered with a large variety of fruit trees. (*CP*, XXXIV, 18-21; pp. 346-7)

Here and there in Pampaskhetra were hermitages headed by learned sages who, apart from engaging in religious activities, rites and sacrifices, also taught pupils the *Vedas, shastras, agamas, puranas*, etcetera. (*CP*, XXXIV, 25-7; p. 348)

5.8 Names of Virupaksha

The *Virupaksha Shataka* mentions the various names of the deities worshipped at Vijayanagara and the temples or shrines dedicated to them, without, however, giving any further details:

Hampeya-mangala-murti (deity of Hampe conferring auspiciousness) (*VS*, I, 2; p. 1); Pompapathi Virupakshe (Virupaksha, lord of the goddess Pompa) (*VS*, I, 29; p. 4); Pompadisha (the lord of the goddess Pompa) (*VS*, I, 34; p. 5); Hemakutadisha (lord of Hemakuta) (*VS*, I, 74; pp. 9-10); Hemashaila-nivasa, (the god who resides on Hemashaila) (*VS*, I, 74; p. 10); Hemadhama (the god who resides on Hema hill) (*VS*, I, 74; p. 10); Hampeya-Yoga-Vibhu, (omnipresent or great yogi of Hampe) (*VS*, I, 123; p. 15).

5.9 Names of Pampadevi

Shivanamarendri (consort of Shiva) (*VS*, I, 2,3; pp. 1 and 4); Pompambike (mother Pompa) (*VS*, I, 124; p. 15).

5.10 Names of other deities

Bhairava, situated to the right (south of Virupaksha); Durga, situated to the left (north of Virupaksha); Malala Benaka (Ganesha of sandstone); Honna Nandi (gold-plated crouching Nandi); Halavu lingas (many *lingas*). (*VS*, I, 125; p. 15)

Karimukha (elephant-faced); Shanmukha (six-faced); Bhringeshvara; Vrishabha; Virabhadra; Dandahasta (staff-bearer); Nakshatra palaka (moon); Uraganatha (lord of the snakes); Bala-Brahmeshvara; Papa-vinasadevaru. (*VS*, I, 126; p. 15)

5.11 Names of sacred hills

Hemakuta hill (*VS*, I, 124; 15); Matanga-giri (*VS*, I, 24; 4); Matange-parvata (*VS*, I, 128; p. 15).

5.12 Names of the river and town

Tungabhadra river (*VS*, I, 124; p. 15 and 128; p. 15); Pompapura, Hampe (*VS*, I, 134; p. 16).

Chapter 6

FORESTS, FIELDS AND GARDENS

This chapter enumerates the great number of agricultural products grown in the region around Vijayanagara and probably in the other zones of the vast Vijayanagara empire. There is an impressive variety of fruits, vegetables, trees, flowers and shrubs, as well as different kinds of rice. This confirms the various accounts of the foreign travellers in the fifteenth and sixteenth centuries who reported that Vijayanagara was one of the best provided cities in the world.

Mountains, forests and fields

6.1 Mountains and forests

Descriptions of an idealized country, such as the following from the *Sobagina Sone,* a good example of the genre, are found very often in the literature.

The Ratnamekhale hill range was very rich in all respects. It had very high peaks, deep valleys and dales, dense forests with varied vegetation, rivers with perennially flowing water, dramatic waterfalls, ponds and tanks, dens, caves, rock shelters and snow-clad mountains. [....]

It also had mines yielding precious stones such as lapis-lazuli, emeralds, sapphires, rubies and others. (*SoS,* XIV, 32, 36, 37; pp. 184 & 185)

The range was filled with mango trees, areca-nut trees, date palms, coconut trees, jack-fruit trees, twelve varieties of *bakula* flowers, *padari* flowers, sandal-wood trees, *jambu* fruit trees, *gavate* trees and *karpura-vale* trees. There were other trees whose tender leaves, sprouts and fruits, both ripe and unripe, looked like gems of different colours. There were bamboo clusters and plantain stems. It was rich in water sources; one could see tanks, ponds, streams, rivulets, deep pools and waterfalls. There were animals such as musk civets, wild cat, swans, peacocks, cranes, monkeys, parrots, reptiles, boars and pigs, lions, tigers and elephants. Hunters lived there along with their wives and families. They plucked, collected and cleaned *bidirakki* (bamboo rice) for eating. (*SoS,* XIV, 38-66; pp. 185-90)

6.2 Cultivated fields

The *Darmanatha Purana* describes the rice fields and vegetable gardens seen by a prince on nearing the capital of a nearby kingdom.

After covering a good distance through forests, rivers and different lands he was nearing his destination. (*DP,* XI, prose; p. 267).

As he was approaching the capital of the kingdom of Vidarbha he saw the fully grown and ripe paddy fields. There were gardens in which vegetables like *brinjal,* bitter gourd, pumpkin, beans (pulses) and others were grown. In addition, there were groves filled with fruit-bearing and other trees. (*DP,* XI, 12-14; p. 267)

Agricultural products

6.3 Fruit and spices

The *Padmaraja Purana* mentions the following fruit-bearing trees and fruits:

Jack-fruit, mango, coconut, plantain, pomegranate, purple berries, areca-nut, sweet lime, orange, lemon, citrus fruit, grapes, wood apple, cloves and cardamom. (*PP,* VIII, 29-31, 33-7; pp. 142-4 and 59; p. 150)

6.4 Trees, plants and shrubs

The *Pampasthana Varnanam* has the following long enumeration of trees, plants and shrubs that were grown in and around Vijayanagara, in the fields and orchards fed by abundant water from canals.

Dalimba (pomegranate), *palasu* (jack-fruit), *bakkevalasu* (sweet jack-fruit), *ileya* (sweet lime), *herile* (sour lime), *kittile* (orange), *tengu* (coconut), *nimbe* (lemon), *chendengu* (reddish coconut), *narange* (sour lemon), *drakshe* (grapes), *kharjura* (dates), *nelli* (amalaka), *kire-nelli* (small amalaka), *maimmavu* (sweet mango), *madala* (limonium medica Linn.), *matti* (terminalia tormentosa), *muttaga* (flame of the forest), *kadava* (anthrocephalus cadamba), *kodasige* (wrightia tinctoria), *anile* (myrobalan), *atti* (fig), *belliyatti* (white fig), *aranelli* (another kind of amalaka), *nerilu* (syzygium cumini), *kiri-nerilu* (?), *ara-nerilu* (?), *jambu-nerilu* (jambolana, jaman), *bilva* (aegle marmelos), *kallatti* (ficus tormentosa Roxb.), *bevu* (azadirachta indica), *kari-bevu* (murraya koenigii, curry leaves), *tare* (terminalia bellarica Roxb.), *bore* (ziziphus jujuba), *banni* (acacia ferruginea, shami tree), *channangi* (lagerstroemia parviflora), *belalu* (chloroxylon swietenia, satin wood), *bellavatta* (mussaenda frondosa), *hale* (chrysophillum cainito, star apple), *harivana* (erythrinia indica, coral tree), *bale* (musa paradisiaca Linn., plantain), *kallu-bale* (musa superba Roxb., wild plaintain), *karpura-vale* (a variety of plantain?), *kakke* (cassia fistula Linn.), *bikke* (gardenia gummifera Linn.), *ippe* (madhuka longifolia, mahua of South India), *ingla* (balanites aegyptica Roxb.), *molagu* (marsilea quadrifolia Linn.), *mokke* (oroxylum indicum), *tumbura* (zantoxylum alatum Roxb.), *chembe* (erythroxilium monogynum Roxb.), *kaggali* (canarium commune, cashew nut), *chujjalu* (albizzia amara), *ala* (ficus bengalensis Linn., banyan), *kanchyala* (?), *tapasi* (holoptelia integrifolia, Indian elm), *tandasi* (gymnosporia montana), *arali* (ficus religiosa, pipal tree), *arutala* (sapindus emarginatus? soap nut tree), *sirisa* (acacia sirissa), *sirikanda* (sirium myrtifolium, sandal tree), *tariya* (acacia catechu), *tare* (terminalia belerica Roxb., beleric myrobalan), *honne* (pterocarpus marsupium, Indian kino), *surahonne* (calophyllum inophyllum, Pinnay oil-tree), *rudrakshe* (elaeocarpus ganitrus Roxb.), *bhadrakshe* (ganzuma tormentosa, bastard cedar), *madrakshe* (?), *jivarakshe* (?), *sampage* (michelia champaka), *naga-sampage* (mesua ferrea, iron wood), *bakula* (mimusops hexandra Roxb.), *kuravaka* (barlearia cristata), *tilaka* (andenathera pavonina Linn, red wood), *karnikara* (pterospermum acerifolium), *priyangu* (setaria italica, Italian millet), *shoke* (?), *jala* (shorea laccifera), *vattalaja* (macaranga indica?), *tale* (borassus flabellifer, palmyra palm), *bilitale* (sterculia villosa Roxb.), *kendale* (schleichera trijuga, Ceylon oak), *hondale* (?), *ambata* (embelia robusta), *gavate* (albizzia lebbek), *kulimavu* (?), *aramavu* (?), *hugeru* (?), *ankole* (alangium lamarckii), *taduka* (?), *giggula* (vateria malabarica, Indian copal), etcetera. (*PV*, I, 33; pp. 9-10) [....]

In that thick woodland was a pleasure garden with various trees casting a thick shade and a number of flowering plants such as *surahonne* (calophyllum inophyllum), *honne* (pterocarpus marsupium), *kedage* (pandanus tectorius, screwpine), *iravantige* (jarminum grandiflorum, white jasmin), *jadi* (a kind of jasmin), *molle* (lonicera leschenaultii, Nilgiri honeysuckle), *maggige* (jasminum pubescens), *paddali* (?), *maruga* (origanum vulgare), *sevanti* (chrysantemum indicum), *sampage* (michelia champaka, champak flower), *suragi* (ochrocarpus longifolius), etcetera. (*PV*, I, 36, p. 11)

6.5 Fruit trees, flowering shrubs and ornamental trees

The following trees and shrubs are mentioned in the *Sanatkumara Charite*:

Fruit trees: plantain, mango, orange, pomegranate, rose apple, jack-fruit, coconut, lemon, sweet lime, date tree, grapes, bananas, areca-nut trees and clove trees.

Flowers and creepers: *bakula* (red flowers), *madhavi* (spring blossoms), *tamala* (white flowers) and *malati* (jasmine).

Ornamental tree: *ashoka* (red cedar tree). (*SC*, IV, 2; p. 32; V, 34 & 36; pp. 48-9)

Trees and shrubs in the forest: *chandana* (sandalwood tree), *bakula* (a kind of *kesara* tree), *kuravaka* (red cedar tree), *bela* (wood apple tree), *madala* (thorn apple tree), *nimba* (citrus fruit trees), *jambira* (lemon tree), *panasa* (jack-fruit tree), *kramuka*, (betelnut tree), *kittale* (orange tree), *banni* (thorny tree sacred to Shiva), *dalimbu* (pomegranate tree), *ileya* (sweet lime tree), *ippe* (tree with thick foliage), *honne* (large forest tree), *tamala* (tree with dark bark and white blossoms), *padari* (tall trees), *tengu* (coconut tree), *sampage* (tree with yellow fragrant flowers), *bale* (plantain tree), *suragi* (tree with fragrant flowers), *nandhyavartaka* (shrub with fragrant white flowers), *kenjaji* (trees with red flowers), *mallige* (jasmine), *surahonne* (middle-sized tree), *sevantige* (flower cultivated in garden) and *tavare* (lotus flower).

In that forest there was a variety of birds merrily flying around such as parrots which could speak, singing cuckoos, buzzing bees and playful swans. Also there were some animals, which, forgetting their traditional rivalry, played together in the forest: the cobras and the mongoose, the cuckoos and the crows, the tigers and the deer, and the lions and the male elephants. (*SC*, XVII, 15-18; pp. 202-3)

6.6 Agricultural products

Quite a number of agricultural products are mentioned in the *Mohana Tarangini*, though there is no mention of the modes of cultivation. They include the following:

Paddy, *rajanna* (a superior variety of rice), *gandhashali* (a fragrant variety of rice), *jaggery* (from sugarcane), wheat, pulses (*MT*, II, 20, 22, 40, 41; pp. 36 & 40, III, 51-52; p. 54); turmeric, raw ginger, onion, coriander, *karibevu*, lemon fruit, *kugali, hippali* (ingredients used in spicy preparations), tamarind and betel-leaves. (*MT*, IV, 60; p. 71; III, 34; p. 38 & following);

Fruit-trees cultivated for their crops: banana, *kabale* (a particularly fine variety of plantain), pomegranate, dates, grapes, jack-fruits, rose apple, mangoes, *madala* fruits, sweet oranges, oranges, *nerale* (fine variety of oranges) (*MT*, XIX, 55; p. 286); coconut trees, *pombale* (yellow banana), areca-nut, figs and others (*MT*, XXIV, 40, 48; pp. 351-3); lemons and *chakota*. (*MT*, IV, 60, 62; p. 71)

Fruit trees growing wild in the forest: *madala*, jack-fruits, grapes, pomegranates, dates, *bilvatta, belela, ghotaki, bikke, nemi, heggalapi, kadasu, kare, bare, gulavatti, tumbura, nagare* (*MT*, XIX, 56; p. 286); banana (wild type), *dipa-drakshe* (a kind of grapes) and guava. (*MT*, XIX, 21; p. 279)

All the above kinds of fruits from the forest were offered by the tribal ladies to the king who happened to be there on a hunting expedition (see Section 16.7).

6.7 Jaggery production

Information on jaggery production is to be found in the *Mohana Tarangini*.

In the process of making jaggery it was essential to have quantities of white, well-grown sugarcane, sickles to cut them, a mill or crusher for crushing them and extracting the juice, a large round metal cauldron for boiling the juice and moulds to form jaggery blocks.

Pure and fresh jaggery cubes were piled up in rows opposite the jaggery factories; they looked like sand dunes formed by the waves of the big rivers during the floods. (*MT*, II, 50, 52; p. 42)

Square moulds (probably of wood) were used in the preparation of cubes of fresh hot jaggery, so that they were uniform in size and looked attractive. (*MT*, I, 39; p. 31)

Similar information on the preparation of jaggery is found in the *Channabasava Purana* (*CP*, XI, 11; p. 119).

Ornamental, medicinal and sacred plants

6.8 Plants in a pleasure garden

In describing a pleasure garden, the *Shivatattva Chintamani* enumerates the following plants, and shrubs:

That superb pleasure garden [....] had trees and plants bearing ripe fruits, such as sweet pomegranate, sweet oranges, dates, a variety of citrus fruits (*ile, matulunga, kittile* and *herile*), jack-fruits, mangoes, *nerile* (purple berries), areca-nuts and *bakke* (a kind of jack-fruit). On account of this dense vegetation, the rays of the sun could not reach the ground. (*S*, XXXI, 3; p. 247)

There were the following plants and creepers: *uragavalli*, (betel-leaf creeper), *menasu* (pepper creeper), *pippala* (fig tree), *jambira* (lemon tree), *uruva-mankanda* (sweet mangoes), *yelakki* (cardamom), *ambate* (a kind of sour fruit), *drakshe* (grapes), *are-madale* (a citrus fruit of large size), *bellavatte, bel* fruit, *gavate* (?), *chilla* (a kind of fruit whose seed is used for treating water), *nelli* (*amalaka* fruit), *rudraksha* (elaeocarpus ganitrus), *suragi* (fragrant flower), *sampage* (champaka), *bakula* (a flower), *karavira* (a fragrant flower), *sevanti* (a kind of jasmine), *maruga* (a kind of basil), *mudivala* (a tree with fragrant roots), *ketaki* (screw pine), *panchche* (a fragrant plant), *mallige* (jasmine), *iruvantige* and *jaji* (two different kinds of jasmine). (*S*, XXXI, 5; p. 250)

6.9 Trees, honey and other products

The *Mohana Tarangini* mentions the following plants and products:

Ashoka, sandalwood (*MT*, XXIV, 53, 63; pp. 353, 356); *neem* tree, banyan, *bilva* (aegle marmelos), *amalaka*, *pipal* (*MT*, II, 53, 54; p. 42); honey from different flowers such as *padari*, wild jasmine, jasmine and *kedage*. (*MT*, XIX, 57; p. 286)

Other products include *bidirakki*, bamboo, cane and *lobana* (frankincense). (*MT*, XIX, 2; p. 279, and 64 p. 287)

6.10 Floriculture

The *Mohana Tarangini* mentions the following flowers:

Sampige, jasmine, *tavare* (lotus), *kedage, padari, iruvantige, suragi-hu* (*MT*, XXIV, 49-67; pp. 356, 357); *kempu kanagile, nandyavarta, davana, kennaidile, hongedage, adirganti* (*MT*, XVI, 19; p. 224); *sevanti, kanchi, kempu-jaji, madivalada-beru* (fragrant roots) and *goranti*. (*MT*, IV, 42; p. 67)

PART TWO

THE KING

The second part of this anthology revolves around the king, the prime minister and the royal family. Here, too, the poets depict a fictional world in which an ideal ruler governs an ideal state, all citizens are law-abiding, and there is neither discontent nor internal strife. The king and his able prime minister, both of whom follow age-revered rules laid down in the various treatises on law, statecraft and politics, are the twin pivots around which all else revolves. Both irradiate a benign authority that is all-pervasive.

Chapter 7 deals exclusively with the duties of a king, the ethical guidelines which a just ruler has to follow and a number of suggestions: how to deal with queens and women in general, relatives, brahmins, subjects, subordinate rulers and enemies; when to give gifts and support charitable institutions; how to chose a prime minister. These considerations give the authors ample scope to enumerate the essential qualities which a prime minister should possess, displaying thus their knowledge of the various treatises on law and politics. However, leaving theories aside, sound practical advice is also given, such as when explaining the four ways of diplomacy or the workings of the intelligence service (see Sections 7.19 and 7.20).

Chapter 8 is mainly concerned with public courtly ceremonies and formal occasions such as royal audiences and royal consecrations, of which the most relevant are the coronation of Krishnadevaraya (Section 8.12) and the victory celebrations. Of particular interest in these accounts of formal occasions are the descriptions of the king and his female retinue, and of courtly attire and jewellery (Sections 8.1 to 8.3).

The relationship of the members of the royal family with their relatives, as well as the formal reception of distinguished visitors or respected elderly relations, is explored in Chapter 9. Then follows a section which focuses on the rapport between the king or royal couple and various religious personalities. Finally, the chapter closes with an account of the royal gifts bestowed on exceptional occasions such as the birth of a princc.

The private life of the court forms the subject of Chapter 10. The awakening ceremony of the king, the life of the royal ladies and their entourage, their dresses and jewellery are all described in great detail.

Chapter 11 is devoted to different topics connected with the royal family. The education of a prince and his training in the various arts, especially martial arts, are highlighted in the first two excerpts. The character of the ideal prime minister, the choice of a suitable person for this post and a brief review of ministerial posts then follow. The chapter ends with a detailed description of the retinue of a king, queen and princess.

Other dimensions of kingly duties are explored in Chapter 12, including the patronage of the different cults which obtained in the royal territory, as well as the bestowing of honours on worthy citizens. This chapter ends with the brief report of a minister resigning his job in order to embrace a life of meditation.

Chapter 13, the last of this part, deals briefly with overseas trade and expeditions. The aim of the poets here is not the rendition of perilous and fascinating seafaring adventures, but rather the results of these voyages. Merchants with untold riches are ushered into the presence of the king who is fascinated by their merchandise and their reports. Occasionally foreign merchants and envoys appear at court, thereby giving the authors an excuse to dwell on their outlandish garb and manners. The final excerpt in this chapter is the remarkably accurate account of the court of the sultan of Delhi.

Chapter 7

THE IDEAL RULER AND THE PERFECT STATE

Lengthy passages giving advice to kings in all matters, spiritual and practical, are to be found in a number of the works presented here. Since by their very nature these passages contain the same information with only slight variations, the selection has been limited to the most interesting examples.

The chapter is divided into six parts, opening with a brief passage on statecraft. The second part focuses on the king, his personality and duties. In the third part, words of advice to the king regarding his relationship with relatives, friends and enemies are uttered by various persons, including a queen mother. The fourth part concentrates on the ethical principles that should inform his conduct, such as his patronage of charities. The fifth part deals with the personality, character and abilities of the prime minister, the person actually responsible for the smooth running of the state. Up to this point, the authors' views reflect some of the abstract notions laid down in the traditional treatises on law and politics. However, the two excerpts on the traditional four methods of diplomacy and the intelligence service in the sixth part of this chapter are probably grounded in actual practice.

Statecraft

7.1 Ethic principles to be observed by a king

The *Dharmanatha Purana* has the following passage on statecraft.

A king should conquer or have control over the six traditional enemies of human beings. He should follow the predictions of the almanac and act accordingly. He should possess the three traditional powers and always aim at achieving something. He should strive always to enhance the status of the seven traditional branches of the state. He should support needy persons.

A king should be learned; he should be an expert in the four traditional stratagems, be lofty in his thinking, be extremely patient, be of good propriety, and so on. A king should always speak the truth, be charitable and generous, provide protection to those who surrender for safety, be ready to take part in warfare, and be always gracious. A king should never be arrogant towards his subjects; they should be treated equally and liberally. A king should never be greedy of another king's territory.

A king should acquire wealth only for use during adverse times and to protect himself.

A king should appoint right persons for the right jobs and not otherwise.

A king should protect his subjects, help his own kinsmen, take care of the service personnel, etcetera.

In short, a king should rule his kingdom in such a way as to make his name remembered even after his death. (*DP*, XII, 128-36; pp. 331-2)

The king and his duties

7.2 The ideal king

The following excerpt from the *Bharatesha Vaibhava Sangraha* is a good example of this genre of literature illustrating the behaviour of the ideal king. Comparable passages are found in the *Jivandhra Charite* by Bhaskara, the *Sanatkumara Charite* and the *Jivandhra Charite* by Terakanambi Bommarasa.

One day the king sat in the audience hall and was entertained by musicians and singers. Then he turned towards the learned men and poets who were there to listen to their discourses.

The chief amongst them started speaking. He began by blessing the king emperor, wishing him success in both temporal and spiritual matters. [Thereafter, he gave advice to the king on various aspects and duties of a ruler.]

There are two kinds of victory: the one is over the enemy rulers, in order to attain suzerainty; the other is overcoming worldly matters, in order to attain salvation of the soul. These are termed *loukikartha* and *paramartha* respectively. (*BVS*, II, 1-4; p. 97)

Many kings achieve worldly success easily, but attaining spiritual success is difficult, since it requires true wisdom.

The most successful ruler, however, is the one who is able to achieve a harmonious blend of both temporal and spiritual matters in life. The king should strive to become thus.

Being a *kshatriya*, the king should donate liberally, but only to the deserving ones. He should speak only when absolutely necessary and, similarly, he should act in silence. He should not flaunt his riches; at the same time, however, his lifestyle should be in keeping with his status. He should be considerate and friendly towards his subjects and relatives; he should be like a cobra to the enemy kings. He should always be obedient and respectful towards his spiritual preceptor and other pious persons. He should behave like a hero on the battlefield, but not in the company of others' wives. He should be tolerant of faiths other than his own. He should be well acquainted with the classical literature, the treatises and the arts [of his country]. He should have full control over the five senses. He should not yield, like the animals and insects, to the temptations of the senses and then face trouble. The same five senses may become the five fires or the five gems, depending on the control or otherwise exercised upon them by the ruler. One who leads a careful and prudent life will be like a *yogi*, while the other will be like a deceased person. The wise [king] will have no attachment to the body and other worldly things. He should make a clear distinction between the soul and the body; this attitude will keep him free from the fetters of worldly matters. Such a person will be like pure gold which, even when buried in the earth, will not be in the least tarnished, whereas an iron object becomes rusty in no time. He should be sincere and truthful in his behaviour and speech, and be an example to others. He should lead a pure life, though staying among all worldly comforts and riches.

Even while busy with state duties the king should always think of facing the god of death boldly and of attaining salvation. (*BVS*, II, 6-20; pp. 97-9)

He should always listen to the achievements of mythological persons and aim at the salvation of his own soul. (*BVS*, II, 22; p. 99)

He should enjoy thoroughly the performances of dancers, musicians and the words of poets and also he should reward them appropriately. Though living amidst worldly pleasures and comforts, he should be detached and unaffected by them.

He should treat his body as the temple, his mind as the throne and his soul as the Jina himself, and he should always remember the Supreme Being. By constant meditation on the Supreme Being, one can be granted His vision. This cannot happen in one day. Only when *karma* disappears, can one see Him. (*BVS*, II, 25-30; pp. 100-1)

7.3 The appropriate conduct of the ideal king

Further interesting information on the behaviour of the king can be gleaned from the following passage from the *Sanatkumara Charite*.

The king should earn riches to the best of his abilities and in a just manner without, however, causing hardships to the subjects. He should spend only two-thirds of his total income on his army, his comforts and making gifts. The remaining one-third should be spent on religious institutions and for charitable causes. He should never resort to enforced exactions from his subjects, because this will be very harmful. He should never ignore the advice given by good and virtuous ministers, and should never take heed of the words of bad or foolish persons. He should invariably observe the age-old customs and traditions.

The king should arrange for the regular free feeding of the learned [brahmins]. His prime duty is to offer full protection to all the subjects of his kingdom. He should encourage agriculturalists to work hard and produce abundantly for the welfare of the kingdom.

When the enemy kings approach you submissively, show them full courtesy, treat them kindly and also trust their words. With such gracious treatment extended to them, bind them with obligation towards you. Thereafter, you can punish them as per the exigencies and your interest.

Be a brave warrior and never show your back in the battlefield like a coward. Do not trust young ladies; do not rely on riches; do not show much confidence in brothers and other relatives. The king should be fair and not show any discrimination while treating the surrendered enemy kings.

The king should not give occasion to the subjects to complain either that he is unkind, or that his minister is harsh or hard-hearted, or that others of the court are ill-advisers.

The king should worship the Jinas and the preceptors. He should not hurt his subjects; instead he should always protect them. He should spend his wealth for good causes. He should give shelter to virtuous people. Whomsoever observes the [traditional] duties or precepts will attain real salvation. (*SC*, XVI, 41-54; pp. 194-7)

7.4 On kingly duties

The duties of the ideal king are delineated in the following excerpt from the *Jivandhra Charite* by Terakanambi Bommarasa.

The king should supervise all the departments of the administration. He should provide due protection to the citizens and punish the wicked and the bad. He should not lend his ear to tale-carriers. He should never covet the wealth and wives of others. He should be courageous and boldly face the world. The king should not bear ill will or jealousy at the prosperity of others. He should not talk ill of religious persons; he should not argue much with elderly persons; he should not talk ill of others; he should possess good character. He should not be partial to women; he should always be calm and composed; he should be brave and courageous on the battlefield; he should take care of his subjects and protect them.

He should know that kindness is the essence of all religions and act accordingly. He should be liberal in giving charity, but only to those who deserve it. He should be god-fearing and should always respect the [Jaina] preceptors. (*JCT*, VII, 53-61; pp. 53-4)

Words of advice

7.5 Words of advice from the queen mother

This excerpt from the *Ramanatha Charite* contains sound advice from a mother to a son.

The queen-mother told her son that there were seven essential conditions for a kingdom to prosper: an [able] ruler, [able] minister, [trustworthy] servants, territory, wealth, [dependable] relatives and [strong] fortresses. (*RC*, XXX, 14; p. 195, II)

It is not advisable for the royal prince to play with tops, marbles (made from the seeds of a creeper), *lagge* (a ball game) or *hidigavade* (an indoor game played with cowries), because these pastimes are not befitting the princely status. Ball games, especially, suit only the cowherd-boys and are not fitting for those of royal lineage. (*RC*, XXX, 17-18; p. 195, II)

A prince should not: borrow from relatives, injure the feelings of the body guards and service personnel, overlook harmful persons, have a long-term grudge against his brothers, be pompous towards learned persons, be deceitful with his parents, worry much about others, go against the established *dharma*, desire the wives of others, show weakness on the battlefield, be a hypocrite, retract a promise, behave wilfully or disregard the advice of well-wishers. (*RC*, XXX, 27-30; p. 197, II)

A prince should regularly gather information from his spies and consult his trusted ministers before taking appropriate action. He should never take to gambling. He should not fight with his relatives. He should not be arrogant. There is no second mother, father, [river] Ganga, motherland or god. (*RC*, XXX, 35, 40-4; pp. 198-9, II)

7.6 Words of advice to a king

The following words of advice to a king are from the *Karnataka Krishnaraya Bharata.*

The king should be of exemplary character and behaviour since others will imitate him or be guided by his conduct. Hence, on earth, the rulers are supreme. (*KB*, II, 35; p. 65)

The king should post fearless and trusted guards at strategic locations such as his own resting spots, places he frequently visits, roads, bridges, border areas, entrance gateways of the cities and around the palace. Furthermore, he should post trusted spies to observe the foreign kings, his brothers, sons and ministers.

When he finds his position weak, he should take the required initiative and negotiate with the enemy king to retain the kingdom and rule it, even at the cost of payment.

A wise king should never resort immediately to warfare against the enemy. He should first try all the three traditional ways of winning over the enemy and only when they fail should he wage war.

A benevolent king should collect by way of revenue only one-sixth of the produce from his subjects, without harassing them. Out of that revenue he should ensure that the forts are protected and all the divisions of the army are operational.

A good king should avoid indulging in the seven types of sensual pleasures. Instead, he should spend his time in religious practices, charities and similar activities. While discharging his duties as a ruler, he should not be guided by the words of the tale-carriers, but by wise and good ministers.

A good king should excuse the mistakes of others, once they have repented. He should not forget those who were good to him. He should not be miserly or guided by greed. Charity should be one of his priorities. He should not be arrogant; he should keep bad people at a distance. (*KKB*, II, 43-8; pp. 66-7)

7.7 On the relationship between the king and his brahmins

The *Karnataka Krishnaraya Bharata* voices the following opinion.

The king should keep the learned and religious brahmins happy and contented because [they] ensure prosperity to the kingdom, the king and his progeny. (*KKB*, II, 50-5; pp. 67-8)

7.8 On the advice of the brahmins

The author of the *Ramanatha Charite*, however, sees the situation differently.

The words or advice of the brahmins should not be taken for granted, since they can be misleading and spoken with the intention of making money for themselves. Accordingly, their saying that those who died in the battlefield won the hands of the *apsaras* is only a glamorous tale invented by them for the benefit of innocent and gullible persons. (*RC*, XXXIV, 61-73; pp. 461-3, II)

7.9 On subjects, enemies and subordinate rulers

The behaviour of a just ruler towards his subjects, enemies and vassals is thus described in the *Karnataka Krishnaraya Bharata*.

The subjects should be cared for with kindness and at the same time humility. Similarly, those who surrender should be given all protection; the enemies should be eliminated, but peace of mind should be maintained and the path of *dharma* should be strictly followed.

The king should always be alert with his subordinate rulers and vassal kingdoms. He should not torture others for any reason whatsoever. He should respect the brahmins and the gods. (*KKB*, III, 33-8; pp. 309-10)

7.10 On administration

The *Karnataka Krishnaraya Bharata* on administration:

A good king, staying in the city provided with all the amenities and requirements, should have good ministers and provincial governors posted appropriately at various places and forts. They should encourage both agricultural and commercial activities. When collecting revenues, the king should give enough time to his subjects, without causing hardships or complaints. They [subjects] are the backbone of the kingdom and its prosperity; thus [through them] he can increase the income for the state treasury. And the wealth so gathered should be utilised for good causes only and for the welfare of the subjects. (*KKB*, II, 83-91; pp. 72-3)

7.11 On warfare

The *Karnataka Krishnaraya Bharata* on warfare:

A king should never use poisoned weapons, even during a war against an enemy king. Even after victory over an enemy king, the righteous king should not resort to the killing of the brahmins, the destruction of temples and *mathas* and the slaughtering of common people. (*KKB*, II, 101-2; p. 74)

To punish those who act against *dharma* and cause injustice is not a sin for a king. Indeed, it is a meritorious act. For a *kshatriya* king it is fair to kill anyone in the course of a battle, including close relatives. (*KKB*, II, 66-7; p. 53)

7.12 On being a compassionate human being

The *Karnataka Krishnaraya Bharata* has the following words of advice:

A good king should not give up a person who has surrendered seeking protection; he should not betray trusted friends; he should not kill helpless women; and he should not confiscate the belongings of a brahmin, since such acts are against the law of the land. (*KKB*, VII, 62; p. 586)

Of all the good qualities of a man, compassion towards all beings is the most important one, and thus a good king should be compassionate towards all beings. (*KKB*, VII, 65; p. 586)

Moral and ethical precepts

7.13 Ethical guidelines a king should follow

Battaleshvara's *Ramayana* has this impressive list of prohibitions.

Those who indulge in the following vices will not prosper and or attain salvation either during life on earth or after death: one who does not behave in a just manner towards his father; an unfaithful woman; one who runs away from the battlefield, betraying his master; one who is ungrateful towards a benefactor; one who violates the traditions and ancient customs; and one who indulges in intoxicants. (*R*, IX, 6; p. 104)

Moreover, one should avoid the following: forgetting the deity and its commandments, and criticizing the elders out of arrogance. On the other hand, goodness should be recognized in the elders and they should be respected. Honourable persons should be honoured with all reverence. Knowledge should be welcomed, even if it comes from a younger person, and help should be given to the needy (or young). One should never embark on a journey alone, but in the company of a trusted person. One should not be selfish in thought (or deed). One should dine in company. One should not walk through a forest without a companion; similarly, one should always sleep with a companion. Finally, while tackling difficult tasks, there should be someone to guide one.

Again, a king should not take for granted or trust the following: an enemy king, a concubine, a fire, a mistress, a bad friend, deep water (sea), a forest, a mountain peak, a shameless widow and a cobra. (*R*, IX, 23-5; p. 108)

7.14 On charities and gifts

The *Samyukta Kaumudi* on charities:

There are four kinds of important charities that are conducive to the exalted status of a person: offering of protection, medical treatment, food and education. Among these four, the most meritorious is the liberal offering of food. (*SK*, VII, 14; p. 124 and 45; p. 132)

Gifts given to meritorious persons are like feeding a cow; it gives milk, although it is fed with grass only. If an undeserving person is given donations, it is like pouring milk into the mouth of a cobra: it can only give deadly poison. (*SK*, VII, 50; p. 133)

The minister

7.15 On ministers I

The *Ramanatha Charite* has the following words of warning about ministers:

Friendship with a bad king, employment of a wicked minister and life with a woman of loose character are bound to doom a king to a miserable life.

The minister that cannot judge between good and bad orders before carrying them out will, in the end, bring misery to the king.

The post of minister should be given to a brahmin or a *vaishya* and not to a *kshatriya* or *shudra*; [ministers from] the latter two [traditional classes], in the long run, are sure to prove detrimental to king and kingdom.

The first three of the four traditional classes of society always wish for the welfare and prosperity of the king, while the last category, never.

Kshatriya or *shudra* ministers are the worst enemies of the king. Hence, only a brahmin is most suited for the post of minister.

A *shudra* minister will never shirk before the worst kind of crime, will find faults in the king and make him responsible for everything, and will become a traitor as soon as the occasion arises. (*RC*, XXXVII, 80-5; p. 353, II)

7.16 On ministers II

The *Vijayakumari Charite* has the following advice on the choice of a suitable minister:

The king, out of affection for his queen, should not offer a high position [the office of minister] to her relatives; [rather], he should just bestow on them presents. Otherwise it would be as giving a sharp sword to a mad person who would use it not only for his own ends, but also for those of others. It would give the king endless worries and troubles; it would be bad for the kingdom. A person of bad character performing vicious deeds and harbouring vicious thoughts should never be given the post of a minister. Also, the king should not favour an unwise and arrogant person. Instead, the king should choose as a minister a person of good and decent ancestry, wise and well educated, of good character and well known to him. He should be mature, experienced and follow the *dharma* of the land.

The king should be kind and compassionate, listen to the problems of the poor, test his own service personnel and consider favourably the advice of wise persons. His rule should be just and in accordance with the *dharma* of the country. He should respect religious persons and make arrangements for charities to be bestowed upon religious institutions, temples, etcetera. (*VC*, I, 509-21; pp. 54-5)

[One day], the king sitting in the audience hall had to advise his minister as follows: a good minister should work for the strengthening of the *dharma* of the country, the treasury of the kingdom and the army.

A benevolent minister should not make the subjects suffer under heavy taxation, indulge in worldly pleasures and overlook the ancient *dharma*, customs and practices; [he] should respect the religious preceptors and teachers.

A good minister should not allow or encourage the intermixing of the four traditional classes of society; he should put down immoral life in the kingdom and should not harass people who are law-abiding and well behaved.

The established institutions [customs] should be maintained, the brahmins should be given all protection and [the minister] should never listen to bad persons carrying tales.

An able minister should always be alert and ready to protect the royal household, kingdom and army of the king; [he should always] be interested in the well-being of his master, the king.

A good minister should be adept at political diplomacy and should be well-versed in all the branches of knowledge, especially those which are observed and followed in everyday life. (*VC*, I, 529-34; pp. 56-7)

7.17 The ideal minister

The character of the ideal minister is described in the *Karnataka Krishnaraya Bharata* as follows:

A good minister should be bold, courageous, liberal, of good character, popular with the subjects, learned, clever, trustworthy, pure, open-hearted, born into a brahmin family, knowledgeable about all religious and dharmic duties and of smiling countenance. In times of disputes, the king should entrust the responsibility of administering justice to the learned and religious brahmins. They should not succumb to bribes, but should discharge justice according to the *dharma* of the land and punish those found guilty. (*KKB*, II, 76-81; p. 71)

7.18 On the relationship between the ruler and the minister

A passage from the *Karnataka Krishnaraya Bharata*:

A wise and good minister should be trusted completely and the state affairs should be entrusted to him. He will always work for the prosperity of the king, the kingdom and its subjects. (*KKB*, II, 66-8; p. 69)

Diplomacy and intelligence service

7.19 The four ways of diplomacy

The *Channabasava Purana*, apart from the usual words of advice to the king, has a very explicit passage on *chaturopaya*, or the four methods of dealing with adversaries.

The four traditional expedients to be followed by rulers in order to attain success against their adversaries are *samamu* (negotiation on equal terms), *bhedamu* (dissemination of disagreement among the party or camp of the adversary), *danamu* (charitable attitude towards the adversary) and lastly, if the above three methods fail, *dandamu* (open fight against the adversary). (*CP*, XXIII, 19; p. 231)

7.20 Intelligence service

The existence of an intelligence service is highlighted in the following passage from the *Shri Krishnadevarayana Dinachari*.

After being crowned, the king was advised by the important persons of the court to undertake a tour of the kingdom in order to know the people and their conditions. He readily agreed, saying that by staying in the capital he would not learn much about his subjects. Before setting out, however, he wanted to gather information on all the various parts of his kingdom through his trusted secret emissaries. The spies were intelligent, knew many languages and were capable of assuming different disguises, so he despatched them to over nineteen places and to the neighbouring kingdoms. Similarly, he instructed his officers to carry out the duties of watch and ward within the capital and to check whether there were infiltrators. They were also to look into the maintenance of law and order within the city. (*SKD*, I, prose; pp. 10-11)

Furthermore, the king himself, after the evening audience was over, would set out in disguise, accompanied by his trusted companions, and go around the streets of the capital to study the people, their behaviour and so on. When anything unpleasant came to his notice he would question the city guard on the morning of the next day and give proper directions. In this manner, he was able to maintain efficiently law and order in the city. The personal interest of the king made the city guards extra vigilant and scrupulous in discharging their duties. On account of this, even ministers such as Appaji were afraid of talking carelessly in their houses, be it by day or by night. (*SKD*, I, prose; pp. 11-12)

Chapter 8

THE COURT

This chapter is divided into four parts containing a number of descriptions of formal courtly occasions. The first part, which centres on the king and his entourage, commences with a remarkable description drawn from the *Bharatesha Vaibhava Sangraha* of a king enthroned, flanked by his female fly-whisk-bearers and surrounded by his retinue. (Incidentally, the stance and outfit of the king find an exact visual counterpart in the sculptures of the period.) A description of the king's female retinue from the *Mohana Tarangini* concludes this part.

The second and most substantial part of this chapter is devoted to various types of royal audience. It starts with the *Channabasava Purana*'s description of the attire and jewellery worn by the courtiers, the sitting arrangements and the public present in the audience hall. The excerpt from the *Mohana Tarangini* depicts a typical public audience held in the evening. From the *Pampasthana Varnanam* comes a magnificent description of a divine audience at the court of Shiva. The audiences granted to specific groups of professionals, such as ambassadors, provincial rulers and state accountants, are followed by accounts of very special occasions, including a theological debate held at the presence of the assembled court and the king rewarding a scribe for his linguistic talents.

The third part focuses on coronation ceremonies and the gifts presented to the new king. Perhaps the most important of these narratives is that of the coronation of Krishnadevaraya, in which there is mention of the sixteen *mahadanas* (great gifts) made by a king on special occasions.

The chapter concludes with the victory celebrations from the *Mohana Tarangini.*

The king and his entourage

8.1 Portrait of a king

The following account comes from the *Bharatesha Vaibhava Sangraha.*

One day the king, who was young, of a wheaten colour and beautiful, got up in the early morning. He worshipped the deity and entered the audience hall. It was embellished with the nine kinds of gems and tastefully decorated with gold plates. The ruler sat on the golden throne in a posture befitting royalty: his left leg was folded and rested on the seat, while his right foot, with the *pendeya* (anklet of honour), rested on the sandal below the seat. His right hand rested on a short dagger [tucked into the belt] in a golden sheath, while the left [hand] was [placed] on the cushion at his side. He wore the sacred thread, an upper cloth which covered his body and a crown under which a bun of plaited hair was visible. At regular intervals, the panegyrists sang his praises.

He had thick moustache and eyebrows. He had donned glittering ear ornaments, wristlets, pendants and a necklace set with the nine kinds of gems. A silk cloth covered his chest. He sat in state with great majesty. (*BVS*, I, 15-28; pp. 91-3)

A number of attendants held fans and fly-whisks; others were busy with their individual assignments. To his right were the subordinate rulers and the officers, while to the left were the ladies-in-waiting. At the front were poets and scholars; at the back were trusted friends and sandal-bearers. A group of young and beautiful ladies attentively and keenly attended to his needs. (*BVS*, I, 31-3; p. 93)

8.2 The king's female retinue at a royal audience

The following description is taken from the *Mohana Tarangini.* Particularly interesting is the enumeration of the objects carried by the attendants, especially golden staffs, betel-nuts, a napkin and water vessel. (Visual renderings of such formal scenes are often found in the sculpture and painting of the period.)

The king was seated on a throne placed at the centre of that inner hall. The two queen-consorts who stood at his sides looked like golden portrait sculptures. They were so close to him that they seemed like his shoulder ornaments, studded with glittering stones and diamonds. Adding colour to the audience were two rows of ladies carrying the golden staffs of royalty standing in front of the king. Apart from them were hosts of female attendants; some were loudly praising the virtues of the king, in the manner of the brahmin panegyrists. Ready at hand was a lovely lady carrying in her hand a jewelled pouch containing betel-leaves, nuts and other items that the king might require. Another lady was standing with a soft clean napkin in her delicate hands, ready [for the king] on demand. Other ladies standing in attendance were holding a vessel of sweet drinking water and a golden spittoon. He was fanned by a girl rhythmically waving a fan with a golden handle, while another plied the fly-whisk to and fro, to ward off the flies. The next [girl] held a mirror, to be shown to the king when asked for; another was in charge of his golden sandals; the last was carrying a short dagger. All these ladies were part of the regular retinue of the king. Apart from these, there was a number of other ladies for the entertainment of the king and his queens. Among them were those who were proficient in all the 64 branches of knowledge. If some had mastered the art of playing string instruments, others were virtuoso percussionists. Again, some played wind instruments, others percussion instruments. Some had [tame] birds for the entertainment of the king. These ladies, who were in charge of entertaining the king in various ways, were [also] the ones in charge of the 52 assignments. He enjoyed the various kinds of entertainment offered by the ladies, and at the end he thanked all of them by giving them betel-leaves and nuts placed on golden plates and the other usual presents. (*MT*, IV, 3-19; pp. 59-62)

Royal audience

8.3 King, audience hall and public

The description of royal audiences is among the themes the poets loved to explore best. The magnificence of the hall and its golden throne, the distinguished persons attending the audience, the courtesans sitting on either side of the king, the retinue of female servants carrying fly-whisks and fanning the ruler with long white cloths: such are the themes that appear in the *Dharmanatha Purana* (*DP*, VI, 1-7, 9, 15 and interspersed prose; pp. 109-12). All the above mentioned elements were elaborated upon in a number of other works, including the *Channabasava Purana*, from which comes this excerpt giving an insight into the attire, jewellery and sitting order of those present at the royal audience.

The king sat in audience on a high, golden throne. He wore jewels of various kinds. On either side of the king, the governors and other subordinate rulers were seated on seats studded with jewels. Next were the princes who distinguished themselves in war. They were all dressed according to their status. They wore musk *tilakas* on their foreheads. Their bodies had been sprinkled with various fragrant substances. The anklets of honour shone prominently on their ankles. [As a mark of *kshatriya* descent] they held small daggers in their left hands. They wore rings of various types, studded with diamonds, precious stones and/or pearls. Various kinds of long pearl necklaces hung from their necks, cascading on their chests. On their ears and shoulders were ornaments of various designs. Their attire was completed by long glittering swords, a mark of valour, which they held in their hands. (*CP*, VII, 3-5, pp. 73, 74) [....]

The next group of persons seated in that hall, to the right of the king, was that of famous scholars. They were specialized in various branches of knowledge and sat on golden seats. They wore full beards, ear-ornaments studded with jewels, the *yajnopavita* and the sacred signet-ring. (*CP*, VII, 8; p. 75) [....]

Then there were the feudal kings accompanied by their ministers, generals, relatives, diplomats, scholars, physicians, dancers and singers. There were about sixteen such rulers coming from different countries. One after another, all of them were introduced to the king by two masters of ceremonies. (*CP*, VII, 12-18; pp. 76-7)

8.4 An evening's public audience

This account is drawn from the *Mohana Tarangini*.

The king regularly held another public audience in the evening. After sunset the whole palace and the audience hall were well lit by numerous standing lights and torches. Then the king sat on the jewelled throne placed in that part of the palace. Besides the usual retinue of ladies-in-waiting, the audience consisted of men of different ranks, positions, professions and pursuits. Those related to the royal family sat on jewelled seats close to the king. Next to them were the trusted servants and officers of different ranks and positions. The next group consisted of elderly persons and scholars specialized in various disciplines. They were sitting in rows. As usual there were many groups of young ladies who were masters in different performing arts, such as music, dance and drama, and who entertained the assembled court. At the end of the daily audience, the king rewarded liberally and in various ways all those assembled there. The learned persons were awarded with the seven kinds of gifts. The followers of all religions, Shaiva, Vaishnava, Jaina and Ganapatya, the worshippers of Surya, as well as all the other devotees, were equally and generously rewarded by the king. Noblemen, rich gentry, brave warriors and distinguished soldiers belonging to all the four divisions of the army were all honoured by the king. The next people to receive gifts at the hands of the generous king on that day were the ladies who entertained the audience. Furthermore, princes, rich individuals, philanthropists, merchants, wrestlers, priests, door-keepers and porters were also rewarded by the pleased king, who then retired into the palace for the night. (*MT*, XVIII, 8-17; pp. 254-6; XX, 48-60; pp. 302-5)

8.5 A divine audience

This passage from the *Pampasthana Varnanam* describes Shiva and Parvati (here called by her patronymic Girije) in their audience hall surrounded by their divine court. The description of Shiva and his attributes is one of the most remarkable features of this passage.

One day Shiva desired to grant audience to his devotees. He then dressed up for the occasion and wore a jewelled crown on his head, a black dot of fragrant musk on the forehead, ear-ornaments in the shape of a cobra, a necklace of big pearls around the neck, a thick string of pearls across the chest, a trident (or bow) in one hand, wristlets, an elephant skin around the waist, a girdle with hanging tassels, *vibhuti* smeared all over the body, *parijata* flowers in the hair bun, fragrant sandal paste applied on the body, a silk upper cloth and golden sandals. He had staff with a coral-studded handle and [was accompanied by] female attendants with fly-whisks. Thus attired, Shiva, led by his faithful attendant Nandikeshvara, entered the audience hall and sat on a golden seat encrusted with precious stones. His consort, Girije, soon joined him. (*PV*, I, 54-5; pp. 15-17)

A large number of gods, goddesses, semi-gods, other celestial beings, their attendants and associates, as well as other members of various classes of beings, both male and female, who were part of the retinue of the divine couple, had assembled in that hall. Before entering they had to be approved by Nandikeshvara; then they took their places in accordance with their position and status. They saw Shiva wearing the tiger skin, his body smeared with *vibhuti* and decorated with garlands of *rudraksha* beads, with a Shiva *linga* on the head [fixed into the hair]. He carried a *kamandalu* in the hand and held a *japamala* in his fingers; a small sack containing *vibhuti* hung from his left shoulder; his waist was enhanced by a *nagasutra* and a band was tied around his chest. All of them paid their respects to Shiva [who was] seated in audience together with Girije, his consort. (*PV*, I, 58-61; pp. 18-19)

The *Sanatkumara Charite, Kaushika Ramayana, Samyukta Kaumudi* and *Shri Krishnadevarayana Dinachari* also contain descriptions of royal audiences, but these are not particularly original.

8.6 Ambassadors and provincial governors are granted an audience

In the course of a royal audience described in the *Padmaraja Purana*, ambassadors of the proverbial 56 countries pay their tribute to the king and his minister Padmarasa.

The chief minister entered the audience hall and sat on a special seat to the right of the king's throne. Among those assembled were ministers, governors, ministers of subordinate rulers, feudal rulers, members of the royal family, scholars, poets, art critics, learned persons and others. There were also chieftains, leaders, noblemen, musicians, dancers, actors, reciters [of classical literary works], representatives of different classes of society, comedians, bons viveurs, warriors and combatants, service personnel and officers, as well as the representatives of the eighteen departments of the government. (*PP*, V, 2-3 & 6; pp. 77-8)

Emissaries from the 56 countries (Goula, Turuka, Malayala, Konkana, Lata, Andhra, Chola, etcetera) appeared before the king and paid their tributes. The door-keepers of the king ushered them in. They brought, as part of their tributes, elephants, horses, cloths, youthful girls, choicest gems, perfumes, coins and other precious and unusual objects. The king was very pleased at seeing all those gifts. (*PP*, V, 4-5; p. 78)

8.7 Royal accountants are granted an audience

This excerpt, which comes from the *Shivatattva Chintamani*, is one of the few in which administrative matters are mentioned.

Royal accountants submitted [to the king] the various expenditures made from the royal treasury and storehouses. Among these were allowances made to the war-heroes, monthly allowances to the concubines and allowances for the royal horses, elephants, charity houses and the like. They also had detailed receipts of the various types of tribute received by the subordinate rulers. The appropriate ministers accounted for the horses and elephants in the royal stables. Then the army general paraded the princes of the defeated kingdoms who had been taken into custody and ushered in the ambassadors from other countries who had come with large tributes and payments. Having accepted the supremacy of the king, they praised him enthusiastically in various ways. (*S*, XXXI, 39-42; pp. 258-9)

8.8 A theological debate

A somewhat exceptional royal audience is described in the *Padmaraja Purana*. The king invites the interested public to a public debate on religious matters. The occasion for this philosophical discussion was the arrival of a Vaishnava religious leader from Andhra who wanted to demonstrate the superiority of his faith over Virashaivism. His counterpart in the debate was a local staunch Shaiva devotee. The excerpt gives an insight into the various branches of learning current at that time.

Thereupon, the king invited all the experts, critics and interested public from all classes of society to assemble at court.

They were all proficient scholars and authorities specialized in the following branches of learning: *Rigveda, Yajurveda, Samaveda, Atharvaveda*, various branches of philosophy, astrology, *Dhanurveda, Gandharvaveda* and *Ayurveda*.

There were also poets, reciters of literary works, debators, artists, preachers, priests of all religions, respected gentry, philosophers, *tantra-kovidaru, mantrikaru*, actors, singers, musicians, warriors, dramatists, merchants, courtesans, feudal kings, governors, princes and men of the king's cavalry.

The king sat on the throne and sent for the contenders in order to start their debate on the philosophies, principles and ideals of their respective faiths. (*PP*, IX, 18-22; pp. 166-7)

8.9 A scribe decodes a document written in a foreign script

The *Amalabasava Charite* uses the setting of a royal audience to show how the linguistic proficiency of a scribe is rewarded.

The king was seated in the audience hall. There were some rulers from neighbouring countries who had brought rich tributes. All in all, there were about 1,00,000 persons gathered there. Among them were 8,000 rulers, princes, their ministers, nobles, personnel in charge of the 72 kinds of service, linguists, artists proficient in the 62 arts and others. By chance, the king happened to come across a document written in a strange script. He handed it over to his ministers, but since it was written in an unusual script nobody could read its contents. Among the experts who were there and tried to read it were astrologers, mathematicians, scribes, astronomers, scholars, specialists in the *Agamas*, musicians, learned persons, wise people, arithmeticians, epigraphists and so on. It was then the turn of the linguists, who were specialized in the 56 languages obtaining in the different countries and in the 23 different scripts. None could decipher the document. Thereupon, the king declared that whoever could read it and reveal its contents would be honoured and rewarded by the office of the chief treasurer of the government and the ministership. (*AC*, VII, 2-10; pp. 96-8)

At last, by the will of the god, one of the court scribes was able to decipher and read out the document. On hearing its contents, the king was pleased. He hugged that learned person and made him sit on the throne at his side. (*AC*, VII, 24-5; p. 101)

Thereafter, that person was presented with the customary gifts of honour: ornaments encrusted with gems, silk clothes and others. He was paraded to the sound of music through the main streets, riding one of the choicest elephants. (*AC*, VII, 41-4; pp. 105-6)

After passing through the main streets of the place, the procession returned to the palace. The king received [that person] and made him chief minister and head of the royal treasury. He was then given a separate palace to live in. (*AC*, VII, 47-8; p. 106)

Coronation

8.10 The coronation of Dharmanatha

This elaborate description is drawn from the *Dharmanatha Purana*.

The king decided to crown the prince and entrust the kingdom to him. He then sent for his commander-in-chief and ordered him to erect a pavilion for the celebration of the royal consecration. That pavilion was to be tastefully decorated. (*DP*, XII, 96; p. 324)

The officer chose a suitable place at the centre of the vast multi-storeyed royal palace. (*DP*, XII, prose; p. 324)

The walls of the pavilion were decorated with blue sapphires. It was embellished with festoons, pot-shaped finials, flags and banners, strings of pearls, mirrors and coins. It looked like a marriage pavilion. All the auspicious items necessary for conducting the ceremony had been placed in the required order on the platform at its centre. There was a golden throne glittering with precious stones and diamonds. On all four sides were tassels of different kinds of leaves, umbrellas of honour, long pearl garlands, white fly-whisks with golden handles, etcetera. The royal sword, duly decorated according to the ritual, was set up in front of the throne. At another place, also in front of the throne, was a decorated auspicious vessel. (*DP*, XII, 97-103 & prose; pp. 325-6)

Kings, emperors, close relatives, noblemen, men of distinction, subordinate rulers, ministers, generals, respected men, other subordinate persons and a host of others had assembled there to witness the function, as well as the personnel in charge of the [72] services. The whole hall was vibrating with activity and resounding with voices. (*DP*, XII, 105 and prose; p. 326)

The king entered the pavilion holding the right hand of his son. They were followed by all the dignitaries participating in the ceremony and by young ladies who carried the various auspicious objects and other items required in the course of the ritual. (*DP*, XII, prose; p. 327)

On reaching the golden throne the king sat down, thus signalling to the dignitaries and the ladies to take their respective seats. (*DP*, XII, 107; p. 327)

An astrologer approached the king and the prince, who was sitting at the side of his father, announcing that the auspicious moment had come. Father and son got up and occupied the glittering [golden] plank [for the rituals]. (*DP*, XII, 107 and prose; p. 327)

The king, elderly religious persons and close relatives took the auspicious golden vessel. (*DP*, XII, 108; p. 327)

When the whole place resounded with chanting, the king performed the ritual, pouring over [his son] water mixed with sandal paste and other auspicious substances. Then it was the turn of the ladies to pour auspicious water from their vessels onto the prince. (*DP*, XII, 110-12 & prose, 113; p. 328)

To celebrate the occasion, flowers of various kinds were showered [on the public assembled there]. (*DP*, XII, 114; p. 329)

After all the rituals were over, the crowned prince stood up and put on sandals, which were studded with corals. He was given new clothes with painted designs and sixteen kinds of ornaments, all studded with precious stones. Then he was led by his father to the royal throne, which was placed at the centre of the platform, and was invited to sit on it. Thereupon the auspicious *arati* lights studded with the nine gems were shown to him, and different kinds of fruit such as coconuts, citrus and others were given to him. (*DP*, XII, prose; p. 329)

[While] the pavilion was resounding with instrumental music, singing and chanting of auspicious *mantras*, the father placed on the head of the prince the royal crown. At that, the prince became the crowned king. (*DP*, XII, 116-17, prose; pp. 329-30)

His father pronounced him as being the owner of the state treasury, the state horse, elephant, sword and seat, the white umbrella, etcetera, and enjoined him to rule the kingdom following the tenets of *dharma*. Then he also entrusted him with the care of the members of the royal household, ministers, subordinate rulers, governors, close relatives and other relatives. After that, the father introduced to him some of the neighbouring rulers and asked him to honour them and their kingdoms. He also introduced [him to] some other [rulers], who were there standing with their tributes, and requested his son to welcome and honour them appropriately. With all this, the coronation function terminated. (*DP*, XII, 121-5; pp. 330-1)

8.11 Gifts bestowed upon the king

The *Jnanachandrabhyudaya* adds some interesting details at the end of the description of a coronation ceremony, which is otherwise similar to the foregoing example, by mentioning the presents given to the newly crowned king.

He [the king] then sat on a throne decorated with precious stones and gems, and the crown was set on his head among good wishes and blessings from the brahmins. All the dignitaries and learned men gave him presents: fragrant substances, perfumes, pearls, precious stones, diamonds and other valuable objects. As an important part of the function, two brahmins gave the crowned king fly-whisks, a glittering throne and a white umbrella [all insignias of royalty]. After this, all the guests took leave of the king and left. (*J*, VI, 106-7; p. 191)

8.12 Krishnadevaraya's coronation

The next excerpt, from the *Shri Krishnadevarayana Dinachari,* describes the coronation of Krishnadevaraya. Of interest here is the mention of the *shodasha-dana* (or sixteen *mahadanas)* and the munificent charitable gifts such as the equivalent of the ruler's weight in precious metals, gems, etcetera.

The minister at the court of Vidyanagara [i.e. Vijayanagara] respectfully suggested to Vira-Narasimharaya, then king, to nominate Krishnaraya crown prince. The king requested the minister to make the necessary arrangements, and at an auspicious moment he handed over his signet-ring. The preparations for the coronation ceremony were completed in due course. Present at the ceremony were the king's officers, nobles, scholars, learned persons of the court, astrologers, ascetics, elderly and young persons.

Then, as prescribed by the scriptures, the king was asked to give away valuable objects as an act of charity [by performing] the *shodasha-dana.*

The king also gave in charity the equivalent of his own weight in silver, pearls, gems and fabulous wealth; furthermore, he instituted gifts for some thousand families and others.

After that he was bathed in the holy water brought from the four oceans and from the rivers Ganga, Yamuna, Sarasvati, Narmada, Godavari, Sindhu, Kaveri, Tamraparni and others.

Then gems were poured over his head. He donned a yellow silk cloth and was anointed with sandal paste, musk, saffron paste and *agaru* (yellowish fragrant paste). He put on jewels set with the nine kinds of gems. He then visited the temples of Vitthala and Virupaksha and paid his respects to the gods. He also paid homage to the elders.

A golden band was tied on his forehead; he was taken to the state treasury and made to touch, as an auspicious act, the nine kinds of gems, heaps of which were stored there. Similarly, he was taken to the arsenal, to touch the weapons.

He was then led to the throne and sat [for some time] in audience. Finally he took leave of Narasimharaya and of [the minister] Appaji. Afterwards he dined in the company of his sons-in-law, sons, close relatives, torch-bearers and others. (*SKD*, I, prose; pp. 5-6)

Other brief descriptions of similar coronation ceremonies are to be found in the *Nemijinesha Sangati* and *Vijayakumari Charite.*

Victory celebrations

8.13 Celebrations on the return of the victorious army

The following passage drawn from the *Mohana Tarangini* describes the rejoicing on the occasion of a successful military campaign.

After having vanquished the enemy, the king and his army returned to their own territory. On reaching the outskirts of the capital, they halted for some time in its pleasure garden. The city was decorated for this occasion. All the streets were embellished with numerous festoons of flowers, leaves, tender branches of trees, plants, floral wreaths, tapestries and the like.

The victorious army was welcomed by their relatives and citizens who had come with a band playing various tunes. The *sumangaliyaru* (auspicious wives) who were in the welcoming party, carried various auspicious objects: *arati* lamps, pots, mirrors and others. They waved them before the faces of the victorious men. Thereafter, the king and his nearest relatives took their places in the palanquins and the procession started. At the head there was a group of brahmins reciting appropriate sections and verses from the ancient scriptures; there were also the panegyrists loudly proclaiming the various titles and achievements of the king, while a number of *mangaleyaru* (auspicious ladies) were singing.

After some time, the procession approached the lavishly embellished gate of the city. It was decorated with mirrors, arches, tassels and banners. The ground had been liberally sprinkled with red powder. The main streets leading from the gate were lined with storeyed buildings, many of them with projecting balconies. Colourful festoons, tassels and tapestries hung from the balconies. For this purpose the buildings were fitted with artistically-wrought pegs in the form of elephant trunks and other motifs on which the hangings were fastened. The halls, too, were equally carefully decorated.

The citizens stood in front of the shops on the street level and enjoyed the sight of the victorious king and his army passing through. They showered freshly-plucked flowers and petals on the soldiers. Some brought gold plates filled with red-coloured cooked rice for honouring the king and his men. As the party moved on, long cloths adorned with exquisite embroideries were spread on the ground under the feet of the marching party [in order to protect their feet from the dust]. The shopkeepers whose warehouses were on the main streets brought out from their shops large quantities of musk, saffron and camphor powder, as well as handfuls of gold coins and precious stones, and strew them all over as a sign of joy and appreciation for their king. (*MT*, XLII, 19-28; pp. 572-4)

All along the route of the procession were beautiful dancers performing to the accompaniment of musicians, while brahmins, panegyrists and others were engaged in their respective activities until the convoy reached the palace. There the king rewarded with honours, clothes, jewellery and other gifts all those who had accompanied him in the campaign. [He then] dismissed them. The musicians, singers, brahmins, scholars and other performing artists were then [similarly] rewarded and dismissed. After the army and other men departed, two lady-servants of the king placed before him the golden sandals. The king slipped into them and ascended the steps to his palace which, on this occasion, was richly decorated with colourful banners, flags, festoons, tassels, tapestries and such like. Once again, he and his limited retinue were received and welcomed by the auspicious wives, who repeated the rituals of *arati*, *nivali* and others. After this, the feet of the king were washed with fragrant warm water and then he stepped into the palace. Throughout, the king was accompanied by a host of relatives, elderly persons, young maids and servants. Thereafter he retired. (*MT*, XLVII, 44-9; pp. 577-8)

Chapter 9

ROYAL RECEPTIONS AND VISITS

The themes of this chapter are formal visits, paying due respect to mendicants and holy men, and bestowing of gifts on the people on special occasions.

The first three excerpts, which are drawn from the *Airavata,* deal with invitations and receptions connected to a religious function, the *Airavata Nompi*: in the first, Bhima visits his cousins, the Kauravas; in the second, a dignitary arrives and is welcomed by the Pandavas; in the third, Kunti, the mother of the Pandavas, invites the elder queen Gandhari to attend. All these occasions highlight the formal and ceremonial manner of the parties involved.

The respect of the court for mendicants, holy men and religious personalities is revealed in the descriptions of their reception and entertainment, and the numerous benefactions given to them. The most detailed accounts are those from the *Dharmanatha Purana, Jnanachandrabhyudaya* and *Bharatesha Vaibhava Sangraha* reproduced below. The theme connecting the first two excerpts is the desire of the king or royal couple to beget offspring, a wish which the holy men readily fulfill.

The announced birth of a prince, as his actual birth, were occasions for public rejoicing and special celebrations such as the distribution of gifts from the royal treasury to the citizens.

Formal visits, receptions and invitations

9.1 A visit to royal cousins

This excerpt and the following two examples are drawn from the *Airavata.*

Bhima went to the palace of his cousins. When he arrived, the gate-keeper informed the princes seated in the audience hall and ushered Bhima into their presence. Amid the praises and chants of the panegyrists, Bhima proceeded, escorted by the bodyguards. On seeing him, his cousins rose from their seats, welcomed and embraced him and made him share the throne with [the eldest of] them. They then enquired about his welfare, then honoured him by offering the customary betel-nuts and leaves placed on a golden plate. In turn, the prince strew auspicious rice on their heads, inviting them to attend the *nompi* (religious function) performed by his mother, Kunti. (*A*, III, 1-5; pp. 28-9)

9.2 Reception of a dignitary

On reaching [the palace], Arjuna sent word to his brothers to come out and welcome the dignitary. All the kings, rulers, relatives, learned men and others who had assembled there set out and reached the square in order to receive the dignitary with all the honours. There was also a host of beautifully dressed young ladies who stood holding many varieties of auspicious lights to solemnly welcome that honoured person. The receiving party rode on well decorated chariots, elephants and horses, and was accompanied by the infantry and a band of musicians who played enthusiastically and joyfully. (*A*, IV, 30-5; pp. 45-6)

They received him with all honours [by] performing different types of *arati,* twice pouring handfuls of gems at his feet and [finally] paying their respects. (*A*, IV, 37-8; p. 47)

The learned brahmins, while chanting Vedic hymns, offered auspicious rice and blessed him. Then relatives, citizens and others, such as ladies, children and elderly, paid their respects. Elephants and chariots drawn by horses were paraded before him as a mark of respect. (*A*, IV, 41-3 & 45; p. 48)

Then the dignitary walked towards the palace, assisted by elderly relatives, while auspicious ladies spread all kinds of luck-bearing items along the way and waved *arati* lamps. Eventually, they entered the palace. (*A*, IV, 47; p. 49)

Once there he was requested to sit on a jewelled seat. His relatives washed his feet with Ganga water and worshipped [him], as was the practice. Their mother, too, came out, paid her respects, praised his good qualities and welcomed him. (*A*, IV, 49-50; pp. 50-1)

9.3 An invitation to an elder queen

Kunti was asked to go to the palace of the elder queen and invite her for the special religious function that she was about to perform. Before going on this errand she returned to her own palace in order to get ready. Her ladies-in-waiting applied oil to her hair, her whole body was perfumed with musk and she was bathed in fragrant water. She went to the dressing room and put on splendid garments and ornaments of various kinds. She was sprinkled with various perfumes. Then she put on her sandals and went out [to the accompaniment of] music played by her followers.

She stepped into a golden palanquin and reached the abode of the elder queen. At the entrance she alighted from the palanquin, walked in, prostrated herself before the elder queen and invited her to participate in the religious function performed by her in her own palace. (*A*, VI, 20-5; pp. 65-6)

King and queen pay homage to holy men

9.4 The king honours a Jaina mendicant

This excerpt drawn from the *Dharmanatha Purana* describes how the news of the arrival of a Jaina holy man and his followers is conveyed to the king. The king, his retinue and the city population prepare to welcome the visitors who take up residence in one of the royal gardens on the outskirts of the capital.

One day the king and his queen consort were seated in the assembly hall. (*DP*, III, prose; p. 48)

At that time, the gardener in charge of the royal pleasure gardens on the outskirts of the capital approached the king and told him that a Jaina mendicant with his 500 followers had arrived and was camping in a marble pavilion inside the garden. There he was lecturing to his followers and explaining the Jaina creed to his disciples and the public. It was spring time and the flowering plants and creepers of the garden were looking beautiful. (*DP*, III, prose; pp. 50-1)

The moment the king learned about the presence of this distinguished Jaina mendicant, he rose from his seat, folded his hands respectfully and, as a mark of reverence and respect for that holy person, made seven steps in the direction of the encampment. (*DP*, III, 13; p. 51)

The gardener, who had come with presents of fruits and flowers, was given valuable presents. The king decided to meet that holy person and ordered his resolve to be publicly announced to the beating of drums. (*DP*, III, prose; p. 51)

The citizens rejoiced in hearing this news. The ladies cleaned the frontages of their homes, decorating them in various ways. They dressed themselves in their best clothes and, in readiness for the holy visit, held in their hands auspicious pots, mirrors and other objects. (*DP*, III, 14-16; pp. 51-2)

Other citizens, either on horses or in chariots, arrived and assembled in the courtyard opposite the king's palace. (*DP*, III, prose; p. 52)

The king, superbly attired, set out with his queen on the royal elephant. All around him were attendants holding white umbrellas, fly-whisks and other royal insignias. There were also persons reciting passages from religious texts, playing various instruments, chanting sacred verses, praising the king in different ways, etcetera. In the royal retinue was a host of princes, subordinate rulers, ladies, attendants and others. (*DP*, III, 18-29; pp. 53-4)

While on his way, the king saw from a distance the royal garden filled with dense vegetation and various kinds of trees, some bearing fruits, some in full bloom. As the royal party and the army neared the garden, all the birds, such as parrots, *koyil* and others, darted up into the sky, offering an enchanting view. On reaching there, the king commanded the army and his retinue to wait outside. He entered the garden with folded hands to meet the holy person who was camping there. He saw a group of followers of the saintly man engaged in studies, discussing the tenets of their religion and commenting on ancient treatises, philosophy, metaphysics and other subjects. (*DP*, III, 37-41; pp. 56-7)

Then, in their midst, he saw that distinguished person. (DP, III, prose, 43; p. 57)

The king reverentially circumambulated him three times with folded hands. As prescribed in the scriptures, he worshipped his holy feet, using the auspicious objects brought in containers of gold and silver studded with gems. Then he sat humbly on the floor in front of him. (*DP*, III, 48; prose, p. 58)

The king prayed in various ways, and confided to that holy person his sadness at not having a son. (*DP*, III, prose; pp. 59-60)

On hearing him, the mendicant blessed him and told him that soon he would become the father of a soul destined to be one of the great Jaina *tirthankaras* (Dharmajinadhisha) and who would be greatly revered. This announcement made the king extremely happy. (*DP*, III, 63; p. 61)

The *Prabhulinga Lile* also gives a detailed description of the reception of a holy man, a Virashaiva. However, since the account is very similar to that from the *Dharmanatha Purana* quoted above, it has not been included here.

9.5 The royal couple pay homage to a holy man

In the following passage from the *Jnana-chandrabhyudaya* the king and the queen honour an ascetic.

One day, at the end of the fasting period, a Jaina holy man arrived at the king's palace looking for alms. When the king saw him approach the palace, he stepped down from the throne and went to welcome him. He paid his respects by circumambulating him with folded hands. Thereafter, he led the holy man inside and requested him to take his place on a seat located in a prominent position. There his feet were worshipped according to tradition, by bathing them in holy water, anointing them with sandal-paste, sprinkling them with sanctified rice, etcetera. At the end, pure and simple fare was offered to him.

The king, who had no issue, begged the mendicant to bless him with descendants. The mendicant immediately agreed. Not only this, but he foretold the birth of a son of outstanding character and beauty. Eventually the king and his retinue saw him off, following him for some time and paying him their respects. (*J*, I, 11-19; pp. 5-7)

9.6 The king feeds the holy men

This particularly detailed account, which gives an insight into the king's role in the ceremonial feeding of religious mendicants, comes from the *Bharatesha Vaibhava Sangraha.*

[While the king was seated in the audience hall, a conch was blown indicating that the time for dinner had come. So he stood up and proceeded towards the dining hall.]

The king observed the practice of not partaking of food unless he had first fed the holy men. Accordingly, he went to the hall where the religious persons were assembled. (*BVS*, II, 43-7; p. 103)

He discarded the marks of his royal status, such as the umbrella, fly-whisk, sword, sandals and others. He left behind all his servants and attendants and walked barefoot. Instead of his royal dress he wore only a silken lower garment, tying the upper cloth around his waist.

He carried all the requisites for worshipping the preceptor in bowls and jars. In all humility he walked barefoot and alone to meet his *guru*.

He proceeded without looking left or right, with his mind fixed on meeting his *guru* and the other holy men, and eventually he reached the front court where they were assembled. He stopped and stood on one side of the entrance. He placed the vessels and bowls he was carrying on a gold-sheathed plank and stood humbly at the side of a gold-sheathed pillar, eagerly hoping to meet the holy men. (*BVS*, III, 1-20; pp. 104-6)

He believed that offering cooked food to an image was *upachara-bhakti* (formal homage), whereas feeding holy men was *mukhya-bhakti* (real devotion). (*BVS*, III, 23; p. 107)

At last, after much waiting and to his great joy, two *munis* appeared. On seeing them, the king took the objects required for worship and honoured them in the customary manner by circumambulating them three times and then prostrating himself before them as a mark of respect. Then he led the two mendicants to his palace, which had been cleaned and decorated as usual. As they walked through, the king's attendants and servants, including ladies, stood on both sides. The king himself led the holy men, sometimes taking them by the hand while climbing up or down the steps and so on. (*BVS*, III, 24-38; pp. 108-9)

The mendicants moved on in silence, appreciating the devotion of the king. At some point the bejewelled queens came forward to welcome the two *munis.* They received them with the usual showing of lamps and coloured water and singing of auspicious songs. Finally they prostrated themselves at their feet. Then the *munis* were led to the dining place, which had been thoroughly cleaned and brightly lit. There they were offered raised seats. The king and the queens worshipped their feet, set before them golden plates and gave them cooked food with great pleasure and devotion. They ate to their full satisfaction. After that they were requested to sit on a couch and offered betel-nuts and leaves for chewing. (*BVS*, III, 44-52; pp. 110-11)

The two mendicants, Chandragati and Adityagati, blessed the king, to his great happiness; the queens, too, were also blessed by them. (*BVS*, III, 55-7; pp. 111-12)

Thereafter, the holy men stood up, ready to go. The king accompanied them, occasionally leading them by the hand. After some distance, the *munis* requested the king to go back, but he did not. On reaching the last doorway, the mendicants requested him to return to the palace after blessing him yet again and then they went on. The king stood at that spot until the holy men were out of sight. Then he returned to the palace wearing the golden sandals studded with jewels and the other royal insignia. (*BVS*, III, 59-68; pp. 112-13)

Distribution of gifts

9.7 The king bestows gifts upon his subjects

The *Jnanachandrabhyudaya* describes how the king, on learning that he would soon become the father of a son, distributes gifts to his subjects.

A Jaina mendicant told the king that he would be blessed with a son. The overjoyed ruler sat granting audience, surrounded by poets, singers, scholars, subordinate kings, governors and a host of other persons, flanked by young lady attendants waving fly-whisks. He gave orders for the distribution of generous gifts to the inhabitants of the city. The citizens were allowed to take as much as they wanted from the enormous riches of the state. In the meantime, the king listened to religious discourses and accounts of the life of the Jaina prophets and preceptors or to music, enjoying himself to his heart's content (*J*, I, 20-1; p. 8)

9.8 Gifts on occasion of a royal birth

On the occasion of the birth of a child, it was customary for the royal couple to give gifts to the brahmins, as described in this brief passage from the *Prabhulinga Lile*.

After having prayed to the gods for many years, the queen gave birth to a baby. On that happy occasion, the king and the queen made gifts of gold [coins], clothes, precious stones and diamonds to the brahmins and all the others. (*PL*, III, 12, p. 23)

Chapter 10

PRIVATE LIFE AT COURT

The private life of the king and the royal ladies is the theme of this chapter. The first part deals with the king: excerpts from the *Dharmanatha Purana* and *Shri Krishnadevarayana Dinachari* describe in great detail the king's levee and his various morning activities before entering the audience hall. His attire and jewellery are the subject of a detailed passage from the *Ramanatha Charite.* The *Sanatkumara Charite* has a lively account of the reception awaiting a prince on returning after a long absence, during which he conquered many rulers and married a good number of princesses. He arrives with his wives, a large retinue of male and female attendants and a vast quantity of riches that the princesses' parents had given him. The decoration of the town, the welcoming party and finally the reunion of the prince with his own immediate family are all vividly rendered.

The life of the royal ladies is dealt with in the second part of this chapter. Here too, pride of place is given to topics such as the awakening of a princess, from the *Prabhulinga Lile,* and the ornaments worn by the ladies of the royal household, from the *Ramanatha Charite.* The latter text and the *Mohana Tarangini* both offer insights into the daily life of the queens, their intellectual and other pastimes and artistic activities. The attentions lavished on the pregnant queen by her entourage are described in the passage drawn from the *Dharmanatha Purana.*

Morning activities of the king

10.1 The king's levee

The first excerpt, which is taken from the *Dharmanatha Purana,* deals with the ceremonial awakening of the king and his subsequent morning routine. A similar account appears in the *Sanatkumara Charite.*

At daybreak, the king woke to the sound of auspicious music, singing, recitation from the sacred texts and the ringing of bells in the temple. (*DP,* V, prose & 47; p. 92)

Afterwards he brushed his teeth and bathed. He dressed in clean white garments and set out to the [Jaina] temple accompanied by a number of distinguished persons and nobles. He circumambulated the building accompanied by artists playing, singing and dancing. He then washed his feet and entered the temple with his hands reverently folded, chanting the names of the deity. He prostrated himself before the image and performed six types of ritual. Then, facing the god, he sang his praises 1,000 times. (*DP,* V, prose, 48-55; pp. 93-4)

Thereupon he worshipped the preceptor and other Jaina teachers. Every day he bestowed upon them gifts such as gold, clothes, cows, etcetera. For a short while he sat listening to the recitation of religious texts and eventually he returned to the palace. Once there he washed and then ate. He ended his meal chewing nuts and leaves mixed with fragrant edible camphor. He proceeded to the private audience hall and sat there in audience surrounded by ministers, governors, army generals, chief minister, court priests, subordinate rulers, army chiefs, important relatives and other close associates. (*DP,* V, prose; p. 94)

10.2 The king's attire

Great attention is lavished on the dress and adornment of a prince in this passage from the *Ramanatha Charite.*

At dawn, the prince woke to the sound of melodious recitations, looked into the jewelled mirror and then bathed in warm water. He wore a white lower garment, put on the sacred ash marks, *rudraksha* beads and golden sandals and then proceeded towards the temple enshrining the Shiva *linga* [his patron deity]. There he prostrated himself and prayed. (*RC*, XXIX, 35-7; pp. 178-9, II)

After engaging in worship for some time, he left the temple accompanied by his young lady-attendants and went to the dressing room. The ladies helped him to dress and tie the different ornaments. A turban was tied on his head, a *tilaka* of musk was drawn on his forehead and he was handed pearl earrings and necklace, another necklace, shoulder ornaments, diamond armlets, golden waist band and a chain with a gem pendant. He wore the *pendeya* (anklet of honour) on the right ankle and a golden shawl [across his shoulder]. His body was anointed with fragrant *javadi*. (*RC*, XXIX, 48-59; pp. 180-2, II)

He then left the palace and reached the front court hall, which had been lavishly decorated with pearls. There he sat on the throne, which was studded with all kinds of precious stones, while different categories of personnel attended on him: governors, ministers, feudal rulers, generals, commanders, nobles, war heroes, distinguished cavalry men, bodyguards, poets, learned men, ambassadors, panegyrists, court jesters, musicians, singers, performing artists and many friends. (*RC*, XXIX, 62-71; pp. 183-4 II)

10.3 Krishnadevaraya's morning activities

The most exhaustive description of a king's awakening ceremony followed by an audience is that found in the *Shri Krishnadevarayana Dinachari*.

The king [Krishnadevaraya] woke up from sleep one hour before sunrise to the recitations of the names of gods, saints and preceptors, hymns, [parts from] the *Bhagavata* and praises of ascetics such as Muchukunda. He also listened to the ethical aphorisms of philosophers such as Sanjaya, Vidura and Chalukya (Chanakya). He then listened to [the recitations of] scriptures on statecraft such as *Vairagya-shataka*, *Niti-shataka*, *Vaidya-niti*, *Raja-niti* and such like.

After this he touched a cow of brown colour. Then, again as a good omen, he looked at the faces of two brahmins and dismissed them. He then washed his face. He sat and started chanting the names of various gods and other saintly persons. He was then offered the *prasada* and *tirtha* bought from 108 Vaishnava and 77 Shaiva temples. He stood up and with devotion and respect lifted the offerings to his head.

He received with all honours learned Vaishnava and Shaiva priests and invited them to sit down. He then made enquiries about the gifts that had been granted in order to conduct the rites and festivals at Shriranga, Shrimushnu, Venkatachala, Totadri and other places, and whether these were sufficient and regularly supplied. The priests replied that the king's officers at the respective places were carrying out their duties regularly and with precision. They also told the king that the temples enshrining the five elemental *lingas*, [known as] Ekambaranatha [earth], Jambulingeshvara [water], Arunachaleshvara [fire], Kalahastishvara [air] and Chidambareshvara [ether], also received their allowances regularly and promptly. The priests confirmed that these temples enjoyed such privileges, along with 77 Shaiva and 18 Shakta centres.

The king then sent for the officer in charge of the charities for religious institutions and temples. He reported to his master that the *agraharas* in the regions of Tigulanya, Telunganya, Morasanadu, Karnataka, Melunadu, Ghattadasime, Choladesha, Pandyadesha, Malayaladesha and others were thriving and that the residents were actively engaged in the study of religious texts such as the *Rigveda*, *Yajurveda*, *Samaveda*, *Atharvaveda* and other religious classics. They also were generous in entertaining guests and organizing the free feeding of the needy. In conclusion, they were happily leading a pious and devout life.

At this point, the king sent for the general who reported that all the forts in the kingdom, be they hill-forts, those surrounded by water or those on the land, were well guarded, protected and efficiently maintained. Moreover, everybody was safe in the kingdom and there was nothing special to report on the activities of the subordinate kings since all of them were quiet.

Next came in the officer in charge of the metropolitan city. He prostrated himself before the king and paid his respects. Then, along with the general, he reported to the king that in the city of Vidyanagara (Vijayanagara) and its outskirts the watch and policing systems were very effective thanks to the efficiency of the police. He further stated that the residents of the city, who belonged to eighteen different groups, lived in perfect harmony, understanding and happiness. They were frequently in a celebratory mood, as indicated by the festoons of green leaves seen everywhere.

Thereafter, the persons in charge of the temples of Virupaksha and Vitthala presented themselves before the king, informing him that the daily rituals in these temples were conducted regularly and without any problems. The person in charge of the Virupaksha temple said, further, that it was the day of the car festival and that the flag-hoisting ceremony had taken place to mark its commencement. It was therefore appropriate for the king to visit the temple and have *darshana* of the deity. The minister then informed the temple officer that the king would participate in the function and that he should come back to the king the moment the processional image of the deity was taken out [of the shrine] and placed on to the chariot.

The king sent for the nine accountants of the office who came and presented the accounts pertaining to eighteen subordinate rulers.

At that point, the king was informed that envoys bringing messages from various parts of the country were waiting at the entrance to the palace. On hearing this, the king sent for the chief minister and general. They had a consultation in the privacy of the council chamber. Having completed this, the king came out to hold a big [public] audience which lasted for four *galige.* The king's sons-in-law, his sons, subordinate rulers, nobles, ruling chieftains, officers of the palace, close relatives, officers, dependents, poets, cultured persons, scholars, priests, religious teachers, heads of religious institutions, sages, astrologers, physicians, cavalry men, elephant trainers, panegyrists, singers, bards, scientists, dramatists, physiognomists, artists and other representatives of the 72 branches of the arts all attended the audience. (*SKD*, I, prose; pp. 1-3)

10.4 A prince returns after a long absence

The theme of the next excerpt from the *Sanatkumara Charite* is the reception of a prince.

He travelled on the aerial chariot and alighted in the grove which was outside the palace. (*SC*, XII, 50; p. 137)

On hearing of the arrival of his son and his wives, the king gave orders for the city to be decorated and for a grand welcome reception to be organized for the prince [who was] returning after a long absence.

The orders of the king were made public and the city was adorned in various ways. All the buildings with their various storeys and towers were whitewashed. At the appropriate places were erected arched gateways [made] of fresh leaves, branches and flowers, and gateways in the shape of *makaras,* which were a special sign of distinction, and embellished with mirrors, flags, banners, festoons of cloth bands and golden pot-shaped pinnacles. The pavements of the streets were sprinkled with water mixed with musk and other fragrant substances. Their borders were decorated with saffron-coloured bands, while auspicious diagrams and other motifs were painted on to the pavements with pure white pearls.

Virginal young girls, youthful ladies and concubines were singing joyful songs at the reception. With them were other young and beautiful ladies carrying the usual auspicious mirrors, pots, fly-whisks and the like. (*SC*, XII, 58-60; p. 139)

In the welcoming party were dancing girls accompanied by musicians playing the *vine, tabor, maddale* and *tala.* There were singers, debators, poets, learned persons and others, together with the four divisions of the army, the infantry, elephants, cavalry and chariots and their respective generals, [as well as] subordinate kings, citizens from all classes, musicians, etcetera.

The whole procession reached the garden of the city where the prince and his retinue had alighted. They met the prince, paid homage to him and expressed joy at his return. (*SC*, XII, 58-62; pp. 139-40)

[Then the procession commenced its return journey with the prince and his retinue].

The musicians started playing on drums of different kinds: *pataha, bheri, mridanga, tambata, dindima* and others. Along with the trumpeters, they all produced a tremendous din. The wives of [respectable] elderly citizens performed auspicious rituals such as *arati.* They poured upon the [heads] of the prince and his wives honey, curds, coloured rice and parched grain, and swung around their heads auspicious objects like lemons, etcetera, and blessed them. As the procession neared the main street of the city, the ladies of the palace out of curiosity climbed onto the towers, terraces and balconies to have a look at the prince and his party. The king was waiting at the main gate of the palace to receive his son. He was flanked by young ladies holding fly-whisks and umbrellas. On reaching the palace, the moment the prince saw his father he jumped down from the chariot and prostrated himself at his feet. Thereupon the king embraced his son. The wives of the prince, too, paid their respects to the king by bowing to his feet. Then all, with tears of joy, entered the palace. There they met the queen-mother and bowed to her feet also; this brought tears of joy to her eyes. Similarly, the princesses also paid homage to the queen-mother, expressing their affectionate sentiments. The queen then blessed them with great warmth. (*SC*, XII, 64-72; pp. 140-2)

At the end, all those who had accompanied the prince and his party were given clothes and ornaments and were eventually seen off. On an auspicious day, the prince was crowned and the office of viceroy was conferred on his closest friend. The usual presentation followed. Thereafter, the king retired. (*SC*, XII, 64-74, pp. 140-3)

Royal ladies

10.5 Ladies' apartments

The information on the ladies' quarters and on the daily life of the princess in the next extract is drawn from the *Mohana Tarangini.*

The royal ladies lived in the upper apartments of the palace. They moved from one apartment to the other and went up and down according to their needs and whims, but always escorted by their ladies-in-waiting and attendants. Occasionally the royal ladies climbed the tall towers where they sat in a room and talked in private with their companions. (*MT,* XXVII, 29-32; pp. 383-4; XXVIII, 7, 28, 33; pp. 393, 397 & 398)

10.6 Everyday life of the princess

At sunset the lights were lit throughout the palace, including the private apartments of the princess. At that hour, she worshipped Shiva. After that she dined with her friends and slept on a beautifully decorated bed. At daybreak, she woke to the singing of auspicious songs by the learned ladies who recited select texts from the *Vedas* or sang songs in praise of Shiva. On awakening, she looked into both her palms and observed the auspicious lines on them. Then she had a bath, worshipped Shiva and had a sumptuous lunch with her companions and assistants. Chewing *pan,* the princess and her young and beautiful attendants and friends entered the private audience hall in order to spend the day in a pleasant manner.

The attendants flanked the princess. In their hands were vessels containing drinking water, betel-leaves and nuts, spittoon, fan, fly-whisks, mirror, napkin and such like. Then a host of female entertainers joined the princess in the audience hall. They were experts in the traditional 64 disciplines. Some recited from the classic literary works; others retold graphically the wars between the gods and demons as narrated in the epics. Some recounted in great detail the stories of the great kings, such as Harishchandra, while others told the legendary stories of the past sixteen emperors. Occasionally the princess listened to discourses on Hindu epics. Those who were proficient in playing various types of instruments entertained the princess with their skills. Similarly, the dancers, along with their [accompanying] musicians, pleased her with their performances in various styles. Those who were virtuoso players of special types of instruments, such as *rudra-vine, dhanur-vine, tumbura-vine, kurma-vine* and *svara-mandala,* displayed their art before her. Also for her entertainment, performances of plays were staged. There were even magicians organizing shows of magic. She watched all these shows, one after the other. At the end, all the artists and performers were rewarded by her with suitable gifts and they were all pleased.

She turned then to play indoor games such as the game of dice in its various forms: *letta, pagade* and *chaduranga.* Being an adept in these games and using her intelligence and skill, she invariably won all the games. However, to encourage her playmates and in order to boost their morale and please them, she wantonly lost the games at times and accepted defeat. Thus she spent the day joyfully playing in the company of those ladies. (*MT,* XXVI, 37-40; p. 376, XXVII, 1-16; pp. 378-81)

10.7 The awakening ceremony of a princess

Dress, makeup and jewellery of the royal ladies provided the authors with endless scope for enumerations. The next passage, which is drawn from the *Prabhulinga Lile,* is a perfected version of a similar passage in the *Sobagina Sone.* Here the princess wakes up and proceeds to her elaborate morning toilet.

While the musicians played on their instruments, the princess woke up. She first looked at her palms and then into the mirror. Then, slowly, she stepped down from her bed. The attendants in charge of various kinds of services, such as holding clothes, perfumes, golden mirror, fly-whisks, etcetera, gathered around her, ready to be at her beck and call. They applied *javadi* (oil mixed with musk) to her hair and gave her a bath with water to which fragrant sandalwood oil had been added. She was dressed in fresh clothes and golden sandals were put on her feet. She sat down on a low stool encrusted with diamonds. Her hair was then loosened to dry. Once dried, it was plaited and decorated with *kadamba* flowers arranged in such manner as to cover the full length of the plait. Various ladies-in-waiting adorned her with a variety of jewels. Each lady was in charge of one type of ornament. She wore toe-rings, anklets, foot-ornaments, waist-ornaments decorated with tassels, a long, thick pearl necklace, a choker consisting of many strings of large pearls, bracelets, finger-rings for both hands, armlets, nose-ornaments set with pearls, round ear-ornaments studded with the nine gems and a pearl ear-ornament. Another attendant applied the customary *tilaka* of musk on the forehead of the princess. Then a string of pearls was tied as a headband around her head. Another lady-in-waiting applied black collyrium to her eyelashes. To avert the evil eye, some drawings were traced on her cheeks and breasts with fragrant substances such as *kumkuma,* musk and sandal paste. The princess donned a garment painted in various colours and the ladies helped her to tie it in an attractive manner. When all the dressing and makeup were over, an attendant held a mirror before the princess so that she could check her appearance. She looked like [the goddess] Rati. (*PL,* IV, 19-23; pp. 34-9)

10.8 The queen's attendants and their specific tasks

The *Dharmanatha Purana* describes the retinue of the pregnant queen as follows.

The pregnant queen, who was to give birth to the [fifteenth] Jaina *tirthankara,* was seated on a throne placed in the middle [of a hall] in the company of ladies only. (*DP*, VI, prose, 52; p. 120)

Since she was pregnant with an important being, she was surrounded by a group of lady attendants and servants. The latter were drawn from the 72 kinds of service. (*DP*, VI, prose; p. 128)

The queen appointed each of the lady-assistants to fulfil a specific task, which they accomplished with great skill and attention. These tasks were to dress her with colourful lower garments; to paint her feet with reddish herbal colour; to put toe-rings on her toes; to dress her with silk clothes, the edges of which were seamed with small tinkling bells; to help her to put on a necklace of bright and beautiful pearls, armlets studded with the choicest of gems, wristlets studded with blue diamonds and finger-rings set with gems; to draw decorative figures on the cheeks with fragrant herbal colours; to assist her while putting on a nose-ornament of pearls and ear-ornaments set with gems of various colours; to apply collyrium to the eyes and a dot of musk on the forehead; to apply fragrant musk powder to her hair and then dress the hair in a bun; to carry umbrellas, fans and fly-whisks; to serve her betel-leaves and nuts; to carry the spittoon for her; to please her with music played on the *vine*; to entertain her with dance performances and a variety of vocal music; to play beautifully the *dakke muraja, kahaḷe, shankha* and other instruments for her happiness. (*DP*, VI, 66-94 & prose; pp. 123-8)

After that, all of them sat on a platform and spent some time in casual and witty conversation, [enjoying] riddles and jokes. (*DP*, VI, prose, p. 129)

10.9 Ornaments worn by royal ladies

The *Ramanatha Charite* has a remarkably detailed account of the jewellery worn by royal ladies. As the story goes here, a young queen is preparing to meet her lover.

The queen was told in private by a trusted confidante that arrangements had been made for her to meet her lover that day and that she should get ready. Then the young queen went to the bathing house and sat on a seat decorated with the nine kinds of gems and shaped like a lotus flower. Her attendants applied scented oil to her long thick hair and then gave her a bath with warm water laced with fragrant *kumkuma* and musk.

She was then dressed in a lower garment. Her hair was tied in a big bun and on her forehead was applied a pearl-coloured dot. She wore the following ornaments: a pearl nose-ornament, a golden bangle, wristlets set with blue sapphires, a thick long necklace, diamond earrings, a garment set with beads, anklets, a net of pearls for the hair bun, waist-ornaments, a jewel to be pinned in the centre of the bun, shoulder-ornaments, a large pendant (on a chain), a twisted bracelet to wear on the wrists, loose ornaments for the wrists, a golden chain, a finger-ring set with a ruby, diamond-ear ornaments, a hair net with pearls, a golden flower shaped like the screw pine [to pin in the bun], anklets, a signet-ring, armlets, twisted chain ornaments for the wrists, golden bangles, another kind of armlet, a *pendeya* (anklet of honour), a waist-girdle with hanging chains and others. (*RC*, XXIX, 81-99; pp.185-7, II)

10.10 The queens' artistic activities

Among the inmates of the king's harem were numerous gifted performers, as described in this passage from the *Ramanatha Charite.*

Some queens of the king's harem were as beautiful as Rati; they were not only charming but also intelligent and clever. There was one who was an excellent actress; a number of others were good dancers and musicians; some had a deep knowledge of literature and other classical works. All of them were endowed with feminine charm and grace in their talk, behaviour, smile, gait and other qualities. (*RC*, V, 21-6; pp. 80-1)

Chapter 11

ROYAL FAMILY AND COURTIERS

This chapter deals with three topics: the education of the princes, the qualities of the ideal ministers and the splendour of the royal retinues. The education of young princes is a theme explored in various texts, such as the *Nagakumara Charite* and *Ramanatha Charite*, both of which give an idea of the various subjects a prince was expected to learn, at least in theory. Similar information can also be found in other texts, like the *Kaushika Ramayana*.

The personality of a minister has already been discussed at length in Chapter 7. Here, the *Ramanatha Charite* celebrates the qualities of an exemplary minister, not in abstract, but referring to an individual, Baichappa. Another theme discussed in theory in Chapter 7 is the choice of a minister: the passage from the *Padmaraja Purana* reproduced here exemplifies what probably happened in practice. The *Amalabasava Charite* lists the various ministerial posts.

Finally, excerpts from the *Channabasava Purana*, *Ramanatha Charite* and *Mohana Tarangini* give accounts of the retinues of the king, queen and princess.

11.1 Education of a prince

This account is drawn from the *Nagakumara Charite.*

[In the course of a function], the king named the prince Nagakumara. After the completion of his fifth year of age, he started his education. He was taught various subjects: the *Bharata-shastra*; different scripts; composing works with nine kinds of characteristics; interpreting omens; knowledge of gems; different languages; handling arms and weapons; warfare; gambling; art of painting; knowledge of vehicles; *mantras* and *Tantras* of various kinds; knowledge of textiles [?]; [various] religions; the traditional 64 arts; the traditional four types of diplomatic expedients; how to handle horses and elephants; how to make love; and archery. (*NC*, I, 103-9; p. 317)

11.2 A prince is trained in the use of weapons

The *Ramanatha Charite* stresses the importance of the prince's training in the martial arts.

[In the course of time], the son of the king grew up. Considering that the proper time for the education of the prince had come, the king appointed a well-learned teacher. The education of the boy commenced on an auspicious day. He was made to learn various branches of knowledge. He was further taught to become an expert in the use of different kinds of weapon: long and short swords, daggers, steel clubs, shields, long spears, bows and arrows, heavy wooden clubs [and others]. He was also trained in riding horses and elephants. He was made to learn the tricks of mock fighting, to the appreciation of all the proficient teachers and others. Meanwhile, he became a youth. The king was happy and very pleased to see his achievements in learning the arts of warfare and other subjects. (*RC*, VIII, 79-90; pp. 141-2)

11.3 Description of the ideal minister

The qualities of an ideal minister, such as Baichappa, are enumerated in the *Ramanatha Charite.*

Baichappa, the king's minister, was faithful like the wife of Indra; he was firm in his attachment, strong in his decisions, of agreeable temperament, pure in action and thinking, adept in the traditional seven paths of statecraft and far away from the traditional six enemies (bad qualities). He was the confidant of the king and thus was responsible for counselling him wisely; he was very close to him. (*RC*, V, 30-1; p. 82)

11.4 Choice of a prime minister

The difficult task of finding a suitable minister is the theme of the following passage from the *Padmaraja Purana.*

The senior minister died. On hearing that, the king sent for all [important] relatives, near and dear persons, sons, brothers, sons-in-law, etcetera, in order to select an efficient person to succeed to the post of chief minister.

They suggested nominating the son-in-law of the deceased minister since he was well read, of good character and behaviour, and also good looking. On hearing this, the pleased king sent for his trusted attendants and ordered them to go to the residence of the minister-designate, carrying a golden palanquin, and to inform him of the wish of the king. They met this person, paid their respects and conveyed the wish of the king. The offer was accepted with great humility.

He considered the offer, which would entail him being at the head of the administration, the state treasury, the royal retinue, the close relatives [of the royal house] and the divisions of cavalry, elephants and chariots, and being responsible for guarding [all of the state interests] and subjects. He then paid his respects to [various] religious persons, took leave of them and proceeded to meet the king in his palace. He travelled in a golden palanquin. On hearing of his arrival, the king came forth and received him with all honours and dignity, led him to the assembly hall and made him sit on a special seat which had been placed to the right of his throne. There he was nominated head of the royal treasury, the [stocks of] food-grains, clothes, jewellery, royal horses, elephants, chariots, army and all other state property. Furthermore, the king told the minister to strive for the welfare and prosperity of the kingdom and his subjects. Finally, the king celebrated the investiture ceremony.

The property of the deceased minister was handed over to him and he was given leave to go to his own place. Once there, he bade farewell to his followers and entered his palace. (*PP*, IV, 2-13; pp. 59-62)

11.5 Ministerial posts

The *Amalabasava Charite* briefly lists the various ministerial posts.

The king had the following officers: royal household minister, royal priests, army general, prince, chief writer, minister of the granary, treasury officer, chief gate-keeper, stores officer, chief or permanent officer, minister of peace and war, army commanders and other ministers, to a total of eighteen. (*AC*, XXXIX, 22; p. 391)

11.6 The king's retinue

The *Channabasava Purana* describes the personal attendants of the king (or minister) entrusted with various kinds of service. They followed their master wherever he went and attended to his needs until they were asked to retire for the day. These servants were generally young and beautiful ladies who were part of his retinue.

There were the one entrusted with the pouch containing betel-nuts and leaves; the one who carried the [metal] spittoon and made it readily available for use; the one who carried a metal vessel containing water used by the master [particularly for washing the mouth after chewing of betel-nuts]; the one who carried a fan and fanned the master; the one who carried a fly-whisk used for warding off the flies; and the one who carried the sandals of the master ready for use, whenever required. (*CP*, V, 45; p. 51)

11.7 The queen's retinue

The *Ramanatha Charite* enumerates the personal retinue of the queen.

There was a lady carrying a pouch, others carrying a spittoon, a fan, a fly-whisk (or fly-flạp), a mirror, sandals, yet another spittoon and others. An attendant put anklets on the feet of the queen; another enhanced her eyes with collyrium; a third applied a beautiful *tilaka* of fragrant musk on her forehead; and a fourth helped her to put on pearl earrings. (*RC*, VIII, 26-31; p. 133)

11.8 The princess's retinue

The *Mohana Tarangini* has the following information on the retinue of a princess.

For pleasure and for the sake of a change, the princess sometimes left the palace and visited the city. She was usually escorted by a retinue of companions and ladies-in-waiting. Before setting out, she was carefully dressed and made up by her maids. When she was ready they descended from the upper apartments and entered the open courtyard, and from there they went outside.

The princess and her close companions travelled

separately in beautifully decorated palanquins carried by bearers, while the attendants followed them. The opening of each palanquin was screened with a thin cloth.

When the cortege passed through the main streets of the city, the citizens stood on the balconies of the storeyed houses in order to catch a glimpse of the princess.

The attendants of her retinue were all young and beautiful. They were elegantly dressed in tights, long garments, breast-bands and bodices. They wore different types of jewellery on their bodies and some of the ornaments had small rattlers which tinkled melodiously as they moved. Each of them fulfilled a special duty. They carried various items for the requirements of the princess, such as a cane basket containing betel-leaves, a purse for betel-nuts and other accessories and ingredients. In addition, they carried a napkin, a thick and soft carpet, a pair of golden sandals, fly-whisks of different types, a fan made of fragrant smelling roots, another of palm-leaves and a third of redolent jasmine flowers, a water container, a number of small vessels, a mirror, a spittoon, a camphor box and a big bowl containing sandal paste mixed with water, all for the use of the princess in the course of the outing. (*MT*, X, 7-10; p. 132; XXIII, 7 & 55-6; pp. 333 & 342-3; XXIV, 2-10; pp. 344-5 and 20; p. 347)

Chapter 12

PATRONAGE OF CULTS AND BESTOWING OF HONOURS

The first part of this chapter deals with the duty of a king to extend his patronage to religious institutions. The first excerpt, which comes from the *Bharatesha Vaibhava Sangraha,* depicts a Jaina king participating in the ceremonial unveiling of the statues of the Jaina prophets. In the second, from the *Channabasava Purana,* a minister funds the building of Virashaiva *mathas* (religious establishments). The last passage of this section, giving an account of royal and courtly benefactions extended to cults, is from the *Samyukta Kaumudi.* It describes the invitation, accommodation and entertainment of a large group of brahmins entrusted with the performance of a complex ritual, the *shata-yagam* (100 sacrificial rites).

The second part of the chapter focuses on the various honours bestowed by the king on a number of distinguished personalities, ranging from generals and ministers to scholars and poets. The chapter ends with the account of an able minister deciding to renounce worldly honours for a life of meditation.

Patronage of cults

12.1 The king unveils images of the Jinas

The *Bharatesha Vaibhava Sangraha* describes the royal patronage extended to the cult.

On the orders of the king, an officer named Bhadramukha constructed 72 monasteries in which stone statues of the Jinas were enshrined. On hearing that the work was completed, the king unveiled the images on an auspicious day. In his retinue were his ministers, friends, sisters and their husbands, queen-consort and other queens. Together they paid homage to the Jinas. Then, along with his numerous wives, daughters, daughters-in-law, sisters, he paid homage to the Jaina mendicants and gave them presents. They returned to their place and entered the palaces in a happy frame of mind. (*BV,* LI, 10-36; pp. 431-5)

12.2 Patronage of the Virashaiva cult

This passage from the *Channabasava Purana* deals again with religious patronage and the building of monasteries.

[As an act of patronage in favour of the Virashaiva faith and its propagation], the minister gave orders to build monasteries in the vast open area in front of his own palace. These structures were to be located on either side [of the main street]. Then some thousands of Virashaiva religious leaders were accommodated in these newly built monasteries, where they were to perform their religious activities. (*CP,* VI, 18; p. 61)

12.3 The king entertains the brahmins

The *Samyukta Kaumudi* mentions a king's *shata-yagam* (100 sacrificial rites). The following passage deals with the reception and honours bestowed upon the brahmins invited to perform the ceremony. (A similar description is found in Section 18.5.)

One day the king sent for learned scholars and told them that he had heard about the great merit one would earn by performing the 100 religious sacrificial rites, and expressed the wish to perform them. Thereupon, the ceremony was publicly proclaimed by the beating of a drum, so that the brahmins could come and participate. They turned up in large numbers and went to the king's palace. Among them were those well versed in the *Vedas* and Vedangas, philosophy, teaching, debating, interpreting the classical treatises, delivering discourses and much more, to the great joy of the king. For the convenience of the learned men assembled there, the king had arranged at numerous places charity-houses to supply water and other beverages, sumptuous and rich food, daintiest dishes and choicest preparations, besides providing gifts. There were also [numerous] halls for performing the sacrificial rituals.

The king welcomed the brahmins as they approached the palace, prostrating himself and paying his respects. They blessed him and, in turn, he presented them with suitable gifts. Then he called his officers and gave instructions for making arrangements for their stay, which had to be as comfortable as possible. Accordingly, the guests were invited to take a bath and then to participate in a feast in the dining hall. (*SK*, VII, 16-22; pp. 125-6)

Honours

12.4 The king honours a general

In the following passage, the *Dharmanatha Purana* describes the reception of a general on his return from a victorious campaign. On this occasion, the king bestows upon him lavish gifts.

The general returned after a victorious campaign. The whole city was decorated for his arrival. Auspicious ladies carrying pots, mirrors and all kinds of auspicious things were ready to receive him. With them were also, as usual, singers and dancing girls. The general entered his palace accompanied by all of them. Afterwards he bade goodbye to the subordinate rulers, princes, and others. Then he washed, ate and spent a pleasant evening in the company of the ladies of the palace, entertaining them with his battlefield experiences and other stories. The next day he sent for all those rulers and princes he had conquered and who had surrendered to him and told them that he wished them to live happily. He then sent for the horses and camels that had been captured in the course of the campaign and was pleased in reviewing them. After having spent some time there, on an auspicious day he set out to meet his master, the king. He travelled for some time and set up a camp at some distance from the metropolitan city. (*DP*, XIII, prose; pp. 371-2)

Meanwhile, a messenger announced to the king that the victorious general had arrived. The king was pleased and eager to receive him. The general entered the city and reached the main gate of the king's palace. He then requested his followers to stay there and, in the company of a trusted few, went towards the audience hall with his hands full of choicest gems.

On entering, he respectfully touched the feet of the king and gave him the rich presents that he had brought with him. (*DP*, XIII, 128-31, prose; pp. 372-3)

The king, then, as a mark of honour, offered him *tambula* (camphor mixed with betel-leaves and nuts) of superb quality. (*DP*, XIII, 131-2; p. 373)

After that, the general presented the king with all the valuable and exquisite things that he had amassed in the course of his military campaigns in other countries. Moreover, he narrated to the king in great detail his experiences on the battlefields. (*DP*, XIII, prose; p. 373)

On hearing all these accounts, the king was very pleased and praised his trusted general. He rewarded him with most valuable gifts which included choicest gems, ornaments, cloths, vehicles and, once again, the *tambula*. (DP, XIII, 133 & prose; p. 373)

The general took leave of the king, came out of the palace and, accompanied by the followers he had left at the entrance-gate, returned to his own palace and retired [for the day]. (*DP*, XIII, 134; p. 373)

12.5 Honours conferred on a scholar

The *Shivatattva Chintamani* narrates how a document written in an unknown script was brought to the king. None of the assembled persons could decipher it. Eventually, it was decoded by a scholar who was related to one of the ministers. (A similar story is set forth in the *Amalabasava Charite*, see Section 8.9.)

The king was very pleased and wanted to show his appreciation to the scholar. He decided to celebrate the occasion in a sumptuous manner. The entrance doors of the palace, the shops in the city, the houses of the concubines, the mansions of the high-ranked officers and the homes of the pontiffs were all decorated in the grandest possible manner with flags, festoons, tassels, artistic works, pot-shaped pinnacles and mirrors. In addition, the front courts were sprinkled with fragrant water and sweet-smelling flowers. Thereafter, *rangavalli* were traced on the prepared ground; the patterns were embellished with white pearls and borders of saffron and musk. Expert musicians played on different musical instruments, and the singers sang various melodies. All the while, young dancers displayed their performing talents. All this was going on in the upper apartments of the buildings, which were suitably decorated with golden pinnacles. At the appointed and auspicious time fixed by the court astrologers, the king sent for this famous intellectual. On his arrival, the king honoured him by presenting him with the royal signet-ring, other auspicious objects, and a richly caparisoned state elephant. Before the presentation, the court astrologers performed different rituals in order to endow the signet-ring with sanctity, auspiciousness and fame. Thereafter, this honoured person, who had been raised to the rank of a minister, set out with his retinue. There were servants with fly-whisks, fly-flaps, umbrellas [of honour], soldiers and other attendants, a troop of horsemen and elephants and palanquins, all in large numbers, loudly shouting in praise, joy and enthusiasm. They moved noisily on either side of the dignitary.

The king followed the procession. The citizens and the auspicious ladies, well attired in rich garments and bedecked with jewellery, lined the whole route, blessing that honoured person and joyfully showering auspicious rice on him. Further along, handsome ladies of different walks of life, all wearing beautiful ornaments, waved before the dignitary the auspicious lights they held in golden plates. All along, they sang auspicious songs that were suitable for that occasion. They wore wristlets, bracelets, earrings and necklaces; some wore pendants on a string, fillets, anklets and other jewels. They wore colourful flowers and areca-nut flowers in their hair and had perfumed themselves with sandal paste and the like. The vanguard of the procession consisted of musicians who played loudly the auspicious tunes on percussion and wind instruments.

As the procession proceeded through the main street, there was a large number of followers of the minister revelling and rejoicing; they played and sprinkled on each other sandal powder, camphor, *sadu*, fragrant water and saffron powder. At the same time, citizens belonging to all walks of life presented themselves before the minister and offered him tributes. Once the procession reached the palace, the minister took leave of the king and entered his [own?] palace.

Later, the pleased king gave the daughter of his younger brother in marriage to the minister. The ceremony was performed with grandeur. (*S*, XXXI, 49-67; pp. 260-5)

12.6 Honours conferred on a poet

Scholarship was highly valued, and references to honours conferred on scholars and poets are relatively frequent. One such example is the following passage from the *Proudharayana Kavya*.

A poet, in accordance with the challenge he had accepted, composed 101 poems every day for eleven days and at the end of that time the work was completed. It was then brought and presented to the king, who not only expressed surprise but also paid his deepest respects to that work. (*PK*, XXI, 31; p. 299)

At the request of the king, a minister [the poet's patron] read out that [literary] work, explaining its meaning and commenting upon it, to the great appreciation of the ruler. The king, in return, bestowed lavish gifts on that minister. On the minister's suggestion, the poet was similarly rewarded for having composed the work. Among the gifts [he received] were ornaments studded with jewels, a three-stringed necklace [of pearls], a bracelet of distinction, silk garments, a chariot and five villages with rent-free rights. Furthermore, the poet's patron organized a procession, in the course of which the [literary] work was placed on the royal elephant and paraded [through the streets of the capital]. (*PK*, XXI, 32-4; p. 299)

12.7 Insignias of a minister

As a mark of distinction, the following attendants and insignias were conferred on a minister. The passage is drawn from the *Vijayakumari Charite*.

The minister was entitled to a number of honours which were conferred upon him by the king: he was to be accompanied by attendants carrying with them a pouch (or box) containing betel-leaves and nuts, a fly-whisk of yak tail, a water jug, a spittoon and sandals; servants [were also in this retinue]. (*VC*, I, 10, 28; p. 110)

12.8 The minister renounces worldly honours

The *Padmaraja Purana* recounts how a minister leaves his position and surrenders to the king all the insignia of his office.

The chief minister wished to leave his office in order to take to religious life. He politely announced this resolve to the king, saying that from now on his services were reserved for God and his devotees and no longer for humans. He then surrendered all the trappings of royal honour that had been conferred on him as a minister: all possessions and property, wealth, gold, jewelled ornaments, official dresses and ceremonial clothes, headdress of distinction, staff of office, official seals, keys and locks, and service personnel. (*PP*, VI, 102; p. 118)

Chapter 13

OVERSEAS TRADE AND FOREIGN VISITORS AND COURTS

Overseas journeys, trade and foreigners are mentioned in the *Nemijinesha Sangati*; however, no specific details of the journeys are given. As in the first excerpt here, the exotic environments are used as a backdrop to the story, rather than being the main subject of the narrative. Tales of hurricanes and miraculous survivals from shipwreck are also narrated in the same text (*NS*, X, 176-87; pp. 217-18), along with accounts of profitable overseas expeditions (*NS*, IV, 10-15, pp. 66-7).

Reception of foreigners by the king, a frequent occurrence at the Vijayanagara court, is described in some detail in both the *Dharmanatha Purana* and *Mohana Tarangini*. Particularly interesting here is the account of the dress and appearance of the foreign guests. The chapter closes with one of the most important excerpts of this selection, from the *Ramanatha Charite*, giving a vivid account of the exotic court of the Delhi sultan.

Overseas travel

13.1 Travels of a prince

The following brief account is drawn from the *Nemijinesha Sangati*.

In the course of his adventures, the prince entered a city called Parshvaka. There he met a person of Persian origin who knew many languages. He met him to enquire about the island of Ratnadvipa and the ways of reaching it. (*NS*, X, 253-5; pp. 228-9)

Foreigners

13.2 Reception of a foreign envoy

The *Dharmanatha Purana* has this vivid description of a foreign messenger.

One day, the king was seated in audience in the upper storey of the palace, which was decorated with various kinds of lustrous gems and finials set with diamonds. Along with the king, were the crown prince, governors, ministers, subordinate rulers, army generals, important officers, members of the king's retinue, distinguished relatives and others. (*DP*, X, prose; p. 230)

An envoy from another kingdom arrived with a written message. He was dressed in a long overcoat and wore a conical cap on his head, all of pure white cloth, and carried a staff in his hands. He brought valuable presents for the king. On seeing him, the gate-keeper went in to inform the king. When audience was granted, the gate-keeper ushered the foreign guest to the king's presence.

On entering the audience hall, the messenger paid his respects and took the seat meant for him, placed to the right of the king, but at some distance. Thereafter, the king made enquiries about the purpose of his visit. At this point the envoy presented the gifts that had been sent by his master and handed over the message. The scribe of the king read out the contents of that letter, which was about the proposed marriage of his daughter, the princess. (*DP*, X, 3-6; pp. 230-1)

The messenger then produced a portrait painting of the princess, which had been executed in five colours and drawn with great skill and sensitivity. (*DP*, X, 8, prose 9-10; p. 232)

13.3 Reception of a foreign merchant

The following account is drawn from the *Mohana Tarangini*.

One day a merchant arrived on a ship. He anchored his vessel and entered that town [situated on the west coast of India]. Walking through the city, the merchant admired its richness and its beauty, thinking that there was no other city on earth to rival it. While looking around and being much impressed with the elegance and wealth of the place, he reached the gates of the palace where he saw a crowd of persons waiting [there] for an interview with the king. On seeing him, the gate-keeper led him to the presence of the king. The king was dressed in bright gold-coloured silk clothes and wore sparkling diamonds. This very sight awed the merchant, who paid his respects to that glorious ruler in all humility and presented him with various gifts, among which were some extraordinary objects. Thereupon, the pleased king offered him a suitable seat and made enquiries with the due courtesy and honours. (*MT*, XXVI, 2-8; pp. 643-4)

Then the king sent for a bag of choicest gems and presented them to the merchant as a farewell gift. The merchant stayed in the city for some more days and then left for other places in the interior [of the kingdom]. (*MT*, XXVI, 2-10; pp. 643-4)

A foreign court

13.4 The court of the Delhi sultan

The *Ramanatha Charite* describes thus the splendid entourage of the Delhi sultan.

On the next day the ruler [of Dilli] set out for the audience hall accompanied by a host of female attendants. Some of them were blowing the curved horns of animals and conches. Some others, carrying staffs in their hands, shouted commands whilst moving. The ladies who were at the front had long plaited hair, wore socks and tight breast-bands and were armed with bows and arrows [in quivers], short daggers, swords and shields. Others carried swords of different sizes and shapes, spears, spikes, *kakkade* (weapons with serrated edges), battle axes, lances and the like. They looked beautiful, dressed as they were in the native style. Some of those ladies were Muslim; they wore bodices embroidered with pearls; their plaited hair was decorated with tassels and daggers were tucked into their waist-bands. They moved closely grouped around the sultan. Other *bibbiyaru* (Muslim female attendants) numbering 7,000 followed the ruler on horseback. He was also accompanied by ladies who carried small vessels, water pots, mirrors, containers with fragrant camphor or sandal paste, pouches and other objects; in short, anything that their master could require. The ruler entered the audience hall accompanied by this vast number of attendants. At the same time many female panegyrists chanted loudly [in praise of their master]. He then occupied the royal seat, which had been lavishly embellished with precious stones.

Thereupon the *vajiras* (viziers), *khans* (officers), *malluks* (subordinate rulers) and others entered [the hall]. There were also *khan-malluks* (feudal rulers) dressed in silk garments with short daggers in their waist-belts, slippers on their feet and long plaited hair decorated with tassels. There were slaves dressed in trousers and long overcoats, as well as rulers from neighbouring kingdoms, whose gem-studded turbans indicated their status.

When some of the lesser rulers were stopped at the entrance by the door-keepers, the cunning ones bribed them with heaps of gold coins, thus managing to enter the assembly hall. A host of rulers and officers, coming from different places and variously dressed, had assembled there.

At the orders of the sultan, a great number of elephants and horses of different breeds brought from various countries were assembled [outside the audience hall]. Moreover, there was a large gathering of valorous soldiers and warriors dressed for the occasion and armed with weapons of various kinds. They had come from different countries and regions.

Then the moment came for the ministers and ambassadors to make the presentations to the sultan. Among the presentation items were silk cloths, horses, elephants, young dancing girls and actresses and a special kind of bow of extraordinary strength that was capable of discharging an arrow with enough force to pierce through seven metal sheets. (*RC*, XVIII, 14-63; pp. 333-41)

That special bow and its strength were successfully tested by one of the generals, named Badur, under the appreciative eyes of the sultan and all the others. (*RC*, XVIII, 87-92; p. 345)

In return, that hero was honoured with the title *malluk* (nobleman), clothes, the command over a region and betel-leaves and nuts. (*RC*, XVIII, 96-8; p. 346)

Thereafter, the sultan presented the ambassadors with golden ingots and several boxes filled with jewellery. He then bade them farewell. (*RC*, XVIII, 101; p. 347)

PART THREE

POLITY

The two chapters of this part deal with several subjects related to the state, such as administration, internal policies, army, armaments and warfare: Chapter 14 gives an insight into administration, diplomacy, internal politics and intrigues at court, while Chapter 15 contains a wealth of information, both theoretical and practical, on military campaigns, enrollment tactics and intelligence services. Particularly interesting in the latter chapter is the account of the strategic formations of the army in various forms, such as the lotus, *garuda* (divine eagle) and *chakra* (wheel). The organization of the facilities and provisions of the camp and the band of traders, tradesmen, harlots, entertainers and others that follows the army on the march make for absorbing and entertaining reading. Great care is devoted to the description of arms and armour, as well as an extraordinary array of magical weapons, before passing to the grim descriptions of the actual siege of towns or fortresses and the devastation of the surrounding countryside.

Chapter 14

ADMINISTRATION AND POLITICS

The first part of the chapter focuses on the workings of the state administration and the names and details of the various types of towns and settlements. Several topics relevant to state politics are addressed in the second part. Diplomacy is touched upon in a passage from the *Bharatesha Vaibhava Sangraha*, which describes a failed mission (ending eventually in a duel between the two kings; see Section 5.12). Court rivalries provide an interesting story about a king and his very capable city commander, as found in the *Samyukta Kaumudi*. The last excerpt, from the *Vijayakumari Charite*, gives an account of an attempt on the life of the king and the subsequent apprehension of the killer.

14.1 Reforms in the kingdom's administration

This excerpt is drawn from the *Padmaraja Purana*. Padmaraja, also known as Kereya Padmarasa, was chief minister at the court of the Hoysala king Narasimha Ballala where he introduced a number of reforms

[The newly appointed chief minister went to his mansion, performed the prescribed religious rites and then proceeded to the secretariat.]

He entered the secretariat, sent for sixteen administration clerks and [with a view to introducing a number of reforms] asked for an update of the [state's] revenue, expenses, receipts (?), balances, adjustments and all the transactions that had taken place in the past. Then he ordered them to write down the income and expenses correctly. These reforms brought order in [the accounts of] the king's treasury, exchequer, storehouses, granaries and artisans' workshops. He also examined the provisions made for the maintenance of the [royal] elephants, horses and service personnel. He then looked into the various sources of income [of the kingdom], including customs, taxes, movable income, etcetera. He took decisions and issued orders after having examined each individual case. He kept the personnel of the armies happy and took care that his commands were respected throughout the kingdom. The king soon acquired a good amount of wealth, fame and prosperity [while the minister proved to be his right hand].

His administrative reforms, faultless character and pious and exemplary private life earned him the praises and appreciation of the learned men. Furthermore, the minister was sincerely involved in devotional pursuits. (*PP*, IV, 23-7; pp. 65-6)

14.2 Types of settlements and towns

The *Sanatkumara Charite* enumerates various types of settlements:

grama (small town), *nagara* (city), *madamba* (province), *kharvada* (district headquarters from 200 to 400 small villages), *kheda* (small fortified town), *pattana* (city) and *drona* (town on an island). (*SC*, III, 20; p. 27)

The *Ramanatha Charite* elaborates the topic further, adding to the above-mentioned list *durga* (fort) and *dronamukha* (headquarters for 400 villages?). According to this text, *kharvada* is a town surrounded by hills. (*RC*, XVII, 108; p. 327)

However, the most extensive discussion on administrative divisions of the kingdom and classification of settlements according to position and inhabitants is found in the *Mohana Tarangini*.

The metropolitan city was called *nagara*, while other big towns without much political importance were called *pattana*. *Kharvada* were those towns surrounded by or close to hills, while the others were called *pura*. Smaller towns were known as *grama* and villages as *halli*. Habitations which had been gifted to learned persons or philosophers were known as *agrahara*; those given to heroes were also called *pura*. Settlements which had become particularly prosperous and had expanded were called *upagrama*. (*MT*, II, 16-18; p. 35)

14.3 A failed diplomatic mission

The *Bharatesha Vaibhava Sangraha* has an interesting account of unsuccessful negotiations between the king and one of his brothers. The king, a Jaina, returned to his capital after having conquered many kingdoms and married many princesses. In his campaign, which lasted long years, he simply followed the way indicated by the *chakra-ratna* weapon. The kings in whose territories the *chakra-ratna* appeared were supposed to surrender to him.

The army followed the *chakra-ratna*. The troops carried silken flags and banners bearing the symbols of the sun and the moon. They were near the city of Poudanapura, which was ruled by the younger brothers of the king.

The king questioned the minister about it and was informed that unless all his brothers surrendered, the *chakra-ratna* would not move and the army could not proceed. Since they were his own brothers, he wanted to win them over by means of diplomacy. Hence, he sent to all of them a written message, asking them to surrender. They, accordingly, renounced the kingdom, which they had inherited from their father and chose to become ascetics. Thus, 93 brothers took to asceticism, but the king was not too pleased. (*BVS*, XLI, 1-8; pp. 366-7)

Only one brother remained, but he was as powerful and stubborn as the king himself. His name was Kamadeva. The king entrusted his clever minister, Dakshinanki, with the task of fetching him.

The minister, carrying all the insignia of royalty, went to the palace of Kamadeva, along with his retinue. When he arrived at the palace he sent word through one of the attendants and was eventually ushered into the presence of Kamadeva, who was sitting in audience. (*BVS*, XLI, 10-14; pp. 367-8)

The king was seated on the throne, on a cushion made of soft swans' feathers, and was surrounded by ministers, lady-attendants and others. The emissary was led to the presence of the king. Thereupon, Kamadeva received him with all courtesy and made him sit close to him. He bade all the lady-attendants to go away. He asked the emissary about his king-brother and his campaigns. After having heard all the news in great detail, he gave him some gifts and asked him to rest for that day. (*BVS*, XLI, 25-39; pp. 368-71)

Next day, after briefing Kamadeva's well-wishers and ministers, [the emissary] requested Kamadeva to meet his king who was his eldest step-brother and his step-mother who was also camping near the city. He said that such a meeting would be much appreciated by their followers and armies. He did all this in a very diplomatic way in order to avoid a fight between the brothers, blood-shed and so on. All these clever and diplomatic moves were understood by Kamadeva. He politely expressed his resentment. (*BVS*, XLII, 1-13; pp. 372-3)

He told the emissary that although his brother had vanquished a number of kings and expected him to surrender, he was not prepared to take such a course of action. The mission did not succeed. (*BVS*, XLII, 13-14, 20-1, 46-50; pp. 373-9)

14.4 Shrewdness of a city-commander

A story revealing the attempts of the king to thwart the popularity of the city commander is narrated in the *Samyukta Kaumudi*.

The king, accompanied by a vast army, left the capital on an expedition aiming to check the intrusions at the borders. Before leaving, he entrusted the city commander with the responsibility of protecting and administering the capital in his absence.

On his return, the victorious king enquired from his subjects about the conditions of the administration during his absence. They replied that it had been very good and that they had been very happy. Noticing the popularity of the city commander, the king entertained some suspicion that he might, someday, usurp the throne and take power into his hands.

So the king sent for his minister and for the royal priest and conferred with them, expressing his unfounded fears. The three of them devised a plan to curb the popularity of the city commander.

The next day they sent for the commander and told him that some thieves had made a hole through the wall of the palace and had stolen valuables from the king's own treasury. It was his responsibility to capture the burglars and recover the valuables. He was given eight days to solve the case. The truth of the matter was that the king, his minister and the priest had jointly committed this [supposed] theft in order to put the blame on that officer, aiming at making him unpopular and proving him inefficient. The officer was also threatened with punishment if he did not catch the thieves in the time allotted.

The commander then went to the treasury and found that the king had inadvertently left there his sandals, the minister his ring and the brahmin his sacred thread. He then had proof of the conspiracy, but waited for the appropriate moment to make the fact public. (*SK*, II, 6-24; pp. 20-5)

14.5 An attempt on the life of the king

In the *Vijayakumari Charite*, a minister who belonged to a different faith, devises a scheme to kill the king.

After subduing an insubordinate ruler, the king returned to his capital with his victorious army. On the way he halted and set up camp on the bank of a river. A saintly person appeared there and presented the king with a mango fruit of a special variety. It was, however, a poisoned fruit Having eaten the fruit, the king realized that he was going to die. He tried antidotes for the poison and then took to religious life. Eventually, when there was no hope of survival, he sent for another trusted minister of his own faith and instructed him to crown the prince his son. (*VC*, I, 892-901; pp. 96-7)

After his coronation the prince discovered the plot and changed his personal guards, replacing them with trusted ones. He took into confidence his new minister and consulted with him in private. The new minister placed before the newly-crowned king a detailed plan of how to get rid of the treacherous minister and his followers. They would construct a temple, install the deity worshipped by the minister and organize a celebration inviting him and his followers. For that purpose they planned to build a large temporary pavilion with only four heavily-guarded entrances. While the guests would be engrossed in feasting with their leader, the treacherous minister, fire would be set to the building so that all of them would be killed at once. There should be very loud music in order to prevent their cries being heard outside. But the king, who was a non-violent and pious Jaina, did not endorse this plan in the least, arguing that it did not befit a *kshatriya* ruler. (*VC*, I, 1003-16; pp. 107-9)

After some days, however, when the king was sitting in audience, his soldiers produced the person who had poisoned and killed his father. As a threat, torture instruments, such as a leather whip, saw and pincers, were placed before him and he was forced to disclose the names of the persons involved in the plot. Moreover, he was also made to confess the persons behind the scheme. According to his statement, he had been intensively trained in the use of the 32 kinds of weapon, how to pretend to be a pious and religious person and how to observe the tenets of Jainism so as to impress the victim and to win his confidence. Later, he was given the poisoned mango fruit and sent out on that mission. The angry king declared all the conspirators outlaws and sent them away. (*VC*, I, 1020-6; p. 110)

Chapter 15

ARMY AND WARFARE

The texts contain many descriptions of military campaigns and equipment, encampments, battles and sieges. The first part of the chapter presents excerpts dealing with military campaigns in general, before passing onto the recruitment of the best army personnel available, among whom were a number of foreigners such as Turks and Khorasanis. The passage drawn from the *Shri Krishnadevarayana Dinachari* mentions spies able to move at the speed of wind or to operate with the swiftness of thought.

The second part of the chapter concentrates on the encampment: great care is lavished on the description of its layout, the various tents with their colourful emblems, the kingly apartment and the other camp facilities, including shops selling an amazing variety of eatables and drinks like arrack and toddy. The *Ramanatha Charite* mentions drugs, such as hemp and opium, among the items available at the camp, as well as the presence of "thousands of concubines" and other ladies who accompanied the army, along with the traders and merchants. An impressive number of personnel was attached to the army. The *Channabasava Purana* vividly describes the numerous bullock carts involved in the transport of equipment of various kinds, including battle gear for war-elephants and horses. The same text mentions the various tradesmen employed by the military, ranging from barbers, water-carriers and washermen to cobblers, blacksmiths and silversmiths. An unusual passage from the *Bharatesha Vaibhava Sangraha* is concerned with the private life of the king in the course of a long military campaign: the hostilities are momentarily suspended on occasion of the birth of a prince and initiation ceremony of another prince.

Strategy and the tactical deployment of the army are dealt with in the third part of the chapter. This opens with a description from the *Bharatesha Vaibhava Sangraha*, in which two royal brothers fight against each other. However, being Jainas, bloodshed must be avoided at all costs and the duel is fought by unconventional means, such as staring at each other and lifting one another. A fascinating insight into the traditional formations of the army, like the *garuda* and *chakra*, is found in the *Nemijinesha Sangati.*

The fourth part of the chapter is devoted to the description of weapons, from conventional mechanical contrivances to firearms, bombs (?) and special armour. The *Channabasava Purana* has an extensive section on magical weapons or *mantras*, capable of conjuring up the hills, wind, fire and wild animals.

The fifth and final part of the chapter concentrates on defensive equipment and the attack and siege of fortified cities. The authors here rely on observation rather than poetic inspiration. The passages drawn from the *Ramanatha Charite* and *Channabasava Purana* convey a vivid picture of the assailants kept at bay with bales of burning grass, showers of hot mustard-seeds, boiling oil or porridge and hot limestone and baskets filled with poisonous snakes and other horrors thrown down from the ramparts. The closing passage from the *Mohana Tarangini* gives a lively account of a victorious army and its followers.

Generalities on military campaigns

15.1 Preparations for a military campaign

This excerpt from the *Karnataka Krishnaraya Bharata* describes an ideal military campaign.

The end of the rainy season is the most appropriate time for a military expedition. The rivers are easily fordable and there is abundant vegetation. The army should comprise chariots, elephants and horses, and soldiers who are well equipped with bows, arrows, swords, armour, etcetera. The troops should march to the accompaniment of a band playing military music. Spies should be sent in advance to report on the enemy's movements, and to look for suitable places for the overnight camps. All the four divisions of the army [chariots, horses, elephants and infantry] under the command of the king should take strategic positions. The king, with encouraging words and promising generous rewards, should inspire his forces to feats of daring and valour. Before starting on a campaign, omens revealed through birds, animals and the wind should be carefully observed. (*KKB*, II, 2-9; pp. 75-8)

15.2 Beginning a military campaign

This passage from the *Bharatesha Vaibhava Sangraha* is the most comprehensive treatment of the theme in this selection.

The king decided to start a military campaign at an auspicious moment on the tenth day of *Navaratri*. First of all he went to his mother's palace to pay his respects, give her the appropriate gifts and be blessed by her. She hugged him and wished him every success and a safe return. Then the king's wives [who accompanied the king on his military campaign] met the queen-mother and took leave of her. She blessed all of them with great affection. (*BVS*, XIX, 1-9; pp. 249-50)

Then the king went to the temple of the Jina to worship [the deity] and make offerings. The ascetics who accompanied him blessed him, wishing him a victorious return. [In the temple] the crown was placed on his head and then he gave homage to the Jina again, paid his respects to the holy men and departed on the royal elephant to the chanting of priests and the drumming of the band. All around him marched servants carrying the royal umbrella, fly-whisks, flags and banners. (*BVS*, XIX, 16-24; pp. 251-2)

As he passed through the streets of his city, all the citizens assembled to watch the grand procession of their king. (*BVS*, XIX, 26, 27; p. 252)

As he came out of the fort gateway, he faced the *banni* tree on which the *chakra* was to be seen. On seeing it, he stopped the elephant on which he was riding and reviewed the vast army assembled there, ready to undertake the expedition. It consisted of all the four traditional branches: infantry, cavalry, elephants and chariots. The generals informed him that they were ready for the march. The king and his impressive army marched on, amidst the joyous and loud music produced by the *bheri, nissala, pataha, shankha* and other instruments and the bursting of numerous crackers.

As he proceeded round the sacred *banni* tree in clockwise direction, the *chakra* moved ahead of him, showing him the way to follow. Different battalions were headed by separate generals. (*BVS*, XX, 1-13; pp. 254-5)

Army personnel

Descriptions of army personnel are a theme in which the poets delighted. Works such as the *Ramanatha Charite* and *Shri Krishna-devarayana Dinachari*, which are quoted below, as well as the *Mohana Tarangini* and *Channaba-sava Purana*, have interesting information on recruitment tactics and the intelligence service.

15.3 Enrollment tactics

From the *Ramantha Charite* comes this account of the means of recruitment employed by a prince.

The prince made valuable gifts to particularly brave warriors and men of the cavalry, wherever they were, to encourage them to join his army. By means of tactful words and skilful negotiations he persuaded them to enlist. Thus, famous warriors who had no job prospects in the armies of cowardly rulers deserted their employers and joined the prince. (*RC*, IX, 3-5; p. 153)

15.4 Intelligence service

The *Shri Krishnadevarayana Dinachari* mentions two particularly specialized intelligence personnel:

Behina vayu-hanumanthayya were spies who were able to go everywhere with the speed of the wind; *manovega-purusha-mrigayya* were those who operated with the speed of thought. (*SKD*, I, lines 4-5; p. 31)

15.5 Preparations for battle

Battle preparations are described in detail in the following excerpts from the *Ramanatha Charite*. Particularly interesting in this excerpt is the mention of the various nationalities of the mercenaries, such as Turks and Khorasanis serving the local kings, as well as the detailed description of costumes and weapons.

On hearing that a border fort had been captured by the ruler of Kampila, the emperor was furious. He summoned his general and dispatched letters to his most trusted subordinate rulers, ordering them to come with all their forces, elephants, horses and infantry. Soon, armies arrived from different kingdoms such as Kongu, Kodagu, Maleyala and Tigula. The emperor reviewed this vast army [and decided to fight the ruler of Kampila] [....]

Upon that, the prince [son of the ruler of Kampila] went to the court hall along with the general-minister and issued a proclamation of war. At once the preparations commenced. Elephants and horses were readied for the battle; their caparisons were reinforced with steel plates and they wore armour, coats of mail, saddles and decorations. The soldiers equipped themselves with different kinds of weapons, such as bows, arrows, swords, spears, shields and double shields of lead, and then set out for the war singing war-songs. The warriors of Kannada origin were keen to fight bravely and earn different kinds of reward at the end. Those soldiers had with them young horses (or elephants?), white, red and yellow garments of honour, umbrellas, girdles with bells, elephant trunks [denoting a high status], two-faced mirrors, golden or silver coats of mail, daggers set with gems, hand-lances, golden weapons, etcetera.

Along with the above warriors, the soldiers of Islamic faith [horsemen who were employed by the Hindu king] were also ready for the battle. They donned jackets decorated with tassels and festoons and broad waist-belts, carrying with them horns, spears and such like. They wore [steel] armour, round [steel] helmets, [steel] shoulder-pieces, daggers and wooden quivers for the arrows. A number of them rode on fully-caparisoned war-elephants. In addition to their masters, some elephants carried on their backs big kettle-drums and trumpets of various kinds. (*RC*, XI, 25-9; p. 190)

The elephants, standing close to each other, were to form an impregnable front line. The infantry, wearing a tight low garment and [steel] armour and equipped with screen-like shields fitted with tassels, a variety of weapons, shields decorated with silver or gold plating, and others, were then in full alert. There were also some distinguished nobles with their wristlets, anklets and *pendeyas* (anklet of honour) prominently displayed. Among the gear carried by the soldiers were nets, cloths, long ropes, whips, wooden torches, heavy logs and instruments producing a wild noise to scare the enemy. The archers had bows embellished with gold- and silver-work, quivers for arrows and swords with golden hilts. They marched to the battlefield dressed in tight shorts, armour and wristlets of honour.

Then there were the lancers. They held short daggers and wore tight lower garments with hanging tassels. They had big hair-buns and had applied sandal paste over their bodies. Next came the bodyguards; they dressed in tight shorts, gold ornaments, silk [turbans], anklets, etcetera. They also carried glittering swords and shields. Some of them carried new shields and a new kind of sword called *kaditale* ("chop off the head").

Other infantry personnel, too, set out for the battle. They had leg-ornaments, *pendeyas*, special armlets and necklaces with pendants. In that army were also boatmen, experts in jumping and scaling [walls, and others]. They had neatly dressed up their hair in buns and they wore tight lower garments and golden ornaments. Their wives wished them a successful campaign and promised to die or commit *sati* should they die in battle. (*RC*, XI, 1-46; pp. 186-93)

Various trusted staff of the royal entourage and subordinate rulers with their men, money and equipment also joined the army. When the whole army consisting of all the traditional divisions had assembled [in the required order] between a valley and a tank outside the fort, the chief minister informed the king, who was seated in the audience hall on the jewelled throne.

The king, with the help of the royal priest, determined the auspicious moment for commencing the campaign. He then went out of the fort amidst the loud din of drums, trumpets and other instruments. He was accompanied by his crown-prince, subordinate rulers, ministers, generals, other high officers, [influential] citizens, priests, relatives and others.

Descending from his fort and accompanied by the prince, the king reviewed the vast army. Then the troops proceeded to fight against the army of the enemy. (*RC*, XI, 53-83; pp. 194-9)

15.6 The army of Ballala

The same text proceeds to describe the army of the enemy.

The army of the enemy king [Ballala] was [equally] well organised and arrayed. Constituted by the armies of the king and of the governors of the various provinces, it, too, included princes, generals, commanders, chieftains, brave warriors and others. On the right was the mass of soldiers of the *shudra* caste, and on the left was an army of able swordsmen. Apart from the above, there were innumerable war-horses, elephants and men all well arrayed and ready for the fight.

At the forefront was the division of the *bedas* (professional warriors or hunters). Behind them was the battalion under the prince's command, which included skilful warriors. Further [away] there were Muslim generals, Kannoji from the Odiya kingdom, and others from Gurjara and Lata. There were also servants attending to menial jobs. (*RC*, XII, 31-40; pp. 206-7)

The encampment

15.7 Layout of the encampment I

Among the various descriptions of encampments, the following from the *Dharmanatha Purana* is the earliest in this selection.

[A prince went to another kingdom with all his retinue and all the four branches of the army to win the hand of the local princess.]

As the convoy neared the capital city of that kingdom, the prince summoned the commander of the army and gave order to pitch the encampment. The commander selected a suitably large area and soon he created a beautifully laid-out temporary town with main and secondary streets, markets, stables for horses and elephants and other [features]. At the centre of the camp he built a seven-storeyed palace. This beautiful town, built in such a short time, looked like a work of magic.

The prince entered the camp to the sound of auspicious music, the chanting [of passages] from sacred texts and the fluttering of banners placed above the buildings. He visited all the elegantly built quarters and finally entered his palace. He then took leave of all the governors, subordinate rulers, princes and personnel of the four classes of the army, requesting them to go to their respective accommodation.

He changed, bathed, ate and then, suitably attired, spent some time in the company of the ladies [artists] of his retinue. (*DP*, XI, 20-6, & prose; pp. 269-71)

15.8 Layout of the encampment II

From the *Mohana Tarangini* we learn the following details.

The encampment mainly consisted of cloth tents, with tops adorned with golden pinnacles, glittering in the bright sunlight. The king's tent was placed at the centre of the camp, and around it were those of the royal princes, subordinate [rulers] and other distinguished persons. Above each one fluttered a banner on which [painted] emblems proclaimed the status of the occupier.

At the centre was open ground, similar to a square, where four main roadways [laid out in the four cardinal directions] converged. These were lined by rows of shops stocked with various kinds of merchandise managed by merchants who followed the army and catered to its needs. (*MT*, XXXVI, 66-71; pp. 447-8 and XXXVII, 3; p. 449)

15.9 Camp facilities

The *Ramanatha Charite* gives information on the provisions that were available at the camp.

Skilled workers constructed a beautiful camp. [....]

Separate quarters were provided for the treasury, for storing cash, sleeping, bathing, dining and for the chief of the army to hold audience. There were also [rows] of shops stocked with items such as arrack, hemp, toddy, *rotti*, sugar, *ghee*, jaggery, wheat flour, rice and mutton. The tents of the harlots stood out by their colourful appearance: green, red, yellow and others. Close to these were some shops where fragrant substances, such as sandal [powder or paste], musk, camphor and the like were stored in large containers to be sold. There were separate rows of tents for the subordinate generals and commanders. (*RC*, XXXXII, 54-65, pp. 430-2, II)

15.10 Camp provisions

The same text has the following information on the intoxicating drinks and other substances that were available at the camp, as well as on the ladies accompanying the army on the move.

There was fried *bhangi* (hemp), *uri-singi* (an intoxicating, medicinal plant), *bitti* (seeds taken along with drinks), *unmattada-bija* (opium seeds), *sure* (arrack carried in leather bags), *surida-pini* (toddy juice), *vatsa-nabhi* (poisonous preparation from aconite), *kavala* (a fried food) and *ganga-sara* (arrack carried in leather bags). (*RC*, XXXXI, 52-4; p. 415, II)

There were thousands of concubines seated in palanquins provided with screens. There were 10,000 beautiful young women with petal-shaped eyes. A large number of clever ladies riding horses and young attractive girls on foot playing all sort of pranks followed the soldiers. (*RC*, XXXXI, 56-61; p. 416, II)

15.11 Personnel following the army

The *Channabasava Purana* gives an exhaustive picture of the army on the move, its equipment and camp organization.

Following the proclamation of war, the army moved towards the fort of the enemy and set up camp in its proximity. A number of tents of various sizes were pitched in rows. (*CP*, XLII, 12, 13, p. 445)

The equipment of the army was transported by bullock carts, animals such as bullocks and buffaloes and slaves. It included horse-saddles, reins, bridles, metal armour for horses, whips, face-guards and other defensive items. Then there was elephant gear such as chains, ropes, bells and leather straps. For the infantry and other personnel there was armour, shoulder-plates, face-guards, helmets, weapons, sandals and others. (*CP*, XLVII, 44; p. 520)

The camp was very busy with the elephants, horses and soldiers in their glittering armour and weapons of different kinds all milling around.

Some rows of tents were set up by merchants selling edible grains and other items to soldiers and others. [At one end] there was an open ground for the training of horses and elephants. The drivers of golden chariots drawn by bullocks practised there also.

The king, subordinate rulers, nobles, ministers and other officers were purposefully going from one place to the other. The ladies, too, were carried about in palanquins. (*CP*, XLII, 14-15; p. 445; XLVII, 32-9; pp. 517-18)

The essential requirements of the army, such as food grains and other edible items, gold, dresses, clothes, ornaments, fragrances, perfumes, golden utensils, silver, big vessels, cots, mattresses and pillows, were carried to the camp either by bullock cart or large numbers of bullocks. (*CP*, XLVII, 40; p. 513)

There were traders, businessmen, goldsmiths, cloth merchants, jewellers, professional cooks, flower merchants, sellers of betel-nuts and leaves, vendors of dairy products, oil merchants, tailors, cobblers, sharpeners of weapons, barbers, washermen, hot water suppliers, gamblers and others.

There were blacksmiths who manufactured and repaired steel axes, pick-axes, crow-bars, sickles, spikes, swords, daggers and other bladed weapons. Sweepers and water-carriers attended to their respective duties, helping in the upkeep of the camp. There were also bangle-sellers who exchanged the old bangles on the wrists of the ladies for new ones. There were also bawds and aged go-betweens. There were shops selling eatables: *dose*, pickles, sugar, ginger, jaggery blocks and others.

In the camp there were artists who had mastered the 64 traditional branches of knowledge, which included poetry, singing, dancing, logic, literature, humour and satire. There were also persons who were engaged in the six traditional kinds of profession: accounting, business, agriculture, warfare, cattle-breeding and menial service. The people camping there belonged to the eight traditional races and 101 castes. (*CP*, XLVII, 41-3; p. 519)

Various kinds of non-vegetarian dishes prepared from the meat of different kinds of birds and animals, all mixed with tasty ingredients [and spices] and cooked in various ways, were also transported to the camp. There were also other kinds of food preparations, intoxicant drinks made from the sap of the palm trees, etcetera. (*CP*, XLVII, 45-6; p. 520)

The camp was provided with a number of lamps and torches for lighting the area after sunset and there were watchmen patrolling at night. (*CP*, XLVII, 47; p. 520 and XLVIII, 33; p. 530)

15.12 Life in the royal camp

The *Bharatesha Vaibhava Sangraha* has lengthy passages describing the life of the ruler and his entourage at the camp.

On the morning of the next day the king attended to the *puja* and then sat in audience where musicians, singers, bards and other learned men entertained him in various ways. At that moment, Mandakini [one of the ladies-in-waiting] appeared with a prince. The king played affectionately with the young boy for some time, to the delight and appreciation of all those who were present. (*BVS*, XXIII, 1-6; p. 274)

In the meantime, a lady-in-waiting came running from the harem to announce that the elder queen, Kusumaji, had given birth to a prince. On hearing this, the overjoyed king presented her with a garland of pearls. Then he went to see the child and its mother. (*BVS*, XXIII, 39-41, 43; pp. 279-80)

On that occasion, the whole camp was lavishly decorated and everybody celebrated the joyous event. Throughout the kingdom, special *pujas* were held and presents were distributed. The usual birthday functions, including the [ceremony of] naming of the child on the twelfth day, were performed in a grand style. (*BVS*, XXIII, 46-8; p. 280)

Since the newly born child required time to grow and gain strength to undertake the journey, the king remained in that camp, provided with all the comforts of his capital, for six months. (*BVS*, XXIII, 53; p. 281)

After six months, the king and his army marched towards the South Sea. On the way they halted at suitable places for spending the summer and the rainy season. At last they set up the camp on the shore of the South Sea. There [the king] followed his usual routine of performing religious functions and spending time in the company of his numerous wives and the young princes. (*BVS,* XXIV, 2-5, 11; pp. 282-3)

At that time, the eldest prince (Arkakirti) attained the appropriate age to undergo the ceremony of religious purification and receiving the *yajnopavita-kalyana* (sacred thread). The function was carried out with all the necessary pomp and circumstance. (*BVS,* XXIV, 42; p. 288)

Strategy and warfare

15.13 A duel

An unusual duel between two royal Jaina brothers is described in the *Bharatesha Vaibhava Sangraha.*

[The king, who was on a military campaign, and his step-brother readied themselves to wage battle against one another with their vast armies.] (*BVS,* XLIV, 43; p. 395)

Before the commencement of the fight, ministers from both sides met in the middle of the battlefield to deliberate how violence and blood-shedding could be avoided and how the conflict might be resolved. They approached the kings, pleading with them not to become the cause of violence [and to avoid] any fighting with swords [or other deadly weapons]; rather they should fight a *dharma-yuddha.* They proposed that [instead of involving the armies] only the two kings should fight, without injuring one another. They should stare intently at each other (*drishti-yuddha*), splash water to each other's face (*jala-yuddha*) and lift one another (*malla-yuddha*). By this method, the winner would be decided. The kings accepted these conditions and stood facing each other.

At that point, the elder king appealed to his younger brother in a number of ways, begging him in all humbleness to refrain from resisting and to recognize his sovereignty. When all his appeals failed, he offered to acknowledge his defeat and surrender the whole kingdom instead of fighting with him, even in a non-violent way. Moreover, he blessed his brother and his kingdom, wishing him peace and prosperity. (*BVS,* XLV, 1-38, pp. 396-401)

This last move succeeded. The younger brother was humbled at the magnanimous gesture of the elder king and decided to relinquish the kingdom and take to asceticism, thereby attaining salvation. (*BVS,* XLV, 40-8, pp. 401-2)

15.14 Strategic formations of the army

Of the texts in the present selection, the *Nemijinesha Sangati* has the most detailed description of strategic deployment of the army.

The king ordered the first commander to place the troops of the various vassal kings in the form of a thousand-petalled lotus. The armies of [the most powerful] kings were posted in such a way as to form the pericarp of the lotus, at whose centre was the king surrounded by numerous war-elephants. (*NS,* XXVII, 10-16; pp. 670-1)

On the opposite side, the king ordered the commander-in-chief to deploy the army in the form of the *garuda* (divine eagle). Accordingly, the forces of ten kings, consisting of the four traditional branches of their armies, took their positions and formed the left wing of the *garuda.* Similarly, some other rulers and warrior-brothers of the commander-in-chief, along with the four branches of their armies, formed the right wing of the *garuda.* In the same fashion, some others positioned themselves as to form its beak, neck and tail. At the centre were posted distinguished warriors seated on elephants. It was an impregnable military formation. (*NS,* XXVII, 22-34, pp. 672-4)

[The battle lasted for several days. One day] the army was arrayed in the form of a *chakra,* an intricate formation similar to a large [circular] embankment, at whose periphery were numerous chariots. (*NS,* XXVIII, 14, 17, 31,120; pp. 689, 692 & 708)

Types of weapons

An array of weapons, both conventional and magical, is mentioned in the *Padmaraja Purana, Shivatattva Chintamani, Sanatkumara Charite,* Battaleshvara's *Ramayana, Ramanatha Charite, Mohana Tarangini, Vijayakumari Charite* and *Channabasava Purana.* The last of these texts provides the most exhaustive information.

15.15 Mechanical contrivances

Battaleshvara mentions the following mechanical contrivances and other defensive devices:

Goblin device, mechanical hawk, mechanical (rotating?) steel hook, mechanical obstacles, mechanical lions, hot sand, bombs(?), explosive materials, a mechanical big tiger, spikes and catapult. (*R,* XVI, 39; p. 200)

15.16 Firearms

According to the *Ramanatha Charite*, firearms of various kinds were transported by carts to the battlefield. Among them were:

Muskets, rockets, bombs(?), various kinds of explosive devices and saltpetre. (*RC*, XXXXI, 49; p. 415, II)

15.17 Arms and armour I

The same text mentions:

Armour or coat of mail, helmet, shoes and sandals, iron club or rod, bow, quiver, weapon with a serrated edge, wooden club, various types of sword, shield, arrows for the bow, gloves [of leather], battle axe, iron or stone balls, blow gun, hand-bars, etcetera. (*RC*, XIX, 17-21; pp. 362-3)

15.18 Arms and armour II

A similar list of weapons is found in the *Mohana Tarangini*.

The most common weapons, however, were bows and arrows of various types; spears and lances, clubs, swords and daggers of different sizes and shapes, stones for slings, discus and others. A special type of arrow had a crescent-shaped tip. (*MT*, XXXIV, 18-23; pp. 463-4)

Apart from the above, it appears that, on the whole, the soldiers used whatever was at hand or was readily accessible, as indicated by the following list from the same text:

Stone in a sling, sharp-edged stone, square heavy stone round stone, and others. (*MT*, XL, 37-73; pp. 542-9)

Elephants were used for breaking open the strong shutters of the fortification gates. (*MT*, XXXIV, 5; p. 461)

15.19 Arms and armour III

The *Channabasava Purana's* description of weapons runs as follows:

The horses were equipped with saddles, reins, bridles and stirrups, and the elephants with protective metal plates and the usual caparisoning; the choicest horses were harnessed to the chariots. These were embellished with flags, banners and bells and driven by charioteers. A variety of weapons was given to the infantry, along with double armour (?) and hand-guards to protect their bodies. Talismans were tied on their upper arms.

There were other divisions in the army, such as the band with drummers, trumpeters and bugle-blowers. There were those who plied fly-whisks and held umbrellas for the benefit of the leaders. There were also panegyrists who sang eloquently the praises of their masters.

Swords of different shapes and sizes, daggers, maces, hammer-like weapons, spears, spikes, clubs, sticks, axes, bows and arrows and discus were among the weapons used. (*CP*, XXIII, 25-38; pp. 233 & 236; XXXVIII, 38; p. 403)

15.20 Magical weapons

The following array of magical weapons is specified in the *Channabasava Purana*.

Besides the above-mentioned conventional weapons, there were *mantrastras* (magical weapons) of different types. These created illusory objects such as hills and mountains, fire, wind, darkness, snakes, storm winds, water, rain or deluge, thunderbolt, bright light, *sharabastra* (mythical animal) and others. (*CP*, XL, 9-19; pp. 418-20; XL, 29; p. 423)

A list of *mantrastras*, along with their opposites, appears at a later point in the same text:

Uragastra (snake-weapon) and *garudastra* (eagle-weapon), *parvatastra* (weapon creating mountains) and *vajrastra* (thunderbolt-weapon), *meghabana* (weapon creating clouds) and *vayuvyastra* (wind-weapon), *timirastra* (weapon creating darkness) and *bhanushara* (weapon creating light). (*CP*, XLIII, 22-8; pp. 459-61)

Other weapons which created illusory or magical effects were the ones producing tigers, lions, bears, snakes, wild bisons, crocodiles, whales, rain, thunder, lightning, cyclones, stormy winds, cold, fire, smoke, rivers, goblins, unbearable light, glaring heat and many others. (*CP*, L, 11-12; pp. 555-6)

15.21 Defensive equipment of a fort

The *Channabasava Purana* also describes the defensive arrangements of a fort, which consisted of strong and stout bastions with battlements and towers. On them were placed the following defensive devices.

Marulkai ("deceptive hand", a mechanical contrivance), various types of firearms and explosive substances, strong and long steel swords, boiling lime in large containers, hot sand, boiling pap, boiling oil in large containers, big stones, heaps of stones for slinging, slings, spears and lances, *pandidale* (contrivance called "boar's head"), large bundles of hay, large wooden logs [and others]. (*CP*, XLII, 11-12; p. 444)

15.22 Preparations to resist an attack

Accounts of how the defensive equipment in a fortress is readied are found in the *Sanatkumara Charite*, *Ramanatha Charite* and *Channabasava Purana*. The following passage is drawn from the *Ramanatha Charite*.

The moat, walls, ramparts, bastions, posterns, towers, scaffoldings, battlements, buttresses and "tiger-faces" were all strengthened, reinforced and kept in good condition. Moreover, arrow-holes and holes for firearms were strengthened and the fort gates provided with new locks and strong new wooden bolts. Flagstaffs, balls to be thrown, logs to be dropped, long clubs to attack the scaling soldiers and other defence equipment were kept in readiness and in plenty. In addition, there were thick wooden clubs, spikes, stakes, stones, heavy stones, fire-powder, mechanical devices for shooting, bows, ropes, nooses, arrows, scissors, oil-vats, etcetera. There were heaps of scalding sand, large quantities of boiling porridge, hot limestone, grass [to be set on fire before dropping], red hot coals, stacks of nets of different types, ropes, thick ropes, mortar pieces and steel shields.

There were specialists skilled in repairing quivers, bows, arrows [and other] arms. There were also carpenters who could manufacture and repair the wooden equipment. There were blacksmiths for making weapons such as axes, pick-axes, *marulkai*, swords, bars and similar. There were masons who could attend to stone and masonry works, others who could sharpen swords, daggers and spears and tinkers who made or repaired armour, helmets and face-guards. Besides these there were also large numbers of brave soldiers. (*RC*, XXXVII, 50-63; pp. 347-50, II)

15.23 Siege of a fort

A detailed account of a siege is given in the following passage from the *Channabasava Purana*.

The order arrived to lay siege to the fort. The commander-in-chief was accompanied by his ministers, subordinate rulers and generals. As usual, the retinue following him included those carrying the royal umbrellas, fly-whisks, banners and flags and the panegyrists of the court. He rode on a white elephant, followed by the others. The [war-]elephant and horses had been provided with protective metal armour and caparisons. The chariots were drawn by horses wearing armour. Likewise, the infantry, too, was fully equipped. At the forefront was the band playing loudly on their musical instruments such as *bheri, dakke, doudhe, nissala, dundubhi* and *bombuli*. (*CP*, XLII, 17-19; p. 446)

The fort of the enemy had towering walls with a number of bastions, buttresses, towers and palisades [at regular intervals]. Its main gate was known as *pulimukha* ("tiger face"). Colourful banners and flags, some of which were painted, fluttered from tall posts on the towers and ramparts. There was also defence equipment such as mechanically operated contrivances called *pandidale, marulkai* and *tugu-dole* (logs in swinging position). There were also conventional defences such as swords and stones of different sizes. (*CP*, XLII, 21-2; p. 447)

A (military) formation known as "moving fort" proceeded towards the fort wall amidst a loud noise produced by drums, bugles and trumpets. Movable platforms and tall ladders were placed against the towering walls. Many carts transporting big wooden logs [meant for breaking open the closed fort gates] moved at the front. The elephants, which had protective metal plates on their sides, moved towards the main gate. Some soldiers hid behind those large metal plates fixed on the elephants' sides and moved forward unnoticed and unharmed. Other soldiers, braving the stones thrown from the top of the wall with slings and other devices, moved stealthily towards the secret passage. When it came to scaling the fort wall using the movable platforms and ladders, the defence placed on the ramparts repulsed the assailants, pushing them down by hurling stones, logs of wood, burning rubbish and hay and the like. Both armies fought face to face, using all their skills and displaying bravery. A rain of stones and weapons fell on the attacking army. During the violent fighting, the moat was completely filled with bodies and the materials used in the course of the battle. From the top of the ramparts, the defending army used the mechanical *marulkai* and shot at the assailants. Stones were hurled and boiling oil, hot sand, melting lac, hot mustard-seeds [to make the ground slippery], boiling stone-lime, heated stones, boiling flour pap, burning chillies and tobacco, foul smelling urine of rams and goats and whatever else came to hand rained down on the enemies. Firearms were also used in the defence of the fort. (*CP*, XLII, 24-32; pp. 448-50)

In spite of all, some soldiers succeeded in scaling the walls with ladders. Prior to that, attempts had been foiled by pushing down the climbers, by throwing on them burning bundles of fodder and hay and by using weapons such as the *pandidale*, swords, daggers, arrows, axes, maces, clubs, wheels, discs, explosives and others. They also used red-hot coals and boiling wax, as well as nets and big ropes with nooses to capture them; thick smoke was created [to hamper their progress]. Ultimately, however, the assailants climbed over the wall into the fort. (*CP*, XLII, 34-43; pp. 450-2)

Now the two armies faced one another. The fight became very violent.

[At this point in the text, a magical arrow is referred to.] When it was taken out of the quiver it looked like a single arrow, but when it was strung to the bow it split into ten and, on discharge, those ten arrows became a hundred. While in flight they became a thousand, while destroying the arrows of the enemies they became one *lakh* (1,00,000) and, finally, when that one *lakh* of arrows fell onto the opponents they multiplied further. (*CP*, XLIII, 16; p. 458)

15.24 The victorious army and its followers

The *Mohana Tarangini* presents a vivid tableau of the victorious army on the march at the end of a military campaign. Particularly interesting is the enumeration of the various people who followed the troops.

At the vanguard of the returning victorious army was the military band playing loudly the *dindima*, *bheri*, *tambate* and others. (*MT*, XXXVII, 6-9; pp. 49, 500 & 509)

There were some men holding aloft banners and flags of various kinds. They had on them [painted] emblems of elephants, rams, buffaloes, men, mythical beasts, bulls, *garudas*, scorpions or mice, which represented the mounts of the *ashta-dikpalakaru*, [as well as the gods] Vishnu, Bhairava and Ganapati respectively. (*MT*, XXXVII, 48; p. 508)

Other banners had different painted emblems: kite, conch, discus, elephant, lion, tiger and fish. (*MT*, XXXVI, 40; p. 492)

Young ladies, marching in two rows along with the army, held umbrellas topped by golden finials, fly-whisks, pouches, skin-flasks containing drinking water, thick tassels (?), spittoons, fans and the like, [all] for the use of their masters. (*MT*, XXXVI, 39; p. 491)

Besides those lady-attendants, ministers, councillors, accountants, expert astrologers and others seated in palanquins followed the army. Some were carrying with them a huge quantity of wealth and money. In this procession, the king, the princes and other rulers and officers were the most prominent.

The victorious army consisted of brave fighters who were specialized in various branches of warfare. Some were experts in the use of bows and arrows of various types, while others were adept in the use of firearms.

In that caravan were load-carrying oxen, civil labourers, wrestlers, boxers, singers, merchants, business people selling gold and other precious things, vendors selling betel-leaves and nuts, some elderly advisors, etcetera. (*MT*, XXXVI, 39-43; pp. 491-2)

PART FOUR

PLEASURES OF THE COURT

The following five chapters that comprise this part deal with courtly pastimes such as hunting expeditions and garden outings, ceremonies relating to royal weddings and formal banquets, and artistic activities, especially literature, dance, music and painting. A new element pervades this section: the attention of the poets is centred on women. As with the king, the minister, the capital and the court, women, too, are for the most part idealized. The main concern of the courtly ladies is to please their husband, the king; they are able to divine his wishes; they unquestioningly obey his orders. In short, they are the incarnation of the ideal woman: beautiful, elegant, always obedient.

Chapter 16, the first of this part, centres on hunting and hunters: their settlements in the forest, rough way of life, dress and caps made of leaves, weapons and hunting techniques are all described in detail. Particular attention is paid to the hunters' wives in a number of excerpts, for instance that drawn from the *Proudharayana Kavya*. The informal and relaxed atmosphere pervading these passages provides the ideal foil to courtly ambiance, in which every gesture assumes an almost ritual significance.

Visits to the royal pleasure gardens, an important element of courtly life, forms the subject of Chapter 17. Although these were generally formal affairs involving the king, his queens and other courtly personages, the *Jaimini Bharata's* description of a "ladies' only" outing in a garden, followed by water sports and the consumption of "a mildly intoxicating drink" (see Sections 17.1 and 17.2), seems to suggest that even courtly ladies knew how to be merry and enjoy themselves once the straitjacket of courtly etiquette was lifted. In general, however, the ladies follow the king around the garden, admire its flowers and shrubs, participate in water sports and are eventually rewarded by the king with new clothes and jewellery.

Chapter 18 is perhaps one of the most intriguing in this part. It contains a wealth of detail, not only on the elaborate bill of fare typical of courtly banquets, but also on the way of serving food and the seating arrangements and lighting of the dining halls. A passage from the *Bharatesha Vaibhava Sangraha* gives an account of the protocol followed by the king when inviting his mother to dinner (Section 18.8). The same text describes how the king must persuade his queens to join him for dinner, instead of merely waiting on him, as would normally be the case (Section 18.9). This chapter ends with a small selection from a cookery book, the *Supa Shastra*, one of the very few surviving traditional texts on courtly cooking. This work, written by a Jaina author, was probably addressing an audience of professional cooks, since there is no indication of the quantities and proportions of the various ingredients.

Chapter 19 revels in endless accounts of royal weddings, in which the bride and her ladies-in-waiting play a major role. This theme gives the poets ample scope to dwell on a number of details regarding the preparations for the ceremony, the dressing of the bride and the groom, their way to the sumptuous marriage pavilion and the pomp and pageantry of the wedding ceremony itself. Each of the texts consulted has at least one account of the above-mentioned topics: the present selection is restricted to the most exhaustive passages. Particularly interesting are the details regarding the reception and accommodation of the guests, from the *Sanatkumara Charite* (Sections 19.9 and 19.10), the list of items in the brides' dowry, from the *Mohana Tarangini* (Section 19.19), and the enumeration of the presents bestowed on the departing bride by her parents, from the *Dharmanatha Purana* (Section 19.20).

An insight into the intellectual and artistic life at court is provided in Chapter 20, the last of this part. Here again, the courtly ladies, a number of whom must have been extremely well educated, play a pivotal role. The first set of excerpts, on literature, opens with a long account of the composition and recitation of a poem composed by one of the queens, drawn from the *Bharatesha Vaibhava Sangraha* (Section 20.1). The passage from the *Karnataka Krishnaraya Bharata* reproduced here, in which Krishnadevaraya commissions a poem, deals with theme of royal literary patronage (Section 20.2). The second set of excerpts in the same chapter concentrates on music and the dramatic arts, highlighting the role of the queens as accomplished musicians and dancers. Particularly engaging is the extract from the *Bharatesha Vaibhava Sangraha* describing a theatre and its discerning audience (Section 20.3). The third and last collection of excerpts in this chapter considers the art of painting, particularly portrait painting and the choice of appropriate themes for murals (Section 20.11).

Chapter 16

HUNTING AND HUNTERS

Hunting was one of the most popular courtly pastimes. Most of the texts cited here mention hunter settlements and give details on hunter communities. There are stereotypical descriptions of the hunters' appearance, "of stout frame and dark complexion, with long arms, thick moustaches of a reddish colour and bushy hair" (see Section 16.6), as well as their dress and headgear made out of leaves (a detail which is confirmed in the visual arts) and their rough manners. There is admiration for the ability of the hunters to negotiate jungle paths and their accurate markmanship and stamina in pursuing the prey. Their exuberance is vividly rendered in their talking loudly, making noise while on the move and drinking. According to the quotation from the *Proudharayana Kavya* (Section 16.4), their wives are equally bold and demonstrative: they follow their husbands through the forest, helping them to spot wild animals and retrieve the arrows; they are filled with admiration for their husbands' prowess. Throughout, the authors show a keen awareness of the alien forest environment in which the hunters operate.

The last three excerpts describe royal hunts and hunting parties. The first, from the *Shivatattva Chintamani,* has an impressive portrayal of Shiva as *kirata* and his entourage all dressed as hunters. The second, from the *Ramanatha Charite,* focuses on the wild animals of forest and the equipment of the hunters, while the third, from the *Mohana Tarangini,* has again a wealth of detail on dress and hunting gear, as well as the hounds of the participants. At the end of the hunt, as a mark of respect, the royal party is welcomed by the "ladies of the forest" and the ascetics. They pay homage to the king and offer him and his followers food and appropriate presents such as fragrant substances, medicines and rare animals.

16.1 A hunters' settlement

The *Dharmanatha Purana* contains a detailed description of the life of the hunters. On his way to a distant kingdom, the prince and his retinue pass through a dense forest inhabited by hunter communities.

The hunters, who lived in huts, were all of a black and shining complexion. They were busily knitting nets, preparing nooses, looping ropes, making slings and bows, sharpening arrows, arranging them in quivers and fashioning pegs of wood and other implements required in their profession.

In another part of the settlement the womenfolk were cleaning and pounding bamboo-rice. While working, they sang songs. For pounding rice they used mortars made of sandalwood and pestles fashioned out of an elephant's tusk.

Other women were plucking fruits, digging out sweet potatoes and collecting bamboo rice and other items for daily consumption. At another place, a hunter and his wife had set out on a hunting expedition. He carried a bow and had packed his arrows in a leather bag strapped around his waist. His wife wore a skirt made of leaves and ornaments of wild seeds. Her hair-bun was decorated with peacock feathers and her necklaces were made of bamboo pearls. She, too, carried a bow and both walked together in the forest. (*DP,* X, 100-8; pp. 251-3)

In due course, a wild boar was killed. Other wild animals, including lions, tigers and their cubs, bears, hares and pythons, fled on seeing the hunters approaching. The hunters, however, tracked them down and captured them with their nets, nooses and dogs. Finally, they killed their prey. (*DP,* X, prose 111-16; pp. 253-4)

The hunting expedition continued some time until they were tired. They found a beautiful spot in the forest and stopped there to rest and to have some intoxicating drinks. The hunters and their ladies sat in a circle, at whose centre were containers filled with drinks. They were joined by the ascetics and their wives who lived in the same forest and who were keen to partake of the drinks. The ascetics wore snake skins around their necks and antelope horns on their heads. They were clad in blankets made of rags and carried with them cups made out of skulls.

The ladies invited all to sit in a circle. They drew a diagram in the centre on which they scattered *vasanti* flowers. There they installed and invoked their deity, Gandabhairava. They then spread mango leaves on the ground and placed upon them many pots full of drinks of various kinds. Thereafter, they worshipped the goddess Madhu Devata by chanting *mantras* in accordance with their customs and sprinkling with their fingers some drops of liquor in all directions. After that, they partook of the drinks, the oldest first, the youngest last. Close to them were plantain leaves on which were piled preparations of mutton and fish fried in bear fat, which were served by the ladies. They drank from flat shallow bowls, round shells of pot gourds, new glass vessels and cups. The ladies took care to repeatedly fill the containers when emptied. Eventually they, too, started drinking and enjoying the liquor. (*DP*, X, 123-33; pp. 255-7)

16.2 The hunters in the forest

In the *Sobagina Sone* are several passages dealing with the life and activities of hunters, hunting parties and royal hunts.

While marching in the forest, the hunters created a loud noise with their bow-strings, hunting dogs and their own rude and loud talking. They were accompanied by their wives who were of a dark complexion, similar to dusky clouds; their occasional smiles were like the lightning in dark rain-laden clouds. Their complexion was so black that the forest looked darker, the darkness spreading even to the sky. They saw the tracks of lions, tigers, elephants and boars, and followed the footprints and other traces of these animals near the ponds, among the water-flowers and in thickly-grown grass. They keenly observed the movements of bears and bisons. (*SoS*, XI, 28-34; pp. 128-9)

They talked aloud about the various types of hunting tactics and strategies, so that the whole forest resounded. They spotted deer, antelopes, bisons, wild pigs, various birds and hares. Their wives stood by the side of their husbands, helping in various ways. They supplied them with arrows, pointed out birds and other animals, collected the prey and killed rabbits. Moreover, they retrieved the discharged arrows and shot at birds and hares. They hunted lions, wild pigs, tigers, elephants, bisons and bears. They collected the pearls that fell from the severed heads of the elephants and presented them to their wives. (*SoS*, XI, 36-43; pp. 129-30) [....]

Birds, such as parrots, bottle-birds, *kukuil, gouju, kakkara, sore, pulledeand kiruvakkis,* were killed in large numbers by the unerring arrows of the hunters, falling like *amalaka* fruits from the tree. In addition, they killed wild animals, such as elephants, bears, lions, *sharabhas*, bisons, deer, antelopes, stags, camels and small pigs. (*SoS*, XI, 50-1; p. 132)

The ladies appreciated the valour shown by the hunters in killing tigers, wild pigs, bears, bison and lions and carried the prey with their husbands. (*SoS*, XI, 53; p. 132)

They carried the killed game in various ways. Small birds were put in a kind of net-bag and carried on their back; other [live] birds were transported in baskets and cages. Among the captured animals were birds and their chicks, peacocks, mice, squirrels, tortoises or turtles and crabs. They carried hares tied to poles, iguanas and similar creatures in net-bags and some others on their heads. (*SoS*, XI, 55; p. 133)

16.3 A boar hunt

In the course of a boar hunt, a prince comes to the help of the hunters. This passage is drawn from the *Sobagina Sone.*

A wild boar appeared in that forest. The hunters bravely confronted and surrounded it. First they let loose their dogs, which barked and checked its charging speed. (*SoS*, XI, 60 & 62-4; p. 134)

The enraged boar charged more violently, killing some dogs and some men and creating confusion among the hunters. (*SoS*, XI, 66-70; pp. 135-6)

Undaunted, the hunters attacked the ferocious animal from all sides, spreading strong nets which were quickly loosened. After some time, the prince who was resting in that same forest came to the help of the hunters. (*SoS*, XI, 71-5; p. 136)

[Eventually, the prince killed the boar.] The delighted hunters praised the prince and presented him with unique objects and various kinds of wild birds and animals. (*SoS*, XIV, 7-8; p. 179)

Among these were deer, antelopes, wild cats, mongooses, black apes, mountain monkeys, big wild dogs, civets, wild pigs, different kinds of forest birds, peacocks, hares, pearls collected from the heads of the elephants, lions, tails of yak, wet musk, tusks of elephants, teeth of wild boars, horns of rhinoceros, tiger claws, fruits, honey and a unique bird. (*SoS*, XIV, 7-14; pp. 179-80)

16.4 Hunters' prowess

Yet another royal hunt, in which the marksmanship of the hunters and the hunting skills of their wives play a prominent role, is described in the *Proudharayana Kavya*.

One day the king, wishing to go hunting, set out for the forest together with the four traditional divisions of the army. The hunters assisted him by briskly looking for game in shrubs, bushes, trees and other hideouts. As the hunters were busy killing the wild and ferocious animals of the forest, their wives followed them, admiring their brave and valorous feats and praising them in glowing terms. At this, the hunters rejoiced and, thus encouraged, pushed forward searching for the game. The ladies assisted their husbands in the hunting expedition: they spotted the characteristic marks and footprints left behind by wild animals, such as lions, elephants, wild boars, wild bisons, and others, encouraging them to follow the trails and kill the animals.

They proceeded through ravines, valleys, streams, rivers, bushy terrain, and shrubs and creepers and sometimes they climbed on tall trees for reconnoitring the forest. When they spotted fat and healthy wild animals, all the hunters together noislessly trapped or killed them with spears. Thus they hunted wild boars, elephants, bisons, tigers, lions and swines. Their wives encouraged and helped their husbands by retrieving the arrows and other weapons. [....]

Thinking that the pearls found in the heads of the elephants were originally stuck in the claws of the lions, they killed a large number of them, as well as innumerable other animals. While they were proceeding with the killed game, they were attacked by a ferocious lion at a narrow spot. Seeing the roaring animal jumping towards them, the frightened wife of a hunter tightly embraced her husband; the hunter released himself quickly and, in an instant, stabbed the lion with a sharp weapon.

At one spot, a doe was playing with her young fawn. On seeing them, a hunter shot an arrow at her, whereupon she jumped forward to shield her fawn. Noticing this, his wife embraced him, beseeching him to save both the doe and fawn. The hunter immediately shot an arrow which intercepted the first one and saved the deer. His delighted wife embraced him again and kissed him affectionately, praising his skill in archery.

Another hunter fought boldly against a wild horse while a bison attacked him from behind. At once he seized the bison by its horns and tore them from its body. Then he killed a tiger with a club. Seeing his gallantry, his lady embraced and kissed him in appreciation of his valour and strength. At another spot, a wild boar attacked a lady and carried her off. At that, her husband shot a single arrow and rescued his wife unharmed. Finally, the hunters presented to the king tiger claws, gems found in the heads of lions, pearls from the heads of elephants and a beautiful deer. The king was immensely pleased and rewarded them handsomely. (*PK*, VIII, 16-25; pp. 101-3)

16.5 Shiva's hunting expedition

In the *Shivatattva Chintamani* it is Shiva in his aspect as *kirata* who goes on a hunting expedition. Of particular interest here are the descriptions of the outfits worn by the participants.

The chief [Shiva] dressed himself for the hunting expedition. He decorated his hair with peacock feathers and wore a colourful short garment trimmed with tender leaves, twigs and flowers suitable for the occasion. He wrapped his body in a green-coloured shawl and armed himself with a bow and arrows. He also donned necklaces of wild scarlet seeds and pearls collected from the [heads] of wild elephants and boars. The necklaces had pendants of emeralds. The hunting party included dogs and a number of followers. They were also dressed like their chief in a manner befitting the occasion. The consort of the chief, her associates and assistants, all dressed like huntresses, joined the party. On reaching the hunting grounds, the party went into action. The dogs were placed in strategic positions and the nets were set up at appropriate spots. The hunters talked, discussed, shouted or communicated by signs about the ways and means of stalking different animals such as elephants, lions and lionesses, tigers, wild boars and bisons.

In the course of the hunt, a wild boar of formidable build and ferocious looks appeared and attacked the hunters, throwing some of them on the ground. The assistants cried in distress and the chief shot a single arrow at the ferocious and defiant boar. It ran away and fell at some distance. (*S*, XXIII, 10-21; pp. 157-60)

The *Nemijinesha Sangati* contains an enumeration of nets, traps, nooses and other hunting equipment which, however, is elaborated upon in the following passage from the *Ramanatha Charite*.

16.6 A royal hunt

Among the most relevant accounts of hunting expeditions is this extract from the *Ramanatha Charite.*

One day the king was in the audience hall, sitting on the gem-studded throne. With him were his ministers, feudal rulers, governors, nobles, heroes, warriors specialized in the use of various kinds of weapons and the usual panegyrists. The chief hunter arrived there, paid his respects to the king and informed him that wild game was abundant in the nearby forest. The king was pleased and, as customary, rewarded him. Then, on order of the ruler, the impending hunting expedition was announced and soon a host of professional hunters assembled there. Characteristically, they were all of stout frame and dark complexion, with long arms, thick moustaches of a reddish colour and bushy hair. They presented the king with some special items such as tiger skins, fawns, peacock chicks, bamboo tubes containing honey, tusks of wild pigs and the like. They had a large number of dogs and hounds of different breeds and colours, all well trained in the art of hunting. (*RC*, XXVII, 23-42, pp. 134-8, II)

The hunters brought nets of different kinds such as: *hebbale*, (big net), *tere-sire* (screen-like net), *kalkanni* (noose type net), *bellara* (snare-net) and *habbugevale* (spreading net). They carried animals and birds that had been tamed and trained to be used as decoys to entrap game, falcons, tigers, hawks, elephants, bisons, deer and so on.

They had sickles, swords, axes, hatchets, long clubs and long and short spears and carried camping equipment which included round tents, canvas, side-canvas, boxes, pots, bedding, cots and spittoons. (*RC*, XVII, 43-6; p. 138, II)

[When all was arranged], the ministers informed the king. Special provisions were taken for guarding the fortress in the king's absence. After sending word to his eldest son to join him, the king set out amidst loud music played on bugles, trumpets and drums of various shapes and sizes. He was accompanied by a convoy of elephants, horses, soldiers, hunters and dogs. After marching for some time, the party entered the forest of the place, Hosamale.

In this forest was a large variety of trees, plants, bushes, shrubs and creepers and animals such as bisons, wild buffaloes, wild boars, bears, wild horses, deer, hares, reptiles, mongooses, monkeys, musk-deer, antelopes, tigers and birds.

The hunters moved about following the tracks left by the different animals. In the course of the hunt they used all the equipment they had with them, their strategy being to surround their prey. The hunters' wives participated in the expedition. They wore a short garment and breast-band and their hair was tightly plaited. They had slings stuck at their waist and a short sword in their hand. They followed their husbands wherever they went. (*RC*, XXVII, 48-73; pp. 140-3, II)

They hunted bears, boars, bisons, deer, tigers, foxes, jackals, wild buffaloes, wild cats, and others, by making use of their tamed decoy animals and dogs. Similarly, they hunted many kinds of bird, too. (*RC*, XXVII, 48-92; pp. 140-9, II) [....]

The hunting expedition continued for about eight days. When they returned they carried jackals, deer, tigers, antelopes, stags, wild cats, mongooses, rabbits, bears, bisons, parrots, cuckoos, peacocks, doves and other such prey, all in plenty. (*RC*, XXXIV, 2-3; p. 267, II)

16.7 Aniruddha's hunting expedition

Yet another vivid account of a royal hunt is the following, exceptionally lengthy extract from the *Mohana Tarangini.*

The king set out on a hunting expedition in the early hours of the morning. Brave and adventurous noblemen accompanied their chief, whom they followed, riding on the choicest of steeds. The attendants of the king and the other princes carried umbrellas and fly-whisks, following their masters in rows.

Large numbers of *bedas* were both at the front and at the rear of the party. They were dressed in short lower garments which had golden borders. On their arms they wore wristlets and on their ankles they wore anklets of honour and other metal ornaments. Around their waists were chains with rattles that made a tinkling noise as they marched; leather sandals protected their feet while hunting in the jungle.

They carried long strong ropes of various sizes, nets of different types, bells, swords, axes, bows and arrows, spears and lances, large sticks and other weapons required in the course of the hunt. Along with the hunters there were numerous dogs, which had metal or leather collars with long chains or ropes held by the hunters. The animals wore on their back coverlets of red or painted cloth decorated with jewels. The dogs and their masters marched with great enthusiasm and vigour towards the forest.

The hunters carried with them different types of net that were required in the course of the hunt. Each type had its own specific use: so, for example, *kalvale* (net with nooses to catch wild animals by the legs), *koralvale* (net with nooses to catch the prey by the neck) and so on.

On nearing the forest, the king and his associates changed their dress for an outfit more appropriate for the occasion. They wore tight-fitting green coloured garments. Over their heads were fixed twigs and small branches plucked from the mango trees. They armed themselves with bows and arrows and wore leather sandals on their feet. All these changes were made in order to blend in with the surroundings and avoid scaring the wild animals.

When everything was ready, the hunters made a loud noise on one side by beating the drums and shouting as the dogs barked, while the king and his companions waited on the other side. The animals, birds and reptiles, terrified by the noise, fled from their hiding places, dens, nests and holes. Thereupon, the hunters unleashed ferocious dogs, which pursued, attacked and killed the fleeing animals.

The released dogs pounced, caught some of the animals and started devouring them. It was hard for the hunters to make them release their prey. They had to forcefully drive thick sticks into their mouths to retrieve the dead game and continue the hunt.

The king and his retinue killed various animals. The king, using his sword or arrows according to the situation, killed lions, tigers, elephants, bisons, yaks and others. Everybody admired the king, and the panegyrists who were part of the hunting party sang his praises. The king chased wild pigs and killed them by piercing them powerfully with his long spear. The other (hunters) killed fleeing deer, pigs, elephants and others. Some of the animals, such as hares, jackals, fawns and iguanas, were caught alive using the appropriate nets. Parrots, doves, partridges and hawks were caught in the same manner. Because of their association with various deities, swans, kites and peacocks were spared.

By noon it had become quite hot and the hunting party was tired. They rested under shady trees on the banks of sweet-water ponds and in the forest. First they washed their hands and feet and drank water from the tanks. Then some of them were given cold camphor for applying to their feet, which were tired or swollen on account of their running and of the stones and thorns of the forest path.

The forest was full of fruit-bearing trees and plants such as wild plantains, grapes, guavas and mangoes. The party plucked various kinds of fruits and ate them to their hearts' content. Among these were jack-fruits, grapes, pomegranates, dates, sweet orange, wild banana, orange, sweet mango and many others.

They collected beehives full of honey and drank it to their fill. The sweet honey collected from various trees had different flavours such as wild jasmine, jasmine, *padari* and *kedage*.

There were also trees giving fragrant substances and others, like the *tobana*, exuding gum: they collected these substances. As a mark of refined taste, they plucked unusually shaped sticks from the bamboo bushes.

The chief of the party not only partook of the fruits, honey and other delicacies brought by his retinue, but also, as a mark of honour, presented these items to his followers, along with the customary betel-leaves and nuts and flowers.

On seeing the king and his hunting party, the forest-dwelling ladies presented themselves before the king. These damsels were all young and beautiful. As was their custom, they were clad in leaves and twigs. They approached the king, singing auspicious songs in his praise and wishing him well. They offered him various kind of eatables: bamboo rice, sweet honey, dates, grapes and ripe fruits, having just fallen from the trees. They also presented him and his party with mementoes that they had collected in the forest: horns of wild buffalo and bison, tusks of fully grown elephants, lion and tiger claws, rare feathers of the *bherunda* (mythical bird) and many others. They gave him rare percussion instruments made out of elephant hide. In addition, they presented him with fragrant and aromatic substances gathered in the forest, such as musk, *punugu* and *goraja*, and young birds and animals to be brought up as pets such as peacocks, *chakravaka* birds, lions, tigers, swans, singing *kogile*, talking parrots, young and beautiful deer and jumping rabbits.

The ascetics who had their hermitage in that very forest, on seeing the king and his party, came out and presented the king with auspicious and rare objects such as *ekamukha-rudrakshi* and medicines (herbal and mineral) [that they had] found in that forest. Then the party took leave of them all. In the evening, they returned to the city bearing all the gifts of the ladies and ascetics of that forest. They also proudly brought the game they had caught or killed during the hunt. The slain animals were covered with green leaves to ward off the flies and dust. They were tied to long poles so that they could be easily carried by persons bearing the ends of the poles on their shoulders. Their march towards the city was a memorable sight; they were preceded by a band of musicians who played loudly all the way. (*MT*, XIX, 6-87; pp. 276-92)

Chapter 17

PLEASURE GARDENS AND WATER SPORTS

Descriptions of the arrival of spring, the outings of the king and his entourage to the pleasure gardens on the outskirts of the capital, and the various celebrations connected with the *Vasantotsava* (spring festival) are among the themes that the poets deal with in great detail. No doubt, these topics provided them with a welcome opportunity of contrasting the formality of the invitation extended to the king by the chief gardener, or the splendour and pageantry of the royal cortege on its way to the garden, with the carefree atmosphere surrounding the king and his ladies as they are shown around the garden by the chief gardener. After admiring at length the trees, flowers, orchards and shrubs, the party revels in *jala-krida* (water sports), squirting coloured and fragrant water on one another, bathing in the pools, listening to music and poetry, flirting, swinging on decorated swings made from branches and foliage and having fun on merry-go-rounds. Particularly interesting is the reference to elaborate landscape architecture such as the "artificial hillocks, caves and valleys" noted in the excerpt from the *Jaimini Bharata* (see Section 17.1). The gardens had a number of splendidly decorated pavilions designed for different activities. Hydraulic devices with elaborately decorated outlets to regulate the level of water in the pools are briefly mentioned in the *Mohana Tarangini* (Section 17.5).

17.1 A pleasure garden

The first description of a royal pleasure garden in this selection comes from the *Jaimini Bharata.*

The royal pleasure garden was on the outskirts of the capital. It was spring. The mango trees were covered with new leaves and in full bloom and below them it was shady and cool. There were bowers made of different kinds of plants and creepers. The ground was covered with clean and cool sand. There were artificial hillocks, caves and valleys. Seats covered with stone slabs embellished with glittering gems and diamonds were placed at appropriate places. A pond skirted by beautiful marble steps was filled with lotus flowers.

Around the pond gathered birds of various kinds, all pleasantly warbling as they flew around. The fragrance of numerous flowering trees, plants and creepers permeated the garden. (*JB*, XXIX, 44-8; pp. 366-7)

17.2 The *jala-krida*

The description of the garden just quoted followed by an account of the *jala-krida* of the princess and her friends.

They divided into two groups facing each other and splashed water at one another. One party was headed by the princess, the other by her friend. They played in the water until they were tired and then they came out and stood on the steps in their wet clothes looking like beautifully sculpted statues placed along the edge of the pond. They changed into colourful clothes, dried their hair over fragrant smoke, put on their jewellery and applied the dot on the foreheads with a mixture of musk and saffron. They perfumed their bodies, coloured their feet, applied collyrium to their eyes and *makarika* on the cheeks and body and hung garlands in their hair. After this, they had some mildly intoxicating drink and chewed betel-nuts and leaves mixed with edible camphor before again walking about in the garden, playing pranks, singing, dancing, joking and drinking. (*JB*, XXX, 12-18; pp. 370-1)

17.3 The Chariot of Spring garden

The *Channabasava Purana* has the following account of a pleasure garden, whose name is

Chaitra-ratha-vana (Chariot of Spring), situated near the king's capital.

There were reservoirs, small tanks, ponds, wells, streams and channels with flowing fresh and cool water. (*CP*, XI, 14; p. 123)

Shady and cool pavilions, made of tender sprigs, leaves and branches, were erected at suitable intervals. There were swings and merry-go-rounds for the pleasure-seeking ladies. (*CP*, XI, 24; p. 123)

It was customary to make special decorations on festive occasions when the king and his retinue of dignitaries made a pleasure trip to that garden. All the necessary arrangements were carried out by the head gardener. (*CP*, XLV, 25; p. 487)

Rows of festoons, arches, temporary gateways and banners made of twigs, branches of trees, leaves, flowers and flowering branches were set up [at regular intervals] along the paths and passages throughout the garden. There was a series of statues decorated with colourful flowers of various kinds; they carried sprinklers out of which flowed water.

There were pavilions, bowers, canopies, resting platforms and swings, all made of foliage, branches and creepers. The channels flowing through the garden were filled with sweet-smelling water. There were also pavilions that supplied drinking water to the thirsty and food to the hungry of the party. (*CP*, XLV, 27; p. 487)

17.4 A formal visit to a pleasure garden

The king and queen and their entourage visiting a pleasure garden is a formal occasion that is painstakingly described in the following passage from the *Dharmanatha Purana*. (A lengthy account of the coming of spring from the same source has been omitted here.)

The king sat with his queen on a throne placed in the centre of a pavilion on the seventh floor of the palace. The pavilion, decorated with pearls, had a beautiful outlook onto the gardens at the rear of the building.

With the king and the queen were the usual ladies-in-waiting and attendants, ministers, poets, writers, comedians, female performers and a group of cultured and intelligent men and women.

The king had applied fragrant substances to his body: a mixture of saffron, camphor and red sandalwood paste. The queen had drawn floral and other designs on her body, using a paste of black musk. Amid pleasant talk, the queen offered betel-leaves and nuts, which the king happily accepted.

From the pavilion, the king enjoyed the sight of the pleasure garden in full bloom. Gardeners, garland-makers and young ladies entered the pavilion and gave him garlands of flowers of different kinds. Then they sat on the seats reserved for them, Two of the many female performers, Vasantamala and Kamalate, stood up: they first recited the poem *Vasantakalada-baravam* (Welcome to Spring) and then presented their play *Vasanta-viharana* (Pleasure of Spring). Their compositions vividly rendered the splendour of the spring season and the pleasures that it brought, expressed in poetic words and set to pleasant music. (*DP*, XIV, 33-7; pp. 382-4)

In the course of the performance, these two artists hinted that it was time for the king to visit the garden and enjoy the pleasures of the spring season. (*DP*, XIV, prose; p. 384)

The king gladly accepted this suggestion, praising them and rewarding them with clothes, gold and jewellery as a token of appreciation for their outstanding compositions and performance.

The king then requested the queen to accompany him to the pleasure garden, to which she gladly consented. He left the upper storey of the front court room of the palace, [known as] the *Lakshmi-mantapa*, and gave the order to announce publicly, to the beating of the drum, his excursion to the garden. Accordingly, the officer in charge carried out the order. Thereupon, a large number of citizens donned colourful clothes, put on fashionable jewellery, perfumed themselves with all kinds of scents and assembled in the forecourt of the palace. (*DP*, XIV, prose 38-43; pp. 384-5)

The king and the queen-consort sat on the royal elephant followed by their entourage. Some of them rode on an elephant and wielded the glittering royal staffs; some [waved] fly-whisks and others [held] umbrellas trimmed with pearls and edged with pearl tassels.

Other elephants were used by the princes; the concubines took their places in chariots while the chief ministers, other queens and *sumangaliyaru* (auspicious wives) rode on horses, all in attendance around the king. The king proceeded on the elephant amidst the music played on various instruments. (*DP*, XIV, 48-62 & prose; pp. 384-6)

The sons of subordinate kings, concubines, door-keepers, comedians, poets and performing artists all formed part of the large royal cortege. They rode either in chariots or were carried in palanquins, solemnly progressing through the streets of the town.

The slowly moving procession reached the pleasure garden. Everybody's heart was refreshed at the pleasant sight of it. On arriving there, the king and the queen descended from the elephant and entered the garden accompanied by close associates. The ladies-in-waiting, too, alighted from their palanquins and entered the garden. Before the arrival of the king and his party, the garden had been carefully inspected by the door-keeper. (*DP*, XIV, prose; pp. 386-9)

The umbrellas and other royal insignias were stacked at an appropriate place and the elephants were stationed at the perimeter of the garden. The head gardener guided the royal party through the grounds, pointing out the varieties of trees and fruits such as oranges, lemons, citrus fruits of various kinds, coconuts, areca-nuts and flowering plants. The ladies, hand in hand, followed the king. As they proceeded further, the gardener showed them rows of plants of *naga-kesara, jambuka,* sandalwood and clove trees. (*DP*, XIV, 63-8; pp. 390-1).

The party finally reached a spot covered with cool sand. Then one of the comedians stepped forward and observed that the groves surrounding it inspired amorous feelings. At this, the king smiled in appreciation. They reached a place where fragrant jasmine plants were in full bloom. A comedienne described the plants and the flowers in suggestive and poetic language. The king, taken with her talent, gave her some gifts and proceeded further to enjoy the beauty of the garden. (*DP*, XIV, 69-72 & prose; pp. 391-2)

After some time they reached the centre of the garden where, in an open space, [stood] the *vasanta-mantapa* (pleasure pavilion).

For the occasion of the king's visit, the pavilion had been richly decorated with fragrant cooling roots of *vetiver*, cut stems of plantain trees, mango leaves, a profusion of flowers such as *champaka*, lotus, jasmine, *sevantige* and *chenganile*, garlands and curtains of flowers and flower buds tied in various shapes. In addition, the pavilion had been painted [with red ochre] and sprinkled with camphor water and fragrant pollen. In short, it looked like a picture.

The king, the queen and their retinue took their places in the pavilion, which resembled that built for the marriage of Kanthu and Rati. They sat on seats, which had been treated with fragrant camphor and other perfumes and covered with sweet-smelling petals of different flowers. It was the most inspiring place for performances and other pastimes. (*DP*, XIV, 77-9 & interspersed prose; pp. 393-4)

To the great pleasure of the king, a musician played melodious music on the *vine.* While the king was enjoying the music, the ladies wandered about the garden, attracted by the beauty and fragrance of the flowers and the variety of trees and creepers. They walked merrily, sometimes picking those fruits and flowers which took their fancy and enjoying themselves in various ways. They sat in the green-houses, decorating their bodies with the flowers that they had gathered. Eventually, they returned to the king. Thus decorated with flowers and young leaves, they looked like a cluster of walking creepers. On arriving, they presented him with various kinds of beautiful flowers, wreaths and bunches of fruit. The king graciously received these gifts and wore some of the flowers [himself]. Thereafter, the king, the queen and the ladies left for the *jala-krida* (water sports). (*DP*, XIV, 79-106 & interspersed prose; pp. 394-400)

The pond for the water sports was situated in the middle of the garden. It was beautiful, being surrounded by flowering plants and creepers in full bloom. Marble steps on its four sides gave access to the water. All around the pond were rows of sheds with exquisitely decorated golden seats. There were also boats whose exteriors were encased in silver. The water had been perfumed with a mixture of saffron, camphor, musk and red sandalwood paste.

The king and the ladies stopped at the edge of the water and took the syringes and hollow-curved bones [to be used as dippers]. The king waved his hands and the ladies lowered their sprinklers into the coloured water and sprayed each other. The king watched the play of the ladies and, at a certain point, squirted a syringe full of saffron and musk water on the queen, drenching her completely. The queen, in return, armed with a golden sprinkler, sprayed fragrant water on her husband for a long time, without interruption. Then the other ladies playfully sprayed the king with water of various colours and fragrances.

When they had exhausted the coloured water, which was stored in large containers on the banks of the pond, the king gave a signal and everybody jumped into the pond and played joyfully in the waist-deep water. When it became cold in the water, the king and the ladies left the pond and stood on its banks.

The chief household-officer produced clothes of superior quality and ornaments set with gems, which were donned by the queen and the other ladies. They decorated themselves with flowers from the garden. Then the gardener was sent for and the king gave him many handsome gifts.

Finally, the contented king, together with his queen-consort and their retinue, left the pleasure garden on the royal elephant, followed by war-elephants, horses and soldiers. On entering the capital through the main gateway, the royal party was welcomed by the citizens. When the king reached the palace, he alighted from the elephant and was greeted by the auspicious waving of the five varieties of *arati* lights. Once inside, he sat on the golden throne encrusted with gems, placed in the middle of the *mantapa.* Loud music was played, the ladies sang auspicious songs and the court priests chanted sacred verses. He listened with reverence to the chants and prayers and received the holy rice, scattering it on his head. He then spent some time watching performances by comedians, dancers and others. Finally they were dismissed and the king bathed, dined and retired for the night. (*DP*, XIV, 112-66 & interspersed prose; pp. 401-13)

17.5 The *Vasantotsava*

The same themes are elaborated upon in the descriptions of the spring celebrations in the *Padmaraja Purana* and the *Jivandhra Charite* by Bhaskara. The passages from the *Mohana Tarangini* reproduced here are the most elaborate renderings in this collection; they extend over the next three excerpts.

Some tanks were built of white marble, others of finely-dressed stone. (*MT*, XIV, 28, p. 199)

Pools of various dimensions with different shapes and ornamentation were near the royal palaces and within the citadel. They were for the use of different persons, separately, according to their rank and lineage. Groups close to the king went there to enjoy themselves. (*MT*, XIV, 34; p. 200)

The pools were fitted with well-designed inlets for controlling the admission and flow of water. These were a type of mechanical contrivance, operated by female attendants. The inlets were works of art in their own right. Some were shaped like an elephant's trunk.

Before the water sports took place, the water of the pools was coloured by means of red flowers and perfumed with fragrant substances. The royal ladies, accompanied by their consorts and ladies-in-waiting, entered into the coloured water and played in it: they splashed it on one another, sometimes using syringes. Occasionally, they played in the water with balls fashioned out of flowers or sandal paste. (*MT*, XIV, 34-40; pp. 200-02)

17.6 The *Vasanta-puje* (homage to spring)

When the party had played happily in the pools for a long time, the king ordered them to come out of the water and worship the god Vasanta. Coconuts, various kinds of fruits and sweetmeats, auspicious rice and flowers were collected and appropriately arranged. In the course of the ritual, some ladies sang various traditional tunes, while others played the accompaniment on the *vine*, *tabla* and other [instruments].

The queen sprinkled coloured water and sandal paste mixed with water on the king and on her companions. He, and the others as well, reciprocated, to the general merriment of all present. After some water squirting, the two queens were asked to stand together with their youthful and attractive ladies-in-waiting in two rows facing each other. At a given signal, the two groups started spraying one another. They held gold vessels and syringes filled with coloured and fragrant water. They competed against each other keenly, amid great mirth and loud cheering. Percussion instruments and conches were played loudly throughout. (*MT*, XIV, 47-67; pp. 203-7)

The heat of the play was so great that the two rows broke up in no time. The fun and merriment, however, remained unabated. Along with syringes, sprinklers and vessels, they threw balls of flowers and fragrant sandal paste at each other.

Then, they turned to the swings and to the merry-go-rounds, all of which were richly and tastefully decorated.

The spring festival ended with the king giving costly clothing, ornaments and jewellery, as well as sandal paste and flowers to the lady participants. Then he bade them farewell and retired to the palace with the queen and their retinue. (*MT*, XIV, 88-92; pp. 211-12)

17.7 Swings and merry-go-rounds

At the centre of the garden was a pillared pavilion. Life-size female figures of young and bejewelled ladies standing in different dance postures were sculpted onto the pillars. Some held vessels in their hands; others held sticks, [such as those] used in the stick dance. The pavilion was decorated with flowers, floral garlands, sweet-smelling branches and leaves of different trees. The air was filled with fragrance. There were balconies decorated with cloths and tapestries of different kinds, colours and shapes.

At a short distance there were many swings of different sizes, decorated with garlands, twigs and tapestries. (*MT*, XIV, 28-32; pp. 199-200)

The merry-go-rounds were used by the royal couples and their ladies-in-waiting. The couples sat in them, while the attendants rotated them at a great speed so that the pearl strings, bead necklaces and other jewellery worn by the players were scattered all over the ground. (*MT*, XIV, 88-9; p. 211)

17.8 The *Vasantotsava* of Shiva and Girije

In this extract from the *Channabasava Purana*, the newlywed couple, Shiva and Girije, celebrate the spring festival.

For the festival, a large pool measuring 10,000 *yojana* was prepared under the supervision of the bride's father. The flooring was of shining marble and the steps were encrusted with various kinds of sparkling gem such as red rubies, diamonds, beryl, stones of reddish colour, rubies of the colour of the lotus flower and corals of the choicest variety. At appropriate places were large metal cauldrons filled with coloured fragrant water mixed with saffron powder, sandal paste and musk.

After a sumptuous feast, the newlywed couple, accompanied by close relatives, dignitaries and other guests, reached the pavilion that was near the pool. The couple sat on the golden throne decorated with gems, which was at its centre. The bride gave the signal for the commencement of the *Vasantotsava* by taking some sandal paste into her hands, mixing it with water and throwing it at her husband.

In return, the groom sprayed perfumed water on the bride and she retaliated. Thereafter, all those gathered there started spraying coloured water at each other using the syringes and golden containers. Amid great merriment and laughter, the water play went on. The wives of the dignitaries and some young ladies joined the festival. They enjoyed themselves greatly, indulging in revelry, giggling, laughing, chuckling, flirting, joking and quarrelling for fun. Some swam, dived or jumped into the coloured water.

After much enjoyment, they climbed out of the pond and donned various sorts of clothes and ornaments. Eventually, all the participants were given as a mark of honour betel-nuts and leaves mixed with edible camphor. They went to the palace of the bride's father, where he gave the usual gifts to his son-in-law and his daughter. Clothing and ornaments were given to all present and everybody dispersed. The couple, riding on a bull and accompanied by a host of musicians and followers, reached their destination. On arrival, they were greeted by the waving of the auspicious lights. They descended from the bull and sat on a golden throne. It was now their turn to give appropriate presents to all those who had participated in the various celebrations throughout the wedding. After this, the crowds went away and the couple retired to the inner apartments. (*CP*, XXXVII, 62-84; pp. 387-93)

17.9 The *jala-krida* of Shiva and Girije

The last excerpt of this chapter, which is devoted to the water sports of Shiva and Girije, also comes from the *Channabasava Purana.*

The pool was large and provided with a series of steps at different levels, all encrusted with precious stones. The pool, covered by lotuses floating above the clean water, was inhabited by a large number of fish and swans. (*CP*, XLV, 45; p. 492)

The colour of the water changed from place to place: it was greenish at one spot, reddish at another, darkish at a third. For the occasion of the water sports it had been mixed with yellow pigment, saffron-coloured powder and musk.

The heroine and her ladies-in-waiting, all dressed in sheer garments, descended into the pool and stood on different steps. Accordingly, some of them were in the water up to their knees, while others were up to their thighs, waists, navels or breasts. They held in their hands the gem-studded syringes, which had been made to look more attractive by being shaped like a swan, heron, parrot, water-bird, partridge, cuckoo, elephant, horse, deer, *sharabha* or *bherunda.* The ladies were waiting for the signal to start the water play.

The signal came as the hero sprayed coloured water on the heroine's head. She stood there looking like a sapphire statue. In return, the heroine surreptitiously took a jewelled vessel filled with a dark mixture of musk and water and emptied it onto the head of the hero. Then everybody poured, splashed and sprayed coloured water freely, smearing one another with sandal paste and other perfumed substances and coloured powders.

At a given moment, the heroine and her associates took the syringes and the sprinklers and started using them. During the heat of the play, they pushed each other, pulled one another under water, swam at great speed, dived and played hide-and-seek, while singing and shouting at the same time. After playing to their hearts' content, they climbed out of the water onto the banks of the pool. They squeezed the water from their long hair and the wet garments which stuck to their bodies. They changed into new dresses and started their makeup. They decorated themselves with flowers and perfumed themselves with various fragrances. As they stood on the banks of the pool, they looked like *naginis* of the nether world or mermaids from the watery depths. (*CP*, XLV, 52-65; pp. 494-7)

Chapter 18

FOOD AND DINING

The passages of this chapter deal with food in various contexts. Pride of place is given to formal banquets, as described in the *Airavata*, *Sanatkumara Charite* and *Mohana Tarangini*. The entertaining of brahmins by the king is discussed in detail in the *Samyukta Kaumudi*. A number of accounts focus on private occasions, such as the dinner of a newly wed couple taken from the *Dharmanatha Purana*, the formal reception of the king's mother and a long description of the king dining in the company of his wives, both from the *Bharatesa Vaibhava Sangraha*, and a brief account of the king's meal from the *Samyukta Kaumudi*.

While all these texts describe in painstaking detail the bill of fare, they also offer insights into the setting, eating etiquette and rituals, as well as the serving and seating arrangements. The most intriguing excerpts in this regard are those from a work on cookery, Mangarasa's *Supa Shastra*, which is a collection of recipes used in a royal kitchen.

Free feeding-houses along the main roads of the country are charitable institutions generally connected with charity water-sheds. They are mentioned in a number of texts, particularly the accounts that have already been given from the *Channabasava Purana* (see Sections 4.18 and 4.19).

Royal banquets

18.1 The king's dining hall

This description is drawn from the *Jaimini Bharata*.

Rows of bright and lustrous diamonds illuminated the king's dining hall. The king sat on an elegantly fashioned seat surrounded by a fair number of relatives. His mother served food to him, while his queens stood on either side, fanning him with fans made out of palm-leaves and fly-whisks. In the course of the dinner he conversed pleasantly with all his guests, while enjoying the tasty preparations. These were served in golden plates and bowls studded with gems and diamonds. The menu included *syalyodana*, soup, *ghee*, *bhakshya*, *payasa*, *paradi*, *madhu*, *sarkara*, *palidya*, *sikharane*, *shaka*, fruit juice, fruit salad, pickles, *krusari*, *kachchadi*, milk, curds, etcetera. (*JB*, VI, 44-6; pp. 71-2)

At the end of the meal, he had *tambula* mixed with edible camphor. (*JB*, VI, 55; p. 74)

18.2 A banquet

A festive occasion is thus described in the *Airavata*.

The time came for the grand feast. The princes [sons of Kunti] invited Krishna. He came and sat in the company of kings, rulers, citizens and others who had been invited to that occasion. (*A*, VIII, 34, 36; pp. 88-9)

Golden plates, bowls, spoons and other vessels, some of which were encrusted with rubies and corals, were used to serve food to the dignitaries. The others were served their meal on plantain leaves and in leaf bowls. Oil lamps on stands set with precious stones were placed at both ends of the rows of diners. Young girls distributed fragrant sandal paste and auspicious rice and poured water from golden vessels for each guest.

Attractively dressed young ladies carried serving-bowls filled with various kinds of cooked food, their ornaments tinkling pleasantly as they moved. The food was prepared according to the *shadrasa* (six tastes) as follows: *nimbi* (lemon fruit), *bella* (jaggery), *huli* (tamarind), *kayi* (nuts or raw fruits), *menasu* (pepper) and *lavana* (salt). (*A*, VIII, 37-42; pp. 89-90)

Similarly, there were various food preparations: *kalasu*, *sasivigayi*, *kusumbhari*, *holegayi*, *mekkiyakayi-sikharane* (of both types, sweet and sour), *happala*, *sandige*, *gouli*, *paradi*, *sevige*, *souti-bija*, *kadubu*, *holige*, *bella-mandige, hidigadubu, laddige, garige, vade, tailadholige, surali-holige, bisu-holige, biliya-karachi chakkuli, sanna-sevige, chini-palu, unde, murunde, rajanna, ghrita, payasa, rasayana, halogara, butti, kshira-sakkare* and *kalasogara.*

At the end of the sumptuous feast, the guests washed their hands and assembled in a hall. There, a golden plate containing colourful pieces of betel-nut, crystals of [edible] camphor and fresh betel-leaves was placed before them. (*A*, VIII, 52-4; p. 93)

At the close, the guests took leave of the host, blessing him heartily, and then returned to their respective homes. (*A*, VIII, 67-8; pp. 96-7)

18.3 A formal dinner

This description is drawn from the *Mohana Tarangini.*

On reaching the dining hall, the guests were greeted by the attendants who washed their feet and hands with warm water and ushered them into the hall. They sat on rows of low individual stools that had been covered [with cloth] for that occasion. The hall was lit by standing lamps.

When there was a mass feeding, the guests sat on long narrow strips of white cloth arranged neatly on the floor. Straw mats, cotton [quilts?] or wool were also used. The food items were served in shallow metal platters placed in front of the diners on three-legged stands or low stools either of brass or wood. Occasionally, the food was served on plantain leaves spread in front of the diners, who were seated on mats. Preparations such as *payasam* were served in cups fashioned out of plantain leaves. Drinking water was provided in metal jugs. The food was prepared and served from large metal bowls by specially trained *bonagittiyaru* (young and attractive ladies).

The bill of fare included a variety of dishes, both sweet and savoury, mainly prepared with rice, wheat, pulses, milk and milk products, fruits, sugar, jaggery and honey; [they were] all vegetarian.

Rice of the finest quality was cooked in a variety of ways, such as *toyanna* (preparation of *dhal* and rice) and the like, as well as *tovve* (a dish of cooked *dhal*) and *huli-saru* (hot soup laced with spices). To make the *huli-saru* taste better, asafoetida fried in *ghee* was added just before serving. There were vegetables cooked and seasoned with various spices, raw vegetables cut or diced and mixed with curds such as *palidya* and *dadhi patra mala,* and sweet preparations made out of milk and rice or other ingredients such as *gavali, paradi sanna sajjike* and *gulige.* In addition, there were flat cakes like *bhakshya, holige* and *pheni,* round solid sweets such as *unde* and *sukhinunde,* similar fried solid sweets such as *garige,* fried savouries such as *vade,* fruit juice of a thick variety called *sikharane,* pickles made out of various kinds of fruits like lemons and mangoes, rice cooked and mixed with curds, curds with cream, and *majjige* (buttermilk) of both the thick and thin varieties.

There is no mention of non-vegetarian items except for a sole instance, relevant to the narrative, in which fish is prepared. A lady cuts a big fish into small pieces. This operation is done on a wooden plank. The pieces are then threaded onto skewers and roasted by holding the skewers over red-hot live coal. The fish is then served in a sauce (?) called *sandige.*

Throughout the dinner the guests were fanned by lady-attendants standing near them. At the end of the feast, after the washing of the hands, they were offered betel-nuts and leaves mixed with edible camphor for refreshing the mouth. (*MT,* III, 54-9; pp. 54-5; XI, 47; p. 149; XIV, 3-16, pp. 194-7; XXVI, 4-16; pp. 369-72)

18.4 A wedding feast

The banquet that follows the wedding ceremony yet to be described in the *Sanatkumara Charite* (see Section 19.17) is given here.

[The marriage banquet took place on the fifth day after the marriage. It was a feast in honour of all the guests, in particular the royal ones. The host ordered the preparation of numerous dishes.]

In accordance with the wishes of the host, the following dishes were prepared in great quantities: piles of *hurige,* ponds of *payasa,* lakes of *tuppam,* seas of curds and hillocks of *kajjaya.* There were also varieties of *shadtasa, pachchadi* and *puri* and vegetables of various kinds.

The marriage pavilion had been sanctified by the smoke emanating from the various rituals such as the *homa.* Narrow golden cloth spreads were laid out in rows for the royal guests participating in the banquet. After observing the formalities [washing the hands and feet], the guests entered the hall and took their seats on the spreads. The attendants placed before them golden plates, jewel-studded bowls, cups and vessels, leaves and the like.

Beautiful young ladies, all very elegantly dressed, served the food. Their graceful movements produced a pleasing sound from their wristlets, anklets, toe-rings and other ornaments. This enchanted the guests, particularly when they poured *ghee* on each serving of fragrant smelling rice.

The ladies [each wearing a different perfume] served a kind of cooked rice seasoned with a mixture of sesame seeds, black gram, grated coconut, lemon juice, mustard-seed powder, spices and sugar, all fried in pure *ghee*. The following vegetables were added to another rice preparation: *hire* (sponge gourd), *hittila-avare* (a kind of bean), *suvvara* (a kind of pumpkin), pumpkin, *bale* (plaintain), *badane* (aubergine), *karaveli* (bitter gourd), *avare-kay* (beans), *bimba* or *tonde* (a kind of gourd) and others.

The *sambaru*, which was very tasty, had been prepared using vegetables such as *susalugayi, tumbugayi, masegayi* and *bennegayi*, already cooked or stuffed in different ways.

That elaborately prepared vegetable *sambaru* was served with cooked rice that had been mixed with *uduregayi*. In addition to that was served a very spicy and strongly flavoured dish called *melogara*, tasting sweet, sour and salty at the same time. [There was] another favourite and tasty dish called *badnekayi-baji*. It was made of egg-plants stuffed with a mixture of powdered sesame-seed, black gram, grated coconut, curry-leaves, cardamom, lemon juice, salt and edible camphor.

The next [dish] was *pachchadi*. The *sarva-pachchadi* had been prepared with raw vegetables cut into small pieces and mixed with mustard seeds, salt and lemon juice. There was also a variety of pickles made of large lemons, generous sized *amalaka* fruits, *hirale* (sour lemons), *maguli-beru* (mangoes of a sourish taste) and many more [fruits]. Those elegant ladies served cooked rice as if they were dishing out faultless pearls, so white and fragrant it was. Thereafter, they served a thin soup of golden hue. (*SC*, XIV, 2-13, pp. 161-3)

They also served pure *ghee* of a yellowish colour. Before dining, the guests observed the prescribed *aposana* ritual [taking a small quantity of water into the right palm, circling the food on the plate or leaf, while uttering *mantras*, then sipping the water and taking a few grains of cooked rice].

The diners relished all the tastily prepared dishes together with the pungent side-dishes, pickles and *papad*. In between the rice servings, they enjoyed the *pachchadi*. (*SC*, XIV, 15, p. 163)

They also relished rice dishes mixed with cooked *dhal* (*toye*), *ghee* with *pachchadi*, curds with *palidya* and others. There was the following variety of sweet preparations: *sajjige, paradi, hurige, gavale, garige, sevage, sukhinunde, paramanna*, soft *chakkuli, uddina-kadabu* and *kajjaya-payasa*. Throughout, the ladies served milk, *ghee* and curds in abundance, which were greatly appreciated by the diners.

At the end of the dinner, buttermilk laced with lemon juice, salt, cardamom, curry leaves and edible camphor was served in golden vessels. The diners then observed the prescribed *uttaraposana-etti* ritual, got up, washed their hands, mouth and feet and left the dining hall. They entered a hall with painted walls and took their seats. The host presented all of them with perfumes, sandal paste, auspicious rice, clothes, jewellery and the customary betel-leaves with nuts and then bade them goodbye. (*SC*, XIV, 15-24; pp. 164-5)

18.5 The king feeds the brahmins

The *Samyukta Kaumudi* describes a banquet in honour of the brahmins who were invited to perform a special ritual on behalf of the king;

[A large group of brahmins were invited to attend the king's *shata-yagam*. The king gave orders to prepare everything to make the stay of the guests as agreeable as possible.]

Banana leaves and cups made of leaves were placed in front of the brahmins seated in the hall. The bill of fare included the following preparations: *sannakkiyogara, hesara-tovve, ghee, happala, horakam, shakabalu, kavaleya palidya, pittu, payasam, kalalu, allam, vade, undalige, hurige, sanna-sevige, yereyappa, iddali, bona, dosa, bella-garige, karajige, kayi-dose, yenne hurige, sakkare burude, sajjige payasa, kajjaya, badanekayi-baji, mulangi, maguli, kara-genasu, kajjari*, buttermilk, fruit salad of *panasu, mavu* and *kajjura*.

The brahmins partook of all those dishes to their hearts' content, talking pleasantly among themselves and praising the cooks. After the feast the king made various gifts to the brahmins, who [in return] blessed him and completed the rituals. (*SK*, VII, 29; p. 128)

18.6 The king's dinner

A second excerpt from the *Samyukta Kaumudi* describes the king eating in his private apartments.

Attractive lady-servants carried tasty preparations to the dining hall, where the king was dining that day. The king sat between gem-studded lamp stands. In front of him were low tables decorated with the nine auspicious gems. Upon them were placed golden plates, bowls and a [special] large bowl (?). The queens served the cooked food from the new golden vessels. That day the king was served the following fare: pickles, hot rice, *toye, ghee, talila, palidya, kajjaya, sakkare-payasa, rasa*, thick fruit juice, *kattugulu*, warm milk, curds with cream and other [items]. (*SK*, IV, 9-10; p. 65)

18.7 The newly-wed couple dine together

The following passage comes from the *Dharmanatha Purana*.

After the marriage rituals were over it was time for the newly-wed couple to dine together for the first time. They sat side by side. [The lady attendants] placed before them a single gold plate and a drinking vessel studded with gems. (*DP*, XI, 172; p. 301)

They were served various dishes both sweet and savoury, such as *sanna-saravali, paradi, payasam, puri, garigé, vade, ghee, iddalige*, different types of rice preparations, soup and various vegetable preparations, all mixed with fragrant edible camphor, saffron and other spices.

The couple partook of that delicious fare [in the same dish] and enjoyed the feast. Then they washed their hands with water laced with sandal paste. After that, they chewed betel-nuts and tender leaves mixed with edible camphor and spent the time happily. (*DP*, XI, 172-8; pp. 301-3)

18.8 The king invites his mother to dinner

In this excerpt from the *Bharatesha Vaibhava Sangraha*, the queen-mother is invited to dine at her son's place.

[On the appointed day of the *vrata*, the king and all his queens fasted. At daybreak on the next day, after their usual morning routine, they worshipped their deity.] (*BVS*, XVII, 9-13; p. 229)

On that [same] day, after having fed the Jaina ascetics as usual, the king decided to invite his mother to dine in his company. (*BVS*, XVII, 25; p. 231)

So his wives went to the palace of the queen-mother, paid their respects and informed her of her son's wish. (*BVS*, XVII, 28-33; pp. 232 and 40; p. 233)

On hearing this, the queen-mother, accompanied by her daughters-in-law, left [the palace] and went to meet her son halfway. (*BVS*, XVII, 42-4; p. 234)

The king paid homage to the queen-mother and led her to his palace doors, where he washed her feet. Once inside the palace, she was honoured in various ways, as in the case of an elderly person or a deity. Then she took her meal in the company of her son and all his wives. Thereafter, the queen-mother was invited to lie on the swinging cot and was gently rocked by the king. (*BVS*, XVII, 59-66; pp. 236-7)

Later, she returned to her palace in a palanquin with hundreds of boxes containing silk garments which her son had presented to her. (*BVS*, XVII, 68, 69; p. 237)

18.9 The king dines with his wives

Dining etiquette is the theme of this excerpt from the *Bharatesha Vaibhava Sangraha*. Generally wives do not eat together with their husband, but later.

Having fed the holy men as was his daily habit, the king entered the palace in order to have his dinner. Immediately, he called a trusted person, gave him a heap of gold coins and bade him distribute them amongst the poor, the beggars and the needy.

His numerous wives were waiting for his arrival in the dining hall. On seeing him they were all pleased, particularly since he was in a pleasant mood, which prompted the wives to comment amongst themselves on this and guess its probable reason. They indulged in varied and pleasant talk, exchanging amusing ideas expressed in imaginative and pleasant ways. Hearing their talk, the king also joined in and invited them all to dine with him. The ladies strongly objected, each advancing various reasons to support their arguments, because the general custom was for them to feed their husband first and then take food on their own. But the king insisted that all of them should sit together and dine happily, at least on that day. (*BVS*, IV, 1-22; pp. 114-17)

At last the ladies agreed. They washed his feet with water from a golden jar and then led him into the inner parts of the palace. (*BVS*, IV, 22, 23, 27; p. 117)

He sat on a beautiful cushion on a seat, flanked by his wives who were seated in rows to his left and right. Some of them were seated to dine in his company while others were busy arranging and serving the food. The utensils used on this occasion were all made of gold or silver and set with diamonds and other precious stones.

A big golden plate was placed before the king. Around it were smaller bowls, and in those bowls were spoons [whose handles were] encrusted with glittering rubies. (*BVS*, IV, 28-33; p. 118)

The food was served by ladies whose anklets and rattlers produced a pleasing sound as they moved about. They carried food in serving bowls and vessels with spoons, all made of gold. (*BVS*, IV, 35-7; p. 119)

The king washed his hands using a perfumed ball, rinsed his mouth, and then sat on a wide cushioned seat. For a few moments he sat in yogic posture and closed his eyes while invoking the *siddhas*. After praying for a few moments he opened his eyes and then placed his right hand in the golden plate, into which food had been served, and offered it all to his deity with joy and devotion. (*BVS*, IV, 42-6; p. 120)

He started eating and in doing so he glanced at the wives sitting in rows. Noticing that they had not started their meal, he asked them what was wrong. Thereupon the seated queens called the serving ladies and whispered something into their ears. These [ladies] came to the king, collected a morsel of food from his hands and distributed it to the seated wives. Thus satisfied, they started eating from their plates. In this way they showed their devotion to their husband. The king consumed 32 morsels and satisfied himself. He washed his hands and the ladies did the same. The king requested the queens who were busy serving, to take their food, while those who had already dined with him were in charge of the service. While the second batch of his wives was eating, served by those of the first group, he closed his eyes in yogic contemplation. After all was over the king opened his eyes, saluted the Jina, stood up, covered his body with an upper cloth, put on his sandals and went towards the inner courtyard of the palace. There he sat on the swing, leaning against the backrest.

The ladies came in a hurry, spreading and sprinkling fragrant substances and water and waving fans. Some of them pressed his feet, while others offered him betel-nuts and leaves, all standing around him. He requested them to sit on the soft couches that were there and they indulged in pleasant games of various types and other entertainments. (*BVS*, IV, 48-61; pp. 120-2)

18.10 Food types and preparations

Popular food preparations are described in detail in the *Supa Shastra*. Since the author was a Jain, only strictly vegetarian dishes are discussed.

Preparation of wheat flour and grist: A good variety of wheat from the new harvest should be cleaned by removing stones, mud, husk and dust. It should then be soaked in fresh water for some time and then allowed to dry. Thereafter it should be pounded in a stone mortar till the husk is separated from the grains. The wheat should be completely free of husk and this can be achieved by using a winnowing basket made out of bamboo. It should then be pounded again in the mortar until white flour and grist of different grades are obtained. The grist so obtained would be of three varieties: fine or nice, medium and thick or rough. The grist and flour would be used in the preparation of a variety of dishes, mostly sweet ones. (*SuS*, I, 9, p. 6)

Chunchchu-roti: A measure of wheat grist of the fine variety should be mixed with one-sixth part of butter, a cup of milk and some water and kneaded into a dough, which should be allowed to rest for some time. Then a small quantity of dough should be flattened with the hands and baked on both sides in a hot pan. These *rotis* should be stacked one above the other. Some thick sugar syrup should be prepared and seasoned with *ghee*, edible musk and camphor. With the help of a stick, the baked *rotis* should be dipped into the syrup for some time, until it is absorbed. Thereafter they are ready to be eaten. They are known as *chunchchu-roti*. (*SuS*, I, 10; p. 7)

Milk: Boiling milk should be transferred to three small clay pots which should be kept on red hot coal. No smoke should emanate from the coals. While the milk continues to boil it should be stirred continuously to avoid it sticking to the bottom of the pots. To make it taste different it should be reduced to one-quarter of the original quantity in the first pot, one-sixth, in the second pot and one-eighth in the third. Once it is cooled it is ready for consumption. (*SuS*, II, 2; p. 54)

Curds: The inside of a clean clay pot should be smeared with the juice of a well ripened mango fruit. This process should be repeated three times. Thereafter warm milk should be poured into the pot. After some time it will turn into curds with a pleasant taste. This is known as *chuta-amra-dadhi*. (*SuS*, II, 8; p. 59)

Rice: Well-cooked and drained rice should be spread on a wide plate. To it should be added thick cream made of milk and creamy curds, salt, finely chopped garlic and ginger and ground cardamom. This is called *kattogara*. The same kind of cooked rice, when mixed with curds, salt, ground pepper, finely sliced onions, ground cardamom, chopped raw ginger and diced unripe mangoes, is called *mavina-kayi kalasu-kulu*. (*SuS*, III, 15; pp. 111-12)

Aubergines: Fully grown aubergines should be smeared with oil and then placed on the red-hot coals. When they are properly roasted, their charred skin can be removed. They should be then mashed. Add lime juice, salt, raw ginger, coriander, asafoetida and *ghee* and cook again. Put a small quantity of ground pepper, spices, chopped ginger, etcetera into boiling oil. Add this to the aubergines before serving. This dish is known as *battarika-badane-kayi*. (*SuS*, IV, 25; pp. 150-1)

Chapter 19

ROYAL WEDDINGS

Descriptions of wedding ceremonies are one of the most popular themes with the authors represented here. Looking for a suitable bride or groom, sending the invitation to the guests, sprucing up the town, setting up accommodation for the guests and their parties, and erecting the marriage pavilion where the ceremony will take place are subjects which allow the authors to dwell at length on a variety of details. Enthusiastic attention is devoted to the construction and decoration of the marriage pavilions: floors strewn with perfumed powders; walls adorned with statuettes and paintings; garlands and wreaths hanging from the ceilings; rafters encrusted with precious stones. Equally painstaking are the precise accounts of the bridal toilet and dress, the ornaments worn by the bride and groom and the processions from their respective homes to the marriage pavilion. The narratives reach a climax in the reports of the actual wedding ceremony, which vary slightly according to the authors' different religious traditions.

The chapter concludes with two accounts, one from the *Mohana Tarangini*, recording the bride's dowry, and the other from the *Dharmanatha Purana*, in which a newly married daughter, laden with gifts, leaves her parents' home to follow her husband to his country of origin.

Marriage proposals

19.1 An astrological consultation

The following passage from the *Sanatkumara Charite* describes an anxious king looking for a suitable groom for his eight daughters.

The king wished to select a groom for his eight daughters who were to be married. He sent for the astrologer and asked him to consult the relevant treatises and interpret the signs correctly. Thereupon the royal astrologer took out the book on that subject and worshipped it using sandal paste, auspicious rice, flowers and ripe fruits. Then he took out cowries and dice. Following the indications given by the cowries and the dice, and all the while offering prayers to his patron god, he opened the text. He calculated the positions of the planets, computed the time in different units, compared and corroborated all the information and eventually arrived at the prediction. He told the king that the probable groom [a prince] would appear before him within fifteen days. (*SC*, IX, 5-6; p. 86)

19.2 A formal marriage request and subsequent ceremonies

The *Shivatattva Chintamani* gives an insight into the transactions preceding the actual wedding, such as the marriage request on the part of the groom. The couple in question is none other than Shiva and Girije.

Once the groom had approved of the girl in private, he deputed some wise old men to visit her parents in order to make a formal proposal. On reaching the abode of the bride's father, they were received with due honours. Their request for the hand of the girl was readily agreed, since the proposal came from a groom of distinction. Thereupon, the negotiators returned to the groom's place and reported the happy news. The bride's father summoned the [divine] architect and in no time he built a most beautiful pavilion of untold splendour.

Gifts and tributes received from different kingdoms [as well as] auspicious objects and exquisite food were arranged with superb taste, according to the traditional order. (*S*, XV, 13-15, p. 97)

19.3 Adornment of the city and marriage pavilion

Themes such as the decoration of the city and the construction of a marriage pavilion are found in a number of texts. One of the finest descriptions is the following, drawn from the *Jivandhra Charite* by Bhaskara. Especially interesting here is the reference to the temporary accommodations reserved for the important guests attending the wedding. (This topic is further developed in a later extract, from the *Sanatkumara Charite*; see Section 19.8.)

[On the occasion of his daughter's wedding the king decided to beautify the city and to build a marriage pavilion.]

The *surya-vidhis* and *chandra-vidhis* of the city were decorated with festoons, garlands of beads and precious stones, flags and banners. In the other streets, the lower parts of the buildings and front courtyards were all embellished using fragrant and colourful musk, *sarane*, saffron, *javadi* and fragrant water.

The whole city was shining: the roofs of the buildings were adorned with golden pinnacles, the walls were embellished with paintings and arrangements of beads hung from the canopies. The pillars of the marriage pavilion were covered with gold and various kinds of precious stones, while on its walls were mirrors and bells. The ceiling of the pavilion was studded with gems and mirrors. Jewelled bands, golden chains, floral wreaths, banners, rows of flags and fly-whisks from Nepal had been used in the decoration; in short, the pavilion resembled the abode of Indra.

The air was perfumed by the fragrances exuding from the trees which had been used in its construction, such as mango, *mandara*, plantains, camphor, betel-nut and *ashoka*, and from the leaves of the lotus. A number of golden cauldrons, caskets, storage jars and other vessels containing fragrant water, sandal-paste, *sadu*, musk and other perfumes were placed there. There were cartloads of different flowers, cloths of fine quality, various kinds of jewellery and food grains. There was a [magical] statue fitted with a mechanical contrivance, which on request could fulfil any wish.

Temporary accommodations for the most distinguished guests, such as the rulers of other countries, were built in the royal gardens on the outskirts of the city. They were imaginatively decorated using the nine kinds of gems and other precious stones. (*JCB*, VII, 21-32; pp. 108-11)

19.4 Marriage pavilion I

One of the most detailed accounts of the actual process of constructing the marriage pavilion, together with its paintings, decorated floor and fragrant wreaths, is found in the *Vijayakumari Charite*. (This is followed by a description of a wedding ceremony according to the Jaina tradition; see Section 19.19.)

Artists and skilled craftsmen commenced the preparations for the function. They erected a temporary *pandal* (decorated pavilion) using bamboo poles, coconut leaves and twigs, tastefully decorating it with colourful cloths. At appropriate places they fixed golden pinnacles, mirrors, festoons, tassels, bunches, fly-whisks and the like.

At its centre was the main dais, the *vedika*. It was provided with golden pillars [at the four corners, in order to support a canopy]. [....]

At either side of the pavilion there were smaller pavilions, tastefully decorated, providing accommodation for the royal guests and other invited rulers. There were temporary sheds where food and drinks were provided for the guests.

The walls of the pavilions were embellished with paintings showing dancing girls in various postures, humorous scenes and narratives. (*VC*, I, 366-71; p. 39)

Wreaths were liberally used for decoration. These were made of various kinds of fragrant flowers and leaves, such as lotus, jasmine, *molle*, *jaji*, *sampige*, *maruga*, *mudivala*, *surahonne* and *ketaki*, which filled the pavilions with fragrance. The floor of the main pavilion was treated with perfumed substances like musk and saffron. On the floor were diagrams traced with white pearls. The whole place had been sprinkled with sweet-smelling water, [thereby] attracting swarms of bees.

A number of beautiful ladies gathered in the palace, arranged the pots, drew auspicious designs on them, filled them with sacred water and, having formed a procession, carried them on their heads [to the marriage pavilion]. At the head of the procession were other ladies who carried mirrors, pots and other auspicious objects. Further ahead, ladies were singing appropriate songs to the accompaniment of instruments of different kinds, including conches.

On reaching the pavilion, the procession circumambulated the dais from right to left, and the ladies placed in front of it the objects they were carrying. They further decorated the main pot with flowers, tender leaves, *darbha*-grass, fruits, sacred rice and *dande* (floral garlands); they also placed there *bagina* (auspicious gifts). (*VC*, I, 366-81; pp. 39-40)

19.5 Marriage pavilion II

The *Channabasava Purana* gives a detailed account of the marriage of Shiva and Girije. Here is the description of the marriage pavilion with its paintings and other decorations, as well as the buildings surrounding it, and the facilities provided for the guests.

An expert architect was entrusted with the building of the marriage pavilion. The building, once completed, was exquisite.

Its pillars were embellished with diamonds, the beams with different kinds of rubies, the capitals with gems of reddish colour. The floor had been specially treated and attractively coloured by using blue sapphires. Similarly, the central platform was decorated with sets of pure beryl. The roof-eaves at the entrance were hung with tassels, festoons and strands of pure pearls and topaz. The walls were embellished with lotus-coloured rubies. In addition, sculptures and paintings were displayed at the appropriate places; they depicted animals and birds, such as lions, tigers, elephants, *sharabha* and *bherunda*, as well as musicians and dancers in different postures. There were other types of decoration made with ribbons, flowers, festoons, tassels and banners. A number of large mirrors hung at the appropriate places. The whole pavilion was filled with fragrant smoke of burning frankincense and other perfumes. The floor was decorated with drawings made with sweet-smelling powders and pastes.

[Around the central pavilion] were a number of golden-storeyed pavilions, tents, shelters and encampments, pleasure gardens and parks, ponds and tanks filled with flowering plants and creepers, and artificial mounds and hillocks.

There were vessels with sweet-smelling grass, jars containing civet musk, troughs filled with musk, caskets of fragrant camphor, containers of fragrant pollen collected from flowers of various kinds, large boxes with all kinds of fragrances mixed together and small channels with perfumed water flowing in them. At a number of places, the architect had arranged for a number of beautiful ladies to give water to the thirsty, fruits and sweets to the hungry, and *gandha*, *kasturi* and *karpura* (fragrant substances and perfumes) to the invitees. [They were] also to hold up mirrors [for the use of the visitors], extend hospitality in various ways and to heartily welcome [the distinguished guests].

Once the work was finished, the architect was aptly honoured and rewarded with many rich gifts. (*CP*, XXXVI, 24-31; pp. 369-70)

19.6 Wall paintings

The *Sanatkumara Charite* gives numberous interesting details about the marriage pavilion, such as rows statuettes inlaid with precious stones and portrait paintings "encrusted with precious stones" embellishing its walls (*SC*, IX, 11, p. 87). In its description of the marriage pavilion, the *Ramanatha Charite* specifies the themes depicted in wall paintings.

On the walls of the pavilion were paintings of celestial couples such as gods, *kinnaras*, *kimpurushas*, and others. Narrative paintings depicted scenes from the *Ramayana* and the *Mahabharata*. (*RC*, VIII, 113-15; p. 146)

Reception and accommodation of the guests

19.7 Reception of the royal guests

The *Sanatkumara Charite* has this account of the reception of the royal parties. In the following extract, from the same source, there is a description of the other guests invited to the wedding and of their accommodation.

In the other part of the [marriage] pavilion the royal guests who had come from different kingdoms were received by the host with all due respect and honour. They were provided with bearers of umbrellas and fly-whisks [as a mark of honour] and presented with a variety of jewelled items and clothes. Finally, [they were] led into the pavilion, where they occupied special gold-plated seats in order to witness the splendid function. (*SC*, XIII, 50, p. 155)

Among the guests were learned scholars, poets, writers, priests, religious preceptors and preachers, representing all the traditional classes of Hindu society. There were young ladies, musicians and dancers engaged in various performances and panegyrists singing the praises of their masters and lords. (SC, XIII, 51-2; pp. 155-6)

19.8 Accommodation of the guests

A number of tents made of colourful cloth and embellished with the nine kinds of precious jewels were pitched in the royal grove on the outskirts of the city. As soon as the tents were ready, the king sent envoys to the other kings with letters of invitation to attend the wedding ceremonies of his daughters.

On receiving the invitation, the kings set off to take part in the celebrations. Their queens and daughters accompanied them, travelling in palanquins. Their retinue, as usual, included all the four branches of the army, a band of musicians, panegyrists and others. (*SC*, IX, 15-20; pp. 88-9)

On reaching their destination they were received by their kingly host with all due honours. He made polite enquiries about their welfare. Thereafter, he led them to the luxuriously equipped tents and accommodated them there. (*SC*, IX, 22, p. 90)

The bride and the groom prepare for the wedding ceremony

19.9 Ritual bath in sacred waters

Details of the elaborate bridal makeup can be gleaned from this passage drawn from the first chapter of the *Jivandhra Charite* by Bhaskara. This mentions the water carried from holy places used for the ritual bath of the brides and groom, and the *makarikas* (decorative patterns) drawn with fragrant paste on the bodies of the brides.

[The hero marries eight princesses.] The brides were given a bath in sacred waters, specially brought from holy places and stored in golden vessels. When the bathing ritual was over, they were dressed in the finest garments, given various ornaments studded with the nine kinds of gems as well as with pearls and their bodies were anointed with fragrant substances such a turmeric and sandal paste. Then they applied the dots to their forehead. The lady-artists skilfully drew with a fragrant paste of musk and *kesari* the traditional designs on the arms, cheeks, breasts and other parts of the brides' bodies. (*JCB*, I, 115; p. 31)

19.10 Bridal dressing

The time had come for the brides to be dressed and made up. The ladies-in-waiting fetched fragrant-smelling oil in golden bowls and applied it on the heads [and bodies] of the brides, whilst singing pleasant songs. They perfumed them with other substances such as camphor, musk, saffron-powder and others. They bathed them in sweet-smelling water poured from golden vessels to the accompaniment of propitious songs.

After the bathing rituals were over, the princesses were dressed in white garments. Their hair-buns were decorated with fragrant flowers. They wore earrings, nose-studs with pearls, hair-nets encrusted with big pearls and a dot of musk was applied to their foreheads. Their eyes were enhanced with black collyrium and figures were drawn on their cheeks. Among their ornaments were pearl necklaces and central pendants studded with the nine precious stones; on their forearms were wristlets studded with gems, and around their waists golden girdles. They wore golden chains with small rattlers which produced a light and pleasing sound when they moved about. Bodices covered their breasts, and their long hair was plaited. The ladies-in-waiting gave the groom a ceremonial bath, dressed him in new clothes and decorated him with jewellery. (*SC*, IX, 28-49; pp. 91-6)

19.11 The groom is led to the marriage pavilion

The following three extracts describe the groom and the bride on the verge of leaving their respective homes for the wedding ceremony with their escorts. The first account is from the *Padmaraja Purana*.

In his home, the groom took an elaborate bath in holy water, applied the sacred ash to his forehead, put on a garland of *rudraksha-mala*, fixed a sacred flower in his hair-bun and dressed himself with great care. With royal grace he chewed betel-nut mixed with edible camphor. He then distributed offerings to various saintly persons and finally worshipped his god. Then, accompanied by his mother [his father was no longer alive], he set out in a golden palanquin [to the place where the marriage was taking place]. (*PP*, III, 48 & 50; p. 49)

On hearing about the arrival of the groom's party, the bride's father, accompanied by his retinue, went to receive them.

The groom was invited to sit on an elephant and a procession was formed. As it moved on, a number of attendants took care to fan him, to wave fly-whisks around him and to shade him with white umbrellas. The flags and banners fluttered. More than 75 musical instruments accompanied the welcoming party. (*PP*, III, 50-3 & 56-9; pp. 50-2)

The dancing-girls displayed their art in various ways to the great delight of the bride's father and the other spectators. Along with them were bards, various classes of panegyrists, relatives and wives of the performers, as well as concubines, lovers, young and flirtatious men and young ladies attractively dressed [together with] their mothers. (*PP*, III, 65-8; pp. 53-4)

In order to gain a full sight of the procession and of the groom, the public, particularly the young ladies, the concubines and their mothers and the fulfilled and disappointed lovers, positioned themselves on the rooftops and roof pavilions, on the uppermost storeys of the buildings and on high platforms. At last the procession reached its destination. The groom descended from the elephant, entered the pavilion, paid his respects to the holy men assembled there and took his seat. (*PP*, III, 69-70; pp. 54)

19.12 The bride is led to the marriage pavilion I

The *Sanatkumara Charite* describes the bride and her entourage thus:

By now the bride was ready and was invited to take her place in a palanquin. She was escorted by ladies carrying fly-whisks, mirrors, pots, umbrellas and canopies made of tender young leaves. (*SC*, XIII, 56-7; p. 157)

Some other ladies carried *vine*-shaped musk caskets, containers of camphor, bowls of saffron-powder, sandal-paste in big shells, boxes of black makeup paste, curved amulets containing fragrant substances such as musk, small cases containing black collyrium for embellishing the eyelashes and wreaths of various kinds of flowers. There were virtuoso lady-musicians playing on string instruments of various types such as *dandige, kinnari, mukha-vine, rudra-vine, tambura, vine* and flutes. (*SC*, XIII, 56-9; p. 157)

All of them walked along with the palanquin of the bride. On reaching the marriage pavilion she came out of the palanquin and entered the hall, accompanied by her associates and attendants. She then stood on the plank prescribed for the function, which was placed at the side of the groom [who was already there]. (*SC*, XIII, 60; p. 158)

19.13 The bride is led to the marriage pavilion II

And finally, this account from Bhaskara's *Jivandhra Charite*:

When the dressing was over, she was made to look at herself in a mirror. As usual she was shown the *manimayadarati* and *upparati* (auspicious lights) to ward off the effects of evil spirits. Then she was invited to sit in a palanquin studded with the nine kinds of gems. With her were the lady-assistants carrying fans, umbrellas decorated with precious stones and other things. A party of musicians headed the convoy. (*JCB*, VIII, 24-6; p. 125)

The ladies carried with them all that the bride might require: fans, fly-whisks, sandals, pouches, spittoons, mirrors. As they moved on with coquettish gait, the ornaments they wore produced an attractive jingling sound. (*JCB*, VIII, 30-42; pp. 126-9)

The wedding ceremony

19.14 Wedding ceremony I

This description of a wedding ceremony from the *Jaimini Bharata*, although relatively simple, contains a number of themes such as the procession accompanying the groom, the gifts presented to the groom by the bride's family and the various ceremonies celebrated in the four days following the actual wedding day. All of these are elaborated upon and expanded by later poets.

The bridegroom arrived in a palanquin accompanied by a long procession of torch-bearers, *sumangaliyaru* singing songs appropriate for the occasion, a number of young ladies carrying auspicious objects such as pots and mirrors and a band of musicians playing music befitting the occasion. On reaching the marriage pavilion, the groom was first received by the *sumangaliyaru* waving the auspicious lights around him.

The mother of the bride, as a sign of welcome, washed the feet of the groom with water, offered him a drink of honey and milk, [the father being absent], and welcomed him according to the custom. Thereupon, the priests that were present asked the groom about his family and lineage, to which questions he aptly replied. At the appropriate moment, the brother [of the bride] arranged for the cloth screen which was held between the couple to be removed and a mixture of cumin seeds and jaggery was showered on their heads. The [couple] was invited to stand on the *mettakki* (heap of auspicious rice) and a cotton thread was wound around them; water was poured onto the palms of the groom.

While the priests were chanting the auspicious *mantras*, the bride took a garland of *mandara* flowers and laid it around the neck of the groom. At this point they became husband and wife, and he took hold of her hand. Afterwards, they proceeded to the platform where other rituals such as the *homa* were performed. The *sumangaliyaru* waved the *arati* lights, which were placed on golden trays around the couple. Then the brother of the bride presented the groom with a great number of cows, buffaloes, horses, elephants, chariots, bedsteads, mattresses, various vehicles, perfumes, young and bright female servants, silk clothes, ornaments, necklaces studded with diamonds and the like. Finally, he gave valuable gifts to the priests, brahmins, relatives, friends, poets, singers, actors, dramatists, court panegyrists, musicians and many others, according to their position and status. At night he hosted a splendid feast for the relatives and the newly wed couple. After pleasing everybody, he retired to rest contented.

On the next day, the newly wedded couple were taken out in a procession. A new pavilion was built and decorated with colourful banners and fluttering flags and embellished with tassels and bunches of diamonds and gems. On that morning the couple were bathed ceremonially in fragrant saffron-water. Their foreheads were adorned with *basigas.* The *sumangaliyaru* sang appropriate songs, while the priests chanted *mantras.* The rituals and celebrations continued for three days. The fourth day, called *nagavali,* was the last day of the marriage festivities. Once the ceremonies were completed, the king hosted a magnificent feast and made gifts to all the relatives and others guests and priests who attended the celebrations. Flowers, fruits, betel-nuts, sandal, musk, *javadi,* clothes, ornaments and gold coins were liberally distributed. (*JB,* XXXI, 14-25; pp. 382-5)

19.15 Padmaraja's wedding celebrations

The marriage of Padmaraja is vividly described in the third book of the *Padmaraja Purana.* This full-fledged description of a marriage ceremony contains numerous details on the embellishment of the town, the building of a marriage pavilion, the attire of the bride and the groom and the reception of guests. Especially interesting is a pointed reference to the Virashaiva doctrine (*PP,* III, 67-8). Here, the father of the bride, true to Virashaiva tenets, proceeds with the wedding ceremony without taking into account the traditional times, since, according to the Virashaivas, any time is auspicious.

[Having decided to celebrate the marriage of his daughter with his sister's son], the minister gave orders to decorate the whole town and to build a marriage pavilion. Its floor was covered with colourful spreads and embellished with drawings made with white powder and flowers. Beautiful arches were set up at various places, its parts enlivened with flags, banners, festoons of tender leaves and flowers, vividly coloured paintings and the like. The minister inspected the completed work and, pleased with it, suitably rewarded all those involved. He arranged for additional service personnel, such as *sumangaliyaru* and concubines, to attend at the ceremonies. A community feeding, organized with great care and devotion, was part of the celebrations. (*PP,* III, 39-40, p. 47) [....]

The father of the bride, [who was] a true follower of Virashaivism, was persuaded that any time [of the day] would be equally auspicious. He summoned his daughter, who was of immaculate character, and invited her to pay her respects to the holy persons. Then he took her hands and put them into those of the groom, thus sealing their union. The *sumangaliyaru* came forward, waved the *arati* lights before the couple and blessed them to the sound of auspicious music. Then the couple stood up, paid homage to all the guests and, in return, were blessed by them. They distributed money, jewellery, clothes, floral garlands and perfumes to all the guests and took leave of them.

Finally, they worshipped Shiva, took the *prasada,* chewed *tambula* and left happily. (*PP,* III, 67-78; pp. 54-6)

19.16 A divine wedding

The *Sivatattva Chintamani* describes the wedding of Shiva and Girije.

A number of important persons, their wives, and learned men were in the groom's party, which was headed by musicians playing loudly on various instruments.

On reaching the place of the bride's father, the groom's party was welcomed with due honours. The groom was offered the *basiga* and entered the marriage pavilion. In the pavilion were numerous girls, *sumangaliyaru,* both youthful and mature, who carried in their hands auspicious pots and mirrors and who sang.

The priests were discussing among themselves and calculating the appropriate moment [for performing the ceremony]. Following the tradition, both bride and groom were standing on heaps of rice and between them was a cloth screen.

At the proper moment, amidst the loud sound of percussion and wind instruments, including the flute and conch, the screen was removed. At that divine moment, the groom, with both his hands, showered cumin seeds mixed with brown sugar over the head of the bride and the bride [did the same] over the head of the groom to the great joy of all those gathered there. Next, the couple showered pearls on each other's head. This added to the happiness of the bride's father who presented the groom with new clothes of fine quality, gems, diamonds, money, cows, servants and others. The newly wed couple were then invited to sit on a raised golden platform. The elders, learned men, priests and others blessed them and wished them well by showering rice over their heads. At the end [of all the remaining ceremonies], the bride and her husband were led to their home amidst the chanting of joyful songs and praises. (*S*, XV, 13-29; pp. 97-101)

19.17 Wedding ceremony II

The actual wedding ceremony and the rituals of the following days are narrated in this brief excerpt from the *Sanatkumara Charite.*

Then the ceremony began. The father of the bride washed the feet of the son-in-law, while his queen poured water from a golden vessel. He then performed the offering of water, following the prescribed ritual of self-purification which made him fit to offer presents to the groom. The father gave him ornaments and clothes, while the priests offered him honey mixed in milk.

At the appointed propitious moment the father of the bride gave his daughter away and then he blessed both the bride and groom by strewing auspicious rice on their heads. At the same time, the *sumangaliyaru* waved the *arati* lamps and sung auspicious songs. (*SC*, XIII, 61-5; pp. 158-9)

The needy persons who were assembled there were given jewels, ornaments and clothes by the king [and then dismissed]. On the fourth day, there was yet another function called *nagavali.* (*SC*, XIV, 1-2; p. 160)

On the next day a marriage feast was arranged. It had been organized in a grand style A large variety of dishes, sweets, vegetables, milk preparations and others were served liberally. (See Section 18.4)

At the end [of the feast], the father of the bride presented his newly wed daughter with hundreds of lady-attendants and a quantity of precious jewels, ornaments and clothes. Then he affectionately hugged his son-in-law, took his daughter's hand and placed it into that of the groom. Finally he blessed them, took leave of all and returned to his own palace. (*SC*, XIV, 25; p. 166)

19.18 Royal wedding in a military camp

Among the many accounts of wedding ceremonies in the *Bharatesha Vaibhava Sangraha*, the following one takes place in a very unusual setting as the king marries one of his many brides while on a military expedition.

[In the course of his campaign the king had married hundreds of ladies, the daughters of the kings who submitted to his rule.]

The military camp was decorated and suitably prepared for the celebration of this prestigious marriage. A temple for the Jina was built especially for that occasion. The ceremony was conducted with great pomp. First the Jina was worshipped, then the learned persons and other guests were fed and given presents of gold jewellery, cloths and betel-leaves mixed with edible camphor and sandal paste. (*BVS*, XXXVI, 1-2, p. 341-2)

At the appointed time, the bride and the groom stood on two heaps of rice, opposite each other, separated by a temporary cloth screen. While the ladies were singing the appropriate songs and the brahmins were chanting the *mangalashataka*, the screen was removed. Then the bride and the groom poured rice on each other's heads and exchanged floral garlands. (*BVS*, XXXVII, 2-7, pp. 348 & 349)

The brother of the bride poured the sacred milk to solemnize the marriage. As part of the function, the groom took the bride by her hand and proceeded around the sacred fire. (*BVS*, XXXVII, 9-10; p. 349)

Thereafter, the king bade farewell to the subordinate kings, ministers and all the others who had assembled on that occasion. Holding the bride by the hand, he entered his [private] palace in a contented mood. (*BVS*, XXXVII, 12; p. 349)

19.19 A Jaina wedding ceremony

From the *Vijayakumari Charite* comes this account of a wedding ceremony and the celebrations which took place in the following days.

At the crucial moment while the musicians were playing auspicious music and the Jaina priests chanting the appropriate *mantras*, the cloth screen was removed; the bride and the groom stood facing each other beaming with happiness. Thereupon, the groom applied a dot of sandal paste to the forehead of the bride [following the Jaina practice], while the bride put a floral garland around the neck of the groom. Then the father of the bride joined the palms of the couple and poured *dhare* on them. Finally, the couple showered handfuls of auspicious rice over each other's head. Under the direction of the Jaina priests, the newly wed couple performed the *homa* according to the Jaina custom.

On completion, they paid their respects to the fire-altar, priests, teachers, elders and relatives and received their blessings in return. Then they presented the *muttaideyar* with auspicious objects. (*VC*, I, 403-14; pp. 43-4) [....]

On the next day, the *nagavali, shantika* and *poushtika* rituals were celebrated. Then, at a special place, the Jaina priests drew five diagrams of different colours surrounded by an eight-petalled lotus flower. In addition, they drew the palm of a hand, a bull, a horse and other symbols, invoked the nine deities to descend [into the diagrams] and performed the appropriate rituals. [Afterwards], the couple went to the temple of a Jina where they prayed and paid their respects to the deity, the preceptor, and were blessed. They then returned to their palace amidst resounding music.

The couple gave presents to the learned persons, relatives, subordinate rulers and all the other guests who then, happy and contented, returned to their respective places. Thereafter, the couple spent their time joyfully, enjoying a comfortable life. (VC, I, 416-29; pp. 44-7)

19.20 The bride's dowry

An account of a bride's dowry is given in the following passage drawn from the *Mohana Tarangini*, in which the goddess Rati and the god Kantu move into their own home.

Before their departure, the couple were given all the necessary articles for setting up a new home: gold-laced silk garments, upper garments, jewellery, necklaces of pearls of high quality, golden headgear, jewelled ornament to be worn in the hair-bun, cots with silver legs, golden three-footed stands, soft mattresses, chairs encrusted with gems, jewelled [embroidered?] carpets, pillows, garments of silk, big bowls of metal, plates, small pots of metal, small bowls, mirrors, standing lamps with *hamsa*-motif, an ordinary standing lamp, oil container, pots for carrying water, metal vessels for boiling water, cauldrons for bathing, kitchen utensils of various sizes, pulses and other grains of various kinds, a palanquin, a miniature pavilion encrusted with gems [probably for the *puja* room], fly-whisks, spittoons, female attendants, an elephant, a horse, milching cows, milching buffaloes and others. Then the couple were made to sit on a richly-caparisoned elephant. The party started [probably after sunset] in a procession. On either side were persons carrying lit torches of different kinds. A large number of female attendants followed the party. Before setting off on the journey, the couple were shown the customary *arati* lamps by the *sumangaliyaru*, some of whom sang auspicious songs fit for the occasion. A band of musicians playing different instruments headed the procession. Behind them was a group of learned brahmins carrying their gifts of gold, coins, silk garments, upper garments with golden borders and others; occasionally they chanted *mantras*.

There were also attendants carrying fly-whisks, umbrellas, banners of different colours and flags of different types. The procession passed through the main streets of the town along which were many buildings. Most of these were storeyed and had roof terraces and pavilions from which young ladies watched the progress of the parade. Every now and then, on reaching important landmarks, the procession stopped in order to allow the dancers, musicians and singers to display their talents so as to please and entertain the assembled crowds.

On arrival at their residence, the couple was assisted to alight from the elephant. Again there was the customary waving of the auspicious *arati* lamps and showing of *nivali*. Thereupon the couple entered the house accompanied by their female attendants. All these ceremonies were performed in accordance with the prescriptions. The building had been lavishly and tastefully decorated for that occasion. (*MT*, XV, 13-38; pp. 219-20)

19.21 Bestowing of gifts on a daughter

The *Dharmanatha Purana* gives an account of the presents a king bestows on his daughter on the occasion of her leaving her own home.

One day, as the young prince was seated with his wife on a golden throne, a messenger arrived at the gate of the palace. He had come with a letter from his father. He wore the characteristic white upper garment. From the palace gate he sent word to the prince of his arrival. (*DP*, XII, 2, and prose p. 304)

On being shown in, he rushed into the prince's presence, sat at his feet and informed him about the welfare of his parents. He then handed him the letter that contained the happy news that he should return to his palace immediately. (*DP*, XII, 3-4; pp. 304-5)

After having read the letter, the prince gave detailed instructions to the commanders of his army to return to their own country with the whole army and its equipment. He discussed his plans with the king, his father-in-law and his wife. Then the king gave the bridal presents to his newly married daughter. First he requested a number of ladies-in-waiting to accompany his daughter. They had to accomplish different tasks such as carrying fans, pouches, spittoons, mirrors, plates, cooking pots and pans, sandals and others. In short, they had to perform all of the 72 kinds of service. (*DP*, XII, 4 & prose; p. 305)

The king presented her with silk clothes of different varieties and ornaments studded with all kinds of precious stones. He also gave her a large number of choicest elephants and horses and, in addition, a retinue of female singers, actors, witty speakers, good debators, comedians, clothes and ornaments. (*DP*, XII, 5-7, p. 305)

After the couple had been blessed by the father and mother of the bride, they set out at the propitious moment accompanied by auspicious singing and chanting of hymns and the music of trumpets, kettle-drums, big drums and other instruments, all playing at full volume. Rice and pearls were poured over their heads as a blessing, and the parents of the bride accompanied them for some time. (*DP*, XII, prose, pp. 305-6)

At one stage, the father-in-law stopped and approached his son-in-law, requesting him to take proper care of his daughter. Thereafter, he and the queen approached their daughter and gave her the appropriate advice on how to take care of her husband, his parents and all the others in their family. After that they returned to their palace with a heavy heart. (*DP*, XII, 8-10 & prose, p. 306)

Chapter 20

ART AND ARTISTS

As mentioned in a Chapter 10, numerous talented artists were to be found among the queens and other ladies of the king's private houshold. This chapter focuses on the varied artistic activities of the court. It opens with an exceptionally long passage from the *Bharatesha Vaibhava Sangraha* highlighting the literary gifts of the queens, in which a concert is given, a new poetic work is recited before the king and a queen displays her musical virtuosity on the *vine*. An insight into literary patronage is given in the excerpt from the *Karnataka Krishnaraya Bharata*, where Krishnadevaraya commissions a poetic work. Detailed information on actors, musicians and dancers is found in the excerpts from the *Pampasthana Varnanam*, which describe an entertainment at the court of Shiva, and in similar passages from the *Sanatkumara Charite* and *Amalabasava Charite*. The second part of the chapter deals with paintings, especially portraits. The extracts briefly mention murals as well as paintings on cloth.

Literature, music and dance

20.1 Artistic activities of the queens

Although interspersed with lighter passages, this narrative drawn from the *Bharatesha Vaibhava Sangraha* gives an insight into the formal, almost ritualized courtly life of the time.

One day the king got up, as usual, at an early hour of the day and worshipped the Jaina prophets. He then moved to *meru-soudha* (upper apartment), which was decorated with gold and jewels, and granted [private?] audience. In the palace precinct there was also a pavilion studded with the nine kinds of gems, with the golden throne where the king sat in dazzling splendour [in public audience?]. Female attendants flanked the king. They looked like statues, carrying the water vessels, fly-whisks, caskets and spittoons that the king might require. Then, a learned old lady, the *pandite* (teacher) of the king's wives, appeared with folded hands before him, requesting his permission to present the day's programme. Soon all the queens, some thousands of them, appropriately dressed and bejewelled, ascended to the *meru-soudha* carrying presents for their beloved husband. (*BVS*, V, 1-7; pp. 123-4) [....]

The king could hear their approach by the tinkling of their anklets and girdles. (*BVS*, V, 19; p. 125)

The queens, who varied in complexion, stature and gait, had different characters, talents and dispositions; with folded hands they paid their respects to the king and stood according to the hierarchical order. One after the other they presented their husband with different "gifts of love" that they had brought with them. Among these [gifts] were flowers such as nymphaeas, *champaka*, jasmine, the sword-shaped *ketaki* and fresh mango leaves; there were also rubies, pearls, gems, etcetera. Occasionally, the king and the *pandite* made fun of one queen or another, particularly those who were the most shy, when they appeared before him bearing the gifts. Then, with a sign of the hand, he indicated that they should sit, to which they readily complied. He glanced at those who could sing and they began. They displayed their virtuosity by performing in various modes, one tune following the other. Some of the queens accompanied the melodious songs on various stringed instruments such as the *dandige* and *kinnari*. The king not only appreciated the concert, but also, in the course of it, jokingly teased them. (*BVS*, V, 20-63; pp. 125-32)

At the end of the programme, he summoned all the queens and to show his appreciation presented them with clothes and ornaments. The gratified musicians respectfully touched his feet and sat aside in orderly rows, making room for other performers. (*BVS*, V, 65; p. 132)

While the king was still seated among his wives, musing over the concert which had just finished, one of the singers went to the *pandite* and whispered something in her ear. Thereupon, the old lady briskly rose, approached the king with folded hands and announced that a newly composed work was about to follow, should he be gracious enough to listen to it. The king wanted to know who was the author, what was its subject, who had revised it and so on. The *pandite* replied that it was neither composed by an outsider, nor was it about an outsider and there was no one who could correct it. [This was because] it had been composed [by one of the queens] in his household, it was about him and could be corrected only by him. The pleased king asked the *pandite* to announce the name of the author of the work. She replied that on the previous day, a queen, Kusumaji, was playfully reciting her composition to her pet parrot. It was overheard by another queen, Sumaji, who lived in the neighbouring apartment, and she quickly memorized it. While Sumaji was reciting this work to Amritavachaka, her own parrot, she was in turn heard by another queen, Amaraji, who happened to visit her. So what had been originally composed by Kusumaji was set in a proper form by Sumaji and finally was written [down] by Amaraji.

The king happily agreed to listen to the poem and requested the *pandite* to go back to her seat. At that point another beautiful queen came forward with the new book in her hands and sat in front of the king.

Suddenly, just before the recitation commenced, the original poet, the bashful queen Kusumaji, stood up with folded hands and told the king that she had to leave immediately for her palace on the pretext of some religious function. The king readily agreed to her going away and offered her his golden wristlet to wear in the course of the religious ceremony. In so doing, he firmly held the hand that the queen had stretched out for the wristlet and pulled her towards him, questioning her about the religious function of which he knew nothing. In so doing, he forced her to sit by his side [in appreciation of her artistic talent]. He told her that the poem which she had recited to her pet parrot for pleasure had been overheard and enjoyed by other ladies. He assured her that he understood her feelings of embarrassment and her wish to leave the gathering, because what she had told her parrot in the privacy of her apartment had been made public. He then told her that since there was no outsider present and that they were all one [family], there was no need for her to be shy and he requested her to sit near him. (*BVS*, VI, 1-16; pp. 133-5)

At this point the *pandite* intervened saying that Kusumaji was embarrassed, particularly because the king had held her hand and made her sit near him publicly, and suggested that she should be allowed to sit with the other ladies, to which the king agreed.

Then he ordered the reading to start. The reader placed the work on the book rest, untied the fastened cord and held the delicate leaves in her left hand. She tuned her *dandige* with the right hand, while reciting the text in a harmonious manner: it was as if a *koyil* bird was singing. The work was filled with praise, enumerating the noble and sublime qualities of the king who kept all his wives contented and happy. It also described his handsome features and his apparel with a number of figures of speech which entranced the public. At the end of the work Kusumaji, the original author, had requested the parrot not to reveal anything to anyone and further she asked whether it liked the poem or not. The bird had replied that it was not clever enough to assess the king's qualities, particularly from a queen's point of view. (*BVS*, VI, 19-56; pp. 135-41)

The parrot, however, assured the author that all she had described was true and befitting to such a person as the king, renowned as he was for his noble character. [The bird] concluded by saying that the king and all his queens were like a necklace of choicest gems strung together to form a harmonious ensemble; obviously this was the result of divine blessings. (*BVS*, VII, 1-6; p. 142)

After repeating the parrot's words, the reciter requested the king to correct any mistakes and closed the book. The king, who was greatly pleased, was thinking silently on the poem, which had great literary merit. (*BVS*, VII, 29-30; p. 146, VIII, 1; p. 147)

The ladies, however, fearing the criticism of the king, attempted to disown the authorship of the work, arguing amongst themselves. (*BVS*, VIII, 2-4; p. 147)

Eventually, the king broke the silence and said that their work was good; he appreciated it and they should now ask for the reward they wanted. The queens were not keen on ornaments, since they had already enough of them. He then offered something special. Thereupon, two of them stood up, made a sign to the others, approached the king and prostrated themselves before him; the others followed. The surprised king looked at the *pandite*. She then explained that, being noble wives, they did not like the king to give away his own ornaments as rewards and, at the same time, did not want to disobey his order. (*BVS*, VIII, 7-14; pp. 148-9)

At the suggestion of the *pandite*, he smilingly asked them to rise, and they obliged. He then devised a clever plot: he called two of them on the pretext of having a private conversation; when they approached, he made them flank him and hugged them both at the same time as a token of affection. On seeing this, the other queens, including Kusumaji, laughed heartily along with the king. Then all of them had a good time, indulging in witty conversation and commenting on the incident at length.

At last he spoke to the *pandite*, asking her whether it would be more appropriate for him to dine alone in that palace, or in [the palace] of Kusumaji, the author of that day's literary creation. (*BVS*, VIII, 17-37; pp. 149-52)

The *pandite*, although aware of the wish of the king, answered for fun that it would be more proper to dine in the *devara-griha* (sanctuary) of his patron deity. The answer was obviously not the one expected by the king and Kusumaji. Sensing that, the *pandite* closed her eyes for a short time to think of the proper course of action. She proposed that it would be better if the king would dine in Kusumaji's palace that day. This was readily agreed by all. The *pandite* and all the other queens speedily sent Kusumaji home to make the necessary arrangements. (*BVS*, VIII, 17-46; pp. 152-3)

Thereafter, the *pandite* and other members of the royal retinue, consisting of musicians, staff-bearers, service personnel and others, left the palace.

After all had departed, the king closed his eyes and started meditating. In that posture he appeared like a skilled ascetic. In spite of being an emperor married to so many beautiful and talented queens, he was detached from the material world and was not affected by its pleasures. (*BVS*, VIII, 56-62; p. 155)

While the king was thus seated, the time-keeper blew the conch. On hearing it, the king opened his eyes and prayed to his deity. Then the female servants reminded him that it was time to meet the religious mendicants and feed them as was his custom. He descended from the upper storeys of his palace, met the mendicants, led them to his palace, treated them to various cooked dishes and then took leave of them.

Once he had fulfilled the various prescribed duties, he was led to the palace of queen Kusumaji by her younger sister, Makarandaji, a very young girl, who was expected to become a woman in about six month's time. She was not only beautiful and intelligent, but had been taught how to cultivate her looks. The king was resting on the seat of the swing when she arrived, accompanied by some female attendants. From the golden plate carried by one of her companions she took sandal paste, betel-leaves with nuts and auspicious rice and offered them to the king, while intimating that the dining arrangements were completed and he could go to her house. At that point, the king started a witty conversation, saying there was no point in visiting Kusumaji's house immediately and it would have been better to go there in six month's time. The innuendo was immediately grasped by Makarandaji who promptly replied that the invitation was to visit her sister and that he should not tease her in this manner. They continued such flirtatious conversation for some more time. Eventually, since she insisted, he got up, put on his glittering sandals and walked to Kusumaji's palace accompanied by the young girl and other attendants.

The queen, informed by her entourage that the king had arrived, came out and received him by waving the lights before him and spreading a silk cloth upon which he could walk. When she was about to touch his feet he lifted her up affectionately. After that she washed his feet with her own hands, wiping them with the end of her garment.

As soon as he entered the palace, the pet parrot of the queen announced that the master had arrived and that he should be welcomed and provided with a seat appropriate to his rank. The king, appreciating the bird's speech, sat on the seat which was placed there. Then the bird went on talking and enquired about the welfare of the king, asking why he was not visiting the palace of his mistress more frequently and so on. It even went so far to announce that now that [the king] was there, his legs would be tied and he would not be allowed to return to his palace. The king, smiling, listened to this chatter. The bird then went on to describe the excellence of his mistress, the queen, as a source of pleasure and enjoyment for the king, in witty and metaphoric figures of speech. (*BVS*, IX, 1-26; pp. 157-62)

Then it was the turn of the king, Kusumaji and her sister to engage in an entertaining conversation filled with double meanings. The young sister of the queen added to the fun with her amusing remarks and youthful charm. Seeing that the king and Makarandaji were attracted to each other, Kusumaji suggested sending for her father in order to arrange for their betrothal and marriage. At this, all three rejoiced. (*BVS*, IX, 37-80; pp. 162-8)

After this happy exchange of ideas, Kusumaji requested the king to proceed to the upper apartments to dine. He went up holding the hand of the queen. (*BVS*, IX, 84-5; p. 169)

On arrival, the king saw that the queen had tastefully decorated the apartment in honour of his visit. There were many flowers of various kinds, colourful hangings and screens. Gems and pearls had been lavishly used in the hangings, festoons and fillets. The floor was coloured with saffron-coloured bands and designs. Decorative *rangavalli*, too, enlivened the floor decoration. On seeing all this, the king Ahen praised the queen for her intelligence and artistic taste.

The queen then dismissed everybody, except for one lady who was to stay outside the door to signal the time. Then she closed the door and sat near the king. (*BVS*, X, 1-12; pp. 170-1)

She served personally various kinds of cooked food, including rice, vegetables, sweet preparations, *ghee* and beverages, all in golden plates and bowls.

The bell at the door rang to indicate the time. On hearing it, the king placed his hand in the dining plate and devoutly offered all those items to his deity before starting to eat. While he was partaking of the various preparations, Kusumaji stood close to him and waved a fan, sometimes to reduce the heat of the steaming dishes and at other times to make him feel comfortable. She understood his wishes and requirements without being told, serving him according to his complete satisfaction. She served food, every now and then insisting and pleading, even though he was reluctant. (*BVS*, X, 15-24; pp. 172-3)

At the end of the sumptuous meal, he washed his hands, offered prayers to his deity, took his upper-cloth and rose. He followed the queen up the steps which led to the upper apartments of the palace. On the upper storey of the palace they entered a secret chamber which was in the centre [of the apartments] where he stretched out comfortably on a soft bedstead in the shape of a swan. There the queen offered him betel-nuts and leaves, sprinkled cool fragrant water on him, applied collyrium to the lids of his eyes, as well as sandal paste, and gently fanned him. After some time, she sat pressing his feet. Seeing that, the king asked her to have her dinner and return. After she had gone, the king, feeling drowsy after the meal, closed his eyes and slept.

In the lower apartments, the queen ate her food from the unwashed plate on which the king had dined. Then she washed her hands, and stretched on a swinging cot, which was gently rocked by her assistants, where she had a short nap to digest the sumptuous food she had eaten. When she woke up she looked at herself in the mirror and arranged her coiffure and the dot on her forehead in proper order. She applied over her body such fragrant-smelling substances as *kasturi*, *punugu* and *javadi* and placed flowers in her hair-bun. She chewed betel-leaves and nuts to redden her mouth. Then, with some more betel-leaves in her left hand, she joined the king. While approaching the king's chamber she took care not to create any noise with her leg ornaments, so as not to disturb his sleep. (*BVS*, X, 27-38; pp. 173-5)

The king, however, was already awake after his short nap. He paid homage to his deity, wiped his eyes and removed the cloth covering his face. [The queen] then approached the king gracefully and gave him scented water to freshen his mouth and tender betel-leaves and nuts for chewing. All along, they conversed wittily and enjoyed teasing each other. After having fun for some time, the queen started massaging the legs of the king. (*BVS*, X, 40-53; pp. 175-7)

She then took a *vine* and played upon it, exhibiting her virtuosity in singing. She played in many classical modes and sang a number of tunes, pleasing the king with her masterly talent. After enjoying that music to his heart's content, the king asked her to stop. She put the instrument aside and prostrated herself at his feet respectfully. This gave the king the opportunity to hold her and embrace her lovingly. Thereafter, he made love to her, lying on a soft bed made from swan's feathers. After having rested for some time, they got up, washed, put on fresh clothes, had cool drinks and chewed *vileya*, while reminiscing on the time they spent together. At an opportune moment, the queen proposed that he should attend a performance staged that night in the same palace by professional dancers. (*BVS*, XI, 1-35; pp. 178-83)

The king readily agreed. Before leaving the chamber he presented the queen with all the ornaments he was wearing, except the earring made of gold and pearls. He also gave gifts to the queen's sister and the other attendants. By that time it was evening; the king stood up, bathed and went upstairs to pray and meditate. (*BVS*, XI, 1-38; pp. 178-83)

20.2 Krishnadevaraya commissions a poem

The theme of literary patronage is touched upon in the *Karnataka Krishnaraya Bharata*.

One day when Krishnadevaraya was seated in audience, the court poets presented the great epic poem *Bharata*. The pleased king looked at all the poets assembled there and then summoned the poet Timmanna of the Bharadvaja *gotra*, honouring him with a lavish gift of new clothes and ornaments. Thereafter, he requested him to compose the *dasa-parva* (remaining chapters) of the *Bharata* which Kumaravyasa, the renowned poet of the first ten chapters, had left unfinished. This would continue the work of Kumaravyasa, in the same way as the river Ganga continues to flow after the confluence with the Yamuna. The proposal was readily accepted and once the work was completed the poet dedicated it to Krishnadevaraya. (*KKB*, Pithika Sandhi, 24-8; pp. 4-5)

20.3 Musicians, dancers and actors

Music, dance and acting were among the most popular forms of courtly entertainment, as shown in the following six excerpts. The first, from the *Bharatesha Vaibhava Sangraha*, contains the description of a theatre with its decorations and wall paintings, probably one of the many buildings in the palace compound.

In the evening the king spent some time in

meditation. Then a lady attendant approached and told him that it was time [for the performance]. He stood up, came down from the upper apartment and went to the theatre, which was called Vardhanavati. On entering, he sat on a high throne. (*BVS*, XII, 1-4; p. 185)

The theatre was tastefully adorned with a profusion of precious stones. It looked most colourful, and was sweet-smelling since the drawings [on the floor] were made with fragrant substances. On the walls were paintings of handsome men and beautiful women in various postures and expressions. Some of the ladies were shown teaching their pet parrots, playing the *vine*, performing some play and so on. There were also finely-drawn images of the gods and other celestial beings with faces expressing various feelings.

As soon as the king entered and sat on his seat, the artists and other performers, all well dressed and perfumed, entered the theatre.

Princes, scholars, connoisseurs, critics, men of great taste and refinement, subordinate kings, poets and intellectuals were in the audience. All paid homage to the king and sat in rows. Ministers, elderly citizens, officers of the secret service, harlots, actors, dancers, singers and other performers also paid homage to the king before taking their seats in the rows.

Then the chief minister, Buddhisagara, who was quite aged, very learned, wise and efficient in fulfilling his duties, came to pay his respects to the king and then took his seat. The queens and the other ladies of the harem were seated on either side of the king, concealed by screens which had openings through which they could peep.

There were staff-bearing attendants who ushered in the general public and requested them to maintain silence. Other attendants, following the instructions of the king, distributed betel-leaves and nuts together with edible camphor to the seated public according to their status and position.

The orchestra, after tuning their instruments, started playing. When the required pitch was reached, the singers sang in various modes accompanied by instruments. They pleased their king by singing, first of all, the praises of the (Jaina) deities and prophets. Then they moved to the sides and their tunes were picked up and continued by the actors standing behind the curtain. The dancing master appeared before the king and respectfully prostrated himself. He wore a turban whose end-frill was prominently displayed and an upper cloth to cover his body. He modestly said to the king that he had trained two of his daughters, Netramohini and Chittamohini, to the best of his abilities and that he [the king] would be pleased to see them perform; he then he folded his hands.

The moment the curtain slid aside, those two beautiful young girls performed various dances to the accompaniment of vocal and instrumental music. They impressed the king and the rest of the theatre audience. (*BVS*, XII, 1-34, 46; pp. 185-9 & 191)

The king, as a token of appreciation, liberally gave valuable ornaments, jewels and the like to the two dancers, their master and others of the troupe. Moreover, as usual, he gave presents to the spectators too, according to their rank and status. Finally, he bid farewell to all except the chief minister.

The next dance-drama programme was to be performed only in the presence of the king, the queens and the chief minister. (*BVS*, XII, 49-52; pp. 191-2)

The actresses were proficient in all the sixteen types of classical performing arts. They appeared before the king from behind a curtain made of strings of pearls. As they were moving gracefully, their wristlets, waist-girdles and anklets produced pleasant sounds. There were sixteen performers [in all]. (*BVS*, XIII, 1-4; p. 193)

When everything was ready, the *tambura* player appeared and, standing before the backdrop, paid his respects to the king and played skilfully on his instrument to indicate the commencement of the performance. One of his companions played on the *avuja*, while the artists accompanied him in the same rhythm, producing a pleasant harmony by shaking their anklets.

The stage-master then came forward and, stopping the music for a moment, paid his respects to the king by prostrating himself before him. He had a beard; he wore earrings and a lower garment, an upper cloth tied around his waist and a big turban on his head. (*BVS*, XIII, 6-8; pp. 193-4)

Of the sixteen performers, two played the *titti* and the *mukhavine*, while the remainder sang in various modes with variations and embellishments to the tunes, to please the king. (*BVS*, XIII, 10,13 & 14-20; pp. 194-5)

All the sixteen artists were young and beautiful. Each was differently dressed with costly clothes, ornaments and pearls. When the curtain rose they saluted the audience with flowers in their hands. (*BVS*, XIII, 23 & 26-7; p. 196)

They moved about while singing, forming different groups, to the delight and admiration of the king. At one point, fifteen of them retreated to one side, while one, Mangalavati, danced to the accompaniment of the instrumental music. This first dancer [then] retired while, one after another, the remaining fifteen exhibited their virtuosity in dancing. (*BVS*, XIII, 28-40; pp. 197-8)

The king bade them stop by raising his hand after

witnessing the dance performances to his great pleasure [for some time]. (*BVS*, XIII, 59; p. 201)

The stage-master and the musicians retired from the king's presence. When everybody else had left, the king wished to reward the artists who, incidentally, also belonged to his household. All his wives rushed into his presence from behind the screen. (*BVS*, XIII, 67-8, p. 202; XIV, 1; p. 203)

Then he summoned his artist-wives. They were very tired after the strenuous performances and on coming forward they stood wiping perspiration off their faces, etcetera. (*BVS*, XIV, 4-7; pp. 203-4)

On seeing them, the king praised their acts and promised to reward them whenever they wanted. Thereafter, the king and the performers spent a long time in witty and varied conversation, sometimes pretending anger, offence, resentment and irritation and sometimes joy, [but] always with a touch of flirtatiousness. (*BVS*, XIV, 9-62; pp. 204-11)

At the end of that amorous banter, the king presented each of them with exquisite clothes and ornaments and, embracing them in turn, demonstrated his affection for each one of them. (*BVS*, XIV, 64; p. 212)

Soon they heard the bell indicating that midnight had come. So the king with his young wives got up and proceeded towards his sleeping apartments, called *pushkaravati.* (*BVS*, XIV, 66; p. 212, XV, 1; p. 213)

While walking, he teased the ladies, making fun of them in various ways. He was chewing betel-leaves, sometimes sharing them with his wives, amidst jokes and fun.

The sleeping apartments of the king were surrounded on all four sides by those of his wives. The latter were disposed along corridors with porches having rows of projecting posts from which hung oil lamps. When the lamps were lit it looked as if *Dipavali* was celebrated there. All the rooms were beautifully decorated with different gems, diamonds, gold-plated ornaments, etcetera. On seeing the king, the pet parrots which lived in those four corridors loudly announced his arrival. (*BVS*, XV, 2-12; pp. 213-14)

The king entered his apartments with one of his queens, Padmavati, and sat on the bedstead called *simha-vahini.* (*BVS*, XV, 14-15; p. 215)

Then the king and the queen indulged again in playful banter and while conversing they offered each other betel-leaves to chew. Eventually the king embraced her and made her happy. Similarly, he visited the apartments of the other wives, pleasing all of them without showing any favouritism. (*BVS*, XV, 17-31; pp. 215-17)

He had a short nap lying on a swinging cot lined with swans' soft down, while all his wives were sound asleep. (*BVS*, XV, 33,34, p. 217)

Soon after, he started meditating for a time. At dawn, as usual, the lady-musicians appeared, singing and playing instruments. On hearing them the king got up and left for the temple. (*BVS*, XV, 37, 41 & 43; pp. 218-19)

20.4 A divine dance troupe

After giving a vivid account of the palace at Pampakshetra, the *Pampasthana Varnanam* goes on to describe the public audience given by Shiva. However, before passing to the actual performance of the artists, as given in the next excerpt, the performers present on that occasion are carefully enumerated and described.

The troupe of the dancing girls (concubines) consisted of a learned man, a dancing master, the chief of the troupe, a joker, a narrator, nine young ladies, the chief mistress of the dancers, a vocalist, an instrumentalist, an actor and a master singer. (*PV*, I, 73; p. 36)

The young girls were richly dressed for that occasion. [Apart from the normal garments], they covered their heads and faces with a transparent upper cloth. They had *jadi* flowers tied artistically on their hair with pearl-strings arranged on their hair-buns. On their foreheads were the dark dots of fragrant *kasturi.* (*PV*, I, 66; p. 23)

They wore the following jewellery [made of gold and lavishly studded with precious gems and diamonds]: glittering and bright finger-rings, anklets, a long tassel tied to the plaited hair, waist-girdle, diamond necklace, wristlet, twisted ornament for the wrist, necklace, bracelet, armlet, bracelet for the upper arm, shoulder-ornament, nose-screw of pearls, ear-ornament of rubies, a golden flower set with jewels fixed in the parting of the hair and resting on the forehead, golden sandals and a golden casket [for keeping betel-leaves]. (*PV*, I, 66 & 72; pp. 20, 23, 25, & 26)

20.5 A dance performance in the presence of Shiva

As a part of the entertainment at the court of Shiva, the divine dancers, actors and musicians stage a performance.

It was then time for all the courtesans to exhibit their skills to entertain and please the whole assembly. As soon as Shiva glanced at them they started the performance. First the musicians took the big *dandiges,* removed the white cloth covering, tuned the strings according to the selected mode and started playing.

They performed various tunes in different modes, thus displaying their musical proficiency. (*PV*, I, 74-6; pp. 26-8) [....]

Occasionally they used wax cubes for tuning the strings in the required scale, or arranged an additional string treated with wax. (*PV*, I, 78; p. 29) [....]

The dances were performed to the music of four kinds of *tabor* tuned to the required pitch. In addition to the *tabors*, there were also a number of percussion instruments. (*PV*, I, 80-2; p. 32)

Other musicians played wind instruments such as the *kahale*, after having suitably adjusted the mouthpieces. (*PV*, I, 84 & 85; p. 32)

The dancers performed in front of a screen that served as backdrop. They donned elegant bodices embroidered with pearls, glittering upper garments, tights and frilled sashes. They also wore jewellery of various types studded with diamonds and other precious stones, and chains with rattles that tinkled harmoniously while they danced. They were adorned with a number of precious necklaces and sumptuously decorated waist-girdles. Their performance was guided and directed by their *sutradhara* (master). They executed various [dance] pieces expressing the eight *rasas*, [in which] they combined facial expressions with appropriate gestures and postures in the most exquisite manner. The whole audience was enthralled. A number of other pieces were performed. While dancing, they sang along with the musicians. At the end of each piece they froze in the required positions and looked like statues.

Occasionally they changed their costume to impersonate people belonging to different regions and walks of life. Thus, singers, musicians, dancers and actors entertained the assembled audience with great success. (*PV*, I, 90: pp. 32-5)

20.6 A dance recital

A dance performance is the theme of the following passage from the *Sanatkumara Charite*.

The dancing hall was situated in the middle of the royal garden. It looked like the aerial vehicle of Indra, or Kubera's *pushpaka-vimana*, or even the bed chamber of the goddess of love, such was the profusion and the splendour of its embellishments. The pillars were set with glittering emeralds and the beams with sparkling diamonds; on the floor were red rubies; the walls were enlivened with colourful paintings and at the top [of the roof] were golden pot-shaped finials. (*SC*, IV, 8-9; p. 34)

The prince sat on a glittering golden throne at the centre of that beautiful building, watching and enjoying a dance performance by the young and attractive ladies of the court. Female attendants with fly-whisks flanked him. (*SC*, IV, 23; p, 37)

Different dances were performed according to the rules, with all the required talent and virtuosity, to the accompaniment of various types of musical instrument played by the ladies of the court, each a professional in her own right. Some of the important instruments providing the accompaniment were *murjanas* (tambourines), *mridanga* (drums), cymbals of various kinds and sizes and flutes. Two singers accompanied the dancers. The dance-master sat there directing the performers. [In one particular dance] they rhythmically shook the rattlers tied to their anklets, toe-rings and other ornaments on their person. They performed on a raised platform. (*SC*, IV, 10-12; pp. 34-7)

20.7 A dance-drama performance

The *Amalabasava Charite* describes a dance-drama in the presence of the king and an audience of connoisseurs.

One evening the king wished to witness a dance-drama performance. He went to the theatre, which was embellished with gold-plated walls and gems of various kinds. He sent for the court jesters and other attendants and sat with them to enjoy the performances of the different artists.

Among the public were poets, bards, debators, scholars, specialists in Vedic literature and other treatises and commentators. There were a number of ladies well-versed in the performing arts who knew the leading exponents of each branch [of the arts], as well as other learned persons. There were ladies who were experts in playing the sixteen different types of *vine*. The artists were accompanied by a group of ladies who played various types of brass cymbals with which they indicated the tempo, rhythm and pauses. (*AC*, XXXVIII, 4-8; p. 379)

There were artists who played the *mridanga*, flutes, horns and other wind instruments. The singers performed pleasingly various tunes according to the tenets of classical music. While the concert was in progress, to the great joy and appreciation of the ruler and his retinue, the king looked in the direction of the 700 assistants seated along with his queens. Among them were 100 who were particularly beautiful. This glance was an indication for them to start acting a story narrating one of the sports of Shiva. Accordingly they changed, and once suitably dressed they presented the drama. The theme of the drama was the story known as *Bhikshatana-lile*. (*AC*, XXXVIII, 4-14; pp. 379-81)

The play commenced with some singing to the

accompaniment of instruments. The musicians performed behind the curtain, under the guidance of a *nattuvangane* (lady conductor). The actresses, dressed as Shiva and his retinue, stood in readiness behind the curtain. (*AC*, XXXVIII, 19-23; p. 382)

Portrait painting and murals

20.8 Portrait of a princess

The art of painting is repeatedly mentioned, especially in connection with murals and paintings on cloth. Portrait painting was particularly appreciated. A recurring theme in the romantic literature is of the portrait of a princess from a distant kingdom being shown to a ruler who inevitably falls in love with her, as in the following excerpt from the *Nagakumara Charite.*

One day, when the king was seated in [private] audience, a merchant who came from a faraway place appeared at the court and heaped numerous glistening diamonds of lustruous hues before the king. He also produced a portrait of an exceedingly beautiful princess from the kingdom of Surashtra. [In the course of his tour], the merchant had her portrait drawn and eventually brought it there to show to the king. The king was delighted with the portrait and presented the merchant with *vileya.*

Later, when everybody else had been dismissed, the king talked to the merchant in private with a view to marrying the princess. He arranged to depute his minister and the merchant with this undertaking. He gave them various kinds of gold ornaments studded with diamonds and other precious stones and silk garments (*NC*, I, 14-19; pp. 298-9)

20.9 Portrait of a prince

Queens and princesses commissioned artists to paint portraits of the princes they admired. In this case, to please the queen, an attendant sends for a painter to execute the portrait of the prince with whom the queen had fallen in love. The following brief passage is from the *Ramanatha Charite.*

The painting was well done and the likeness was remarkably similar to the prince. It was a superb work of different colours, and a good portrait. It looked alive, being so expressive and full of movement. (*RC*, XXVI, 28-31; pp. 109-10)

20.10 Chitralekha paints Aniruddha's portrait

The most renowned episode in which portrait painting plays a pivotal role is the story of Chitralekha, whose name means "proficient in the art of painting". She was the confidante of the princess Usha, as narrated in the *Mohana Tarangini.*

One day the young princess [Usha] saw in her dream a young and charming prince, and instantly fell in love. She spoke to her companion and described in great detail the features of the young man. Chitralekha assured the princess that she would draw the portrait of the various princes she saw in the course of her travels. [....]

On returning she showed the princess all the pictures, and eventually she recognized the prince she had seen in her dreams and with whom she had fallen in love. [His name was Anirudda.] (*MT*, XXVIII, 36-8; p. 399; XXIX, 4 & 17-22; pp. 401-5; XXX, 6-12 & 18-34, pp. 414-19)

20.11 Murals

The following passage from the *Mohana Tarangini* describes the wall paintings in the king's bedchamber.

The inner apartments of the king's palace were decorated with murals. The sleeping chamber was embellished with richly decorated niches set in the walls at appropriate intervals, hanging garlands, tapestries, festoons of cloths of various colours, pearls, precious stones and beads, statues holding lit torches in their hands, sculptures of deities and others. The murals on the walls depicted the sports of Rati and Madana, the subjects illustrated being suitable for the king's bedchamber. (*MT*, XXII, 12, p. 323)

20.12 Banners and flags

The *Mohana Tarangini* also mentions the practice of painting emblems of various colours on banners and flags. These emblems enabled everyone to recognize the king, subordinate rulers, princes, officers and others of the royal retinue. (*MT*, XXXVI, 40; p. 492; XXXVII, 48, p. 492; see also Section 15.8)

PART FIVE

RELIGIOUS LIFE

The selection of extracts that appears in the two chapters of this part are concerned with the various facets of religious life. Three major festivals are described in Chapter 21. In the passages from the *Airavata* and *Samyukta Kaumudi*, the festivities are merely used as a backdrop, the poets focusing more on the persons involved and the intricacies of the protocol to be followed. The mood changes dramatically in the extract from the *Bharatesha Vaibhava Sangraha*, which is devoted to the *Mahanavami* celebrations: here the festival and the various phases of the rituals are precisely described, as if to remind the reader of the solemnity of the occasion.

Diverse types of devotion are portrayed in Chapter 22. First, there is the description from the *Mohana Tarangini* of the king worshipping his personal *linga* in the privacy of his own apartments, then, on his way to the assembly hall, of bestowing gifts on brahmins, scholars and needy persons. Although a public affair, this rite concludes his private daily worship. Then follows an extremely elaborate account from the *Prabhulinga Lile* of the visit of a princess to a temple. Here the poet delights in the description of the dress, jewellery and hair-ornaments of the princess and her attendants and in the precise account of all the phases of the ritual, including dance and music. More sober are the passages describing the visits of a ruler to a Jaina temple and monastery entailing the worship of the images of the Jaina prophets, as recounted in the *Bharatesha Vaibhava Sangraha.* The *Sanatkumara Charite* elaborates on the same topic, further describing the visit of a king and his retinue to a Jaina monastery, meeting a holy man, and listening to the readings and explanation of passages from Jaina sacred texts. The subject of kingly patronage of temples is explored in the passages describing the provisions of the Virupaksha temple in Hampe, from the *Shivatattva Chintamani*, and a royal pilgrimage to Rameshvaram, in the *Ramanatha Charite.* The chapter is brought to a close with two extracts from the *Bharatesha Vaibhava Sangraha* and *Ramanatha Charite* dealing with renunciation and the self-immolation of a wife on the pyre of her husband.

Chapter 21

FESTIVALS

This chapter describes three festivals: the *Airavata-nompi*, the *Kaumudi-parva* or *Kaumudimahotsava* and the more famous *Mahanavami*. Though the last survives into modern times as a part of the ten-day *Dasara* festival, the other two seem to be no longer current, at least as celebrations in their own right. There were and are a number of rites centering on the goddess Gauri, one of which, observed by ladies only, was celebrated in November-December. During this festival, an image of the goddess was fashioned and worshipped; but it is uncertain if this is the festival referred to in the *Airavata* (see Section 21.1). Information on the *Kaumudi-parva* is more readily available and a number of literary sources, including the *Mahabharata* and the *Vishnu* and *Linga Puranas*, mention it under the name of *Kaumudimahotsava*. According to the *Mahabharata*, the god Karttikeya was feted on this date. The *Puranas* maintain that the festival was dedicated to Indra seated on his elephant Airavata and to Lakshmi. The Shaiva tradition declares this day as sacred to Shiva. The *Samyukta Kaumudi*, which is quoted here (Section 21.2), however, is a Jaina text, and no detail regarding this Jaina celebration can be found.

The *Mahanavami* festival described in the *Bharatesha Vaibhava Sangraha* (Section 21.3) was the most important annual festival at Vijayanagara. It took place in the month of *Asvayuj* (September-October) and was associated both with the goddess Durga and her victory over the *asura* Mahisha, as well as with Rama's final victory over Ravana. It was essentially a festival connected to kingship, army and weapons; the Vijayanagara kings deemed it auspicious to review troops on that day and keep them in readiness for military operations. Generally, military expedition began immediately after *Mahanavami*, when the rainy season had ended and the roads were dry, and there was plenty of food and water available for the army.

21.1 The *Airavata-nompi*

The *Airavata* is a work based on one of the many stories embedded in the main narrative of the *Mahabharata* that refer to the rivalry between Gandhari, the mother of the Kauravas, and Kunti, the mother of the Pandavas. Gandhari performs a solemn rite, the *Gauri-puja*, in which a clay image of the goddess Gauri seated on an elephant, said to bestow immense fame and wealth, is worshipped. As Gandhari omits to invite Kunti to participate in the worship, Arjuna vows to bring Indra's elephant, Airavata, down from heaven, so that his mother can fittingly perform the ritual herself

When the ladies began performing the ritual, Kunti went to bathe in the river Ganga. There, with the sand of the embankment, she fashioned an image of the goddess Gauri. She worshipped it according to the traditional sixteen methods and then offered it some food. In addition, she worshipped Kamadhenu (the celestial cow) and the celestial tree and gave offerings to the *apsaras*, following the tradition. She then approached the celestial elephant Airavata, worshipped it in the usual sixteen ways and paid her respects to the elders and all those who had assembled for this ceremony. The elders were given auspicious rice, fragrant sandal paste, floral garlands, clothes and *bagina*. On this occasion, the brahmins were gifted land, villages, gold, brides, gold coins, clothes, ornaments, cows, horses and elephants.

The ladies were also presented with ornaments for the hands, feet, ears and necks, together with clothes and perfumes and [other] *baginas* in winnowing baskets. Such was the quantity of the auspicious gifts to be distributed to the brahmins and others that they had to be carried on bullock carts, elephants and camels.

Public announcements were made to invite men and women, young and old, to assemble to receive the gifts of the day. The wives of the participating kings and rulers were also generously treated. At the end, Kunti prostrated herself before the elders and sought their blessings.

It was time for the customary procession. By sunset, the howdah on the elephant was lowered to allow the noble Kunti to climb in. It was then replaced on the elephant's back and the procession set off in great pomp and splendour, accompanied by all who had participated in the ceremony, the four divisions of the army and the groups of musicians, singers and dancers. Some of the citizens watched the procession from the roof terraces as it wound its way through the streets. (*A*, VIII, 1-17; pp. 80-4)

At last the procession reached the forecourt of the palace, where it was received with due honour by waving lighted lamps. (*A*, VIII, 26; p. 87)

The lady descended from the elephant, paid her respects to the elders and entered her palace. (*A*, VIII, 30, p. 87)

21.2 The *Kaumudi-parva* celebrations

The first story in the *Samyukta Kaumudi* concerns the king of Maduranagare and his queen. In it is a description of the *Kaumudi* festival as celebrated on the night of the full moon of the month of *Kartik* (October-November), in which only ladies were allowed to participate.

[On the full moon of the month of *Kartik*], the *Kaumudi-parva* festival was celebrated. The king announced through his officers that the queen, her friends, ladies-in-waiting, servants, household ladies and others should set out from the city to reach the pleasure garden before evening. The ladies of the queen's retinue, all young and attractive, dressed with great care and fastidiousness to participate in that festival.

Furthermore, the king made a public order that no man, himself included, was to enter that pleasure garden until the ladies' festival was over. These beautiful young ladies were to spend the whole night, from the rise of the full moon till the morning of the next day, singing, playing musical instruments, dancing and enjoying themselves until the *Kaumudi-parva* festival was over. (*SK*, I, 36-40; pp. 8-13)

21.3 The *Mahanavami*

This description of the *Mahanavami* celebrations, although performed in the Jaina manner, is drawn from the *Bharatesha Vaibhava Sangraha*. It is surprising that, in spite of the importance of the festival during Vijayanagara times, this is the sole description in these source texts.

The king had ruled for a long time. One day, Buddhisagara, the minister, approached him saying that the rainy season was finished and the sky was clear, and that it was the proper time to resume military activities. Furthermore, a *chakra*, the auspicious sign [of the wheel], had appeared [miraculously] in the royal armoury, signalling that the time was ripe for a campaign. The king had to wage war against the rulers of many countries with fortified cities situated on hills, islands and in forests. (*BVS*, XVIII, 3-8; pp. 239-40)

Pleased with this suggestion, the king rewarded the minister. It was decided that the minister would make arrangements for the nine-day religious celebration prior to the departure of the army on the tenth day of the month of *Asvayuj*. The streets of the city were cleaned and decorated with a profusion of festoons made of tender leaves and with banners. Religious ceremonies were performed for nine days: the *chakra* was regularly worshipped; similarly, private individuals honoured their swords and other weapons. Each day during that period, the king visited the Jaina temple in the centre of the town and performed various religious rites. At night he held court in a grand style, sitting on a throne in the front court of the palace. Before him were large numbers of citizens, as well as groups of performing artists such as magicians, jugglers, mimes and comedians. There were also female singers, acrobats and wrestlers, each of whom started displaying their skills at the very moment the king looked at them. At the end, the king generously rewarded them with the *nava-nidhi* (the nine valuable gifts). Soon after, as part of the parade, the royal chariot appeared decorated with flowers and pulled by elegantly-caparisoned horses. Among them was Pavanamjaya, the horse used exclusively by the king. Then came the royal elephant, whose name was Vijayaparvata, carrying on its back the image of a Jina. On seeing this, the king stood up and paid his respects.

Next came four chariots elaborately decorated with banners, colourful hangings, umbrellas, pinnacles embellished with different gems, bells, festoons and the like. These carried the statues of Jaina deities and [were pulled] in different directions to the singing of the ladies and the music of instruments such as the percussion and the *shankha.* On seeing the chariots the king stood up, while his mother appeared on the balcony of the upper storey; both of them paid their respects to the deities. The king's wives waved auspicious lights in front of the images, then the chariots moved on. (*BVS,* XVIII, 10-34; pp. 240-3) [....]

On hearing the bell signalling the appointed time, the king proceeded to the royal armoury. On the occasion of the *Navaratri* celebrations, all the swords had been unsheathed and placed in rows. They were worshipped using various kinds of flowers, especially red ones, [as well as] sandal paste, red sandal-paste, saffron and various other coloured substances. The place was redolent of burning incense, lit by bright oil lamps and decorated with tender leaves. There were large quantities of offerings such as coloured rice, fruits and coconuts. Along with the swords there were other kinds of weapons in the armoury, but the most important were the king's sword Sanandaka and the *chakra.* The king worshipped the *chakra* and placed a lotus on it. He decided that the army should set out on an auspicious moment in the course of the next day and instructed the minister accordingly. He then retired to the palace for the night. (*BVS,* XVIII, 59-68; pp. 247-8)

Chapter 22

CULTS AND RITUALS

This chapter gives an insight into the various forms of worship. It begins with two very extensive descriptions of private worship, drawn from the *Mohana Tarangini* and *Prabhulinga Lile*. Royal visits to Jaina temples and monastic establishments are the themes of the excerpts from the *Bharatesha Vaibhava Sangraha* and *Sanatkumara Charite*. Particularly interesting is the passage from the *Shivatattva Chintamani*, which offers an account of the various funds allotted by Devaraya II for the maintenance of the Virupaksha temple in Hampe and the celebration of the chariot festival there. The excerpt from the *Ramanatha Charite* describes a royal pilgrimage to Rameshvaram, where a childless royal couple go to seek the help of Shiva. A flower falling from the headdress of the image, a popular method of divination, signals that their wish will be fulfilled and a child will soon be born. The last two passages in this chapter deal with a king and a widow deciding to renounce life: from the *Bharatesha Vaibhava Sangraha* comes the description of a king starving himself to death, while the detailed account of a royal widow preparing to commit *sati* is drawn from the *Ramanatha Charite*.

22.1 Worship of the personal *linga*

This excerpt from the *Mohana Tarangini* is an account of the elaborate worship of the personal *linga* by the king.

The king was awakened at daybreak by a band of lady attendants; some sang auspicious songs and others played various tunes on perfectly tuned *vinadandakas*. Others were praising the king with various epithets. On being awakened thus, the king offered the day's first obeisance to Shiva and to his finger-ring, on which was a miniature sculpted figure of the celestial bull. He gazed at the face of his queen and at a brown coloured cow and its calf, [both of] which were good omens to start the day's activities. (*MT*, XXII, 31, 32, 37 & 38; pp. 327-8)

After attending to the morning call of nature, the king was led to the bathing place by lady attendants holding his hands. There he was made to sit on a lotus-shaped seat and given an elaborate bath. He was given silken garments to wear, after which he walked in his golden sandals towards the *puja-griha*. There he sat on a tortoise-shaped jewelled seat. The chamber was lit with a series of bright oil-lamps on stands; its floor was embellished with auspicious drawings. Flanking the king were lady attendants holding in their hands the requisites for the *puja*. Some had golden vessels with pure water and golden pots full of [ordinary] water. Others had containers with sandal paste, bowls of auspicious red-coloured rice, a casket of sacred ash and a golden basket containing flowers of different kinds: *mandara, jaji, mallige, dundu-mallige, sampige* and others. The remaining ladies carried different types of auspicious lights, ready to hand them over to the king when asked during the course of the ritual. Throughout the *puja*, some of the ladies rang the bells and blew the conch repeatedly at the required moments, as prescribed by the ritual.

After occupying his seat in the *puja* room, [the king] removed all the jewellery he was wearing and instead [put on] auspicious garlands of precious stones and *rudraksha* beads. Then, while reciting the *omkara-mantra*, he applied sanctified ash all over his body. After he was thus prepared he began the ritual. He took out his *jyotirlinga* (personal *linga*) from the cloth in which it had been wrapped and tied around his neck and removed the flowers which he had placed on it in the course of the previous *puja*. He held the *linga* in his palms, upon which he had drawn the prescribed diagram symbolizing the celestial bull, the vehicle of Shiva. Then he washed the *linga* with sacred water for 1,000 times from 1,000 vessels and worshipped it, applying sanctified ash, auspicious rice, different kinds of flowers, sacred *bilva* leaves, *davana* (aromatic leaves), etcetera.

The next phase of the ritual was to perform *arati*

before the *linga* held in the palms, with lamps of different shapes. Lastly, he offered it *naivedya* (food preparations) consisting of cooked rice, *ghee*, pulses, creamy curds, cooked vegetables, *saru*, fruits, thick fruit juice, a variety of sweet dishes and finally *tambula*. He offered flowers: lotuses, jasmine, *mandara* and others. He performed other *sheva* (ritual actions) such as [giving the image an] umbrella, a fly-whisk, fanning it, playing instrumental music, singing, dancing and other [services] from the 72 types of service. At the end of all this, he made obeisance by carrying out the *shastange-namaskar* (prostrating himself head-long on the floor) and singing songs in praise of Shiva.

He then put the *linga* in a cloth, encased it and wore it again around his neck. Thereafter he ate and proceeded to give audience to the public. (*MT*, XXI, 4-46; pp. 306-15; XXII, 39-44; pp. 328-9)

After having performed the morning religious rites and before reaching the audience hall, he went to a pavilion called the *dana-mantapa* (charities pavilion), and sat on the throne placed there for his use. Then he ordered charities and gifts to be given to those who were needy. Thereupon, a host of learned persons, scholars, priests, other brahmins, *purohits* and *karanikas* appeared and blessed the king by reciting auspicious *mantras* and strewing sacred rice on his head. All of them were suitably rewarded with cows, money, gold and other gifts according to their individual needs.

By that time, the ministers and princes had presented themselves and joined the king's retinue. Subordinate rulers from the 56 countries also joined them to pay their respects and tributes to the king. A group of ladies with various kinds of duties followed the king's retinue.

After finishing the distribution of charities for that day in the *dana-mantapa*, the king and his large retinue proceeded to the audience hall. (*MT*, XXII, 47-54; pp. 330-1; XXIII, 3; p. 332)

22.2 The princess goes to the temple

This passage from the *Prabhulinga Lile* describes the princess worshipping the family deity.

[After completing her elaborate toilet, the princess was ready to visit the family temple.]

The attendants announced that the palanquin was ready and the princess could set out for the temple. She then stood up from her seat and stepped into [the palanquin] accompanied by a retinue of assistants. In front of the palanquin were some [attendants] holding an umbrella [lined with] white pearls; to the left and the right were others waving fly-whisks and panegyrists shouting loud praises. (*PL*, IV, 24-5; pp. 39-40)

The attendants carried various objects which the princess might require; among these were a pouch [for small toilet items], a money bag, a royal umbrella, fly-whisks, drinking water [in a jug], a fan, a mirror [with a golden frame], perfume [in a container], flowers and sandals. Some others carried pure water, flowers, fragrant incense and cloths, as well as various musical instruments required for performing songs and dances in front of the deity. (*PL*, IV, 27-8; p. 40)

Well dressed for that occasion, they wore a number of ornaments: toe-rings of various designs that produced a pleasing sound, foot-ornaments, wristlets, armlets, necklaces with central pendants, nose-ornaments of pearls, flower-shaped hairpins, coloured lower garments, leggings, pearl ear-ornaments, chokers, necklaces, girdles, coloured scarves, *mudreya-mentike* (toe-rings of a special kind), golden bangles, ear ornaments of conch shells, necklaces of large pearls and white [silken] garments. (*PL*, IV, 29-31; p. 41)

The temple, which had a golden pot-shaped pinnacle, was decorated with banners, flags, festoons and bunches [of leaves]. When the princess arrived, she descended from the palanquin, washed her face, hands and feet and proceeded around the building in clockwise direction. On entering the Shiva temple, she prostrated herself before the deity with folded hands and offered her respects. Then she sat down to worship the deity in the prescribed ways assisted by her attendants. She bathed the image in the *panchamrita* (liquid mixture of five holy ingredients) and *panniru* (fragrant-smelling water), dressed it in a [silk] cloth and applied *kumkuma*, *karpura* and other fragrant substances of eight different varieties. Then she offered auspicious rice, floral garlands and sacred leaves. After that, as part of the ritual, she and her assistants played instruments such as bells, conches, bronze gongs, cymbals, drums, trumpets, *mridanga*, string instruments, *bheri* (large drums), *kamsala* (twin drums) and others. Next she burned fragrant substances and perfumes in front of the deity. This was followed by *arati* of various types amidst the singing of devotional songs in praise of her deity. Then came the offering of diverse food preparations that were kept in large golden bowls: *ogara, ghee, payasa, happala, parpu-shakha, palidya, uppinakayi, dadhi, takra, pachchadi, saru, shikarane, chinipalu* sugar, and others. All the above dishes were offered to the deity by sprinkling water over them. At the end, split betel-nuts and fresh leaves mixed with edible camphor and lime paste were offered to the deity. Then she waved the lights in front of the image.

As the last act of this elaborate *puja*, the princess

fanned the deity with white fly-whisks, waved other types of *arati* in front of it and held up a jewelled mirror in front of it. Finally, she went around the image once more with great devotion, paid her respects to the deity and then came out of the sanctuary into the *ranga-mantapa* (central hall) of the temple. It was the moment in which music and dance were to be performed as part of the ritual. As soon as she entered the hall, the staff-holding attendants ordered silence. Then the princess and the other singers sang accompanied by the instrumentalists. She sang for some time in different tunes and in various styles to the enchantment of the listeners assembled there. Next, beating the rhythm with her toe-rings and bangles, she started dancing. She danced like a goddess and displayed her proficiency in a number of pieces, which attracted the outside public to watch her performance through the perforated window. At the end of the performance, the temple priest offered the princess the *prasada* and a floral garland and blessed her. She accepted these with great devotion and humility and finally sat there [for a while]. (*PL*, IV, 36-63; pp. 41-9)

22.3 The king visits a Jaina temple

The theme of this passage from the *Bharatesha Vaibhava Sangraha* is the visit of the king to a Jaina temple.

[The king had spent the night in the company of his wives.]

Next day, awakened by the songs of the ladies, he got up and went directly to the bathing chamber. After the bath, he wore a silk *dhoti*, applied an auspicious *tilaka* on his forehead, slipped on his silver sandals and walked towards the Jaina temple. With all humility he proceeded towards the shrine. No panegyrists or [other] persons paid homage to him; no attendants carrying the royal umbrella were to accompany him. Only his wives, who had also taken a bath, followed him. The king held in his hand a *madala* fruit to be offered to the deity, while his wives carried the various items required for performing the *puja*. As they were walking they sang or chanted [the names of the god].

The temple was situated in a garden filled with flowers close to the king's palace. On nearing it, the king left his sandals outside. The shrine was similar to the *kalpabhuja* (divine wishing-tree, which can grant any desire of mankind). It had been embellished with pot-shaped finials of pearls and with gems set in decorative patterns. [On its roof] flags and banners were fluttering. In the temple, big bells were loudly resounding and at the appropriate places were the statues of the Jaina *siddhas*. Having folded his hands, the king went round the shrine, keeping it to his right [side]; then he washed his feet and entered. He stood before the image of the Jina, offered it golden flowers and prayed with great reverence. He prostrated himself three times before it; thereafter he sat on a mat of grass [or reeds] and performed the prescribed rituals. While he was thus engaged, the queens prayed for the welfare of their husband. After paying reverence to the Jaina ascetics, the king and his 500 queens performed the *ashtavidha-archane* (eight kinds of worship) before the life-sized image of the Jina. Then, together, they performed *abhisheka*, bathing the statue with pots full of tender coconut water, flower petals, smashed bananas, pure *ghee*, milk, curds, sugarcane juice and the like. All the while, the lady servants quickly removed any *abhisheka* leftovers [from the ground]. The statue was further lustrated with *lajonga-churna* (flour of parched grains), *kumkuma-churna* (saffron-coloured pwder) and basketfuls of variously coloured flowers. Once the *ashtavidha-archane* were celebrated and 108 lotus flowers were placed before the image, the concluding ritual was performed. Though it was a private chapel situated near the palace and not meant for public worship, yet twelve *lakhs* of devotees had gathered there to witness the ritual. At noon, the bell rang and the priests went to their respective monasteries, while the king and the queens continued their religious practices, such as fasting and meditating; [they spent] the rest of the day relaxing. (*BVS*, XVI, 1-51; pp. 220-7)

22.4 The king visits a Jaina monastery

A visit of the king to a Jaina monastery is described in the following excerpt from the *Sanatkumara Charite.*

The Jaina monastery of that city was a beautiful building. At its front was a series of steps embellished with emeralds. Pearls were embedded in its pillars, lustruous diamonds in its beams and red rubies in its sloping eaves.

One day the king [accompanied by his retinue] went to that monastery to pray. First he reverently circumambulated the building. He then entered it and performed the *shirasashtanga-namaskara* to the *guru* [seated there], thereby pleasing him greatly. He prayed and performed various rituals at the holy feet of the deity. He worshipped it by bathing it with *panchamrita*, anointing it with cool sandal paste, pouring over it a shower of pearls, decorating it with flowers of various kinds and, lastly, offering it cooked rice preparations. While the worship was going on, a series of lamps had been lit, and the temple was filled with fragrant smoke because of the burning of incense and other perfumed substances. At the conclusion [of the rituals], he offered the deity sweet ripe fruits, such as *jambu, rasabale* and others, and then paid his respects. (*SC*, X, 10-11; p. 106)

After all the rituals were over, the king met the *charana-guru* (wandering preceptor) named Sumali and requested him to narrate [episodes] from the Jaina *puranas*. He readily agreed and [proceeded to] elucidate the tenets of Jaina doctrine and philosophy. (*SC*, XI, 13-17; pp. 107-8)

22.5 Provisions for the Virupaksha temple (Hampe)

The next excerpt, from the *Shivatattva Chintamani*, gives an account of the arrangements made by king Devaraya II for the refurbishment and maintenance of the temple of his patron-deity Virupaksha, as well as for the celebrations of the car festivals.

[The king Devaraya II] ordered the construction of four beautiful entrance gateways at the cardinal points of the temple [complex] of the god Pampa-Virupaksha. They were all studded with precious stones and glittering pot-shaped finials graced their tops. He made arrangements for the regular daily cleaning of the main [car] streets that ran in front of those gateways, so that they looked well kept and sacred. He also made provision for the [upkeep of] charity houses for the benefit of pilgrims passing along those streets. He also instituted three car festivals in honour of the deities Virupaksha, Pampambika and Ganadhipa, which were regularly celebrated thereafter. [In all this], he was ably advised by his faithful minister, Lakkannadandesha, whose assistance led him to great achievements. (*S*, XXVII, 249-55; pp. 439-41)

22.6 A royal pilgrimage

A royal pilgrimage to Rameshvara is the theme of this excerpt drawn from the *Ramanatha Charite*.

The queen-consort was concerned because she had no issue. One day, the ladies-in-waiting approached the king and reported the matter to him. Thereupon, he met the queen, consoled her and assured her that he would go [on pilgrimage] to [the temple of] Jatayu (Jatilinga) Rameshvara in order to seek his blessings for begetting a son. He ordered his impending pilgrimage to be announced publicly by the beating of drums. Immediately, the royal horse and elephant were [readied] and paraded before him. Meanwhile, the whole city and its streets were decorated with festoons, bunches, arches of bright and colourful flowers, leaves and the like. A lady attendant appeared with a marble casket studded with gems containing the fragrant sandal paste required in the course of the *puja*. Another came forward with a basket filled with blossoms of sweet-smelling flowers of various kinds. The auspicious rice was carried in a small container by yet another. A further attendant had a basket of well ripened fruits, while a whole bunch of plantain fruits of golden colour was entrusted to the next. The remaining ladies brought a jug containing water, more fruits, sandal paste, rice, floral wreaths, [oil] lamps, frankincense in a censer, betel-nuts and leaves, etcetera. All of them walked in front of the king. When the sumptuously-caparisoned elephant was brought forward, the king patted it with affection, mounted onto its back and rode out. The queen followed him seated in a palanquin, accompanied by a host of beautiful young lady attendants and associates. The royal retinue, flanked by the panegyrists [loudly singing the praises of the king] and followed by the four branches of the king's army, progressed out of the gateway of the fortified city amidst great noise. The men and the women of the place, dressed in their best clothes for the occasion, enjoyed the spectacle of the marching procession. The king, with all his retinue, reached the temple of Shiva [Jatayu Rameshvara]. There he worshipped the deity, offering all of the above-mentioned auspicious items. He then devoutly prayed to god to bless him with a son. [As if] in response to the king's prayers, a white flower from the crown of the deity fell down, indicating that his desire would be fulfilled. The king picked up that flower and gave it to the queen, to her great happiness. Then, overwhelmed with joy, they returned to their fortified city. (*RC*, VII, 70-122; pp. 120-8)

22.7 The king decides to enter a life of meditation

The *Bharatesha Vaibhava Sangraha* describes the king's resolve to renounce the world.

After ruling the kingdom for some more years, the king one day noticed one grey hair on his head. He then decided to renounce the world and start a life of penance as his father and brothers had already done. He went to the forest accompanied by his numerous wives, who also voluntarily renounced the pleasures of the world, and started his penance. (*BVS*, LV, 1; p. 452; LVI, 5-7 & 29-36; pp. 455-60)

For that purpose, the king sat on a stone called a

siddhasana (lion throne) and discarded his ornaments and clothes. With closed eyes he sat in meditation completely concentrated, aspiring for permanent salvation. He overcame the 63 types of worldly attachment and eventually attained the status of a Jina. (*BVS*, LVII, 1-13; pp. 462-3)

When the end was nearing, he lay on a stone couch. At that time only his physical body was there, while his soul had ascended to heaven and joined the company of the other *siddhas.* (*BVS*, LVIII, 4-8; pp. 465-6)

At the spot where the king attained the ultimate salvation, his son erected the *homa* (memorial fire-altar) and felt happy. (*BVS*, LVIII, 11; p. 466)

22.8 A *sati* ceremony

The only description of a *sati* ceremony in this selection is in the following passage from the *Ramanatha Charite.*

On the death of the prince and the order of the queen-mother, the minister arranged the *sati*-ritual. Fire-pits were made ready and filled with sandalwood logs. Auspicious substances, such as scented water, camphor, flowers, musk, and *sadu,* were thrown into the fire, followed by potfuls of sweet-smelling powders. (*RC*, XXXVI, 151-4; p. 336, II)

Then the wives of the deceased were elegantly dressed by five ladies. They wore silk garments, royal signet rings, anklets, necklaces of different designs, pendants, pearl necklaces, dots of pearls on the forehead, nets for hair-buns, rings, wristlets, bangles, armlets, shoulder ornaments, diamond earrings, various chains, gold bangles and others, all of gold and set with gems of various kinds, diamonds and pearls. (*RC*, XXXVI, 157-9; pp. 336-7)

After the whole procedure of dressing and makeup was over, those ladies [the wives], holding a lemon fruit in one hand and a mirror in the other, approached the queen-mother, prostrated themselves at her feet and sought her blessing. After taking leave of the queen-mother, the wives, seated in palanquins, reached the fire-pits. They jumped into the fire and sacrificed their lives to the great grief and sorrow of those gathered there [who were] weeping. After that, the fire-pits were closed. (*RC*, XXXVI, 158-65; pp. 336-8, II)

PART SIX

EVERYDAY LIFE, BELIEFS AND PASTIMES

This part is composed of a number of topics of general domestic and personal interest. Chapter 23 focuses on conception, birth and related ceremonies, as well as religious initiation, while Chapter 24 is devoted to the fascinating subject of omens, amulets, talismans and magic spells, before passing on to the classification of ailments and medicines and, finally, to black magic. Particularly vivid, in this regard, are the passages from the *Samyukta Kaumudi* and *Ramanatha Charite*. Chapter 24 ends with an account of animal sacrifice and ritual suicide drawn from the *Sobagina Sone*.

Chapter 25 offers an insight into the most popular pastimes, especially outdoor sports, indoor games and games with bets, as well as the intellectual pursuits of citizens and courtiers.

Chapter 23

CONCEPTION, BIRTH AND RELATED CEREMONIES

Concerned with the early stages of life, this chapter begins with a brief account of the *garbha-dana* (impregnation ceremony) drawn from the *Mohana Tarangini.* One of the chief Hindu sacraments to ensure the birth of a boy, the *garbha-dana* formed part of the complex array of rituals following the wedding ceremony. The next passage, from the *Dharmanatha Purana*, describes the preparation of the queen for her meeting with the king, which results in her conceiving the prince Dharmanatha. The following excerpts from the *Dharmanatha Purana, Nemijinesha Sangati* and *Ramanatha Charite* deal with the queen's auspicious dreams, indicating that she has conceived a boy. The next four passages focus on pregnancy, birth and related ceremonies. The richest in detail are the extracts from the *Channabasava Purana* and *Mohana Tarangini.* The important theme of ceremonies at birth and religious initiation is discussed in two elaborate excerpts from the *Shivatattva Chintamani.*

23.1 The *garbha-dana* ceremony

From the *Mohana Tarangini* comes this meticulous account of the impregnation ceremony.

On the day of the nuptial celebrations, the husband took his place on a jewelled throne placed in the *chandra-mantapa* (hall open to the sky). Around him were a number of attendants: some stood by his side carrying golden staffs to indicate his royal status; others praised his distinguished qualities, skills and abilities. Some ladies were singing melodiously, while others played on the *vine* to keep him happy and pleased. A few others were proficient in all the traditional 64 branches of knowledge (or arts). All of them entertained him while he was waiting [for the auspicious moment]. At the appointed hour he dismissed them after giving them lavish presents.

He entered the bridal chamber with his wife and several close followers. The corridor leading to it had been embellished with metal statues. The walls and the pillars, corbels and ceilings were decorated with festoons, bunches of pearls and flowers of all kinds. Long hanging floral wreaths formed floral screens. The decoration was enhanced by numerous standing lamps.

In the middle of the hall was a lovely golden cot, on which was a soft thick mattress of white swans' feathers. The bedstead had been provided with a white screen. (*MT*, XVI, 3-18; pp. 221-4)

The few attendants who were present placed near to the cot various items which the couple might require at night: a golden plate with scented areca-nuts, a beautifully woven basket containing fresh betel-leaves, a small box of edible lime paste and a casket for edible camphor to be used along with betel-leaves and nuts. There was a jug full of scented water, another big vessel for washing hands, a basket filled with fragrant flowers, a spittoon and a fan. The ladies then left, closing the doors behind them.

When the couple were alone, the lady took the tender white betel-leaves into her hands, removed their ribs with her fine nails, split them into halves, applied the lime paste onto them, added *kasturi-gulige* (fragrant pills) and, finally, offered them to her husband along with the nuts. (*MT*, XVI, 25-35; pp. 226-7)

On the morning of the next day, they were woken by the singing of auspicious songs by the ladies-in-waiting. (*MT*, XVI, 64-5; p. 233)

23.2 Conception

The themes of conception and birth are explored in a number of texts that are similar except for occasional variation in the details. This account is drawn from the *Dharmanatha Purana.*

In the course of spring, the [chief] queen had her period. On the fourth day, the lady attendants stored a large quantity of pure hot water in metal cauldrons. They applied fragrant oils to her body and gave her a massage and a hot bath. She sat in the middle of a square marble bathing pool, while the handmaidens poured on her warm water from small golden vessels. (*DP*, VI, 97-101; pp. 129-30)

After bathing, the queen slowly proceeded towards the dressing room, where her ladies-in-waiting helped her into a lower garment. (*DP*, VI, prose, p. 130)

Next they dressed her in a white garment and her body was smeared with fragrant sandal paste. She then put on all kinds of jewels studded with choicest pearls: armlet, ornament for the hair parting, necklace, bracelet, girdle, anklet, floral wreath, head jewel, ear-ornament, anklet of honour, hair bun ornament, finger ring and toe-ring. (*DP*, VI, 105-08; p. 131)

A garland of jasmine flowers was tied on her forehead and she wore a long pearl necklace. (*DP*, VI, prose; p. 132)

Another lady drew beautiful flowers and creepers on her shoulders using red saffron and vegetal gum. Finally, she was handed a mirror. (*DP*, VI, 112; p. 132)

Another attendant placed a pair of glittering sandals before her. (*DP*, VI, 114; p. 132)

She put on the sandals, entered the temple, performed *puja* and then had her meal. In the early part of the night, she was pleasantly entertained by female performers and then she went to the sleeping chamber. (*DP*, VI, 114-15, prose; pp. 132-3)

It was filled with fragrances such as *vetiver*, camphor-powder, sandal powder, musk-powder and burning incense. (*DP*, VI, prose; p. 133)

There was a gold-plated cot decorated with pictures made with vegetal colours. On the cot were seven mattresses of swans' feathers and over them were sheets and silken covers. (*DP*, VI, 117; p. 133)

The queen sat on the mattresses and gazed at the thick floral garlands decorating the room. (*DP*, VI, prose; pp. 133-4)

There were also betel-nuts treated with edible camphor and betel leaves and edible camphor mixed with *churna* (edible lime paste), all stored in silver containers. In addition, there was cool water in pots and a number of lamps on gem-embellished stands, as well as other objects which might be of use to the couple in the course of the night. (*DP*, VI, prose; p. 134)

The queen, much pleased with the arrangements, lay down on the mattresses and one lady started pressing her feet. Meanwhile the king performed the appropriate ritual [for the occasion]. He wore an exquisitely painted upper garment and various jewels and his body was redolent with different perfumes. He arrived accompanied by a trusted bodyguard. The queen was standing there, ready to receive him. They sat together on the soft bedstead. And then they enjoyed the night together in pleasurable ways. (*DP*, VI, 119-24 prose; pp. 134-7)

23.3 Auspicious dreams I

A popular theme is the enumeration of the auspicious dreams the mother sees in her sleep immediately after having conceived the child. These accounts are drawn from the *Dharmanatha Purana* and *Nemijinesha Sangati*, both Jaina texts, and from the *Ramanatha Charite*. The first excerpt is from the *Dharmanatha Purana*.

And in that dream the queen saw the sixteen auspicious omens, all indicating the birth of a religious leader. Among these were the elephant, bull, lion, the goddess Lakshmi, a garland of fresh white flowers, the moon, sun, a pair of fish, two golden vessels filled with water, a pond with lotus flowers, the sea, a throne, an aerial chariot, the palace of the king of the *nagas*, heaps of gems and the sacred fire. (*DP*, VI, 125-41; pp. 136-8)

In the morning, the queen told this dream to the king and he understood that all these omens referred to the qualities of the child to be born: [thus], elephant (charitable disposition), bull (righteousness), lion (heroic valour), Lakshmi (worshipped by all), garland (spreading fame), moon (purity), sun (splendour and radiance), pair of fish (happiness), pots of water (quenches everybody's desires), sea (broad mindedness), throne (great attraction), aerial chariot (great traveller), the palace of the king of the *nagas* (untold riches), heaps of gems (matchless splendour) and fire (burning, overcoming the effects of *karma*). (*DP*, VI, 145-50; pp. 139-40)

23.4 Auspicious dreams II

This passage is from the *Nemijinesha Sangati*.

After sunset, the young queen put on sandals which were set with pearls and proceeded to the bed chamber of the king. There she sat on the bedstead on which was a soft mattress of swans' feathers.

She enjoyed the night in the company of her husband and in the early hours of the morning, while asleep, she saw sixteen auspicious objects in a dream: an elephant, bull, lion, Lakshmi, floral wreaths, the moon, a golden pot, young fish, pond filled with lotuses, the sea, the abode of the gods, an ant-hill [the abode of *nagas*], heap of diamonds, fire, the sun and a throne. At daybreak, she washed her face, applied makeup, went to her husband and told him what she had seen in the dream. On hearing her report, the king understood that these were good omens, indicating that she had conceived a child and that in nine months she would give birth to a son endowed with outstanding gifts who would become a great man. On hearing this, she was very happy. (*NS*, XXII, 60-88; pp. 512-16)

23.5 Auspicious dreams III

The following two excerpts are from the *Ramanatha Charite.*

The queen had a dream in the early hours of that day. She saw the sun, the moon, a youthful elephant and a lion. (*RC*, VIII, 20; p. 132)

23.6 Pregnancy

After some days, the queen conceived; this could be seen from the changes in her physical appearance. (*RC*, VIII, 39-41, p. 135) [....]

She fixed her mind on noble ideals, which were to have an influence on the child she was bearing. Meanwhile, the king celebrated a ritual which would ensure the birth of a son. He presented the brahmins with valuable and auspicious objects, vehicles, jewels and other ornaments. As the child was growing in her womb, the queen discarded her jewels and wore instead flowers on her wrists and ears. She wore a single-string necklace of camphor balls and garments woven with the filaments extracted from the stalks of lotuses. Her ladies-in-waiting fanned her with broad and cool lotus leaves and occasionally entertained her with music played on the *vine, kinnari* and other such instruments. On an auspicious day, the queen gave birth to a male child. (*RC*, VIII, 44-55; pp. 134-7)

23.7 Birth of a prince

The present passage is from the *Dharmanatha Purana.*

On an auspicious day and hour, the queen gave birth to a son in the delivery house. Numerous *sumangaliyaru* were there and seven oil lamps illuminated the chamber. (*DP*, VII, prose, 17-19; p. 146)

At that time, the sky opened and a divine shower of gems, gold and flowers fell [on earth] to mark the birth of a supreme religious soul. (*DP*, VII, prose; p. 147)

An attendant immediately conveyed the happy news to the king and received a generous reward. Festivities were held in the palace to mark the joyful occasion. The houses and other buildings [in the town] were embellished with flags, banners, tassels and bunches and branches of fresh leaves, while the street pavements were decorated with a great number of artistically executed drawings. The young ladies in charge of the decorations moved briskly about, making pleasing sounds with the jewellery that they wore. Here and there were learned persons reciting passages from classic religious works and chanting *mantras.* Musicians and singers performed tirelessly, providing the accompaniment to the dances of the young ladies. (*DP*, VII, 23-7; p. 148)

On hearing the happy news, many subordinate and allied rulers assembled in the city to participate in the celebrations. (*DP*, VII, 29; p. 149)

All the prisoners, including the enemy rulers who had been in jail for quite a time, were released on that occasion. (*DP*, VII, 32; p. 149)

Similar accounts of a birth of a prince are found in the *Padmaraja Purana* and *Sobagina Sone.* In the latter text, a childless royal couple eventually manages to have a son named Vikrama or Jagasampa, thanks to a divine flower given by Shiva to the king. (*SoS*, IV, 17-25; pp. 39-40).

This theme of a child conceived by divine intervention is taken up again in the *Amalabasava Charite.* Two interesting observation are given here in the account of the first months of life of the child: on the completion of the sixth month, the child is fed with cooked rice; in the course of the eleventh month, his hair is shaven for the first time. (*AC*, V, 76; p. 72)

23.8 Ceremonies at birth

The following excerpt, from the *Shivatattva Chintamani*, a Virashaiva text, dwells at length on the ceremonies performed at birth, as well as on the *upanayana* ceremony that is performed when a boy reaches the age of eight.

A personal Shiva *linga* on a string of *rudrakshas* was given to the child, a *panchakshari-mantra* was uttered into his ears [by a Virashaiva priest], and the child was then given the name of Basava. Thereafter, the ladies waved the *arati* lights, spat to one side to ward off evil, sang auspicious lullabies and blessed the child. They took the child into their arms, showing their affection in various ways. (*S*, XXX, 23-25; pp. 240-1)

[After some days], the child was given tiger-claws and other ornaments in the shape of a *pipal* leaf and a mango fruit, intended to ward off evil. He was also given a waist-girdle with rattlers, anklets with little bells, wristlets, a finger ring and such like. (*S*, XXX, 33-4; pp. 342-3)

The boy grew up surrounded by the affection of his mother and others. At the age of eight, his father planned to perform the *upanayana*. (*S*, XXX, 45, p. 245)

23.9 Celebrations for the birth of a boy

This lengthy account comes from the *Channa-basava Purana*.

On the birth of a boy [Channabasava], the whole city was decorated to celebrate the joyous event. Colourful banners, festoons, hangings and tassels embellished the streets. In front of each house in the main street were towered bamboo pavilions covered with colourful cloths, papers, greenery, flowers and floral wreaths, leafy branches and mirrors. At regular intervals, large mirrors and pinnacles were fitted onto the pavilions. The ground opposite the houses and the pavilions had been thoroughly swept and sprinkled with fragrant water. The streets were filled with the fragrance of incense sticks and powders.

The residential houses, too, had been embellished. The pillars, planks of the roof and sloping eaves in front of the buildings were [all] tastefully decorated with precious stones and jewels of various colours and sizes. Tassels, clusters of stones, bundles of pure pearls and bunches [of leaves] were hung at the appropriate places. Banners and flags of various colours fluttered on the roofs of the houses. (*CP*, V, 2-3; p. 40)

On that occasion, the streets had been magnificently decorated. The pavement was adorned with coloured [drawings made with] powders and pastes; flowers and flower petals had been lavishly spread. Festoons and tassels were hung at regular intervals; fragrant water and sandal paste mixed with water had been sprinkled all over. The citizens, in particular young ladies, who carried vessels and other objects required for the celebrations, were very busy. [At the appointed hour], the mother and the new-born child were made to sit [in a palanquin] and taken through the main streets of the city. The procession was headed by the king and the four branches of his army. He was accompanied by the ministers, notable citizens and *sumangaliyaru*.

At the head of the cortege were the musicians. They played on different instruments, which made a loud din. Ladies waving white fly-whisks flanked the procession, while young dancing girls danced along its route. (*CP*, V, 5-8; pp. 41-2)

As the procession progressed through the streets, throngs of citizens came out of their houses to stand on both sides of the street and enjoy the sight. Crowds of ladies watched the procession, either from the upper apartments of their houses or from balconies, terraces and platforms. They stood in front of the main entrances, sometimes climbing onto the pillars, or placing themselves in rows along the street [wherever there was place to stand]. (*CP*, V, 11, p. 42)

When the procession came near the houses, the ladies waiting at the doors of their dwellings came forward to wave four kinds of auspicious *arati* lamps in front of the new-born baby and to perform the other customary rituals, wishing all the best for the boy. In return, the king generously presented all those ladies with various kinds of jewellery, clothes, necklaces of pearls and the customary betel-nuts and leaves. Gifts were distributed to everybody without partiality or discrimination.

At the end, the procession returned to the palace. Finally, the king, after making the traditional presentations and having blessed the child, returned to his own palace. At this point, different kinds of *arati* lamps held in golden trays and bowls were waved in front of the mother and child. *Tupiridu* (the "act of spitting") was performed in front of them in order to protect the child from the evil eye. They were blessed and their heads sprinkled with auspicious rice. All this was performed by an elderly *sumangali* who was related to the family of the mother. (*CP*, V, 16-19; p. 44)

Later in the night when the child was asleep, the gods [Shiva and Shive] appeared by the side of the bed and by uttering the relevant *mantras* into his ears initiated him into religious life. They also gave him a Shiva *linga*. Furthermore, the child was given a name by Shiva: Channabasavanna. A talisman was tied on the wrist of the child in order to protect him from all evils. (*CP*, V, 24-5; pp. 46-7)

23.10 Birth and education of a prince

The *Mohana Tarangini* has this narrative.

In the course of the pregnancy, the lady was given whichever food items she most relished and desired. Only ladies with children [were around her]; they gave her new clothes, ornaments, flowers and scents to keep her happy and contented. Day by day, her weight increased and her hair split. (*MT*, XVII, 6-11; pp. 236-7)

At the end of the ninth month of pregnancy, she was made to lie down on a bejewelled cot. The *sumangaliyaru* in attendance sent for the midwives and the priests. On arrival, each of them gave the attendants their sacred ring, medicine and *mani-yantra* (talismanic jewel) to place at the feet of the lady in labour, in order to ensure the safe delivery of the child. Standing lamps lit the delivery room. After a night-long labour, a male child was born. The midwife rushed out of the room and to the great joy of all those who were waiting announced the birth of the child. (*MT*, IV, 78; p. 74; XVII, 12-13; p. 237)

The new-born [baby] was placed in a wooden tub and given a first bath in water mixed with cow-dung. The umbilical cord was cut with silver scissors and then buried in the earth together with the afterbirth attached to it. Then the body of the child was anointed with oil. He was given a bath with warm water and then covered in a soft cloth. The customary religious marks of sanctified ash and black dots were drawn between his brows; collyrium was applied to his eyelids in order to ward off evil and the effects of evil eye. On his right arm was tied a talisman encased in a golden casket. Somebody spat at the side of the child [to ward off evil]. He was given drops of sacred water, as well as of ripe lemon fruits. He was then made to lick his finger that had been smeared with sugar and honey [before being] breast-fed by the attendants. Finally, his body was anointed with butter and he was placed by the side of his mother, who had been bathed. (*MT*, IV, 74-5; p. 73; XVII, 17-23, 28 & 30; pp. 238-40)

Thereafter, the midwives and all the other ladies bathed and put on new garments. They gave the mother auspicious items, such as rice, sandal paste, betel-leaves and nuts, and then some *neem* juice to drink. Immediately afterwards, she was offered betel-nuts and leaves to chew. (*MT*, XVII, 27; p. 240)

As soon as the good news was announced by the midwife, the father sent urgently for the brahmin astrologers, who came immediately. They wore light-green *dhotis*, upper garments and *tripundra* marks on their foreheads. On arrival, as customary, they blessed the father of the new born. They were asked to cast the horoscope of the child. Thereupon, they made elaborate calculations, drew up the horoscope and predicted a good future for the prince. In return, they were presented with new clothes, ornaments, money and other items. Presents were given out in charity to mark the joyous occasion.

All the streets of the city were decorated with festoons, arches, floral wreathes, bunches of leaves and other ornaments. The king made gifts to everybody and all the prisoners were set free. Presents of gold coins with auspicious betel-leaves and nuts were sent to every house.

The birth of the prince became an occasion for celebrations. Some ladies, especially the concubines of the city, came out into the streets to throw saffron powder on each other and sing joyous songs. Following the custom, they carried oil in pots and turmeric as presents to the nursing mother and the ladies attending her in order to help them recover from the stress of the delivery. On the twelfth day after the birth, an important ceremony took place: the child was put in the cradle for the first time and given a name. On this occasion, the priests who had performed the *homa* and calculated the auspicious time for putting the child into the cradle received gifts [from the king].

The mother was given an elaborate bath, as prescribed by the scriptures. She wore new clothes and her hair-knot was tied in a yellow cloth; she had black *tilakas* on her forehead to ward off evil spirits and black collyrium enhanced her eyes. She wore various kinds of jewellery. Elegantly dressed, she was busy at the side of the cradle, accompanied by *sumangaliyaru* who held in their plates *arati* lamps of various kinds. (*MT*, XVII, 29-48; pp. 240-4)

The golden cradle was studded with gems. Brass chains connected it to brass hooks fitted into the wooden planks of the ceiling. The child was eventually put into the cradle. The priest standing by its side recited twelve names of god and the child was given one of them. Immediately after, the priests set the cradle in motion and blessed the child amidst the chanting of sacred verses and lullabies.

Then the mother, relatives and other ladies present on that occasion pushed the cradle gently to the accompaniment of various songs. The mother paid her respects to the priests and her husband and to the elderly ladies who gave her numerous presents and left for their homes. Auspicious music was played and sung throughout the ceremony. A further celebration took place after one month. (*MT*, IV, 68-71; pp. 72-3; XVII, 49-60; pp. 245-7)

After the birth of the baby, the mother was assisted by her ladies-in-waiting. She played in various ways with the child and derived unlimited joy from it. At times she removed the dirt from the skin folds of the neck and fingers of the child; sometimes, out of motherly affection, she kissed his private parts; if he had trouble in swallowing her milk, she blew on his head. When the child grew up and started crawling, he was given gold-laced garments and ornaments such as golden anklets with rattlers and the like. (*MT*, XI, 59-61, pp. 151-2; XVII, 63-7; pp. 247-8)

When he grew up, he learnt to dress himself, wear jewellery and play with boys and girls of his own age. He then learned how to read and write. He was taken to the gymnasium and trained in the various sports. He rode horses and elephants. In due course, he mastered all the 64 traditional disciplines.

Occasionally, in the company of other boys and friends, he enjoyed watching fights of birds and animals such as cocks, rams, buffaloes, elephants and others. He mastered the handling of the 22 varieties of arms and weapons and wrestled with professional wrestlers. When he became a young man, he started to enjoy playing and sporting with young girls. (*MT*, XVII, 77-84; pp. 250-51)

23.11 Religious initiation

This detailed passage from the *Shivatattva Chintamani* describes the *diksha-vidhana* (religious initiation) of a devotee following Virashaiva precepts.

[According to the poet, this procedure follows the details given in the *Vatulagama*.]

The preceptor in charge of the initiation of the devotee should be a properly qualified person. He should be very calm and composed, well-versed in all branches of the *Shaiva-agamas*, compassionate, contented, steadily engaged in Shaiva rituals, adorned with *vibhuti* and *rudraksha*, aware of the traditional practices, not greedy, blameless, devoid of all attachments and impartial.

Such a preceptor should for a full year observe the person wishing to be initiated. He should assess his behaviour, character and disposition to be initiated. Only after being fully satisfied with the qualifications of his disciple should he decide on initiating him and blessing him. (*S*, XLIII, 3-4; pp. 484-5)

Then, on the appointed day when the planets have reached the appropriate position, at the appropriate time and with the approval of the preceptor, the disciple should take a bath at sunrise. Thereafter, he should dress in silk garments, decorate himself with *vibhuti*, *rudraksha* beads and flowers and approach the preceptor.

On nearing the preceptor, the disciple should pay his respects and then worship the preceptor's feet. He should offer silk cloth, ornaments, flowers, garlands and fragrant substances such as sandal paste. He should wave *arati* lamps and incense [in the usual manner]. Thereafter, he should respectfully worship the other four priests [who will assist the preceptor during the rituals].

After that, he should respectfully offer betel-nuts and leaves to all those assembled there, according to their status and rank. Respectfully, he should go round to meet the other venerable and elderly persons [invoking their blessings] enter the *diksha-mantapa* (pavilion for the initiation ceremony) and sit at its centre.

The pavilion should be well cleaned and decorated with floor-drawings for that occasion. According to the means of the devotee, there should be five golden, silver, copper or mud vessels, all decorated with auspicious thread. Four should be placed at the main [cardinal] directions, the fifth in the middle. The vessels should contain the *pancharatna* (five kinds of gems), sacred water, fresh leaves, flowers, sandal paste, auspicious rice and garlands and should be covered with silk cloths and worshipped [in the usual manner].The chief priest should be seated in the centre, with [copies of] the *Rigveda, Yajurveda, Samaveda* and *Atharvaveda* [placed] respectively in the east, west, north, and south directions. They should be reciting the *panchakshari-mantra* and performing the usual rituals.

Then all of them in turn, including the chief priest, must sprinkle the disciple three times with the water contained in the five pots, using *darbha*-grass in order to purify him. Thereafter, the chief priest has to place his palms on the head of the disciple, while concentrating on the supreme god, and, at the auspicious moment, initiate him by whispering into his ears the sacred *mantra* symbolizing the greatness of the supreme god.

Throughout the ritual, the disciple should be seated with his hands folded in *anjali-mudra*. Then, in all reverence, he should receive the *linga* from his preceptor, wear it on his body and meditate on it. He should never be parted from it until the end [death]. Thereafter, he should lead a righteous life and regularly worship his personal *linga* three times a day according to the Virashaiva prescriptions. At the end of the ceremony, the initiated devotee should again worship the preceptor, and with all reverence offer *dakshine* and other gifts to the other priests and venerable persons. (*S*, XLIII, 6-25; pp. 485-90)

Chapter 24

OMENS, TALISMANS, DISEASES AND MAGIC SPELLS

This chapter is divided into four parts, the first giving an insight into the fascinating and mysterious world of good and bad omens, talismans and astrology. The most intriguing of these passages is the account of Chitralekha's proficiency in all things magic as given in the *Mohana Tarangini*. The second part begins with a broad systematization of diseases, followed by a succinct passage on the classification of medicines, based on how they were to be taken or on their basic ingredients, together with an interesting report on physicians, their dress, headgear and attendants, all drawn from the *Sanatkumara Charite*. This part ends with a vivid description of a lovesick princess pining for her absent lover, as found in the *Mohana Tarangini*.

Magic and magicians are considered in the third part of this chapter. A passage from the *Samyukta Kaumudi* describes a terrifying Kapalika mendicant and his awe-inspiring practices. A sombre account of black magic performed by a lady-in-waiting on behalf of a lovelorn queen comes from the *Ramanatha Charite*. The fourth and final part of the chapter is devoted to the accounts of animal sacrifice and ritual suicide in the *Sobagina Sone*.

Omens and talismans

24.1 Good omens

According to the *Sanatkumara Charite*, good omens are:

Twitching of the right eye, twitching of the right shoulder, chirping of the lizard on the right side, and a dream in the early hours of the day, in which the goddess Padmavati puts a garland of pearls around the neck of a lion, indicating that the dreamer [the queen] would beget a son endowed with good luck. (*SC*, XII, 44-5; p. 136)

24.2 Bad omens

The *Mohana Tarangini* lists the following, which were considered bad omens, especially on the verge of a battle:

A crow seen to the left of the marching army, a *hanga* bird flying from left to right across the path of the army, a lizard chirping to the right, a kite flying across the path, a throbbing in the left arm of the chief of the army, a twitching in his left eye, and trees falling to the ground along the route [of the army]. (*MT*, VI, 25-6; p. 95)

24.3 Astrological calculations

The same text describes how the astrologers fix a suitable date and time for moving to a new house.

The king [father of the bride] sent for learned and famous astrologers to consult them on the most suitable time for moving into the new house. On arrival, the astrologers blessed the king and offered [him], as was customary, the auspicious grains of rice. Then they requested the king to put forward his question and the king asked them to determine the best moment for the prince and his wife to be occupying a new house. The astrologers made elaborate calculations following the *surya-siddhanta* (established astrological system). At the end of all these detailed calculations, they fixed upon the *tithi* (date), *vara* (day), *nakshatra* (stellar position), *yoga* (conjunction of auspicious stars), *karana* (astrologically auspicious time of day), *graha-gati* (planetary movement) and others, and then informed the king when to take further actions. (*MT*, XIII, 52-5; p. 187)

24.4 The magical arts of Chitralekha

This story from the *Mohana Tarangini* contains information on the use of talismans and magic spells.

Chitralekha, a confidante of the princess, was adept in the art of magical formulae, talismans and the like. When she was on the verge of going away on some mission and of being separated from her princess for some time, she not only gave her detailed instructions about how to safeguard her safety, but also made some incantations, invoking all the planetary deities, including the god of love. At the end of that ceremony, she applied a black dot on the princess's forehead in order to avert all evil from her. In addition, she tied two talismans, one on the arm of the princess and the other on her own. These had the power to ward off any kind of malignant spirits and goblins and to keep them at a good distance from the wearer. Furthermore, [Chitralekha] was such an expert in the art of magical spells that there was hardly any other who could match her ability and her skill. On account of this, she had no fear of anything. She was capable of travelling in the air. All this she had learnt from a preceptor named Shukrachari.

At the same time, she was well informed in exorcisms of a benign nature and capable of invoking auspicious influences and powers. Thus, with their help, she could attain success for good causes. (*MT*, XXIX, 5-6; p. 402; 15; pp. 404 & 29-30; 35; pp. 406-07)

24.5 Talismans

A talisman or *bahupuri* (amulet with a magical spell) was tied on the arm of a warrior by a well-wishing lady. This had the properties of instantly clotting the blood gushing from the wounds caused by the enemy's sword, as well as doubling the wearer's strength and valour in battle. (*MT*, XXXIII, 59; p. 458; XXXIV, 19; p. 463)

Diseases, medicines, cures, black magic and witchcraft

24.6 List of diseases

The following three passages from the *Sanatkumara Charite* deal with diseases, medicines and *vaidyas* (physicians). The list of diseases mentions:

Cough, asthma, catarrh, respiration trouble, scabies, itching, fever, swollen eyes, stomach pain and the other 700 [ailments, the names of which are not mentioned]. (*SC*, XVII, 3; p. 200)

24.7 Classification of medicines

This classification follows the traditional Ayurvedic system.

Liquid medicines, medicines to be taken by licking and medicines in the form of globules were all kept in caskets specifically made for them. (*SC*, XVII, 11; p. 201)

There were other types of medicines: medicines in powder form, medicines made of red lead (?), medicines in the form of purified ash and medicated oils. (*SC*, XVII, 26; p. 205)

24.8 Physicians

The *vaidyas* (physicians) form the topic of this extract.

When called, they went to treat the sick accompanied by their attendants who carried the caskets containing various medicines and also [reference] books. When they went out, the physicians wore a *kulayi* (cotton head-dress) and a cloth covering their upper bodies; in their hands they held coloured napkins. They wore ornaments in their ears, rings on the fingers and necklaces with central pendants. (*SC*, XVII, 12; p. 202)

24.9 "Love sickness"

The *Mohana Tarangini* has an extensive passage describing the "love sickness" of the princess.

The love-sick princess was led by her trusted friends and ladies-in-waiting to the upper apartment of the palace.

She lay down on a bedstead, which had a soft thick mattress. All ornaments were removed from her body and garments that were tight were loosened. Her hair-knot was untied and a broad cloth was wrapped around her head. Her forehead was smeared with musk, her feet were washed with sweet-smelling cold water taken out of a pitcher and fragrant and cool sandal paste was applied all over her body by her companions. [....]

Some attendants fanned her body gently with fans and fly-whisks in order to soothe her. They covered her body with a soft and cool silken blanket. Some dear companions embraced her in their efforts to console her, while others spoke to her in soft and gentle words.

After some time, lacking patience, they all went down the stairs and entered a pleasure garden situated close to the palace. There the princess was made to sit on a swing for a change and to relieve her mind. But this did not bring any solace. Unable to endure the pangs of love, this princess embraced her most trusted friend, Chitralekha.

Again in their efforts to console the princess, her ladies-in-waiting and attendants together took her to a cool and shady bower, where she was made to lie down on a bed of green and cool leaves and fresh twigs from young plants, placed close to a channel of cool and pure running water. (*MT*, XXVII, 29-35, 58-62; pp. 383-90; XXVIII, 5-9, 12-13 & 18; pp. 393-5)

Magic spells

24.10 Black magic

This vivid description of a Kapalika mendicant is drawn from the *Samyukta Kaumudi.*

One day, a Kapalika mendicant arrived at a house [....] begging for alms. He was dressed in a tiger skin and wore garlands of conches and beads. He was stout, his body was smeared with holy ash and in his hands he carried the trident and a small hourglass-drum. His hair was dishevelled, but not too long. He had a shoulder bag containing drugs and sedatives. In short, he was terrifying. (*SK*, V, 27; p. 90) [....]

On the night of the appointed day, he went to the burial ground situated on the outskirts of the city, taking with him all the items required for conducting [black magic] rituals. There he made a dead body sit up, placed a skull into its hands, performed some rituals by chanting and reciting related *mantras* and invoked an evil force. (*SK*, V, 32-3; p. 91)

24.11 Magicians and magic spells

From the *Ramanatha Charite* comes this account of black magic.

The youngest queen saw, in the course of a festival, a son of her husband by an [older] queen, and was attracted to him by his youth and heroic qualities. The young woman pleaded with her lady-in-waiting to arrange a meeting with him.

Thereupon, that lady-in-waiting promised her mistress to make use of witchcraft and some medicines to conquer the prince. She also undertook to invoke the evil powers through black magic. In addition, she suggested imbuing a portrait of the queen with a spell, the effect of which would cause the prince to fall in love with her and desire her passionately at the very first sight of it. (*RC*, XXIII, 49-54; pp. 46-7, II)

Accordingly, [the lady-in-waiting] indulged in practices of various kinds, including the waving of burning camphor, presenting fresh flowers and buds, applying sandal paste to the feet of the goddess and offering silk garments studded with jewels. She also offered to have her mouth closed with a metal lock, to dress only in *neem* leaves and to perform her ritual. She was even prepared to disembowel herself and offer her intestines to the goddess in order to achieve her aim. (*RC*, XXIII, 82-7; pp. 52-3, II) [....]

At last, she promised the lovelorn queen that she would fetch her lover in about a fortnight's time and that she should not become dejected or worried since there were many evil deities who would fulfil her desires and they had to be invoked. (*RC*, XXIII, 94-6; p. 54, II and XXIV, 32-7; pp. 61-2, II)

[Next day], that trusted lady-in-waiting joined the queen in the audience hall and informed her of the various items of black magic that she would obtain. They included the following: a substance inducing attraction for making the dot on the forehead, a substance inducing attraction to be applied to the eye-lashes, a kind of magic ash, a substance to attract the object and a small figure of the inauspicious goddess. (*RC*, XXV, 57-63; pp. 94-5; XXIX, 109-10; p. 189, II)

Accordingly, that lady [-in-waiting] invoked and worshipped various evil deities [goddesses] in diverse ways with offerings that included different cooked items and animal sacrifices. At times she stood naked in the darkness and prayed to the goddesses. At last, the goddesses assured her that they would only arrange for the prince to enter the apartment of the queen; the queen herself would have to win him over. (*RC*, XXVI, 1-16; pp. 105-07, II)

Sacrifices

24.12 Animal sacrifice

The *Sobagina Sone* has several gory passages on animal sacrifice and ritual suicide.

[A female spirit conjured up by an ascetic with his supernatural powers was at large to punish the king and his army who had insulted her.]

The king, in order to pacify that wicked [female] spirit who was causing havoc in the city, organized offerings of food and other sacrifices. Accordingly, 3,000 sheep, 700 bisons, 16,000 large vessels full of cooked food and 8,000 pots of liquor were placed before the spirit, along with red flowers. Then she was invited to partake of food and drinks which she consumed at one stretch. (*SoS*, VI, 45-6; p. 65)

She also devoured 77,000 horses, 1,000 elephants and more. (*SoS*, VI, 50-1; p. 65)

24.13 Ritual suicide

This theme occurs quite frequently in Indian myths, though the device used by the prince to end his own life, as described here in these passages from the *Sobagina Sone*, is somewhat unusual. (Such devices are sometimes also depicted in the sculpture of the period, particularly on memorial-stones celebrating the self-immolation of a person.)

[The prince approached the temple of Mahakali in the middle of the forest].

There he saw the severed heads of humans, sheep and buffaloes sacrificed to the goddess. There were tassels made of the intestines of the immolated [human] beings. The whole area around the temple looked grim with blood stains all over. There were pots of *toddy* (crude liquor) and heaps of cooked food. (*SoS*, XI, 30-2; p. 99)

[When there was no response for his prayers from the goddess], the prince sacrificed his life by putting his head onto a special device. When his head was cut off from the body it sprang into the air. This sacrifice was appreciated by all those gathered there to witness this feat. (*SoS*, XI, 56-7; p. 104)

The brother of the prince, seeing that his elder brother had sacrificed his life, followed his example by jumping into the fire-pit that was in front of the Mahakali temple. (*SoS*, XI, 72; p. 107)

Chapter 25

COMPETITIONS, SPORTS, GAMES AND INTELLECTUAL PURSUITS

This chapter gives an account of the most popular pastimes of the period. Apart from the bullock race, an annual public event celebrated with all pomp and circumstance, as described in the excerpt from the *Amalabasava Charite*, most of the leisure activities mentioned here concentrate on different types of indoor games: playing with dice and cowries, ball games, jumping games and so on. Moreover, various board games seem to have been the most fashionable in courtly and other circles. The *Pampasthana Varnanam* shows how the courtesans, apart from being skilled in board games, also indulged in other amusements, such as painting, singing and acting, and even solving mathematical riddles. Games with bets and other more boisterous pastimes taking place near the quarters of the courtesans are recorded in the *Mohana Tarangini*.

Princely leisure activities also make an appearance in the literature, especially martial sports and also intellectual pursuits, both of which are mentioned in the *Vijayakumari Charite* and *Ramanatha Charite*. The account of diverse honeymoon entertainments given in the *Vijayakumari Charite* includes conventional board games, garden strolls and water sports, as well as animal fights between rams and bisons.

25.1 A bullock race

The *Amalabasava Charite* has a vivid description of a bullock race, here called *kariya-habba*.

On the full moon of *Jyeshtha* (May-June) was a festival called *Kara-parva*, in the course of which a race of young bullocks took place. For this occasion the city was decorated with festoons and banners and there was music everywhere. In short, the whole city looked like the abode of auspiciousness.

People belonging to the eighteen castes of society, the *shudra, vaishya, kshatriya*, brahmins and others, left their homes to enjoy the celebrations, assembling at an appointed place to watch the race. Numerous young bullocks had been brought there to participate in the competition. Their horns were embellished with golden rings and tassels, their chests with rattling bells, their bellies with bigger bells and their backs cloaked with cloths inlaid with small pieces of mirror. Around their necks were strings of pearls, anklets were on their legs and their ears were covered with painted ornaments. Their bodies had been sprinkled with fragrant water, sandal paste and sweet-smelling powder from various flowers. There was a large number of decorated animals, each of a different type, all waiting to take part in the competition; to add to the din, a number of musicians played loudly. The king, his wise ministers, subordinate rulers and others of his retinue arrived and looked on. (*AC*, XXXV, 4-9; pp. 362-4)

The bullocks in the race had to run to a fixed point called *karugallu* (a stone normally fixed at the entrance of the town or village). As expected, the king's bullock won the race. (*AC*, XXXV, 12; p. 364)

25.2 Leisure pursuits of a king

The *Vijayakumari Charite* gives an account of the king's leisure hours as follows.

The king, seated in his audience [hall], used to spend his free time in the company of persons specializing in various branches of knowledge. He was interested in many subjects and enjoyed participating in these meetings. Among the topics discussed were grammar, logic, music, musical performance, poetry, literature, mythology, *yantras, tantras, mantras*, the 64 arts, etcetera. The king composed poems, wrote prose and dramas and took part in debates with the court scholars and learned persons. (*VC*, I, 335-9; p. 36)

25.3 Pastimes of a prince

Among the pastimes of the prince and his friends were sports, indoor games and intellectual pursuits, as described in the *Ramanatha Charite.*

After having his morning bath, etcetera, the prince sent for his friends and went with them to the gymnasium. He spent some time there doing his exercises. He practised the use of weapons, such as swords and daggers of various shapes and sizes, clubs of iron and wood and others. They spent some time watching the fights of bisons, rams, elephants, horses, wrestlers, etcetera. Then they played indoor games such as *netta* and *pagade.* (*RC*, XXVIII, 1-3; p. 155, II)

The prince and his associates played a ball game in two teams. (*RC*, XXVIII, 1-3; p. 155, II)

[The prince and his friends] enjoyed engaging in discussion with learned persons. They debated on literature, philosophy, history, poetry, drama, and on the works of ancient authors such as Bana, Bharata, etcetera. They also spent some time listening to musicians and singers. (*RC*, XXVIII, 3-5; p. 155, II)

25.4 Pastimes of the courtesans

The *Pampasthana Varnanam* lists the following pastimes of the courtesans.

They would sit facing each other on cushions embellished with pearls and pass their time in playing different types of dice games, such as *pagade* and *netta*, *chadurange* (a kind of chess game), or talking in humorous ways, joking, playing with mystical diagrams, singing, reciting classical works, acting, solving quizzes and mathematical riddles, painting and performing dances based on romantic themes. (*PV*, I, 72; p. 25)

25.5 Indoor games

The *Samyukta Kaumudi* mentions a range of indoor games:

Gaduga (a game played using seeds), *hidigavade* (a game played with cowries), *sadugudu* (a game played in teams), *sendu* (a game with balls), *bohari* (a game with tops) and *jigi-halle* (a jumping game). (*SK*, X, 9; p. 183)

25.6 Games with bets

This passage from the *Mohana Tarangini* describes games with bets.

In some parts of the quarter of the concubines there were storeyed houses with spacious halls on the side of the road. These were the places where games with stakes or bets were played. The participants in such games were visitors from the 56 countries. Both indoor and outdoor games were played there. The most popular were: cutting a plantain fruit thrown in the air before it touched the ground; breaking into two a coconut, which oscillated to and fro; cutting a bundle of sugarcanes with a single stroke; and reducing a block of jaggery to smithereens with a single blow. Among the indoor games were: *letta*, *pagade*, *chadurange*, *bohari*, *solle*, *bara*, *guttadoppu*, *saribesa* and others. Quite often arguments and quarrels arose among the players, gamblers, concubines, attendants, drunkards and money-lenders who were engaged in these games. (*MT*, XX, 19-26; pp. 297-8)

25.7 Recreations of the citizens

The *Channabasava Purana* gives the following information on board games.

The popularity of *chadurange* has already been referred to while describing the streets of the concubines. [It appears] that this game was a favourite of the harlots and their callers. The pawns used were called horse, elephant, king, minister and soldier. There was money staking too. (*CP*, X, 46; p. 106)

Another indoor game was *pagadeyata* (a game of dice). It was played with black, red, green and double pawns. It was a popular game with the concubines and their visitors. (*CP*, X, 47-8; pp. 106-7)

25.8 Pet birds

The *Sanatkumara Charite* has the following accounts of royal pets.

The royal palace was a shelter for pet birds, which were kept for entertainment. Among these were parrots capable of reciting what they had been taught and cuckoos with melodious voices. There were peacocks who danced with their tails spread and graceful swans. The bees hovered, making a soft buzzing noise. (*SC*, V, 35; p. 49)

25.9 Honeymoon entertainments

The *Vijayakumari Charite* lists the pastimes of a couple on their honeymoon.

The newly wedded couple spent their leisure hours in the following indoor and outdoor pastimes:

[playing] *netta* (dice), backgammon, *pagade* (chess) and *chadurange*; [watching] animal fights with rams and bisons, and wrestling [matches]; sporting in a garden and in the water of a pool; and listening to music and watching dance performances, etcetera. (*VC*, I, 459-60; p. 49)

APPENDICES

Appendix I

SOURCE TEXTS AND THEIR AUTHORS

The notes that follow give essential summary information about the 27 literary works, from which all of the translated passages in this volume have been drawn. The works are here arranged in chronological order, according to the commonly accepted dates assigned to the authors. Each entry in this list follows a standard scheme: resumé of the life and career of the author; synopsis of the work as a whole, together with a condensed account of the principal narrative; overall format of the work; location of the manuscript consulted and publication details; and index of all the sections in the volume quoting passages from the work.

1 *Jaimini Bharata* (*JB*) by Lakshmisha (*ca.* 1345-47)

The author of the poem, Lakshmisha son of Annamanka, was born in the first half of the fourteenth century in Devanuru, near Kaduru (Chikmagalur District). There, between 1345 and 1347, he composed the *Jaimini Bharata*. It is likely that the poet visited Vijayanagara. Little is known about his life. He was a Vaishnava brahmin of the Bharadvaja *gotra* and possibly a priest. His patron deity was Lakshmi-ramana-svami of Devanuru.

Based on the Sanskrit poem by Jaimini *muni*, the *Jaimini Bharata* narrates the preparations for the *ashvamedha-yajna* which the Pandavas were to perform in order to celebrate their victory over the Kauravas. Before performing the *yajna*, a specially selected horse followed by a huge army was set free to roam. The custom was that if the animal entered another kingdom its ruler had to acknowledge the sovereignty of its owner. Whoever defied this rule was attacked by the army following it. In this way, Arjuna conquered many kings, thus establishing his supremacy over them. Such exploits are vividly narrated in this work.

The *Jaimini Bharata* consists of 34 chapters and 1,907 poems.

There are various manuscripts of this poem, written both on palm-leaf and on handmade paper, copied by several scribes at different times. The material was found in the Chief Epigraphist's Library, Mysore, 294.5923 LAK, Acc. No. 13922.

The work, edited in Kannada by B. Bhimashena Rao, was published in 1973 by T.N. Krishnayya Setty & Son, Chikkapete, Bangalore, and printed at the Sree Satyananda Press, Bangalore. It has not been translated into English.

See Sections 2.1, 3.1, 3.11, 3.12, 4.3, 4.11, 17.1, 17.2, 18.1 and 19.14.

2 *Dharmanatha Purana* (*DP*) by Bahubali Pandita (*ca.* 1352)

Unfortunately, Bahubali Pandita's life is shrouded in mystery. It is not known where the poet lived, nor where his poem was composed. He was a Jaina who lived in the fourteenth century and wrote the *Dharmanatha Purana* in *ca.* 1352.

The poem is a *champu-kavya* (a poetic work with prose passages). The poet shows his ability in using a number of different metres.

The aim of this work was to narrate, for the first time in Kannada, the life of the fifteenth *Tirthankara*, Dharmanatha.

The work begins by paying homage to monks, ascetics, the goddess Sarasvati and a number of eminent Jaina personages, followed by the traditional description of the Bharata and Kosala countries. The story of Dharmanatha then begins.

The ruler of Kosala, Mahasena, and his queen Suvratadevi had no issue. One day the *acharya* Pracheta and 500 disciples arrived in the capital and were served by the royal couple with great devotion. Pracheta was pleased and blessed them, forecasting that they would become the parents of a divine son who would be venerated by the whole world. The king and the queen were extremely happy and requested the *acharya* to give them an account of the previous life-history of the soul to be born as their son.

Pracheta told them that long ago their son had been born as the son of a royal couple of Vatsadesha, king Bhanuraja and queen Manohari, and had been called Dasaratha. On attaining the appropriate age Dasaratha was consecrated king, and his father renounced the world and commenced a life of penance. Dasaratha and his wife, Dayavatidevi, entertained daily members of the Jaina faith, thereby gaining great merit. One night, on seeing a lunar eclipse, he too decided to retire from the life of worldly pleasure in order to attain salvation.

When, after millions of years, Dasaratha returned to earth as Dharmanatha, his birth was blessed by the gods and goddesses. His childhood was happy and at the proper age he was appointed the crown prince. Meanwhile, the *svayamvara* of the princess Shringaradevi of Kundinapura was announced. Dharmanatha participated and won the hand of the princess.

He returned home with her, and in due course his father, Mahasena, renounced the world and Dharmanatha was consecrated king. The princes who had been disappointed at the *svayamvara* then united to declare war on Dharmanatha. They were, however, defeated by the commander-in-chief of the king.

One day, during a royal audience, a meteor fell from the sky. Dharmanatha interpreted this as an indication that the time had come for him to renounce the world. So he took his vows and his son succeeded him.

Dharmanatha eventually attained enlightenment and preached to the gods, the ascetics and the others, seated in the centre of the *samavasarana-mantapa* (preaching hall).

The text contains, in passing, vivid descriptions of the country, the royal court, the education of the princes, the royal ladies, the birthday celebrations, the royal marriages, the various pleasures and pastimes, the water sports of the royal ladies, the king's nightly rounds in the city, the prostitutes, the drinking of intoxicants and the performances of music and dance, most of which were observed by the poet in contemporary society.

The work consists of sixteen sections and 2,485 poems.

There are various manuscripts of this work, written both on palm-leaf and on handmade paper, copied by different scribes at different times. The material was found in the Maharaja College Library, Mysore, K 821.32 BAH dB, Acc. No. 95840.

The work, edited in Kannada by N. Basavaradhya, was published in 1975 by the University of Mysore, and printed by Messrs. Mitra Printers, Mysore. It has not been translated into English.

See Sections 1.1, 3.4, 3.13, 3.14, 6.2, 7.1, 8.10, 9.4, 10.1, 10.8, 12.4, 13.2, 15.7, 16.1, 17.4, 18.7, 19.21, 23.2, 23.3 and 23.7.

3 *Padmaraja Purana* (*PP*) by Padmanaka (*ca.* 1385)

Padmanaka, the author of the work, was born in the second half of the fourteenth century, probably in Ambapura, and died in 1420. He was the tenth descendant of Padmaraja, the main character of his work. It is believed that the poet was based in Ambapura where he composed his poem in *ca.* 1385, and he is likely to have visited Vijayanagara. His ancestors were ministers of the Hoysala kings, and later feudatory rulers. The poet was a Virashaiva and his family deity was Vishvanatha of Varanasi.

The *Padmaraja Purana* narrates the life of Padmaraja, a historic person, popularly known as Kereya-Padmarasa, who was a minister at the court of Narasimha Ballala of the Hoysala dynasty at Dorasamudra. The underlying aim of the work, however, is to establish the superiority of Virashaivism over Vaishnavism. Many long and short tales, told with vivid details and often with poetical exaggeration, are embedded in the main narrative.

The work begins with salutations to god Vishvanatha of Varanasi, other deities and the Virashaiva saints. Then follows a description of the Karnataka country, the birth of Padmaraja and his education, and his marriage to the daughter of Gourappa-dannayaka, a minister at the court of the Hoysala kings.

While narrating these events the poet renders in detail the Hoysala country, the bridal dress and ornaments, the reception of the groom, the wedding ceremony and much else. After the marriage, on the death of his father-in-law, Padmaraja assumes office as a minister under the Hoysala king. Even as minister he continues to lead a religious, pious and righteous life. A good account is given of the king's audiences and of deliberations at the court.

It is claimed that Padmaraja was responsible, in a miraculous way, for the construction of a large irrigation tank near Beluru. When the king goes to check the news for himself, the poet takes the opportunity to describe in detail the large retinue of the king, the appearance of the tank, the usefulness of its water, and the various kinds of trees and crops grown there. The king is pleased and suitably rewards Padmaraja.

Thereafter, Padmaraja turns to pious activities, and charitable deeds such as organizing free-feeding. As part of the urban scene, the poet gives a detailed description of pleasure gardens and of the houses of different merchants, prostitutes and others. The rest of the work deals with doctrinal disputes between the heads of the Virashaivas and of the Vaishnavas.

The last chapter tells how Padmaraja retires from office and proceeds from Dorasamudra to Varanasi, on the way staying in the city of Hampe for some days. Eventually, he reaches Varanasi and there he merges with his patron deity Vishvanatha.

The poem consists of thirteen chapters and 1,270 poems.

There are various manuscripts of this work, written both on palm-leaf and on handmade paper, copied by several scribes at different times. The material was found in the Maharaja College Library, Mysore, K 821.22 PADpH, Acc. No. 29331.

The work, edited in Kannada by R.C. Hiremath, was published in 1958 by the Muruga Matha, Dharwad, and printed at the Lingaraja Art Press, Dharwad. It has not been translated into English.

See Sections 4.8, 4.12, 4.15, 4.17, 6.3, 8.6, 8.8, 11.4, 12.8, 14.1, 19.11 and 19.15.

4 *Virupaksha Shataka* (*VS*) (*ca.* 1410)

The work does not contain any information about the name, provenance or life of the author. However, it is likely that he was associated with the town of Hampe, and a contemporary of Devaraya I, possibly even enjoying the king's patronage. This is corroborated by the fact that the poem mentions the kings of the Sangama dynasty up to Devaraya I. The poet was probably a Virashaiva and his patron deity was Pampapati-Virupaksha of Hampe. The *Virupaksha Shataka* was written there in about 1410. As the title indicates, the poem is in praise of the god Pampapati-Virupaksha, patron deity of the Vijayanagara monarchs, particularly those of the Sangama dynasty. As expected, most of the poems end with the words *Shri Virupaksha.*

The work begins with prayers to Ganapati, Sarasvati and other deities. From the tenth poem onwards, the author addresses his prayers directly to Virupaksha and refers to various mythological incidents such as Shiva killing Andhakasura and the Tripurasuras, and the burning of Madana. In poem 123, the river Tungabhadra, the Hemakuta and Matanga hills, and other local landmarks are mentioned. In some poems, the poet expresses his desire to be freed from entanglement in the material aspects of life.

The *Virupaksha Shataka* consists of 136 poems without divisions into sections.

There are various manuscripts of this work, both on palm-leaf and on handmade paper, copied by different scribes and at different times. The material was found in the Kannada Adhyayana Samsthe, Mysore, Nos. KB 179/1 and KB 384/2. The work has not been edited.

See Sections 5.8, 5.9, 5.10, 5.11 and 5.12.

5 *Sobagina Sone* (*SoS*) by Deparaja (1424-46?)

The biographical details of Deparaja are unknown. However, it is believed that the *Sobagina Sone,* whose title means "Drizzle of Delight", was written by king Devaraya II under the pseudonym of Deparaja. The author lived in Hampe and it is here that he probably composed the work in the first half of the fifteenth century. He was a follower of either Virashaivism or Shaivism.

The *Sobagina Sone* is a poetic work and contains a number of romantic stories told by the poet to his wife. These include vivid descriptions that throw light on contemporary life at Vijayanagara.

The work begins with a description of a country called Chadura, its capital city Sisuvolalu, and its king Jayashekhara, whose queen was Surabhavati. One day, the king and the queen had a romantic encounter in the garden and in due course the queen gave birth to a prince named Vikrama or Jasagampa. He grew up in the company of two noble friends, Madura and Malava.

In the first story Kanjere is abducted by the demon Bagura. Eventually the demon is killed, Kanjere is released and she is married to Vikrama's friend, Malava. In the next story Madura's marriage to Vasanta is celebrated in the Kalika temple. These narratives are followed by a number of other stories containing vivid descriptions of everyday life. The last of these deals with the romance between the prince Vikrama and the princess Patrini. The work, apparently incomplete, ends with the meeting of the royal lovers.

The work comprises 26 to 30 chapters and 2,050 to 2,179 poems. The variations are due to the additions of the copyists.

There are various manuscripts of the *Sobagina Sone*, both on palm-leaf and on handmade paper, copied by several scribes at different times. The material is in the University U.G. Library, Mysore, K 821.31/DEP of S.

The work, edited by B.S. Sannayya, was published in 1970 by the Kannada Adhyayana Samsthe, Mysore, and printed by U.S. Printers, Chamundipuram, Mysore. It has not been translated into English.

See Sections 1.2, 3.17, 4.10, 6.1, 6.3, 16.2, 16.3, 24.12 and 24.13.

6 *Jivandhra Charite* (*JCB*) by Bhaskara-Kavi (*ca.* 1424)

Bhaskara-Kavi, or simply Bhaskara, son of Basavanaka, was born in Penukonda. He lived and probably died there in the first half of the fifteenth century. He belonged to a Jaina family of the Vishvamitra *gotra*. It is likely that he visited Vijayanagara. His work, the *Jivandhra Charite*, was composed in about 1424. It is said that the poet wrote it seated in the Sushanteshvara Jaina temple at Penukonda, of which he was probably in charge.

The narrative, containing many sub-stories, is woven around a prince, Jivandhra, so named because he was found alive in a burial ground by a merchant, Gandhotkata.

The text opens with salutations to the Jaina *Tirthankaras*, preceptors, previous Jaina poets, and so on. The story is presented as if it was told by an ascetic named Gautamadhara to a ruler, Shrenika-Maharaja.

The Hemanga country, whose capital was Rajapuri, was ruled by king Satyandhara. In the same town a wood-cutter, Kashtangara, made his living by carrying wood from the nearby forest and selling in the market. One day, the tired wood-cutter was resting in front of the house of a beautiful young lady, Padmavati. Enamoured of her beauty, the wood-cutter decided to enjoy her company. He was told to have 1,000 gold coins ready for her and, accordingly, he worked hard to save that sum.

Meanwhile, he met a Jaina teacher who forbade him to visit any woman on full-moon days, a direction which he scrupulously observed. Eventually, when he had saved the 1,000 gold coins, he went to Padmavati's house, but when he realized that it was a full-moon day he left, forsaking his money. The honest lady complained to the king. He appreciated the principles and restraint observed by the wood-cutter and appointed him as his minister. Kashtangara proved to be efficient in his office, but as the king had no heir, he soon had ambitions to usurp the throne.

After some time the queen conceived. The angry minister rebelled against the king and killed him in a battle. The queen fled for safety and reached the burial ground where she gave birth to a son, but abandoned it. At the same time, a merchant, Gandhotkata, was in the burial ground with his still-born child. On seeing the abandoned child he took it home, brought him up properly, and entrusted his education to a Jaina preceptor, Aryanandi. It was through his teacher that Jivandhra discovered the events which led to his abandonment.

Then the prince Jivandhra started to plan to take revenge on the usurper. In order to gain strength he began to lead an adventurous life, in the course of which he gained the hand of eight princesses and the support of their fathers. Finally, the wood-cutter was killed in battle and Jivandhra regained his father's kingdom. He re-instated his mother who, in old age, took to a life of meditation. Jivandhra, too, after having ruled for some time, left the kingdom to his son and retired to the forest to attain salvation.

The *Jivandhra Charite* consists of sixteen chapters and 908 poems.

There are various manuscripts of this work written both on palm-leaf and on handmade paper, copied by several scribes at different times. The material was found in the University U.G. Library, Mysore, K 821.32 BHA.K, Acc. No. 166434.

This work, edited in Kannada by P. Nagarajayya and K.N. Krishnamurthy Rao, was published in 1970 by Messrs. Samaja Pustakalaya, Dharwad, and printed by Pratibha Mudrana, Dharwad. It has not been translated into English.

See Sections 19.3, 19.9 and 19.13.

7 *Prabhulinga Lile* (*PL*) by Chamarasa (*ca.* 1430)

The exact dates of Chamarasa are unknown. He lived and worked in the first half of the fifteenth century at Vijayanagara, where he was probably one of the court poets of Devaraya II. He was a Virashaiva, as is clearly demonstrated in the present work. The *Prabhulinga Lile*, which was composed at Vijayanagara around 1430, is the biography of a saint and writer of the twelfth century, Allama-prabhu. The poem also mentions Allama-prabhu's contemporary and close associate Basaveshvara, who was a minister at the court of Bijjala III of the Kalachuri dynasty of Kalyani.

One day, seated in audience on mount Kailasa, Shiva proclaimed that to attain a place of permanent happiness in Kailasa one had to be born as a mortal, lead a righteous life and acquire true knowledge. Parvati asked whether there was any such person on earth. In reply, Shiva uttered the name of Allama, who was already born as a human, and was none other than an aspect of his own self. Wishing to test him, Parvati sent to earth the personified negative aspect of herself, which took birth as princess Maya, the daughter of Mamakara and Mohini of Banavase.

The youthful Maya visited the temple of Madhukeshvara daily and worshipped the enshrined deity. One day Allama went to that temple and played beautifully on his *maddale.* At that, the enraptured Maya, a skilled dancer, sent for him. She fell in love with him at first sight. He was led to the palace and, with the king's approval, he was appointed as dance-teacher to Maya. Maya's advances were not appreciated by Allama and an assistant, Vimale, tried to dissuade her, but failed. Allama fled from Maya.

Meanwhile, the embodiment of Parvati's positive aspect was born as Mahadeviyakka in Udutadi. Its ruler, attracted by her beauty, wanted to marry her but she renounced worldly pleasures and led a saintly life.

On his way to Kalyani, Allama met with other saints: Goggayya, Animisha, Muktayakka and Siddharama of Sonnalapura. With Siddharama he reached Kalyani, where he met Basaveshvara and others. He lectured to all who had gathered in the Anubhava-mantapa on the secret of the *ishtalinga.* He also taught Mahadeviyakka who, in the meantime, had also come to Kalyani.

Allama-prabhu then left Kalyani to wander throughout the country teaching devotees. At Srigiri, he met Goraksha and taught him about *moksha.*

When at last he returned to Kalyani, Basaveshvara met him and offered him the *shunya-simhasana.* He set an example to them regarding feeding the *jangamas* with devotion and humility. He also taught the elements of Virashaiva philosophy to all the followers gathered at Kalyani and led them in the way of salvation.

The work consists of 25 sections and 1,111 poems.

There are various manuscripts of the *Prabhulinga Lile,* both on palm-leaf and on handmade paper, copied by several scribes and at different times. The work has also been translated or rewritten in Tamil, Telugu, Marathi and Sanskrit. This Kannada version was found in the Chief Epigraphist's Office Library, Mysore, No. 08869/294. 5513/CHA.

The *Prabhulinga Lile* was edited in Kannada by a team of scholars and published in 1938 by the Lingayat Vidyabhivridhi Samathe. It was printed at the Lingaraja Art Press, Dharwad. The work has not been translated into English.

See Sections 9.8, 10.7 and 22.2.

8 *Pampasthana Varanam* (*PV*) by Chandrashekhara (*ca.* 1430)

Chandrashekhara, also known as Chandrakavi, lived in the fifteenth century. He was a court poet and his patrons were the minister Jakkanacharya, one of the great personalities at the court of Devaraya II, and the king himself. The poet lived at Vijayanagara where he composed the *Pampasthana Varnanam* in about 1430. He was a Virashaiva and a linguist, and author of another work, the *Gurumurti Shankara Shataka.* Chandrashekhara's patron deity was probably Virupaksha of Hampe.

The work is in *champu* form, a mixture of poetry and prose. As indicated by its title, the *Pampasthana Varnanam* describes Hampe, the seat of Pampa and Virupaksha. It opens with salutations to Pampa-Virupaksha, Siddhi-Vinayaka, Vagdevi and other gods. Then the poet's patrons are specified as the king Proudhadevaraya and the minister Jakkan-charya. Particularly interesting are poems 5, 6 and 7, which give an account of the king. A general description of hills, lakes, river and forests follows. From the fifteenth poem onwards, the theme is restricted to Hampe and its actual environment: the river Tunga-bhadra, Rishyamukha hill, Manmatha-kunda, Hemakuta and the surrounding forests. There follows the rendering of Pampapura, its citizens, the main temple of Virupaksha, the deity and the assembly hall. The last topic is of a festive gathering of young ladies, musicians, dancers, performers and the like, as spectators from all walks of life gathered to witness this great event. Although short, this work is very relevant for its contemporary account of Hampe.

The *Pampasthana Varnanam* is not divided into sections, but consists of 61 poems and 34 prose passages. There are various manuscripts of the work, both on palm-leaf and on handmade paper, copied by several scribes and at different points of time. The material was found in the Kannada Dictionary Office, Kannada Sahitya Parishat, Bangalore, Acc. No. 2095 dt. 21.8.67, Vol. II, pp. 124-25.

This short work of 36 pages, edited by B. Sivamurthy Shastry, was published in 1955 by the Sarana Sahitya Karyalaya, 92 Rangaswamy Gudi Street, Bangalore, and printed at the Swatantra Karnataka Mudranalaya, Bangalore. It has not been translated into English.

See Sections 2.2, 5.3, 6.4, 8.5, 20.4, 20.5 and 25.4.

9 *Airavata* (*A*) by Kumara Vyasa (*ca.* 1430)

There is little information about the life of Kumara Vyasa, also known as Naranappa. He was probably born at the beginning of the fifteenth century in Kolivada, near Gadag. It is likely that he visited Vijayanagara, although the present work was composed in the Viranarayana temple, Gadag. The poet probably belonged to the caste of the *senabavas* (scribes and village officers). He was a *smarta* brahmin and his patron deity was Vira-narayana.

The *Airavata* (Indra's elephant) was written about 1430. The poem is based on an episode from the *Mahabharata.* One day the sage Vedavyasa suggested to Gandhari, the mother of the Kauravas, that she celebrate the worship of "Gauri seated on an elephant" (an image made of clay) which would give her immense merit, fame and riches. In her arrogance, Gandhari performed the ritual without inviting Kunti and the Pandavas. Kunti, grievously offended, was consoled by her sons, and Arjuna vowed that he would bring Indra's celestial elephant, Airavata, to enable his mother to perform the worship of Gauri. He shot a number of arrows into the sky, creating a path on which the elephant could descend from heaven to earth. Kunti and her five sons performed the ritual under the guidance of Krishna and Vedavyasa. Although the Kauravas and their parents, Gandhari and Dhritarashtra, were invited, they did not come. The ceremony was successfully celebrated; thereby Kunti and her sons earned great merit, fame and riches.

The *Airavata* consists of eight chapters and 375 poems. There are various manuscripts of this work, both on palm-leaf and on handmade paper, copied by different scribes at different times. The material was found in the Chief Epigraphist Office Library, Mysore, 294.5923/ Kum. No. 8936.

The work, edited in Kannada by R.S. Panchamukhi, was published in 1949 by the Kannada Research Institute, Dharwad, and printed at the Vasanta Mudranalaya, Dharwad. It has not been translated into English.

See Sections 9.1, 9.2, 9.3, 18.2 and 21.1.

10 *Proudharayana Kavya* (*PK*) by Adrishya-Kavi (*ca.* 1430)

A contemporary of Devaraya II, Adrishya-Kavi, also known as Siddhadrishya, Adrisha, or Adrishappa, was born at the beginning of the fifteenth century in Kolhara. His ancestors belonged to the caste of the oil-crushers and he was the chief of seven villages. He lived in Kolhara where the present work was written, and he is likely to have visited Vijayanagara. He wrote two further works, the *Maleya Malleshana Purana*, a work on the life of his family preceptor Maleya Mallesha, and the *Mugdha Sangaryara Purana*. He was a Virashaiva, and his patron deity was Sangameshvara of Uppalagiri. His remains, along with those of eight members of his family, are entombed at Kolhara.

In this work Jakkanacharya, a prominent Virashaiva minister, narrates the lives of Virashaiva devotees to Devaraya II. A good description of the Kuntala country (around the Vijayanagara city of olden days) and of Vijayanagara city sets the framework for the narrative.

For about nine months a Vaishnava teacher, Mukunda-peddi, and his disciples read to the king a Vaishnava literary work, the *Bharata*. The king, pleased and recognizing the importance of the work, rewarded the teacher and his disciples with gifts and honours. The Vaishnavas then took the *Bharata* around the city in a procession. On seeing this, Jakkanacharya composed a work on the greatness of Virashaiva philosophy and religion. One night, accompanied by his followers, Jakkanacharya walked in procession with his work. The Vaishnavas complained about this to the king, who then decided to arrange a debate between the exponents of the two faiths. The Virashaivas were challenged to present within fifteen days a composition elucidating the principles of their faith. This was accepted and the work was entrusted to an erudite Virashaiva scholar, Chamarasa (author of the *Prabhulinga Lile* 7).

Meanwhile, the minister Jakkanacharya entertained the king each day with the biographies of the Virashaiva saints and other Shaiva devotees. He spoke about the merits earned by arranging charitable services such as free feeding, supplying drinking water and organizing matrimonial alliances. He then spoke of the renunciation of worldly pleasures, the Virashaiva philosophy and the greatness of Basaveshvara.

The poet Chamarasa completed his task in eleven days. He composed one hundred and one poems per day. This work was then presented at the king's court in the presence of the exponents of both groups. Jakkanacharya prepared an annotated critical commentary to Chamarasa's poem. The king was pleased, and lavished honours and gifts on the minister and the poet. The book was then displayed on the back of the royal elephant and paraded through the main streets of Vijayanagara, here called Vidyanagara, the capital of the empire.

In the narrative the poet describes the city, the court and social life, popular festivals and customs. The work contains a total of about 80 stories.

The *Proudharayana Kavya* comprises 21 chapters and 1,133 poems. There are various manuscripts of this work, both on palm-leaf and on handmade paper, copied by several scribes at different times. The material was found in the Maharaja's College Library, Mysore, K. 821.31 ADR pb. No. 424 88.

The work, edited in Kannada by S.S. Bhusanurmatha, was published in 1957 by the Murugha Matha, Dharwad, and printed at the Tontadarya Mudranalaya, Dharwad. It has not been translated into English.

See Sections 1.3, 3.2, 12.6 and 16.4.

11 *Jnanachandrabhyudaya* (*J*) by Kalyana-Kirti (*ca.* 1439)

Kalyana-Kirti was born in Karkala (Dakshina Kannada District), probably at the beginning of the fifteenth century. He spent most of his life working there as court poet, writer and physician. He was patronized by Bhairavarasa, the local governor of Karkala. He wrote both in Kannada and Sanskrit. In Kannada, he composed both narratives such as the *Jnanachandrabhyudaya, Nagakumara Charite* and *Kamana Kathe,* and philosophical works such as *Chinmaya Chintamani, Anuprekshi, Ananda Kandali.* Among his works in Sanskrit are the *Jinagna Phalodaya, Yashodhara Charite* and *Vaidya Grantha.* The present poem was composed in Karkala in about 1439.

The main character of this work is a Jaina king, Jnanachandra, who ultimately acquired *kevala-jnana* (omniscience). He was the son of the king of Kashmira, Jinachandra, and his queen Srikanthadevi.

When he was on a hunting trip with his friends he was abducted by a *khechara* (a tribal) and taken to Ratnapura, whose king was Simhabala. There Jnanachandra was married first to the eight daughters of Simhabala and then to the eight daughters of Shakradhanu, as well as to the other princesses Kanakalate, Kamalate and Sindhudevi. Eventually, the prince was able to return to his parents with his many wives.

One day, a Jaina ascetic, Jayavijaya, arrived at the palace. He was treated with great respect and was given all honours. Religious functions took place in his presence and he was asked by the king to expound the greatness of Jainism, its tenets, principles and beliefs. Thereupon, the ascetic narrated a number of stories to illustrate the points made. He stressed the belief in reincarnation of the soul, according to the good or bad deeds accumulated in the course of its earthly existence.

In the end, Jnanachandra became a devout and sincere ascetic and ultimately attained pure wisdom.

The *Jnanachandrabhyudaya* comprises seven chapters and 909 poems. There are various manuscripts of this work, both on palm-leaf and on handmade paper, copied by several scribes and at different times. The material was found in the University U.G. Library, Mysore, K 821.31 KAL.R.

The work, edited in Kannada by Ha.Ka. Rajegowda, was published in 1976 by the University of Mysore, and printed at the Yechchan Printers, Mysore. It has not been translated into English.

See Sections 8.11, 9.5 and 9.7.

12 *Nagakumara Charite* (*NC*) by Kalyana-Kirti (*ca.* 1445)

This work by Kalyana-Kirti, author of the previous work, was also written in Karkala in about 1445. The poem narrates the life and the achievements of prince Nagakumara of the Magadha kingdom, until he acquired pure wisdom.

Nagakumara, originally named Vikramandhara, was the son of the second queen of king Jayandhara. As an infant he fell into a well inhabited by *nagas.* Since he was protected by the *naga* king, he received the name of Nagakumara and grew up to be proficient in all branches of knowledge, surpassing his stepbrother. In order to eulogize Nagakumara, the poet introduces into the narrative many short stories of various adventures, in which, invariably, Nagakumara happens to marry one or more princesses. A number of such stories are very similar, except for minor details and the names of some of the characters involved. As was the case with the hero of the *Jnanachandrabhyudaya,* the prince with a host of wives returned to the capital and joined his parents. Thereafter he ruled the kingdom for a long time following the Jaina *dharma* and its ideals. In the end he attained *kevala-jnana* (omniscience).

The *Nagakumara Charite* consists of five chapters and 350 poems. There are various manuscripts of this work, both on palm-leaf and on handmade paper, copied by several scribes at different times. The material was found in the University U.G. Library, Mysore, K 821.31 KAL.R.

The work, edited in Kannada by Ha.Ka.

Rajegowda, was published in 1976 by the University of Mysore, and printed by Messrs. Yachchan Printers, Mysore. It has not been translated into English.

See Sections 11.1 and 20.8.

13 *Shivatattva Chintamani* (*S*) by Lakkannadandesha (*ca.* 1450)

Lakkannadandesha, also known as Lakkanna-vodeya and Lakkannamathy, was born in about 1400 and died circa 1470 in Hosapattana (Virupakshapura). He lived in Hampe where he was provincial governor, minister and commander-in-chief of the army under Devaraya II, serving until about 1451. Among his many military feats was a victorious campaign in Sri Lanka. Abdur Razak, the Persian envoy (1443), refers to him in his chronicle. He struck coins in his own name. More than seventeen inscriptions, all published, refer to him; they are found in Chitradurga, Kolar, Bangalore, Mandya, Mangalore, Thanjavur, Tiruchirapalli and Salem Districts. He appears to have lived for some time around Kolar. He constructed the Prasanna Virupaksheshvara temple at Virupakshapura (Kolar District) and gifted many villages to it. Lakkannadandesha was a Virashaiva. Each of his poems ends with salutations to the feet of the Shaiva saints.

The *Shivatattva Chintamani* was probably written in Hampe around 1450.

The first 25 chapters of the poem are devoted to the well known 25 *lilas* (playful manifestations) of Shiva. There follows the usual account of Basaveshvara, his birth, his early life, his appointment as minister at the court of Bijjala III of the Kalachuri dynasty at Kalyani, and some of the famous miracles he performed. The last part of the work gives an exposition of Virashaiva philosophy. However, even the first two parts, although mainly a narrative, have been skilfully adapted to serve the main purpose of the work, the divulgation of the Virashaiva doctrine.

The *Shivatattva Chintamani* consists of 54 chapters and 2,221 poems. There are various manuscripts of the work, both on palm-leaf and on handmade paper, copied by several scribes at different times. The material was found in the Oriental Research Institute, Mysore, Gen. No. 2327.

Edited in Kannada by S. Basappa, the *Shivatattva Chintamani* was published in 1960 by the Oriental Research Institute, Mysore, and printed at the University of Mysore Press. The work has not been translated into English.

See Sections 2.3, 4.4, 5.5, 6.8, 8.7, 12.5, 16.5, 19.2, 19.16, 22.5, 23.8 and 23.11.

14 *Bharatesha Vaibhava Sangraha* (*BVS*) by Ratnakaravarni (*ca.* 1457)

The author of the *Bharatesha Vaibhava Sangraha* is Ratnakaravarni, also known as Ratnakara-siddhi, or Ratnakara-anna. He was born at the beginning of the fifteenth century into a distinguished *kshatriya* family in Venupura (modern Venoor, Dakshina Kannada District). He is likely to have visited Hampe. He lived, however, in Venupura where he was a poet specializing in romantic topics, *shringarakavi*, at the court of the local governor Bhairavarasa. He was a prolific writer; among his Kannada works are the *Aparajiteshvara Shataka*, *Triloka Shataka*, *Ratnakaradhishvara Shataka*, *Adhyatma Gite* and possibly the *Someshvara Shataka*. He was a Jaina who converted to Virashaivism and eventually reconverted to Jainism.

The *Bharatesha Vaibhava Sangraha* was composed in about 1457 either in Karkala or Mudabidre.

The poem deals with the life of the king Bharatesha, the sixteenth son of Vrisha-bhanatha, the first of the 24 Jaina *Tirthankaras*. Bharatesha ruled from Ayodhya. Every day he woke up early, worshipped the deities and gave audience to officers, poets, and musicians. After lunch he spent a pleasant time with his numerous queens watching dance and drama performances, listening to music, resting, and so on. At the same time he paid great attention to the welfare of his kingdom.

Once, during *Navaratri*, a *chakra-ratna* (discus) appeared in the royal armoury, indicating that the time had come for the king to start military expeditions. Following the advice of his ministers and after prayers to the *Tirthankaras*, he set out on the *Vijaya-dasami*

(*Dasara* day) and the *chakra* led the way. A large army followed it. The vast royal retinue included thousands of queens and various entertainers.

Between hundreds of victorious battles, the king enjoyed a pleasant time in his camps in the company of his beautiful and famous queens and his young sons, sometimes celebrating marriages, birthdays of princes and other religious functions.

In the course of a long military campaign he vanquished many rulers, received rich tributes from them and often married their daughters or sisters. On his return journey the *chakra* stopped at Poudanapura, ruled by Bharatesha's younger brother, Bahubali. The king anticipated the acknowledgement of his supremacy by all his younger brothers so that the *chakra* would move on and enable him to return to his capital city. However, while all of Bahubali's brothers had renounced life, Bahubali alone desired to take up arms. The ministers on both sides suggested that the issue could be settled by a duel between the mighty kings, thus avoiding great loss of life and property, in the two armies. This was agreed. Before the engagement, however, Bahubali realized the futility of worldly success, renounced the kingdom, was initiated, and led a life of penance.

Thereafter the *chakra* moved on, leading the king back to his capital. After a long and peaceful rule, the king consecrated his son Arkakirti, renounced worldly life and ultimately attained salvation.

The text gives vivid descriptions of the private life of the king, the *Mahanavami* celebrations and various weapons of warfare, mirroring contemporary courtly and military life.

The work consists of 60 chapters and 9,969 (?) poems.

There are a number of manuscripts of the *Bharatesha Vaibhava Sangraha*, both on palm-leaf and on handmade paper, copied by several scribes at different times. The material was found in Karnataka.

The work was edited in Kannada by T.S. Shyama Rao; the fourth reprint was published in 1986 by the Director, Prasaranga, Manasagangotri, Mysore. It was printed at the Tandavamurthy Press, Irwin Road, Mysore. The work has not been translated into English.

See Sections 7.2, 8.1, 9.6, 12.1, 14.3, 15.2, 15.12, 15.13, 18.8, 18.9, 19.18, 20.1, 20.3, 21.3, 22.3 and 22.7.

15 *Sanatkumara Charite* (*SC*) by Terakanambi Bommarasa (*ca.* 1485)

In all probability, Terakanambi Bommarasa was born in the second half of the fifteenth century at Terakanambi (known also as Kudugalluru or Trikadambapura). He was the son of an *upadhyaya* (religious teacher). An interest in religious speculation and debate ran in the family: his great-grandfather, Nemichandra, was a famous commentator on religious matters at the court of Proudhadevaraya. Terakanambi Bommarasa lived at Trikadambapura, a provincial capital and centre of a merchant guild, where he wrote the *Sanatkumara Charite* and *Jivandhra Charite* (see the following text) in the years around 1485. He was a Jaina and his family deity was Terakanambi Parshva Jinendra.

The present poem was composed to extol the ideals and principles of Jainism, and to establish its superiority over the other religions. The main source of the story of Sanatkumara is the *Vaddaradhane*, a Jaina work in Kannada. Terakanambi Bommarasa, however, elaborates upon the original and vividly describes the contemporary society and living conditions.

The work opens with prayers to the Jaina *Tirthankaras* Parshvanatha, Jinachandra and others.

Shrenika was the king of Magadha. One day an ascetic, Goutama, approached him and told the story of king Sanatkumara. While still a prince, Sanatkumara set out on a campaign to curb the insubordination of some lesser rulers. Soon, however, he was lost in a forest because of his wilful horse. Thereupon his close friend, Mahendrasimha, went in search of him. He was led by a *ventara* (spirit), and eventually he found the prince amidst *khechara* (tribal) ladies. Avalokini, a *vidyadhari*, told him how Sanatkumara lost his way in the forest, how Manohara, a *yaksha*, rescued him, and how he eventually married the eight daughters of king Bhanuvega. Later he also married Sandhyavali and other ladies.

Woven into the main narrative is the short story of a brahmin named Nagachandra, his unfaithful wife, Vishnushri, and her paramour, king Pramukha.

Through Mahendrasimha's efforts, Sanatkumara rejoined his parents. His marriage with the princess Sunande was a splendid occasion, with great celebrations, pomp and grandeur. After ruling for a period, Sanatkumara renounced worldly pleasures, attained salvation and became an *arhat.*

The poem consists of seventeen chapters and 864 poems. There are a number of manuscripts of the *Sanatkumara Charite,* both on palm-leaf and on handmade paper, copied by several scribes at different times. The material was found in the Maharaja U.G. Library, Mysore, K 821.31 BOMSM, Acc. No. 88674.

The *Sanatkumara Charite,* edited in Kannada by G.G. Manjunathan, was published in 1970 by the University of Mysore, and printed at the Basavaraja Printing Works, Bagalkot. It has not been translated into English.

See Sections 6.5, 6.8, 7.3, 10.4, 14.2, 18.4, 19.1, 19.7, 19.8, 19.10, 19.12, 19.17, 20.6, 22.4, 24.1, 24.6, 24.7, 24.8 and 25.8.

16 *Jivandhra Charite* (*JCT*) by Terakanambi Bommarasa (*ca.* 1485)

The second work of Terakanambi Bommarasa presented here, the *Jivandhra Charite,* was written either at Vijayanagara or at Terakanambi in about 1485. The content of this poetic work is similar to that of the *Jivandhra Charite* by Bhaskara-Kavi (see No. 6).

This is a story told by a *rishi,* Goutamagunadhara, to the king of Magadha and his queen.

Rajapuri was the capital of the kingdom of Hemanga of which Satyandhara and Vijayavati were the king and the queen. One day a Jaina *muni* arrived and preached to his disciples on religious and moral conduct. A wood-cutter, Kashtangara, who out of curiosity happened to be there, was greatly impressed and wished to know more about good conduct from that preceptor. The *muni* instructed him never to indulge in sexual pleasure on full-moon days and Kashtangara observed that vow strictly.

One day, the tired wood-cutter was resting in the porch of the house of a beautiful harlot who happened to spit accidentally on the head of the wood-cutter. He looked up and was greatly attracted by her beauty. He immediately decided that he would enjoy her company for at least one day, whatever the cost. With this in mind he started saving money. It so happened that the sandal-wood he had stored in his house was bought for 1,200 gold coins by a rich merchant.

He dressed himself luxuriously and took the gold coins to the house of the courtesan. He was seated on a swing-cot with the lady when, by chance, he overheard one of her assistants saying that it was a full-moon day. Suddenly he remembered the teaching of the Jaina *muni* and his vow, and though he had paid the courtesan a great deal of money he left the place without enjoying her company. The lady placed a complaint before the king, who arranged to trace the wood-cutter. When he was asked why he ran away from the courtesan without enjoying her sexually, he told the king of the teaching of the Jaina *muni* and of his vow. On hearing this, and appreciating his high moral stand, the king appointed him as his minister.

In course of time, the minister became greedy and usurped the kingdom. The king died and his pregnant queen was abandoned in the burial ground, where she gave birth to a son. A merchant chanced to be there to bury his still-born infant. To his surprise he found the live child that the queen had deserted in despair. He took the boy to his home and entrusted the child to his wife. He was named Jivandhra.

When the child had completed his fifth year, he began his education with a preceptor. Once grown up he came to know about the usurper-king and the treacherous murder of his father. He waited patiently for an appropriate time to take his revenge.

During his youth the prince had a series of adventures and at the end of each he was married to a princess.

At last the wood-cutter-king was killed in a battle and the prince was consecrated king. After some time he abdicated in favour of his son and took to the religious life to seek ultimate salvation.

The *Jivandhra Charite* consists of twenty

chapters and 1,511 poems. There are various manuscripts of this work, both on palm-leaf and on handmade paper, copied by several scribes at different times.

The material was found in the Mysore University Maharaja College Library, K 821.31 BOMJ M, Acc. No. 95844.

Edited in Kannada by G.G. Manjunath, the work was published in 1976 by Kannada Adhyayana Samsthe, University of Mysore, and printed by Mitra Printers, Mysore. It has not been translated into English.

See Sections 2.4 and 7.4.

17 *Amalabasava Charite* (*AC*) by Singiraja (*ca.* 1500)

It is not known where Singiraja or Sringiraja, the author of the present work, was born. He was a Virashaiva and his patron deity was Kashi Visvanatha. He composed the present poem, which is also known as *Singiraja Purana*, in the late fifteenth century.

The *Amalabasava Charite* is a biography of Basaveshvara, the reformer of Virashaivism, who lived in the twelfth century and was minister at the court of Bijjala III of the Kalachuri dynasty at Kalyani.

Basaveshvara, who is considered an incarnation of Shiva's bull, Nandi, returned to Kailasa after having completed his mission on earth. However, he had to return to earth again, this time with the blessings of Shiva. He was born as a son of Madarasa and Madalambika in the village of Ingaleshvara-Bagewadi. In order to evade undergoing *upanayana* he moved from his native place to Kappadi, where he joined the preceptor Jatavedamuni.

After some time Basaveshvara went to Kalyani and married Gangambe, the daughter of Baladeva, a minister. One day, the king showed to his assembled court a letter written in a strange script. None of the assembled ministers, scholars and others could read it. Basaveshvara eventually deciphered the script and read it. The king was pleased and nominated him a minister as well as giving him one of his relatives, Nilambike, as his second wife.

The narrative then expands on some 64 miracles performed by Basaveshvara at Kalyani and extols his righteous and saintly life. This work only focuses on that part of the saint's life which took place at Kalyani.

The *Amalabasava Charite* consists of 48 chapters and 1,907 poems.

There are various manuscripts of this work, both on palm-leaf and on handmade paper, copied by different scribes at different times. The material was found in the Chief Epigraphist's Office Library, Mysore, No. 08942/294.5925.

The text, edited in Kannada by H. Deveerappa, was published in 1950 by the Oriental Research Institute, Mysore, and printed at the Government Branch Press, Mysore. It has not been translated into English.

See Sections 2.5, 8.9, 11.5, 20.7 and 25.1.

18 *Ramayana* (*R*) by Battaleshvara (*ca.* 1500)

The author, variously known as Battaleshvara, Bhairava, Nirvana Nayak and Nirvana Linga, was born near Yana (Uttara Kannada District). He lived most of his life in Yana and eventually died there, but the dates of birth and death are uncertain. It is not known whether he visited Vijayanagara. A priest, Sanskrit scholar and poet, he belonged to the Havyak-brahmins. His patron deity was Bhairava of Yana. This Kannada version of the *Ramayana*, or *Kaushika Ramayana* as it is sometimes known, was written in about 1500 in Yana.

The poem commences, as usual, with prayers to Gananatha, Sarasvati and others. In general the story of Rama follows the familiar lines, with some variations on account of the time and place of the poem's composition.

Four sons, Rama, Lakshmana, Bharata and Shatrughna were born to king Dasharatha of Ayodhya. Young Rama and Lakshmana followed sage Kaushika, and killed the demon Maricha and routed his retinue. Rama won the hand of Sita in a *svayamvara*, and then defeated Parashurama. Rama was about to be consecrated king, but at the last moment political intrigues and jealousies prevailed and he was sent into exile accompanied by Sita and Lakshmana.

During their sojourn in the Panchavati forest, Sita was abducted by Ravana. Searching for Sita, Rama and Lakshmana arrived in Kishkindha where they met Sugriva and

Hanuman, who promised to help them. Eventually Hanuman located Sita in Lanka and told Rama. Rama then waged a war on Ravana who was defeated and killed. Sita was rescued and rejoined her husband, after submitting to the fire-ordeal. Thereafter, Rama and his retinue worshipped the Shiva-*linga* at Rameshvara and returned to Ayodhya. The work ends with a vivid account of the coronation of Rama in Ayodhya.

Battaleshvara's *Ramayana* consists of 44 chapters and 2,516 poems. There are a number manuscripts of this work, both on palm-leaf and on handmade paper, copied by several scribes at different times. The material was found in the Maharaja U.G. Library, Mysore, K 821.32 BATK, Acc. No. 36981.

The work, edited in Kannada by Shivarama Karanta, was published in 1966 by Messrs. Harsha Prakatanalaya, Putturu, and printed by Messrs. Udaya Printers & Publication, Mangalore. The work has not been translated into English.

See Sections 7.13 and 15.15.

19 *Supa Shastra* (*SuS*) by Mangarasa III (*ca.* 1508)

Mangarasa III (Rajakavi) lived most of his life at his birthplace, Kallahalli (Hosavritti-nadu, Hoysala country), eventually dying there. He was a local governor known also under the titles of Prabhu-raja, Prabhu-kuladip and Prabhu-kulamanidipa, and belonged to the Yadu or Chengalva dynasty. He was a Jaina. His parents were Vijayendra and Padmajammanni; he was married to Kamalajammanni, and his preceptor was Chikka Prabhendu. He was a prolific writer; his other works in Kannada are the *Samyukta Kaumudi*, *Jaya-nripa Kavya*, *Nemijinesha Sangati* (see No. 20), *Prabhajana Charite* and *Shripala Charite*. He wrote the text of several Sanskrit inscriptions.

The first text by Mangarasa under review here, the *Supa Shastra*, is a cookery book in verses. It was probably written in Kallahalli in about 1508.

The work begins with prayers to the Jinas and then to Sarasvati. The author claims to have written the *Supa Shastra* in Kannada using information he gathered from the available Sanskrit works. Further on, he explains that the satisfaction and contentment obtained from enjoying various tasty food preparations helps people to feel happy in both worlds. For this reason he decided to write on cookery, though admittedly only on vegetarian cuisine.

The first chapter describes dishes made with grain-flours, such as *rotti*, *hurige* and *garige*, and their various methods of preparation. The second chapter focuses on liquid or semi-liquid preparations such as milk products, thick fruit juice or fruit pulp. The third chapter concentrates on various kinds of cooked rice; some eight dishes are described, both sweet and savoury.

The remaining three chapters are devoted to the description of different vegetable preparations: plain, spicy, sour and others.

Though the work describes more than 262 dishes, it appears to be incomplete because some of the items listed at the beginning do not appear in the body of the text.

The *Supa Shastra* consists of six chapters and 358 poems.

There are a number of manuscripts of this work, both on palm-leaf and on handmade paper, copied by several scribes at different times. The manuscripts were found in Karnataka and in Tamil Nadu, the copy consulted here being in the University U.G. Library, Mysore, 641.5954 MANK.

Edited in Kannada by S.N. Krishna Jois, the *Supa Shastra* was published in 1969 by the University of Mysore (Kannada Adhyayana Samsthe), and printed at the Mysore University Press. The work has not been translated into English.

See Section 18.10.

20 *Nemijinesha Sangati* (*NS*) by Mangarasa III (*ca.* 1508)

Mangarasa III, author of the previous text, also composed the *Nemijinesha Sangati* in about 1508 at Kallahalli. As the title indicates, the poem mainly deals with the life of the Jaina prophet Nemi, who eventually became the 22nd *Tirthankara*. In Kannada, the story of Neminatha is the most popular of all the stories about the Jaina *Tirthankaras*. Authors such as Chavundaraya (tenth century), Karnapaya (ca. 1140), Nemichandra (ca. 1185), Bandhuvarma (ca. 1200), Mahabala (ca. 1254) and Salva (ca. 1485) all dealt with this theme. The present work is also called *Jaina Bharata* as the majority of the characters of the *Mahabharata* epic appear in it. Thus, a number of stories related to Krishna, Balarama, the Pandavas and Kauravas are all incorporated in the narrative. It is claimed that Neminatha belonged to the same family as Krishna.

Neminatha, whose great-great ancestor was Yadu-maharaja, lived in Dvarka. Balarama and Krishna were his cousins. On attaining the proper age, Neminatha was to be married to the princess Rajimati. For that occasion, hundreds of animals had been brought to be sacrificed. The sorrowful bleating of the innocent animals made him renounce the world and retire to a life of meditation in the forest. He attained supreme wisdom, and became the 22nd Jaina prophet.

In order to attain this exalted status, Neminatha's previous lives were filled with good deeds and the most noble and compassionate actions. The incidents narrated in the *Mahabharata* have provided an appropriate opportunity to retell the familiar stories from the point of view of Jaina doctrine.

The work consists of 35 chapters and 5,138 poems. There are various manuscripts of this work, both on palm-leaf and on handmade paper, copied by several scribes at different times. The material was found in the University U.G. Library, Mysore, K 821.32 MAN M, Acc. No. 124474.

The *Nemijinesha Sangati,* edited in Kannada by B.B. Mahishavadi, was published in 1979 by the Karnataka University, Dharwad, and printed at the Karnataka University Press, Dharwad. The work has not been translated into English.

See Sections 4.13, 13.1, 15.14 and 23.4.

21 *Samyukta Kaumudi* (*SK*) by Mangarasa III (*ca.* 1509)

Mangarasa III, author of the previous two texts, also wrote the *Samyukta Kaumudi* around 1509 at Kallahalli. As with other contemporary literary works, the purpose of the present poem is to propagate religious ideals of Jainism and to advocate a cultured, humanitarian and just society. A number of works on the same subject were composed in Sanskrit and Prakrit. The *Samyukta Kaumudi* contains 18 stories within the framework of the main narrative.

The work commences, as usual, with prayers to the *jinas, siddhas, acharyas, upadhyayas, sadhus,* the goddess Sarasvati and the pontiffs.

Vira Jina, at the request of the king of Rajagriha, Shrenika and his queen Chelini, tells a series of stories to help them attain *samyuktva* (right perception), one of the three fundamental principles of Jainism.

The first story concerns king Uditodaya of Maduranagare and his queen; it describes the *Kaumudi-parva* (festival of the full-moon night), in which only ladies could participate. The second story tells of an intrigue which took place at the court of king Suyodhana, with a view to implicate Yamadanda, the city officer, in a theft from the palace treasury. The king orders Yamadanda to catch the thief within eight days and to report daily on progress. Soon, however, Yamadanda understood that the king was among the persons behind the intrigue, so he resolved to gain time and to make the king realise his folly, step by step. He invented a number of short stories (Nos. 3-18) and each day he narrated one of them to the king, to bring home the truth about righteous, virtuous and humane living, according to the Jaina faith. The stories centred on various persons and, ultimately, every character attained *samyuktva.*

The work consists of twelve chapters and 785 poems. There are various manuscripts of this work on palm-leaf copied by several scribes at different times. This material was found in the University U.G. Library, Mysore, K 821.32 MANSM, Acc. No. 94879.

The *Samyukta Kaumudi,* edited in Kannada by B.B. Mahishawadi, was published in 1979 by the Karnataka University, Dharwad, and was printed by Messrs. Manohara Mudranalaya, Dharwad. The work has not been translated into English.

See Sections 7.14, 12.3, 14.4, 18.5, 18.6, 21.2, 22.4, 24.10 and 25.5.

22 *Karnataka Krishnaraya Bharata* (*KKB*) by Timmanna-Kavi (*ca.* 1510)

It is not known where Timmanna-Kavi was born or died. He was a court poet at the court of Krishnadevaraya at Vijayanagara, where he wrote the present work. The *Karnataka Krishnaraya Bharata*, which was probably composed about 1510, is also known under other names: *Krishnaraya Bharata Katha Manjari* and *Uttara Bharata*. Timmanna was a brahmin; his patron deity was Tirupati Venkatesha, but he also paid homage to Virupaksha of Hampe.

As stated in its first chapter, this poem narrates the events which occurred after the battle of Kurukshetra, in which the Kauravas were annihilated by the Pandavas.

The second chapter deals with the lamentations of the mothers and wives of the deceased, the various words of consolation and the performance of the last rites.

The next two chapters relate the teachings of Bhishma on kingly duties and responsibilities, on statecraft, on the welfare of the subjects, on leading a virtuous and righteous life and so on, all told through a number of stories and anecdotes in order to strengthen the morale of the dejected Pandavas. Then the Pandavas commenced preparations for the *ashvamedha-yagna* (horse sacrifice), in the course of which there were many incidents and adventures. Eventually, however, the sacrifice was successfully completed.

The next two sections narrate the last days of Dhritharashtra, of Gandhari, of Kunti, of the Yadava clan, of Balarama and Krishna, and of the engulfment of Dwarka by the sea.

Thereafter, Parikshita was consecrated king. The Pandavas renounced the world and went to the Himalayas where they died, one after the other, while Yudhishthira eventually reached heaven and attained the status of a deity.

This work is to be understood as the continuation of an earlier work, the *Bharata*, composed in Kannada in about 1430 by Kumara Vyasa of Gadag.

The present work consists of eight sections, 44 sub-sections and 4,006 (3,736) poems. There are a number of manuscripts of this work, both on palm-leaf and on handmade paper, copied by several scribes at different times. This work was found in the University U.G. Library, Mysore, Acc. No. 129092 K 821.4 THIK.

Edited in Kannada by a team of scholars under V.K. Gokak, *Karnataka Krishnaraya Bharata* was published in 1979 by the Kannada Sahitya Parishattu, Bangalore, and was printed by the Prabha Mudranalaya, Bangalore. The work has not been translated into English.

See Sections 7.6, 7.7, 7.9, 7.10, 7.11, 7.12, 7.17, 7.18, 15.1 and 20.2.

23 *Shri Krishnadevarayana Dinachari* (*SKD*) by Mukku Thimmaya and Mallaya (*ca.* 1509-29?)

Very little is known about the two authors of this work, Mukku Thimmayya and Mallayya. It is very probable that they lived at Vijayanagara and were court poets during the reign of Krishnadevaraya. They were commissioned by the king to record contemporary events. It appears that they were followers of the teachings of Shri Ramanujacharya. The work is not dated, but probably it was composed in the first half of the sixteenth century. The *Shri Krishnadevarayana Dinachari* was written mostly in prose, interspersed with a few *shlokas* (couplets).

As the title indicates, the work describes the daily life of the monarch and the important events of his reign. Starting with salutations to Shri Ramanujacharya, the founder of Shri Vaishnavism, it proceeds to detail the king's daily routine. Then an account is given of the founding of the Vijayanagara empire on the initiative and with the help of sage Vidyaranya. Subsequently, the coronation of Krishnadevaraya is described. There are accounts of the neighbouring kingdoms, of the state treasury, of the king's victorious campaigns against the Muslim rulers and the king of Orissa, of his visit to the sacred places and temples and, finally, of his return to Vidyanagara. There are no divisions in the text. There is only one manuscript of this work written either by Thimmaya or Mallaya at Vijayanagara. It is written on palm-leaves and was found in Karnataka.

The *Shri Krishnadevarayana Dinachari*, edited in Kannada by Dr. V.S.S. Acharya, was published in 1983 by B.M. Sree Smaraka Pratishthana, Bangalore, and printed at Swatantra Mudranalaya, Bangalore, The work has not been translated into English.

See Sections 2.6, 5.2, 7.20, 8.12, 10.3 and 15.4.

24 *Ramanatha Charite* (*RC*) by Nanjunda-Kavi (*ca.* 1525)

Nanjunda-Kavi, or simply Nanjunda, was born in Changala Nadu. He was the son of Madhava, a feudatory ruler. He was a Virashaiva or a Shaiva. Nothing is known of him except his poem the *Ramanatha Charite*, also known as *Kumara Ramana Katha*, composed around 1525.

The hero of the poem is Kumara Rama or Ramanatha, the son of Kampa-nripati/ Kampilaraya and his first wife, Hariharadevi. Ramanatha's father was the king of the Kuntala country with Hosadurga as its capital. Ramanatha had an adventurous and heroic boyhood. One day, while playing a ball-game with his friends, the ball fell into the apartments of his stepmother, queen Ratnaji. When Ramanatha went to collect the ball the queen fell in love with the youth and made passionate advances. The angered Ramanatha forced his way out of her palace. Disappointed and scorned, the queen made wild and false allegations against her step-son and insisted that he should be put to death. The king believed her story and ordered his minister to carry out the death sentence. But the sagacious minister understood the situation and hid the prince in an underground cell, while reporting to the king that the queen's wish had been fulfilled.

On hearing of this incident, the Delhi sultan took advantage of the feuds dividing the royal family and its kingdom, and his troops invaded the Kuntala country. At that critical juncture, Ramanatha appeared from his hideout and bravely fought the invading forces, driving them out of the territory. In the process he died on the battlefield.

This text affords a glimpse into contemporary life, into the different sports and games, hunting, warfare and material culture.

The work consists of twelve parts, 47 chapters and 5,807 poems. There are various manuscripts of this work, both on palm-leaf and on handmade paper, copied by several scribes at different times. The manuscripts have been found in Karnataka and in Varanasi.

The *Ramanatha Charite* was edited in Kannada by H. Devirappa. It is not known when Part I was published; however Parts II and III were published in 1959 and 1964 by the Oriental Research Institute, University of Mysore, and printed at the Government Text Book Press, Mysore. The work has not been translated into English.

See Sections 1.4, 2.7, 3.3, 3.5, 3.6, 3.7, 3.8, 3.9, 3.16, 4.5, 4.16, 5.4, 5.6, 7.5, 7.8, 7.15, 10.2, 10.9, 10.10, 11.2, 11.3, 11.7, 13.4, 14.2, 15.3, 15.5, 15.6, 15.9, 15.10, 15.16, 15.17, 15.22, 16.6, 19.6, 20.9, 22.6, 22.8, 23.5, 23.6, 24.11 and 25.3.

25 *Mohana Tarangini* (*MT*) by Kanakadasa (*ca.* 1550)

Kanakadasa (Timmappa), whose dates are unknown, was born in Bada and died in Kaginele (Dharwad District). His father, Birappa, was a *dandanayaka* (local chieftain) under the Vijayanagara rulers. Kanakadasa is mostly associated with Kaginele, however he also lived in Belur and Udupi and visited Vijayanagara. He was a Vaishnava and belonged to the Beda community. In his youth he was, like his father, a *dandanayaka* at the service of the Vijayanagara rulers. He was a disciple of Vyasaraya, the spiritual advisor of Krishnadevaraya, and later in life he became a poet and a devotee of Adikeshava of Kaginele.

The *Mohana Tarangini*, also known as the *Krishna Charite*, was written in the mid-sixteenth century at Kaginele and is dedicated to the poet's patron deity, Adikeshava of Kaginele. The work is written as if Kanakadasa himself was telling this story to his wife, as mentioned at the end of each chapter.

This romantic poem opens with prayers to the poet's patron deity and other gods such as Krishna, Lakshmi, Brahma, Sarasvati and Vinayaka. A description of Dwarka and the country around it follows; in fact, this is the Vijayanagara capital and its surroundings, with which the poet was familiar. The entertainments at the court of Krishnadevaraya receive special treatment.

Rukmini, Krishna's wife, desired a son. Eventually, she gave birth to Pradyumna, who was none other than the god of love reborn. The demon-king Shambasura, knowing that Pradyumna would eventually kill him, unsuccessfully attempted to murder the child. The child grew up, eventually slew Shambasura, and lived with his wife, Rati, in Dwarka. Subsequently they begot Aniruddha who was destined to marry Usha, the daughter of the 1,000-armed Shaiva demon-devotee, Banasura. The two secretly loved each other and frequently met with the help of one of Usha's companions, Chitralekha. On discovering this secret affair, Banasura was incensed and waged war on Aniruddha, taking him captive. At this point Krishna challenged Banasura and a fight ensued. Ultimately, Shiva intervened to appease both of them and the formal marriage of Usha and Aniruddha was agreed. The celebrations ended and Banasura accompanied Shiva to Kailasa.

The *Mohana Tarangini* consists of 42 chapters and 2,705 poems. There are various manuscripts, both on palm-leaf and on handmade paper, copied by different scribes at different times. The material was found in the University U.G. Library, Mysore, K 821.3 KANMS, Acc. No. 140780.

The text, edited in Kannada by S.S. Kotina, was published in 1984 by the Kannada Sahitya Parishat, Bangalore, and printed by Sri Mira Printers, Mysore. It has not been translated into English.

See Sections 2.8, 3.15, 3.18, 3.19, 4.1, 4.6, 4.14, 4.18, 6.6, 6.7, 6.9, 6.10, 8.2, 8.4, 8.13, 10.5, 10.6, 11.8, 13.3, 14.2, 15.8, 15.18, 15.24, 16.7, 17.5, 17.6, 17.7, 18.3, 19.20, 20.10, 20.11, 20.12, 22.1, 23.1, 23.10, 24.2, 24.3, 24.4, 24.5, 24.9 and 25.6.

26 *Vijayakumari Charite* (*VC*) by Srutakirti (1567)

Srutakirti, also known as Ramachandra or Chandanavarni, was probably born at Kanakagiri (Mysore District). He was the son of Akalanka and the grandson of Vijayakirti. Srutakirti lived and worked at Kanakagiri and does not seem to have visited Vijayanagara. He was a Jaina ascetic, and his patron deity was Vijayanatha of Kanakagiri.

He began to compose the *Vijayakumari Charite* on 25 May 1567 and completed it on 16 May 1568. The present work is a Kannada version of the story based by Srutakirti on the Sanskrit original.

The poet starts by paying homage to the first Jina, the religious ascetics and other teachers who attained salvation, to the learned men and the subordinate deities, and lastly to the heroine of the work, Vijayakumari, who also overcame all worldly temptations through her austere and religious life. There follows a description of the Hoysala country and of its capital Dorasamudra (Halebidu, the birthplace of the young Vijayakumari) with which the poet was well acquainted.

During the absence of Vijayakumari's father on business, she was pledged by her mother to a local merchant, in order to borrow money for the entertainment of recently arrived Jaina mendicants. The father returned, and on learning this he approved of his wife's conduct.

From the age of five until puberty, Vijayakumari was taught the various branches of knowledge. The marriage to her relative, Basava, who was an ardent follower of Virashaivism, was planned. However, being a Jaina she did not agree and, to explain and support her position, she narrated the life of Basavanna of Kalyani, the great reformer of Virashaivism. Understandably, to uphold the superiority of Jainism, the picture of Virashaivism presented by her was totally false and filled with contempt for Basavanna. Ultimately, she renounced the world, became a Jaina nun and attained sainthood.

The *Vijayakumari Charite* consists of a single chapter and 1,305 poems. There are various manuscripts of this work, both on palm-leaf and on handmade paper, copied by several scribes at different times. The manuscripts were found in Karnataka.

The work, edited in Kannada by Y.C. Bhanumathi, was published in 1981 by the Kannada Adhyayana Samsthe, University of Mysore, and printed by the Sree Raghavendra

Printers, Mysore. It has not been translated into English.

See Sections 3.20, 4.2, 4.7, 7.16, 12.7, 14.5, 19.4, 19.19, 25.2 and 25.9.

27 *Channabasava Purana* (*CP*) by Virupaksha-Pandita (1585)

Virupaksha-Pandita's birthplace is not known. He lived and worked at Vijayanagara where he was head of a religious Virashaiva institution (Hiriya Matha). He was active in the second half of the sixteenth century. His patron deity was Virupaksha of Hampe. The poet composed the *Channabasava Purana* in 1585 in Hampe.

The work is a biography of Channabasava, the great saint, philosopher and writer of the twelfth century, and is written as though narrated by Channabasava to Siddharama, another contemporary saint. The work begins with a brief exposition of the Virashaiva philosophy followed by a description of the 25 playful manifestations of Shiva. There follows historical information on the Bijjala rulers of Kalyani, the rulers of Anegondi and the Vijayanagara emperors and their territory, as well as brief biographies of a selection of contemporary Virashaiva saints, preachers and writers. In the context of the narrative there are lively descriptions of the city, the pleasures of the court, and the king's daily life and nocturnal visits to the city. There are insights into contemporary politics and statesmanship, and the planning of military campaigns. These details are especially interesting as the author lived at Vijayanagara during the second half of the sixteenth century while composing the work.

The work consists of 2,906 poems arranged in five main sections and 63 chapters. There are various manuscripts of this text, both on palm-leaf and on handmade paper, copied by various scribes at different times; they were found in Karnạtaka.

The *Channabasava Purana* was edited in Kannada by a team of scholars and published in 1934 by the Lingayat Vidyabhivriddhi Samsthe, Dharwad. An English translation of this work was prepared by G. Worther and published in the *Journal of the Bombay Branch of the Royal Asiatic Society* (1865), pp. 98-221.

See Sections 2.9, 3.10, 4.9, 4.19, 5.1, 5.7, 7.19, 8.3, 11.6, 12.2, 15.11, 15.19, 15.20, 15.21, 15.23, 17.3, 17.8, 17.9, 19.5, 23.9 and 25.7.

Appendix II

GLOSSARY

abhisheka, act of washing sacred images as part of a ritual; sprinkling of water or other sanctified substances on objects or persons
acharya, religious teacher
Agama, sectarian work containing philosophical and mythological information
agamajna, agamika, a person well-versed in the study of the *Agamas*
agaru, a fragrant substance used as perfume
Agni, the god of fire; regent of the south-east
agrahara, village gifted to brahmins or learned persons, generally exempted from paying taxes
akshate, raw unbroken rice coloured with turmeric and *kumkuma* used during rituals
allam, green ginger
amalaka, myrobalan (*phyllianthus embilica*)
amrita, nectar of immortality
anjali-mudra, gesture of salutation in which the palms are joined together
annadana, offering food as an act of charity
aposana-etti, a ritual performed at the beginning of a meal; sipping of water
apsaras, celestial beauties, nymphs
arati, auspicious lights shown to a sacred image, an important personage, or a couple in the course of marriage and other celebrations
arhant, arhat, Jaina ascetic
archana, archane, ritual, worship
arekasu, coin of small denomination; half the value of a *kasu*
arghya, water to rinse the hands and mouth before worship and meals
asana, posture, seat
ashoka, type of tree (*saraca indica*)
ashta-dikpalakaru, guardians of the eight directions of the sky
ashtadasha-jati, the traditional eighteen castes, including groups of artisans and professionals
ashtadasha-pradhanar, the traditional eighteen chief officers at court, each responsible for a different department; see Appendix III
ashtadasha-varnane, the traditional eighteen subjects which are treated in a poetical composition; see Appendix III
ashtavidha-archane, the eight kinds of worship
ashvamedha-yajna, -yaga, the horse sacrifice conducted by kings to declare their supremacy
ashvasa, a chapter or a subdivision in a literary work
Asvayuj, the month of September-October
Atharvaveda, the fourth *Veda* containing hymns, incantations and magic spells
aushadhi, medicine
avare-kayi, beans
avuja, a stringed instrument
Ayurveda, treatise codifying the principles of Hindu medicine

badane, badanekayi, aubergine
badanekayi-baji, egg-plant preparation
bagina, bayina, presents consisting of auspicious objects made to the participants in the course of a celebration
bahattar-niyoga, -viniyoga, the traditional 72 kinds of services to which royal persons are entitled
bahupuri, talisman tied on the arm
bakula, red flower (*mimusops elengi*)
bale, plantain
baluvali, gifts made by the father to the newly-wed daughter when she first leaves for her husband's house
bana-devate, forest goddess
banni, tree (*melia sempervirens?*)
bara, barugutta, indoor game played with marbles or stones
basadi, Jaina temple or monastery

basiga, ornamental fillet tied to the forehead of the groom or bride in the course of the marriage rituals
battalu, metal bowl
beda, professional hunter; community of hunters
bele, coin of small denomination
belevennu, prostitute
bella-garige, sweet
bella-mandige, sweet
bennegayi, vegetarian food preparation
bhakshya, rice preparation; flat cake
Bharata-natya, style of dance
Bharata [natya]-shastra, treatise on dance and theatre authored by Bharata
bhasma, sacred ash used by Shaivas
bhedamu, one of the traditional tactics to deal with an enemy king, such as spreading discontent among his subjects
bheri, percussion instrument
bherunda, mythical bird
Bhikshatana, aspect of Shiva as a mendicant
bidirakki, a kind of rice obtained from the bamboo plant
bila-dvara, narrow passage through a fort wall
bilva, tree sacred to Shiva (*aegle marmelos*)
biliya-karachi, sweet dish
bimba, gourd
bisiyanna, cooked rice
bisi-holige, sweet dish
bogari, bohari, top; game of tops
bombuli, small drum
bona, rice preparation
brinjal, aubergine
bund, dam-wall of a tank (reservoir)
butti, type of food preparations fit to be carried in a container; tiffin

chaduranga, chadurange, a type of chess
chakkuli, sweet dish
chakra, chakra-ratna, disc-like weapon
chakravaka, species of duck (*casarca ferruginea*)
chamara, fly-whisk; insignia of royalty
chamari-mriga, yak, the tail of which was used as a fly-whisk; a kind of deer
champaka, flower (*michelia champaka*)
champu, literary form combining poetry and prose
channangi, type of *dhal*
chandana, sandalwood
chandra-mantapa, moon-hall, open to the sky
chandra-vidhi, moon-street, running from north to south
chandra-shale, see *chandra-mantapa*
chappannaru-deshagalu, the traditional 56 countries; see Appendix III
charana-guru, wandering teacher
charite, charitre, account, biography
chatur-varna, the four main castes into which Hindu society is divided: *brahmins*, *kshatriyas*, *vaishyas* and *shudras*
chaturanga-bala, the traditional four divisions of the army: elephants, horses, chariots and infantry
chaturopaya, the traditional four kinds of tactics; see Appendix III
chauri, fly-whisk; insignia of royalty
chaushashti-kalegalu, the traditional 64 arts or branches of learning
chenganile, flower, lotus
chilupalu, warm milk
chinipalu, boiled milk
chinnavarada, jeweller
chintamani-mantra, particularly powerful *mantra* which "grants all wishes"
chippu-karadige, shell casket
chitra-chavadi, hall decorated with paintings
chitra-mantapa, pavilion decorated with murals
chitragara, painter
chouki, inner court or hall.

dadhi, curds
dadhi-patra-mala, food preparation with leafy raw vegetables and curds
dakke, dakke-muraja, percussion instrument
dakshina, dakshine, gift given to a priest for performing a ritual
damaruga, hourglass-shaped drum
danamu, bestowing gifts; one of the four expedients of diplomacy
dana-mantapa, pavilion in which gifts or charity are distributed
dandamu, (the use of) force; one of the four expedients of diplomacy
dandanayaka, general, local chieftain
dande, wreath of flowers strung in a particular fashion, used in the course of rituals
dandige, stringed instrument
darbar, royal court; royal audience
darbha, grass used in the course of rituals (*feronia elephantum*)
darpana, mirror

darshana, "auspicious sight" of a sacred image
Dasara, tenth and final day of the festival celebrated in Mysore during October
davana, plant with fragrant leaves
devara-griha, sanctuary
devate, deity
dhal, lentils, pulses
dhanur-vine, musical instrument; type of *vine*
Dhanurveda, treatise on archery; science of archery
dhare, *dhareyanere*, act of pouring milk on the palms of the bride and the groom held together, thus sanctioning the marriage
dharma, law, duty, virtue, justice
dharma-yuddha, a fight fought without spilling blood or injury
dharmika, follower of *dharma*; pious, just and law-abiding person
dhoti, length of cloth wound around the waist worn by men
dindima, drum, sometimes used by the royal time-keeper to announce the time.
dipa-lakshmi, statuette depicting a young woman holding an oil lamp in her hands
Dipavali, *Divali*, festival of lights celebrated in October-November
dolu, percussion instrument
dosa, *dose*, pancake made of rice and gram flour
doudhe, percussion instrument
drona, town on an island
dundubhi, type of drum
dupa, incense
durga, fort
durume, percussion instrument
dvarapalaka, gatekeeper, guard

ekamukha-rudrakshi, type of *rudraksha*
entadi, mythical eight-legged animal

gade, club, mace
gaduga, round seeds of a wild plant used for playing indoor games
gadyana, gold coin
galige, time unit of 24 minutes
ganangalu, followers of Shiva, itinerant preachers; see *jangama*
gandha, fragrant substance, sandalwood
gandha-shali, superior quality of paddy
Gandharvaveda, treatise on music and dance
gandharva-vivaha, marriage by mutual consent without ceremonies or witnesses
gandhiga, herbal remedy
ganjiyambali, porridge made of coarse grains or rice
garbha-dana, impregnation ceremony, which takes place on the first night of a wedding
garige, *gharije*, round and solid fried sweets made of wheat or rice
garuda, formation of the army in the shape of an eagle
Garuda, mythical eagle, usually associated with Vishnu
gati, pause or time in music
gatti-mosara-unde, curd rice
gavaksha-jala, ceiling ventilator
gavale, sweet preparation made of wheat cooked in water or milk with sugar
gavate, a kind of tree
ghee, *ghrita*, clarified butter
gidibidi, percussion instrument
giri, muntain peak
giri-durga, fort on a hill
gopura, *gopuradvara*, tall, multistoreyed tower marking the entrance to temple and palace enclosures
goraja, aromatic substance
gotra, clan
gouda, chief officer of a city
gouli, sweet; see *garige*
graha-gati, planetary movement
grama, town
guggula, fragrant substance used as incense
gulige, sweet similar to *garige*, but boiled
guru, teacher
guttadoppu, indoor game

haga, coin of small denomination
halli, village
halogara, milk preparation
halu-sakkare, sugar and milk preparation
hamsa, sacred bird, goose associated with Brahma
happala, see *papad*
harivana, large bronze or brass bowl
harugolu, boat with oars
hasagi, *hasangi*, game board made of cloth on which are squares and lines, used for playing *pagade*
havala, coral
hesara-tovve, green *dhal* preparation
hesaru, green *dhal*

hidigadubu, fried sweet preparation
hidigavade, indoor game played with cowrie shells
hirale, sour lemon
hire, sponge gourd
hittala-avare, type of bean
hittina-adige, food preparation made out of flour
holeya, low-caste person
holgayi, vegetable preparation
Holi, spring festival
holige, flat cakes
homa, ritual act in which libations are poured into the fire
horakam, kind of pickle
huli, tamarind
hulimukha, *pulimukha*, tiger-face motif decorating a fort gateway
hurige, sweet made with wheat *rotis* stuffed with boiled *channa*, jaggery and coconut

iddali, *iddalige*, *idli*, flat steamed-rice cakes
ishta-linga, miniature, three-dimensional *linga* used for personal worship; generally kept in a small casket worn at all times

jagale, cymbal
jagate, bronze gong
jala-durga, island fort
jala-krida, *-kride*, water play; water sport
jambu, rose-apple
jananotsava, birth celebration
jangama, wandering religious mendicant or preacher
japamala, rosary, string of beads
javadi, fragrant substance: civet musk
javagahale, trumpet blown to indicate the time
jave, type of wheat
jigi-halle, indoor game played by ladies jumping along a grid drawn on the floor
jina, Jaina prophet; see *Tirthankara*
jola, millet
jyoti-bottu, auspicious mark applied to the forehead of a person in the course of rituals, after touching the top of the flame
jyotirlinga, "luminous" *linga*; *linga* used in personal worship
jyotishya, science of astrology; astrologer

kachchari, sweet dish
kadabu, *kadubu*, preparation made out of rice or wheat, either fried or steamed.
kahale, trumpet
kai-pidi, small dagger
kajjari, curd-based vegetable preparation
kajjaya, deep-fried sweet made of rice-flour and jaggery
kajjaya-payasa, variety of *kajjaya*
kajjura, date fruit
kalalu, curd or buttermilk
kalasha, *kalasa*, metal finial placed on temple towers, *gopuras* and pavilions; metal vessel used along with *arati*-lamps in the course of rituals
kalasogara, rice and vegetable preparation
kalasu, rice and vegetable preparation
Kalpa, one of the six branches of the *Vedas*, prescribing rules for performing rituals
kalpabhuja, divine wishing-tree
kalyana-mantapa, pavilion or hall where marriage ceremonies, both human and divine, are conducted
Kama, Kamachakreshvara, the god of love; see also Kanthu
kamandalu, water jug used by mendicants
kamsala, twin drums
Kanthu, another name of Kama
Kapalika, Shaiva sect
kara-genasu, preparation made out of sweet potatoes mixed with chillies or peppers
karade, musical instrument
karajige, half-moon-shaped puff with sweet stuffing
karajikayi, sweet preparation, similar to *karajige*
karana, astrologically auspicious time of the day
karana, *karna*, scribe at court
karane, colourful decoration of walls and floors
karanika, accountant at the royal court
karaveli, bitter gourd
karma, fate
karpura, camphor
karugallu, rounded boundary stone placed at the outer limit of a village or town
kasturi, *katturi*, musk
kasu, copper coin of small denomination
kattugulu, food preparations suitable for being carried in a tiffin box.
katturi, see *kasturi*
kaustubha, jewel worn on the chest by Vishnu
kavade, cowrie shells
kavaleya-palidya, curds and vegetable preparation
kavya, poetical composition, literary genre
kay, pawn in chess

kayi-dose, dose with scraped coconut
kayi, unripe fruits or vegetables; pickles
kechara, tribal person
kedage, see *ketaki*
kene-mosaru, curds with cream
kere, water reservoir, mainly for irrigation
kesari, saffron
ketaki, screw-pine flower
kevala-jnana, pure wisdom, omniscience
kevali, person who has attained omniscience
khan, Muslim general or commander
khan-malluk, Muslim chief
kharvada, market town; district headquarters
kheda, small fortified town
khorasani, foreign mercenary, probably of Central Asian origin
khus, fragrant root of a grass (*anatherum muricatum*); also known as vetiver
kimpurusha, semi-divine being
kinnara, kinnari, semi-divine being
kinnari, stringed instrument; type of *vine*
kirata, professional hunter; also an aspect of Shiva in his Kirata-lile
kirita, crown, headgear
kodugallu, large rock formation; boulder
kogile, bird with a melodious voice (*eudynamis scolopaceus*)
Kokashastra, treatise on the art of love
kombu, wind instrument
kopparige, iron cauldron used for making jaggery, or for crossing a river
kote, fort
koyil, see *kogile*
krura-karmi, butcher; low-class person
krusari, rice and sesame-seed preparation
kshatriya, person of the military or royal class
kshiragarige, milk preparation
kshira-sakkare, milk and sugar
kulayi, tall cap which came into fashion in the mid-fifteenth century
kumbala, pumpkin
kumkuma, saffron
kunkuma-rasa, fragrant substance made of saffron
kurma-pitha, tortoise-shaped seat
kurma-vine, musical instrument; type of *vine*
kusumbhari, dhal with salt, pepper and other spices
kutila-devate, inauspicious female deities invoked by magicians or sorcerers.

laddige, laddu, sweet shaped like a small ball
lagge, ball game
lakh, 1,00,000
lamancha, fragrant root of a shrub
lata-mantapa, bower; garden pavilion made of creepers or foliage
lavana, salt
letta, game played with dice
lila, lile, play; divine play or manifestation.
linga, phallic symbol of Shiva
lobana (*olibanum*), gum exuded from a tree

madala, type of fruit
madamba, province
maddale, type of drum
madhu, honey; mildly intoxicant drink
madiga, low-class person
maguli, kind of herb
maguli-beru, sourish herb root
mahadana, generous charitable gifts given by a ruler; can be of sixteen different types
Mahanavami, ninth day of the *Navaratri* festival
majjige, buttermilk
makara, mythical aquatic animal with exuberant foliated tail
makara-torana, festoon with *makara* motif at either end, tied across entrances
makarika, makarika-patra, decorative designs drawn with vegetal dyes on the face, shoulders and other bodily parts of royal ladies
mallige, jasmine
malluk, (Muslim) chief or general
mandara, tree with red flowers *(erythrina indica)*
mangalashataka, hymn consisting of eight auspicious verses
mangaleyaru, ladies whose husbands are alive and whose presence at religious and other functions is deemed to be auspicious; see also *sumangaliyaru*
manjara, musk (from the civet cat)
Manmatha, the god of love
mantapa, mandapa, pavilion or hall used for various ceremonies
mantra, sacred formula chanted by priests in the course of rituals
mantrastra, magical weapon created by uttering a *mantra*
mantikaru, expert in *mantras*; sorcerer
mara, tree, wood, especially sandalwood
maruga, creeper with fragrant leaves
marulkai, mechanical device in the shape of a revolving hand

masegayi, any kind of stuffed vegetable
matha, monastery, religious establishment
mathadipati, head of a *matha*
mavu, mango fruit
mekkikayi-sikharane, type of *shikarane*
melogara, sweet, sour and salty preparation; pickles
menasu, pepper
meru-soudha, upper apartment in a palace or mansion
mettakki, heap of auspicious rice upon which the bride and groom are made to stand during the marriage ritual
mogavine, stringed instrument, type of *vine*
moksha, final emancipation from life; spiritual liberation
moksha-mantapa, pavilion where ascetics meditate to attain *moksha*
mosaranna, curd rice
mridanga, barrel-shaped drum
mriganabhi, perfumed substance
mudivàla, fragrant roots of a creeper
mudrike, signet ring
mukha-vine, stringed instrument, type of *vine*
mulangi, radish
muni, a saintly person
munji, religious initiation of a young brahmin; investiture of the sacred thread
muraja, percussion instrument
murjana, tambourine
murutu, round, laddu-type sweet
muttaideyar, non-widowed woman

naga, male snake deity
nagara, city; capital city
nagasara, wind instrument
nagasutra, snake-girdle
nagavali, ceremony observed on the fourth day after a wedding
nagini, female snake deity
naivedya, food offered to a deity
nakshatra, stellar position
nandana-vana, divine garden, or temple garden
natakashale, *natyashale*, theatre (for drama performances).
nava-nidhi, the nine gifts or treasures
navanita, butter
navaratna, the nine precious stones symbolizing the planets; see Appendix III
Navaratri, the "nine nights" preceding *Dasara*
nayak, chieftain, leader
netta, *nettapagade*, board game; a kind of chess
neem, a tree whose bark, twigs and leaves have medicinal properties (*azadirachta indica*)
nigama, small town
nimbi, lemon fruit
nirukta, etymology; one of the *Vedangas*, or subsidiary sciences
nissala, kettle-drum
nivali, auspicious lights or objects waved ritually before the face of a deity
nuchchu, coarse grist
nyaya, logic, justice

ode, see *vade*
ogara, rice preparation; general term used for eatables
Omkara-mantra, the syllable *Om*; the most sacred of all *mantras*

pachchadi, minced raw vegetables
pachche-karpura, edible camphor
padari, type of flower
padma-pitha, lotus-shaped seat
padya, poem, stanza
pagade, board game
pagadeyata, game of dice
palidya, vegetables cooked in curd and then variously seasoned
pan, betel-leaves and nuts; see also *vileya*
panasu, jack-fruit
panchakshari (-mantra), five-syllable Shaiva *mantra*: *"Nama Shivaya"*
panchamrita, liquid mixture of five holy ingredients: milk, curds, *ghee*, honey or sugar, cow urine; used in rituals
panchanga, almanac
pancha-ratna, the five auspicious kinds of gems; see Appendix III
pancha-vadya, *pancha-mahavadya*, the five auspicious instruments: drum, conch, trumpet, bell, *vine*; related to the five elements: earth, water, air, fire and ether
pandal, decorated pavilion erected for celebrating ceremonies
pandidale, defensive contrivance shaped like a boar's head.
pandita, *pandite*, male or female scholar
panniru, fragrant-smelling water for ablutions and sprinkling in religious ceremonies
papad, pulse flour dough rolled out into paper-

thin circles and deep-fried or roasted; used as an accompaniment to meals

paradi, sweet based on wheat cooked in milk

paradi-sanna-sajjike, small sweets cooked in milk

paramanna, sweet rice preparation

parijata, one of the five mythical trees of Indra's paradise

parivara, retinue of a king

parivara-devata, subordinate deities forming the retinue of a main deity

parpu-shaka, *dhal* preparation

paruguppe, jumping game played by ladies

parva, main division or chapter of a literary work

Pashupatavratam, Shaiva ritual

pataha, percussion instrument

pathakaru, bard, panegyrist, reciter of religious texts

pathika, traveller

pattabhisheka, coronation

pattadane, royal elephant used during the coronation ceremony and other royal functions

pattana, city

payasa, semi-liquid sweet based on milk

pendeya, anklet of honour, worn only on one ankle, as a mark of distinction

pheni, flat sweet cake

pitambara, yellow silk garment

pittu, dish made of wheat flour

pongedage, screw-pine flower

poushtika, ritual

pradhana, minister, prime minister

prakara, enclosure, compound wall

pramatha, minor deity attending on Shiva

prasada, offering of food or fruits to a deity

puja, *puje*, worship, ritual

puja-griha, *puja* room.

pulimukha, see *hulimukha*

punugu, fragrant substance, musk

punyashrama, holy hermitage

pura, city, town, fortress

purana, legend, tale, mythical narrative.

puratanaru, venerable person, Virashaiva saint

puri, deep-fried, bread-like preparation

purna-kalasha, *-kumbha*, pot filled with holy water and/or other auspicious objects, worshipped during rituals

purohita, court priest

pushkarani, temple tank used for ritual purposes

pushpaka-vimana, celebrated aerial chariot of Kubera, the god of wealth

raga, musical mode

raja-marga, king's street, main street

raja-niti, politics, statecraft, advice to kings

rajanna, rice dish

ranga-mantapa, central hall of a temple

rangavalli, decorative design drawn on the ground with powdered white stone

rasa, juice, an extract

rasabale, fragrant, tasty plantain fruit

rasala, mango fruit

rasayana, mixed fruit, fruit salad

ratha, chariot

ratha-vidhi, chariot street

Rati, wife of Kama, goddess of passion

ratna-traya, the three jewels (in Jainism): accurate perception, complete knowledge, correct conduct

Rigveda, first of the four *Vedas*

rishi, ascetic, seer

rotti, *roti*, flat bread

rudra-kankana, special wristlet presented as a mark of rank and distinction

rudraksha, *rudrakshi*, seeds of the *elaeocarpus ganitrus*, used as beads

rudra-vine, type of *vine*

sadhu, ascetic, religious mendicant

sadu, black fragrant substance; paste used for putting a dot on the forehead

sajjige-payasa, sweet dish

sakha-aduge, vegetarian dish

sakkare-burude, half-moon-shaped puff filled with sugar

sakkare-payasa, preparation of milk and pulses sweetened with sugar

sali, rice dish

samamu, friendship; one of the four traditional tactics of diplomacy

samavasarana-mantapa, Jaina preaching hall

Samaveda, one of the four *Vedas*

sambaru, relish of cooked *dhal*, spices and vegetables

samyuktva, right perception; one of the fundamental principles of Jainism

sanatana, ancient, traditional

sandage, *sandige*, sauce, condiment

sandhi, chapter or section of a literary work
sandhi-vigrahi, diplomat; a mediator between opposite parties
sanna-sevige, vermicelli
sannakkiyogara, preparation made from the finest quality rice
saramandala, stringed instrument
sarane, drawings decorating the floors and walls of houses
saravalige, vermicelli
saribesa, indoor game played with tamarind seeds, round areca-nuts or coins
sarkara, *sakkare*, sugar
sarovara, natural lake or pond
saru, *huli-saru*, spicy soup, *rasam*
sashtanga-namaskara, prostrating on the ground to pay respects to gods, saints or elders
sasivigayi, vegetable stuffed with mustard paste
sati, wife who immolates herself on the pyre of the deceased husband
save, kind of millet
senabava, officer, scribe
sendu, ball for playing
sevage, *sevige*, vermicelli
sevantige, flower
shadrasa, the traditional six types of tastes; see Appendix III
shadrasa, fruit juice of six different tastes
Shaiva-vratangal, periodical rituals in honour of Shiva
shaka, *shakabalu*, any vegetable preparation
shakti, literally "power" or "energy"; the supreme goddess
shalabhanjike, statuette representing a young woman
shami, a sacred tree (*prosopis spicigera Lin.*)
Shani-trayodashi, day on which Saturn is worshipped; thirteenth day after both the new moon and full moon
shankha, conch shell used as a musical instrument
shantika, ritual performed as a part of the wedding ceremony.
sharabha, a mythical animal
sharana, devotee of Shiva; Lingayat
shastra, treatise on various topics
shata-yagan, the 100 sacrificial rites
shatsthala, the six stages of spiritual improvement according to Virashaiva doctrine
sheva, *seva*, service, ritual service
shikarane, *sikarane*, pulp of fruits prepared in various ways
shikhara, tower above a temple sanctuary
shiksha-shastra, one of the *Vedangas*
shilpa, architecture, sculpture
shilpi, architect, artist
shirasashtanga-namaskara, performing obeisance by prostration
Shivaratri, festival celebrated in honour of Shiva on the night before the new moon day in the month of Magha (February-March)
shloka, *sloka*, couplet
shodasa-dana, the sixteen gifts given as charity by a king; see also *mahadana*
shriganda, sandalwood
shrihastajala, auspiciously folded hands
shudra, the fourth class of society, servants and menials
shula, trident, three-pronged spike
shunya-simhasana, a throne, in the presence of which Virashaiva tenets and doctrines were formulated
shyalyodana, food prepared with rice of the best quality
siddha, perfected being in Jainism; ascetic conversant with occult sciences
siddha-linga, sanctified Shaiva emblem
siddharasa, quicksilver, mercury
sikarane, see *shikarane*
simha-vahana, lion seat
simha-vahini, epithet of Durga
smriti, traditional code of laws
solle, *solleha*, indoor game played by ladies and children
Somavara, Monday; ritual to be performed on Mondays
soma-vidhi, moon-street; see also *chandra-vidhi*
soppuli, *dhal* with greens
souti-bija, vermicelli in cucumber-seed shape
sthala-durga, fort in a plain
sukhinunde, round solid sweets
sumangaliyaru, ladies whose husbands are alive and whose presence is deemed auspicious
supa, soup, cuisine, cook
surali-holige, sweet made out of dough, stuffed and rolled up
surya-siddhanta, astronomical treatise
surya-vidhi, sun-street, running from east to west
susalugayi, stuffed vegetables
sutradhara, stage manager, principal actor

suvvara, cook
svara-mandala, musical instrument
svayamvara, a ceremony in which a princess chooses a husband from the assembled royal suitors
syalyodana, dish with rice of the finest quality

tabla, twin drums
taila, oil
tailadholige, type of *holige* with oil
takra, buttermilk sweet
tala, cymbals, metal instruments
taladavaru, cymbal players
talige, large metal plate
tambata, tambate, tammata, percussion instrument
tambula, mixture of betel-nut, leaves and lime paste chewed after meals
tambura, stringed instrument
Tantra, esoteric philosophical treatise
tantra-kovidaru, adept in performing ceremonies; expert in the use of magic formulas, incantations and charm; strategist
tappate, percussion instrument
taragu, *dhal* preparation
tarkika, logician, debator, philosopher
tatte, metal plate
ter, chariot; pawn in the game of chess
tilaka, mark applied on the forehead
tilisaru, spicy thin soup
tirtha, holy water, pond or lake
Tirthankara, Jaina prophet
tirthodaka, sacred water
tithi, lunar day
titti, musical instrument
torana, festoon hung over doors and arches
tovve, kind of *dhal*
toyanna, dish of *dhal* and rice
toye, dish based on *dhal*
tripundra, three horizontal lines drawn on the forehead of Shaiva devotees
tula, weighing balance
tulasi, small shrub (*ocymum sanctum Lin.*) sacred to Vaishnavas
tulasi-mantapa, small pavilion where the *tulasi* shrub is grown and worshipped
tumbugayi, stuffed vegetables
tumbura-vine, stringed instrument; type of *vine*
tumudu, musical instrument
tuppam, clarified butter, *ghee*

uddina-kadabu, sweet made with black gram
uddu, black gram
udugore, gifts, especially clothes and ornaments
uduregayi, stuffed vegetables
ukkadagale, percussion instrument
undalige, steamed or baked rice dish
unde, round solid sweet
upadhyaya, religious teacher
upanayana, religious initiation
Upanishads, philosophical texts
upparati, type of *arati*
uppinakayi, pickles
uppugayi, pickles, condiment
utsava-mantapa, pillared hall in which special rituals, such as the betrothal and marriage of deities, are conducted
uttaraposana, ritual observed at the end of the meal

vade, vadai, preparation of soaked, coarsely ground pulses and various spices deeply fried in *ghee* or oil
vahana, vehicle, transport
vaidya, pysician
vaishya, third of the four castes; traders and agriculturalists
vana-durga, fortified city in the forest
vanapalaka, royal chief-gardener; caretaker of the royal gardens
vara, day of the week
varaha, gold coin denomination
Vasanta, Vasantha, spring season; god of spring
vasanta-mantapa, pleasure pavilion in a garden
vasanta-puje, worship or celebration of spring
vasanti, flower
Vasantotsava, spring festival
vastu-krama, architectural treatise
vastu-shastra, architectural treatise
vazir, (Muslim) prime minister; horseman
Vedangas, six treatises on different subjects appended to the *Vedas*
Vedas, the four most revered texts of ancient India; see *Rigveda, Yajurveda, Samaveda* and *Atharvaveda*
vedika, dais
ventara, spirit
vetiver, vettiverru, fragrant root used for making perfumes; see also *khus*
vibhuti, sanctified ash of cow-dung; ball made of ash
vidushaka, court jester
vidyadhara, vidyadhari, semi-divine beings
Vijaya-dasami, another name for *Dasara*

vilaya, vileya, betel-nuts and leaves given as a mark of honour during rituals and functions
vimana, aerial conveyance
vinadandaka, stringed instrument
vine, stringed instrument
Virashaiva, follower of Virashaivism; a Lingayat
Virupaksha, aspect of Shiva worshipped at Hampe
visa, coin of small denomination
Vishvakarma, architect of the gods
vivaha, marriage
vrata, vratam, religious observance
vrishabha-mudre, ring in the shape of a miniature bull
vyakarana, grammar
vyuha, battle formation

yaga, yajna, offerings and rituals made through fire
yaga-shala, -ṣhale, hall where sacrificial rites are performed
yagnopavita, yajnopavita, sacred thread worn by boys after their initiation into religious life
Yajurveda, one of the *Vedas,* dealing with the sacrificial rituals
yaksha, yakshi, semi-divine beings
yantra, magical diagram used as an aid in meditation
yenne-hurige, sweet made of dough stuffed with various ingredients
yereyappa, dough made with sweetened milk or cream, rolled out with coconut and bananas into circles, and then deep fried
yoga, mental and physical discipline
yogadanda, armrest used by mendicants
yoganidre, in *yoga,* a state of half contemplation and half sleep
yogi, one who practices *yoga*
yojana, unit of distance: 25 kilometres
yuvaraja, crown prince.

Appendix III

TRADITIONAL LISTS

References to lists without any itemization appear repeatedly throughout the excerpts given in this Anthology. Here follows a selection of such lists, complete with all entries, which may be of interest to some readers.

***Chaturbala*: the four divisions of the army**
elephants, horses, chariots, infantry

***Chaturopaya*: the traditional four kinds of diplomacy**
sama (friendship), *bheda* (sowing dissent in the enemy's kingdom), *dana* (gifts), *danda* (force). This traditional set of four is elaborated upon in the *Shri Krishnadevarayana Dinachari*, according to which there are seven expedients of diplomacy. The additional three are *maya* (playing tricks), *upeksha* (showing disregard) and *mahendrajala* (weaving a net of illusions). (*SKD*, I. p. 7)

***Pancharatna*: the five kinds of gems**
pearl, ruby, emerald, sapphire and diamond

***Shadrasa*: the six types of taste**
sweet, sour, salty, pungent, bitter, astringent

***Shatkarma*: the six traditional professions**
accounting, business, agriculture, warfare, cattle-raising, menial service

***Raja-saptanga*: the seven essential "limbs" of a kingdom**
king, minister, ally, wealth, country, fortress, army. The following seven elements come next in importance to the ones previously mentioned: vehicles, kingdom, queen, clothes, ornaments, camphor, betel-nut and leaves. (*SKD*, I, p. 7)

***Sabha-saptanga*: the seven essential "limbs" of the court**
poets, intellectuals, reciters of the *Puranas*, saintly persons, scholars, guardians, musicians (*SKD*, I, p. 7)

***Sapta-santana*: the seven eternal [duties] of a king**
progeny, wealth, construction of a temple, planting a forest, constructing a reservoir, composing a literary work, honouring the brahmins (*SKD*, I, p. 7)

***Sapta-vyasana*: the seven vices that the king should abstain from**
women, gambling, drinking intoxicants, company of dubious persons, bad talk, scolding, punishing without reason, unnecessary spending (*SKD*, I. p.7)

***Navaratna*: the nine kinds of gems**
pearl, ruby, topaz, diamond, emerald, coral, sapphire, cat's eye (or moonstone), sardonyx

***Raja-dosha*: the fourteen defects of a king**
being an aetheist, a liar, indulging in self-promotion, being lazy, a spendthrift, short-tempered, talking nonsense, being mentally disturbed, indulging in sensual enjoyments, brooding on trifles, neglecting the [prescribed] duties, not upholding the Vedic *dharma*, neglecting the welfare of the state and the performance of auspicious deeds (*SKD*, I. p. 8)

***Ashtadasha-pradhanar*: the eighteen officers in the service of the king**
purohita (priest, royal chaplain), *dandanatha* (general, magistrate), *adhyaksha* (superintendent, chairperson), *adhikari* (officer,

governor), *manthri* (minister, counsellor), *pradhana* (chief minister, king's counsellor), *mahograni* (chief officer in charge of the stores), *bhandari* (treasurer), *senanayaka* (general, commander-in-chief of the army), *sandhi-vigrahi* (minister of war and peace), *pratihari* (chief guard, bodyguard, jester), *antasthita* (king's confidant, high officer), *dvarapalaka* (gate-keeper, security officer), *karanika* (accountant, chief scribe), *dandapani* (staff-bearer), *kothari, kuthari* (officer in charge of the warehouse), *sthalavara* (city watchman, officer), *yuvaraja* (crown prince)

Ashtadasha-varnane: the eighteen descriptive topics of a poetic work

samudra (the sea), *parvata* (the mountains), *pattana* (the city), *raja* (the king), *vivaha* (royal marriage), *putrotpatti* (the birth of a son), *suryodaya* (sunrise), *chandrodaya* (moonrise), *rithu* (the seasons, usually spring), *udyanavana* (the royal pleasure garden), *jala-kride* (water sports in a pool of the royal garden), *madhu-panagoshti* (the royal drinking party), *surata* (erotic play), *viraha* (the separation of lovers), *mantralochane* (the royal council), *dutapreshane* (the mission of an envoy), *yuddha* (war), *prayana* (the journey)

Chappannaru-deshagalu: the fifty-six traditional countries

Anga, Vanga, Kalinga, Telunga, Konga, Lata, Bangala, Chola, Kerala, Goula, Panchala, Simhala, Kuntala, Nepala, Malayala, Tuluva, Saindhava, Konkana, Kuru, Magadha, Matsya, Vidharbha, Koshala, Surashena, Kashmira, Maharashtra, Karnata, Kirata, Turushka, Shankara, Barama, Trigarta, Nishadha, Madhya, Jaina, Barbara, Bahlika, Lata, Chaina, Karala, Odhra, Ghurjara, Kambhoja, Sourashtra, Sovira, Pandya, Huna, Yavana, Mleccha, Haihaya, Aryavartha, Bhoja, Dvaipa, Amaruka, Uttara Kuru, Graiti (*Kannada Nighantu*, Vol. III, p. 2,926)